Venues:

Art Gallery of New South Wales
1 April to 17 May, 1981.

Queensland Art Gallery
2 June to 19 July, 1981.

Art Gallery of South Australia
14 August to 20 September, 1981

Art Gallery of Western Australia
9 October to 15 November, 1981.

National Gallery of Victoria
2 December 1981 to 17 January, 1982

Catalogue written by
Edmund Capon and Mae Anna Pang

Note: The Pin Yin method of translation has been used
throughout.

Note: Dimensions of catalogue entries
are of the actual painted area.

Copyright: ©International Cultural Corporation of
Australia Limited
ISBN 09594122 0 4

Printed by: Wilke and Company Limited
37-49 Browns Road
Clayton, Victoria.

Front Cover: Seal of the Exhibition, which reads --
Chinese Painting of the Ming and Qing Dynasties.

Chinese Paintings
of the
Ming and Qing
Dynasties

14th-20th century
Second Edition

Sponsored by 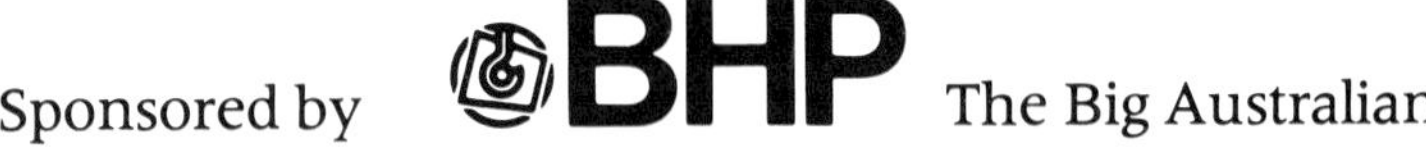 The Big Australian

Arranged by the International Cultural Corporation of Australia Limited.

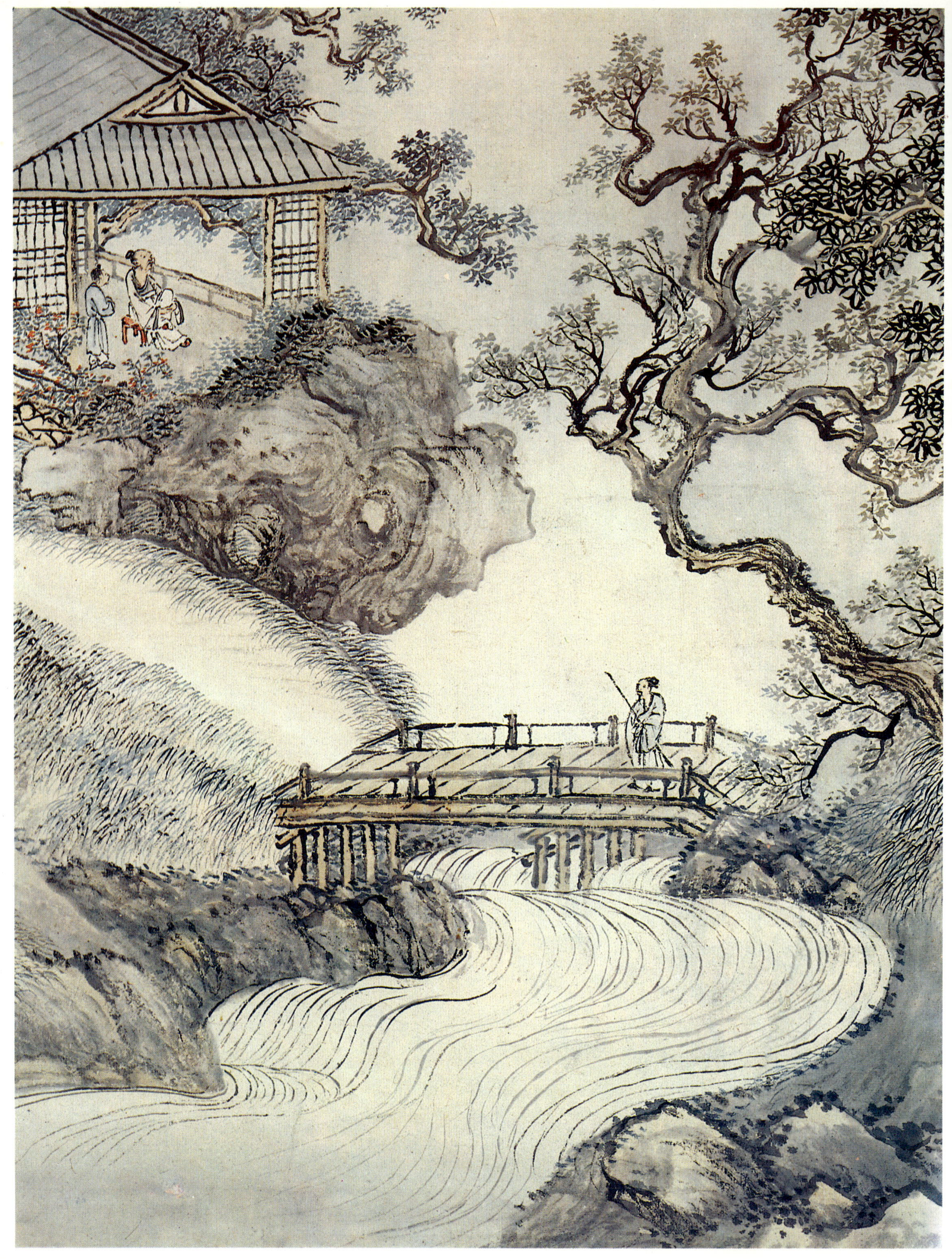

Contents

Opposite: "Ode to the Plum Blossoms in a Summer Moon"
dated 1714 by Wang Hui (1632-1717).

Forewords

The Rt. Hon. Malcom Fraser C.H., M.P.
Prime Minister of Australia.

I am delighted that Australia is host to this magnificent collection of Chinese paintings of the Ming and Qing Dynasties

The exhibition is a significant contribution to the cultural exchange programme between Australia and China which I welcome.

The paintings express the continuous pleasure and delight which Chinese painters have drawn throughout history from the landscape and nature; these responses will be shared by all Australians who view this exhibition.

This is the first major international cultural exchange managed by the International Cultural Corporation of Australia Limited. The exhibition of Chinese paintings of the Ming and Qing Dynasties continues the tradition of cultural exchange between Australia and the People's Republic of China which commenced with the Chinese Archaeological Exhibition of 1977, seen by millions all over Australia. It marks an exciting period in Australia's major touring exhibition programme, the effects of which are far reaching and will immensely enrich our experience in Australia of works of art never before seen outside China.

Financial sponsorship by BHP has been provided on a major scale. To facilitate the arrangements for the exhibition the Government has indemnified these priceless scrolls, thereby removing the insurance burden.

Huang Zhen
Minister of Culture
People's Republic of China.

The exhibition in Australia of Chinese classical paintings is a happy event in the cultural exchange between the peoples of our two countries. The project deserves our congratulations and is a festival of friendship. I sincerely wish the exhibition every success.

The origins of Chinese painting are founded in antiquity. It is a tradition with a long history and its own outstanding characteristics, with works of immortal stature and a vivid national style. Peaks of achievement and high points of art have constantly appeared in the course of its development.

In Chinese painting of the Ming and Qing Dynasties many artists created their own individual styles and formed numerous schools, basing themselves on the traditions of earlier painters. Many of the works in this exhibition are representative ones by outstanding masters of the Ming and Qing Dynasties. Their breadth of themes and richness of content form a marvellous tapestry. Among the aspects of the world of nature depicted are landscapes, animals, flowers, birds, insects and fish, famous mountains and great rivers, mists and groves of bamboo, magnificent palaces and cottage scenes. All of these are included in the paintings. The many facets of social activity are also portrayed in detail – from the fisherman casting his net, the herdboy tending his cattle and the peasant ploughing, to genteel maidens in quiet elegance and literati and scholars drinking and writing poems. The styles of the artists include realistic paintings, characterised by fine brushwork and close attention to detail where each stroke, executed with precision, carries weight; there are also freehand paintings with few strokes of the brush and scattered ink dots. No matter which brush technique is employed, each work expresses the deep love of the artists for nature and for life, so that even with a few brush strokes outstanding artists have been able to impress their inner feelings and individual personalities upon their work.

This exhibition brings together gems of the collections from the museums of twelve provinces and cities including Beijing, Shanghai, Tianjin, Nanjing, Liaoning, Shandong, Guangdong, Zhejiang and Jiangxi, totalling one hundred paintings by over eighty artists. The selection illustrates the general development of painting through the Ming and Qing Dynasties, (mid 14th century to early 20th century), which is one aspect of the rich artistic culture of ancient China. This is the first exhibition of classical paintings to be held abroad since the establishment of the People's Republic. We are honoured to present this Exhibition for the appreciation of the Australian public in the hope of contributing to the friendship and understanding between the peoples of China and Australia.

黄镇

James Leslie, Chairman
International Cultural Corporation of Australia Limited.

The International Cultural Corporation of Australia Limited, the successor to the Australian Art Exhibitions Corporation Ltd., is very proud to present the exhibition:"Paintings of the Ming and Qing Dynasties. 14th to 20th Centuries", from the People's Republic of China.

Following the outstanding success of the Chinese Exhibition in 1977, this exhibition represents a fitting continuation of the cultural exchange between the People's Republic of China and Australia. It is also most suitable as the first major exhibition to be managed by the recently formed International Cultural Corporation of Australia Limited.

The planning and presentation of this exhibition represents a fine example of co-operation between many segments of the Chinese and Australian communities. We are particularly indebted to the Chinese Government for making this exhibition available to Australia; to the Commonwealth Government for its indemnity against loss and to BHP for its most generous and substantial sponsorship.

We offer our thanks and warmest appreciation to everyone involved in mounting the exhibition, particularly the participating galleries and the Australia Council.

Sir James McNeill, CBE,
Chairman of Directors and Directors of Administration, BHP

Australians have much to share with the Chinese people, equally we have much to learn from this great nation. While the early Europeans who settled our country battled with the natural environment of what to them was a strange new land – vast and perplexing -- Chinese scholars continued the centuries-old tradition of capturing the essence of their environment with brush and ink.

The great cultural riches of the People's Republic of China have special interest for Australians. We share the privilege and responsibility of occupying very large land masses. We are each within the geographic area loosely referred to as the Pacific Basin, an area of increasing economic and strategic significance. We have important links in trade and commerce. Strong as these common interests are, one cannot escape the enormity of the differences -- in population, religion, culture and tradition. It is because these are so marked, and yet because the course of development in China can be so important to Australians, that we find this basis for special interest.

It is not that we in Australia have recently discovered China or that it has only recently become a focus of attention for the rest of the world. The history of China takes us back to the earliest recordings of man's endeavours. Chinese artists and artisans have left a very great heritage to remind us of the development of their culture. The brief glimpse which this Exhibition gives us of some of the hidden treasures of China is less than an adequate substitute for travelling through the countryside itself to view the magnificient landscape that inspired the beautiful and tranquil scenes portrayed. For many, however, it will be an introduction which may well stimulate further interest.

BHP has enjoyed a particular relationship with the Chinese people for many years, founded upon the mutual trust and understanding which comes with successful commercial enterprise. It is a relationship which we greatly value and we believe it has helped develop the mutual respect which is evident between the peoples of our two countries.

We are pleased and proud to sponsor the Chinese Classical Paintings Exhibition. I feel, in a small way, it will help benefit China-Australia relations and I commend to you all those concerned with the mammoth task of mounting such an exhibition.

Chinese Painting: an Introduction

Edmund Capon

Any comparison between a Chinese painting, whether a 12th, 15th, 18th or even a 20th century example, and its Western contemporary is a compelling indication of the gulf which separates the cultural and artistic traditions of the Far East from those of the West. Indeed, in the West the evolution of artistic expression has been characterised by periods of radical change prompted by reaction to established notions, rather than by the more gradual evolutionary changes which are familiar to the Far East.

The concept that painting was a means whereby the thoughts, feelings and aspirations of individual man might be expressed is an enduring feature of the art in China from early times. In any representational art the subject is visually described and interpreted, but artistic theory and philosophy in China recognised the need for personal expression far in advance of any such recognition in the West. Painting in the West has been rooted to the concept of fidelity to subject, whereas, it could be said, painting in China is equally founded in the concept of fidelity to the spirit. From these foundations Western artistic traditions concerned themselves with the problems of representation of form, volume, light and colour in their quest for verisimilitude. In China the quest was to capture the spirit or essence of the subject and from this emerged an art composed around the exploitation of expressive line.

As early as the 5th century theoreticians and art critics in China were compiling rules and guidelines for the art of painting which described a philosophical as well as a practical framework around a tradition which, even in such early times, was clearly recognised as a high form of individual expression rather than a representational craft. The consistency of this most fundamental theme to Chinese painting is illustrated in the tenets of the first of the great critics, Xiehe, who in the late 5th century introduced his 'six principles'. The first, and without doubt forever recognised as the vital element, is the requirement for the incalculable quality, 'spirit resonance'. Some twelve centuries later the monk painter Dao Ji (see cat. nos. 59, 60), in his principal essay on painting, the **Hua Yu Lun,** states that the single brushstroke is "the origin of all existence, the root of the infinite representations". As Professor Cahill succinctly states: "In the beginning and also in the end; the line drawn by the brush remains the central fact of Chinese painting throughout its history".

Amongst the enormous volume of literature and critical writings relating to the art of painting in China perhaps we may select one passage in an attempt to paraphrase a whole philosophy. One of the major early essays on landscape painting is attributed to Jing Hao, a landscape painter active in the early Song dynasty (10th-early 11th century). In this attributed work, the **Hua Shanshui Lu** (Essay on Landscape Painting) the author constructs a dialogue, thus employing the familiar 'storytelling' method of Confucius, around the chance meeting in a forest of an old sage and a young painter.

The sage asked the young man: "Do you know the method of painting?" To which I (the author seems to identify himself as the young painter) reply: "You seem to be an old uncouth rustic, how could you know anything about brushwork?" But the old man said: "How can you know what I carry in my bosom?" Then I listened and felt ashamed and astonished as he said to me: "Young people like to study in order to accomplish something; they should know that there are six essentials in painting (these refer but do not precisely echo Xiehe's six principles). The first is called **qi** (spirit), the second is called **yin** (harmony), the third is called **si** (thought or plan), the fourth **jing** (scenery and effect), the fifth **bi** (brushwork) and the sixth **mo** (ink)". I remarked: "Painting is to make beautiful things – and the important thing is to achieve true likeness is it not?" The sage answered: "It is not. Painting is to paint, to estimate the shape of things, to really obtain them; to estimate the beauty of things, to reach it; to estimate the reality (significance) of things and to grasp it. One should not take outward beauty for reality. He who does not understand this mystery will not obtain truth, even though his pictures may contain likeness". I asked again: "What is likeness and what is truth?" The old man replied: "Likeness can be obtained by shapes without spirit, but when truth is obtained, both spirit and substance are fully expressed. He who tries to express spirit through ornamental beauty will make dead things".

The particular outward appearance of things, or indeed their accuracy, was therefore of secondary importance to the capturing of the essence or the spirit of the subject. It was thought that once the essential and fundamental spirit of the subject had been grasped then the natural order of things, in formal design, colour and outward appearance, would follow. We see the implications of this philosophy particularly in the dominant and enduring theme of the landscape. Chinese landscape paintings are patently not precise renderings but the expression of an intellectual ideal. The landscape, the embodiment of nature and representing the forces of the universe, became the natural environment of Chinese thought, philosophy and religion. Nature, in both its general and specific manifestations, thus became the outstanding theme in Chinese painting and the vehicle for the expression and interpretation of those philosophies. Above all, landscape painting in China became the vehicle by which the perpetual and evolving investigation and interpretation of man's relationship with nature, and thus the cosmos, was expressed. Figure and genre painting themes were considered peripheral to this central theme of the landscape and thus became less significant contributions confined to Court or Academic traditions.

It may be said that the Court and Academic traditions which flourished under official patronage had the parameters of their artistic expression limited by the demand of that patronage. These demands were principally those of the Imperial Courts and their concern was primarily one of record rather than philosophical expression. Court and Academic traditions, therefore, tended to the definitive as opposed to the expressive, and the conservative as opposed to the radical. A typical concession to the realism required of such paintings is the greater use of colour compared to the parallel landscape traditions. Nevertheless the emphasis upon line and the expressive qualities of the brushwork were still the cardinal elements.

Painting before the Ming Dynasty

Edmund Capon

The art of Bronze Age China was dominated by the demands of ritual and burial rites in which personal expression played no part. Painting as we recognise the art did not therefore exist in China until towards the end of the Bronze Age (circa 4th-3rd centuries BC) when artists and craftsmen were beginning to take an interest in realism and the representation of natural elements.

The earliest known examples of true painting in China are fragmentary works on silk which were excavated from a 3rd century BC tomb near Changsha in present-day Hunan province. Depicting mythological figures the paintings are executed with fine evenly drawn black ink outlines and flat colour washes. This fundamental and strongly figurative style of painting was to remain basic in China until the true founding of the landscape tradition towards the end of the Tang dynasty in the 9th century AD. A number of, often fragmentary, paintings from Han dynasty (206BC-AD220) and Northern and Southern dynasties (AD420-581) tombs confirm the continued existence of the figurative tradition and the ink drawn outline with colour wash style. The few individual paintings which survive from the pre-Tang era, such as the famous Admonitions handscroll by the 4th century painter Gu Kaizhi in the British Museum and attributed versions of "The Nymph of the Lo River" scroll (for example in the Gugong Museum, Peking and the Freer Gallery of Art, Washington), show some increased expression in the use of inflexions in brushline and modulations in colour washes, but even these developments must be acknowledged as merely amendments to a well-established tradition.

During the later part of the Tang dynasty interest shifted from man to nature and by the early Song dynasty the landscape was firmly established as the foremost theme in Chinese painting. An interest in the landscape, as a subject for artistic expression, stemming from mythological and philosophical concerns, existed as early as the Han dynasty. This interest grew during the troubled and divided Northern and Southern dynasties when men sought consolation and solace from the disturbed world of human affairs in the landscape, spurred on by Taoist attitudes and notions through which poets and painters were inspired by their emotional responses to nature. Surviving paintings, or later copies, of this period suggest that figurative and literary themes still dominated although elements of the landscape were beginning to appear in a supporting context. Another significant influence at this time was the introduction to China of a strong and independent Buddhist painting tradition. Although primarily an iconographic art, elements of the landscape appeared as settings to the illustration of Buddhist texts and **jataka** stories. Here, and above all in the wall paintings at the Dunhuang cave temples in far western Gansu province, the hitherto unfamiliar styles of Central Asia, with emphasis upon strong colour and highlighting, are reflected in Chinese Buddhist painting of the period and were undoubtedly noticed by court and secular artists.

The first true and identifiable landscape painting style in China emerged during the Tang dynasty. Bright, colourful and luxuriant the so-called Tang 'blue and green' style of landscape painting was the perfect mode of expression for the confident and expansive attitudes of the time (for a pre-Tang example see Fig. 1). It was a style which exploited to the full the traditional technique of precisely drawn outline embracing even colour washes. This very precision and clarity was

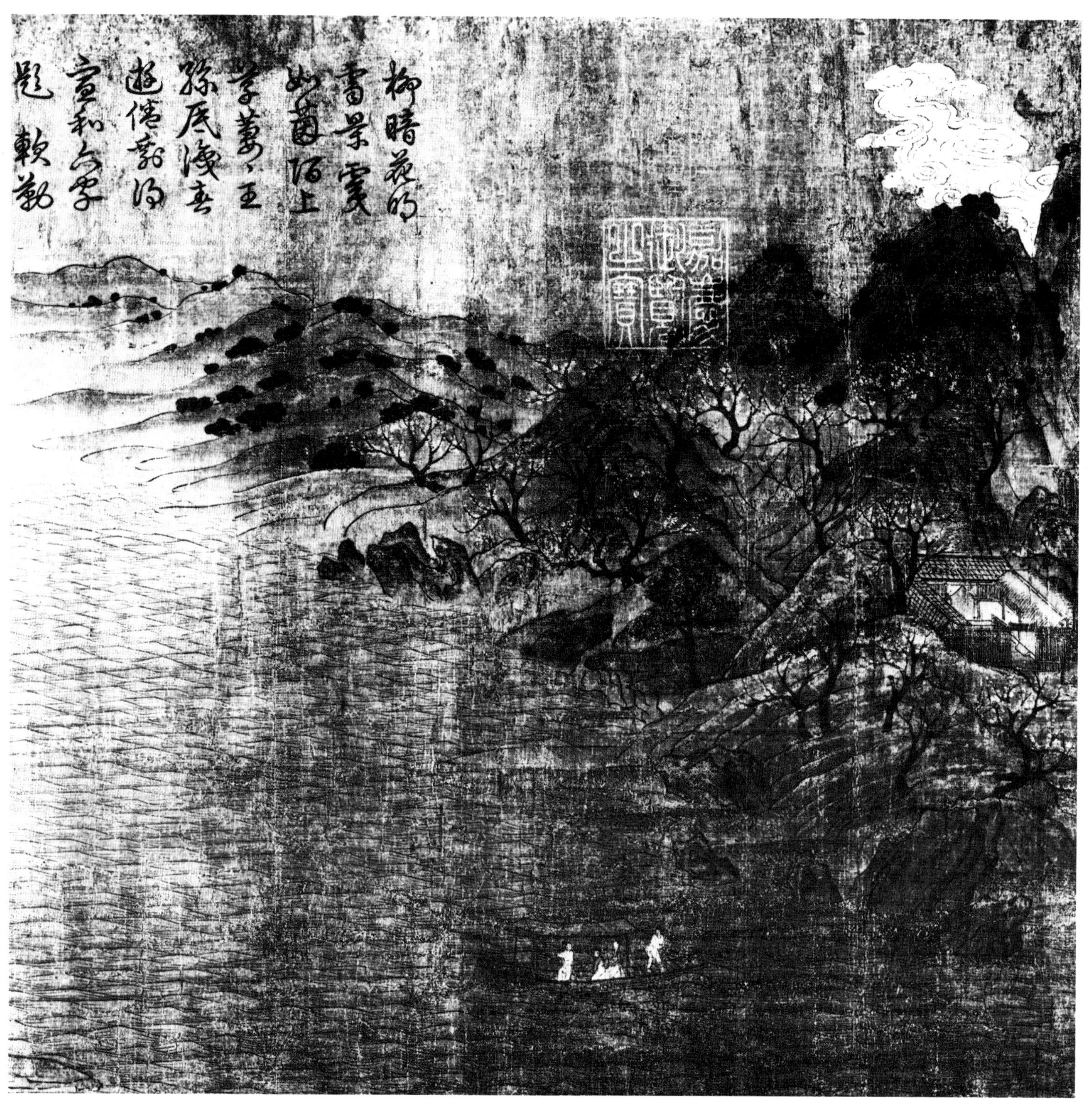

Fig. 1: Detail of handscroll "Travellers in Spring"
by Zhan Ziqian (c. 550-604).
Gugong Museum, Peking.

nevertheless a hindrance to the visual expression of thoughts and emotions, which required mystery, certainty and uncertainty, depth and nearness, shadow and texture, concerning the relationship between man and nature.

The precipitate event in the establishment of the landscape as the pre-eminent theme in Chinese painting was the demise of the brilliant and powerful Tang dynasty. The confidence that had been inspired during three centuries of Tang rule was shattered and artists turned away from figurative and courtly themes, which echoed the Confucian ethic and the world of human affairs, to the unchanging universality of nature. This change of mood and direction was paralleled by developments in brush technique. Tradition, largely through the writings of later critics, credits the 8th century poet-painter Wang Wei (699-759) with the introduction of the innovative **pomo** or 'broken ink' style, which gave variety and emphasis to the brushline, and the **cun** 'texture' stroke, which created a more impassioned surface in contrast to the flatness of the traditional colour-wash. Such brush techniques were to become fundamental to the later development of landscape painting in China and placed yet further emphasis upon the artist's facility with the brush, the expressive quality of the stroke and the texture of the ink.

Painting in the immediate post-Tang era (the 10th century) is characterised by the appearance of the first great landscape tradition. It was a tradition quite unlike the figures in disembodied landscape compositions of the Northern and Southern dynasties or the colourful patchworks of the Tang 'blue and green' style. These early landscape painters sought to paraphrase the enormity of nature in a single scroll. Colour was a subordinate feature, often totally absent, as the use of monochrome ink lent not only imposing sobriety but also unity and continuity. Colour was regarded as a detracting element. The independent features of the landscape which had appeared in earlier paintings were now integral parts of the unending complex structure that is nature.

Many critics have placed the mantle of the greatest landscape painter in China on the shoulders of Li Cheng (fl. 940-67) who was active during the Five Dynasties period (906-960) and the early Song dynasty (960-1279). His monumental landscapes, austere and wintry, powerfully convey the grandeur of nature and the insignificance of man. The great masters of the early Song period, who contributed to the maturing of the landscape tradition at that time, all acknowledge their debt to Li Cheng. In his quest for pictorial unity Li also established a compositional and structural format, broadly dividing the landscape into three distinct parts: foreground, middleground and background, that became as institutionalised as the landscape itself. In such a structure the viewer is led through the painting, sometimes by such a device as a winding path or stream, from the foreground features, generally human in scale, through the middle ground to the often hazily defined distant peaks which so evocatively hint at nature's infinite domain.

The tradition of the monumental landscape, awe-inspiring in its grandeur and gravity, established by Li Cheng was to attain maturity in the Northern Song period in the hands of such painters as Fan Kuan (fl. 990-1030), Guo Xi (c. 1020-90) and Xu Daoning (fl. 1st half 11th century). To lend yet further credence to the magnitude of nature these painters concerned themselves particularly with the representation of implied space and depth. Great use was made of mists and clouds which encircled the distant peaks and often enshrouded those in the middle distance thereby creating a mysterious gulf between the foreground and background elements. The technique of using tones of decreasing strength to allude to recession, known as 'atmospheric perspective', was employed to considerable effect by Guo Xi. These great landscape paintings of the Northern Song dynasty are monuments to the glory of nature and the human presence is always kept to an appropriately humble level.

Towards the end of the Northern Song period a new approach to painting was promoted by the scholar-official class who adopted painting as a medium for personal expression. A rationalisation of this new approach was required and it was a group of scholars, whose leading figure was the great poet, painter, calligrapher and statesman Su Dongpo (1036-1101), that formulated a theory based on a wider appreciation of the arts to include music, poetry and calligraphy in addition to painting.

From this evolved the literary man's painting tradition, or **wenrenhua**, a tradition of great significance in Ming and Qing painting. Central to their thinking was the notion that a painting should reflect the quality, not of the subject, but of the man. Nature thus became the vehicle, or raw material, by which the literati painters interpreted their innermost thoughts and feelings. The emphasis shifted from an interest in portraying nature and man's relationship to nature to a more personal expression of the nature of man. Thus it was that the qualities of brushwork as the means by which the feelings of the artist could be expressed in the most personal and individual manner gained yet greater significance.

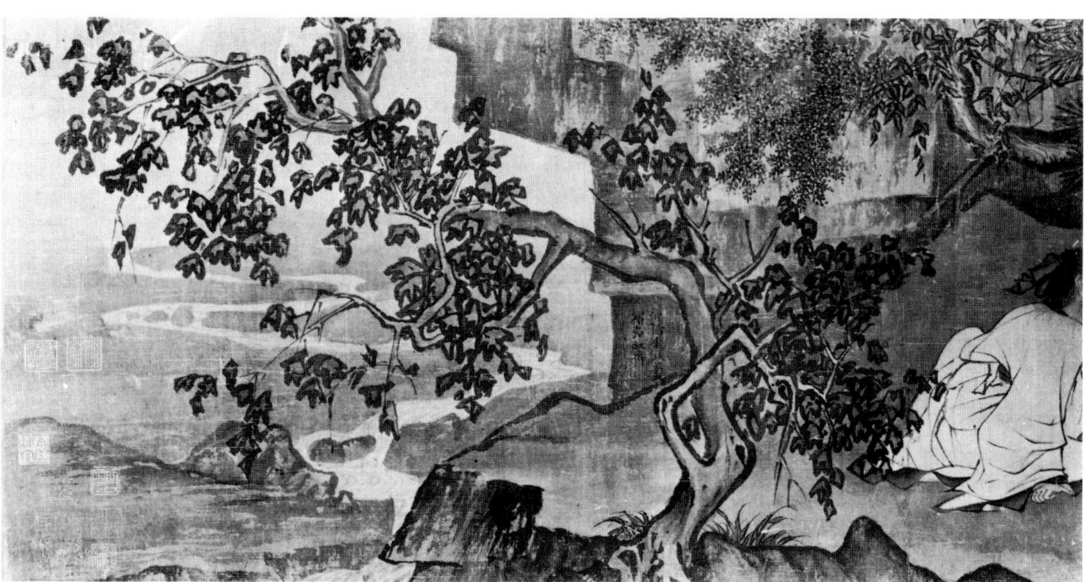

Fig. 2: Detail of handscroll "The Virtuous Brothers Picking Moss"
by Li Tang (12th century), Southern Song dynasty.
Gugong Museum, Peking.

In 1127 the Song dynasty in the north suffered defeat at the hands of the Jin Tartars. The capital was removed from Kaifeng in northern Henan province to be eventually re-established in 1138 at Hangzhou. The rich and luxuriant terrain south of the Yangtze was a fresh inspiration to landscape painters and the initiative in artistic taste and style now centred upon artists working in the region of the new capital. A great influence upon this tradition was the last great Northern Song painter, Li Tang (12 century) (Fig. 2), who served at both the Northern and Southern courts, and laid the foundations for a new, more intimate and less awe-inspiring style that was to later become the feature of Southern Song landscape art. This new intimacy and lyricism found its finest expression in the work of Ma Yuan and Xia Gui (fl. fl. c. 1190-1230) both of whom worked during the Southern Song period. They described a far more intimate relationship between man and nature in oddly assymetric compositions of dissolving mists reaching into infinity and punctuated by craggy rocks and gnarled trees. Man is not subdued by this environment but at one with it. The scholar or poet, invariably present in Ma-Xia school paintings, is shown quietly contemplating the beauty and serenity of nature in a mood of harmony that is in total contrast to the disturbing Northern Song predecessors.

The demise of the Song dynasty in 1279 and the advent of the Mongol Yuan dynasty (1279-1368) prompted, in cultural circles and particularly in painting, a yearning for an idealised past. Painters succumbed to this reaction as their country was being overrun by the Mongol invaders and sought out traditional Chinese values and styles. The two outstanding painters of the early Yuan period, Qian Xuan (c. 1235-1301) and Zhao Mengfu (1254-1322), both sought inspiration from the distant Tang dynasty as their 'blue and green' style landscapes testify. As the far-flung Mongol Empire inevitably weakened China suffered under conditions of political and social instability and uncertainty. Educated men, including painters many of whom had served at the Mongol court, withdrew from public life to seek solace and obscurity in nature. The ideals of the literati were rapidly revitalised in such circumstances and painters once again turned to nature as the one sure and stable feature in an uncertain human world.

It is fitting that this brief introduction to painting in pre-Ming China should conclude with the works of the Four Great Masters of the Yuan dynasty: men who epitomised the literati ideal. Chinese critics have over the centuries unhesitatingly acclaimed Huang Gongwang (1269-1354) (Fig. 3) as the greatest of the Four. His cool, strongly objective landscapes, outlined with a continuous often strained brushline and roughly textured with dry monochrome ink strokes, met the highest literati ideals. As his fellow painter and another of the Four Masters, Wu Zhen, put it, Huang's plain almost virtuous style achieved "flavour with blandness". Similar in technique and style are the paintings of Ni Zan (1301-74), a younger contemporary of Huang Gongwang, who has been accorded almost similar status by the critics. Human isolation is perhaps even more poignantly felt in the work of Ni Zan whose compositions follow a remorseless pattern of foreground, a void for the middle distance and distant peaks which float uncertainly on that indeterminate void (Fig. 4). Ni Zan's distinctive compositional formula was to reappear consistently in Ming and Qing literati painting and is perhaps best reflected in work of Wang Yuanqi (cat.

no. 43). The debt owed to the Four Masters of the Yuan dynasty by landscape painters of the Ming and Qing periods, so well represented in this exhibition, is sufficient comment on the continuity and perpetual evolution of Chinese artistic traditions.

Fig. 3: Hanging scroll "Heavenly Lake" dated 1341 attributed to Huang Gongwang, Yuan dynasty. Gugong Museum, Peking.

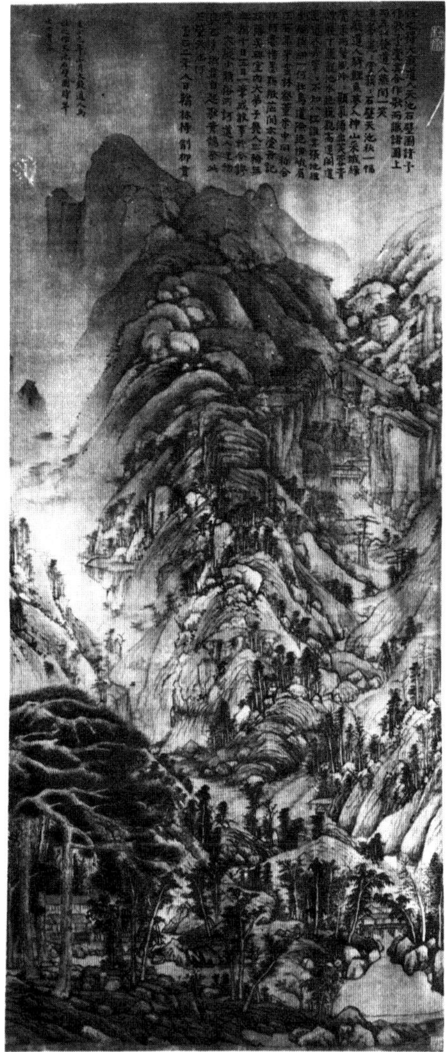

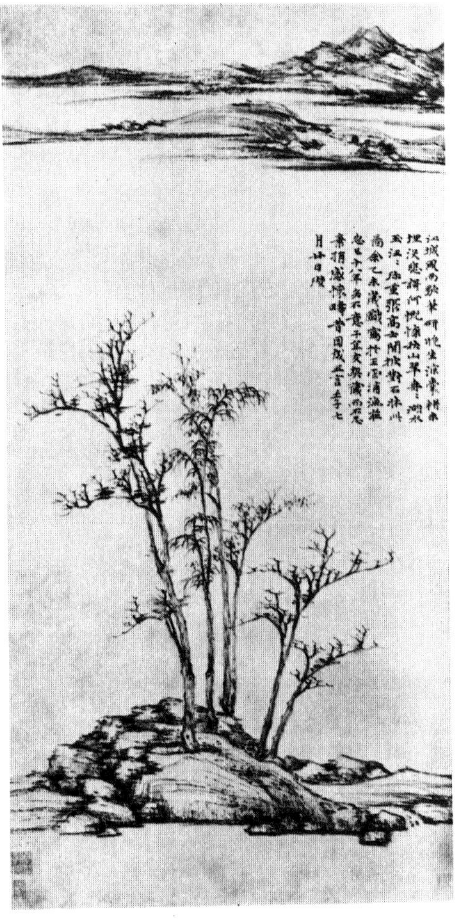

Fig. 4: Hanging scroll "Autumn Clearing Over a Fishing Lodge" by Ni Zan, Yuan dynasty. Shanghai Museum.

Painting in the Ming Dynasty

Mae Anna Pang

The Ming dynasty (1368-1644) was a period of political instability, economic expansion, social changes, and cultural efflorescence. Ruled by despotic and weak emperors, the court was plagued by contending political factions and palace intrigues. For most Confucian scholars, it was a time of disillusionment and alienation; service in the bureaucracy was a dilemma rather than an opportunity. Many scholars withdrew from politics and took refuge in the world of art and culture.

Artists of the Ming dynasty inherited from the past a rich repertoire of forms and styles from which to select their artistic expression. The techniques for the representation of nature had been fully mastered by the court Academy painters of the Song dynasty (960-1279) and the stylistic means of self-expression had been created by the scholar-amateur painters of the Yuan dynasty (1280-1368). It was therefore no longer necessary for the Ming artist to go directly to nature to rediscover what the ancient masters had already discovered. Contemplation of nature was replaced by the contemplation of the art of the past. "Style" and the history of the evolution of styles have become the central theme of Chinese painting of the Ming period.

With the founding of the Ming dynasty in 1368, imperial patronage of the arts was reintroduced, after being neglected by the previous foreign Mongol dynasty. Painters with talent were summoned to court, given official titles, and commissioned by the emperor to paint. The courtly styles of painting that were practised in the Southern Song Academy at Hangzhou were revived in the court of the early Ming: decorative paintings of birds and flowers, figure paintings based on history or legend, and particularly landscape paintings of the school of Ma Yuan and Xia Gui, the two leading landscape artists of the Imperial Academy in the 12th and 13th centuries. Dai Jin (1388-1462) (cat. no. 3), who injected new life into this conservative stream of painting and who may have served in the court of Emperor Xuande (1426-36) at Peking, was credited by Chinese writers of later ages with having founded the Zhe school of painting, named after his native province, Zhejiang province. Zhe school became a loose term that was used to designate painters who followed the style of Dai Jin, and included court painters at Peking and professional painters working in Nanking, with Wu Wei (1459-1508) (cat. no. 4), the most outstanding follower. Nanking, the subsidiary capital in the south, in the 15th and 16th centuries was a commercial and cultural centre. In their reworking of Song styles, both Dai Jin and Wu Wei did not attempt to recapture the naturalism of Song painting, the feeling of empty space, the fleeting effects of light and mist, or to suggest man's emotional response to nature. These Song qualities are replaced by a display of technical skill and virtuosity in the mastery of swift, dashing, animated brushstrokes that resemble the semi-cursive or running script of calligraphy.

Following the decline of imperial patronage, the Zhe school of painting began to lose its popularity, and gradually became defunct by the middle of the 16th century. It was overtaken in importance by another movement, that of the scholar-amateur artists who were living in Suzhou, Jiangsu province. From the beginning of the 16th century, Suzhou, which had become one of the richest areas of China since the Southern Song (1127-1279) and the main centre of literati painting by the late Yuan, gradually replaced Nanking as a cultural and artistic centre.

The literati tradition of painting in Suzhou was revitalized in about 1470 by Shen Zhou (1427-1509) (cat. no. 12), who was regarded as founder of the Wu school of painting. Wu was the ancient name of Jiangsu province where Suzhou was situated. Although Shen Zhou re-established Suzhou as a leading centre of **literati** painting in the Ming, it was the style of his pupil, Wen Zhengming (1470-1559) (cat. no. 14), which dominated Suzhou in the 16th century. While the painters of the Zhe school based their paintings on the court academic styles of the Song period, those of the Wu school drew their inspiration from the scholar-amateur paintings of the Yuan period.

Belonging mostly to the land-owning gentry class, the scholar-amateur painters of Suzhou lived in retirement and did not hold any official posts in the civil bureaucracy. Wealth and leisure enabled them to spend their time in building gardens and libraries, collecting books and works of art, and engaging in painting, poetry, music, and calligraphy. Like the other arts, painting was regarded as a pastime, a means of self-expression and communication with one's like-minded friends. Paintings were given away as presents and were, theoretically, never for sale. Their paintings, mostly landscapes, reflected the secluded world of the scholars and are characterized by a poetic blandness and a great refinement of taste. Not burdened by commercial demands, the literati painter made no attempt to please the uninitiated. To the literary man, who had not undertaken any formal training in painting, technical facility was not held in high regard. Any deliberate or open display of skill and the desire to please was considered vulgar and offensive to the Confucian virtue that "brilliance must be concealed". Technical training, such as that undergone by a professional painter, was regarded as detrimental to the virtue of "awkwardness" (**zhou,** an innate, unspoiled, child-like quality) in a painting. But concealed under the appearance of blandness (**pingdan**) and awkwardness, artistic brilliance drew its inspiration from the other scholarly pursuits of poetry, music, and calligraphy.

Suzhou was also a centre of professional painters, with Zhou Chen (fl. c. 1500-1535) (cat. no. 20), Tang Yin (1470-1523) (cat. no. 21), and Qiu Ying (c. 1515-1551) (cat. no. 24), as its leading masters. Both Tang Yin and Qiu Ying were friends of Wen Zhengming and moved within the scholarly circle of Suzhou.

With the expansion of commerce and industry in the lower Yangtze Valley in the 16th and 17th centuries, economic affluence and increasing urbanisation brought rapid social changes. Education, which became more easily available as the results of the development of printing, was no longer the monopoly of the elite scholar-gentry class. Through education, members of the merchant class, the lowest in the Confucian social order, could now enter the bureaucracy. The class distinctions of scholar, peasant, artisan, and merchant were blurred by social mobility.

The democratisation of education also led to the increasing popularity of scholarly style of painting. Economic prosperity led to its commercialisation, when more people could afford to collect paintings. Professional painters began to adopt the literati style of painting; there were also scholars who did not hold public office and relied on painting for a living. It became more and more difficult to define scholar-amateur painting either on the basis of style or on the socio-economic status of the artist.

The commercialisation and popularisation of the literati style of painting in Suzhou, especially that of Wen Zhengming, are well demonstrated by criticisms made around 1600 by Fan Yulin:

"The men of Suzhou can't recognize a single character and haven't seen a single genuine work by an ancient master. They claim to follow their own minds and create a style of their own. They smear and daub on a mountain, a stream, a plant, or tree, then hang it in the market place and exchange it for a peck of rice. How can their paintings be any good! Among them are some who choose to imitate some famous masters, but the only one they know is Wen Zhengming. They manage a slight resemblance. But with all their copying, they only capture the 'skin' of his external form, without getting anything of his spirit and principle . . ."

Although interesting paintings continued to be produced in Suzhou in the late Ming, the generative force that gave a new direction in painting came from a group of intellectuals gathered around the figure of Dong Qichang (1555-1636) (cat. no. 26), in Huating, Songjiang, which now rivalled Suzhou as an art centre. It was probably about 1593-98, while under the intellectual stimulation of the philosophy of individualism, that Dong formulated his epoch-making theory of the "Northern and Southern Schools" in painting. Chinese painting (landscape) was seen by Dong as developing in two parallel currents, both having their origins in the Tang dynasty (618-906). The distinction is, however, not a geographical one. It is a distinction between two different approaches to painting, in which Dong drew his analogy and philosophical basis from Chan Buddhism. These are, basically, the technical approach of the craftsman (professional painter) versus the creative approach of the artist (scholar-amateur painter). In striving for skilful workmanship and technical perfection, the achievements of which could be measured in stages, the craftsman's approach to painting is compared to the gradual approach to "spiritual enlightenment", advocated by the Northern School of Chan Buddhism. This kind of attainment, according to the Southern (Orthodox) School of Chan Buddhism, is not a genuine enlightenment. The approach of the scholar-amateur artist, on the other hand, is likened to the Southern School's intuitive method of "sudden spiritual enlightenment"; the artist experiences within himself a "sudden awakening" (like a flash of illumination) to his potential for creativity, as he experiences oneness with the Universe and the creative forces of nature. This awakening, although sudden and instantaneous, may be a long and gradual process of self-cultivation. Painting is therefore not only a form of self-cultivation but also self-realisation and self-expression.

The creative approach advocated by Dong Qichang was not an arbitrary kind of creativity, but was based on tradition. The artist creates his own style of painting by transforming the styles of the ancient masters. This is accomplished by carrying on a "spiritual communion" (**shenhui**) with the works of the ancients in which one studies the "mind" (i.e. the conception) of the ancient master and reconstructs the underlying principles of his paintings. Having assimilated and internalised the style of the ancient master, the artist then creates a style of his own which should surpass that of his model. In transforming the styles of the ancients, the artist is also regenerating and transmitting a stylistic tradition. He is, at the same time, finding his place in the history of painting. Through each personal renewal, as with the teachings of Chan Buddhism, the styles of the great masters are passed down as a living tradition. Thus, in his theoretical formulation, Dong has not only drawn a basic distinction between professional and amateur paintings, he has also re-defined scholar-amateur painting and established it as the orthodox tradition.

Paintings by the innovative masters of the late Ming, such as paintings by Dong Qichang, Wu Bin (fl. c. 1568-1621) (cat. no. 28), and Chen Hongshou (1599-1652) (cat. no. 35), are highly expressive and individualistic. By distorting and exaggerating landscape elements into semi-abstract and eccentric forms, and creating formal relationships between them, Dong succeeded in transforming the styles of Yuan masters into a personal style that expressed his intense inner feelings. Wu Bin, in creating his fantastic landscapes, made similar use of the Northern Song style of landscape painting. In the landscapes of both Dong and Wu, tensions are created by such disturbing elements as spatial ambiguity and juxtaposition, as well as by unstable forms. So also, in changing the figure styles of the Northern and Southern dynasties (420-581) into grotesque and awkward forms, Chen Hongshou created an introspective and enigmatic style of figure painting. Thus, by using the styles of the past in a creative manner, the innovative masters of the late Ming introduced a new dimension to Chinese painting.

catalogue no. 1

"Landscapes of Huashan"
by Wang Lu (1332 – ?)

Set of four album leaves. Ink and colour on paper. 34.7 x 50.5cm
Shanghai Museum

Leaf 1: "Jade Spring Retreat"

In the foreground, enclosed by rocky cliffs overgrown with trees and shrubs and hollowed by meandering waterfalls, is a building compound, probably the Jade Spring Retreat. A poetic inscription by the artist reads as follows:

"He who throws away his gourd ladle detests noise
[this refers to the story of someone who hung his ladle on a tree branch, and then threw it away because it made a noise in the wind].
[But] he who listens to rustling pines dislikes quietness.
The two old gentleman are full of wordly concerns, not having reached the state of being at one with nature.
As to identifying with objects of nature and being carried along with natural events, the wonder lies in having no expectations [and hence free of anxiety].
The same spring, like this one, brings different responses.
What the Taoist recluse dislikes, I like.
I wish to recite a poem and inscribe it on the spring.
The recluse laughs [at the idea] and says the spring would not [be able to] know".

Leaf 2: "The Green Dragon Mountain Peaks"

Depicted is a rare vision of mountain peaks immersed in a sea of clouds and mists. A tiny figure sitting on top of a mountain peak contemplating the ephemeral clouds accentuates the immense vastness of nature. Greatly moved by the awesome beauty of nature, Wang Lu expresses in his inscription the view that all the wordly achievements of wealth, fame, and longevity could not compare with that which he was experiencing.

Leaf 3: "Extraordinary Giant Footprint"

On top of a mountain two scholars point at a giant human footprint which, according to legend, was made by Wuwang, the founder of the Zhou dynasty (1027-221 B.C.). The footprint made Wang Lu think of the transience of worldly accomplishments. In his inscription, Wang laments how the sounds (symbolising achievements) made by Wuwang's musical instrument were so loud that they could deafen the ears, and now are heard no more.

Leaf 4: "Below the Jade Goddess Mountain Peak"

Two scholars stand on a mountain top overlooking a ravine which recedes into the distance. The picture is accompanied by a poetic inscription by Wang Lu.

Wang Lu was a native of Kunshan in Jiangsu province. When he was about fifty-two years old, he visited the sacred Taoist mountain site of Huashan in Shaanxi province and he was so inspired by the beauty that he painted an album of more than forty leaves, based on sketches made while travelling. The four leaves in the present exhibition are among the fourteen surviving leaves that can be traced.

In these album leaves, the artist's visual and emotional experience of nature is portrayed with a certain faithfulness to external form and inventiveness in composition. The academic styles of Ma Yuan and Xia Gui are transformed into a scholarly style characterized by heavy lines of tapering brushstrokes that outline the contours of rocks, light ink washes enriched by blue, and sparse texture strokes.

At the back of the entire album is a narrative poem inscribed by Wang Lu to accompany the paintings in the album, which records his travels in Huashan. The inscription is dated 1383. The albums are recorded in **Tiewang Shanhu** (postscript dated 1600) (see Lovell, nos. 30 and 63), **Shibaizhai Shu Hua Lu** (Lovell, no. 69), and published in **Yiyuan Duoying**, 1978, no. 2.

Leaf 1

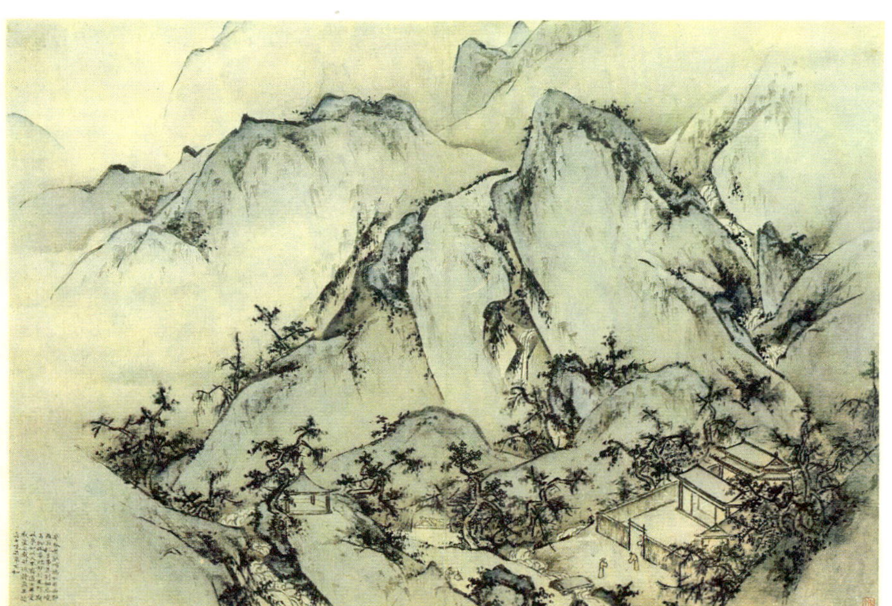

Leaf 2

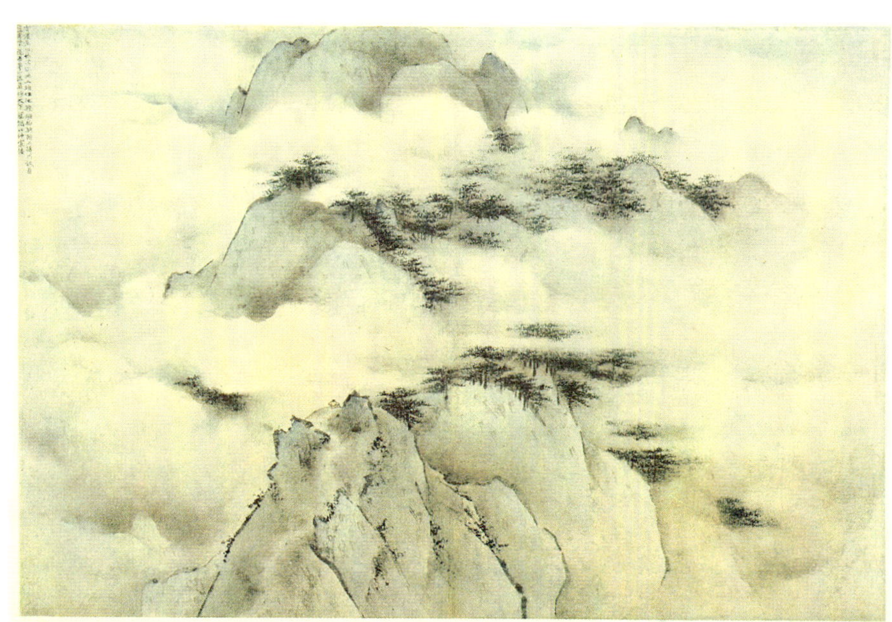

Leaf 3

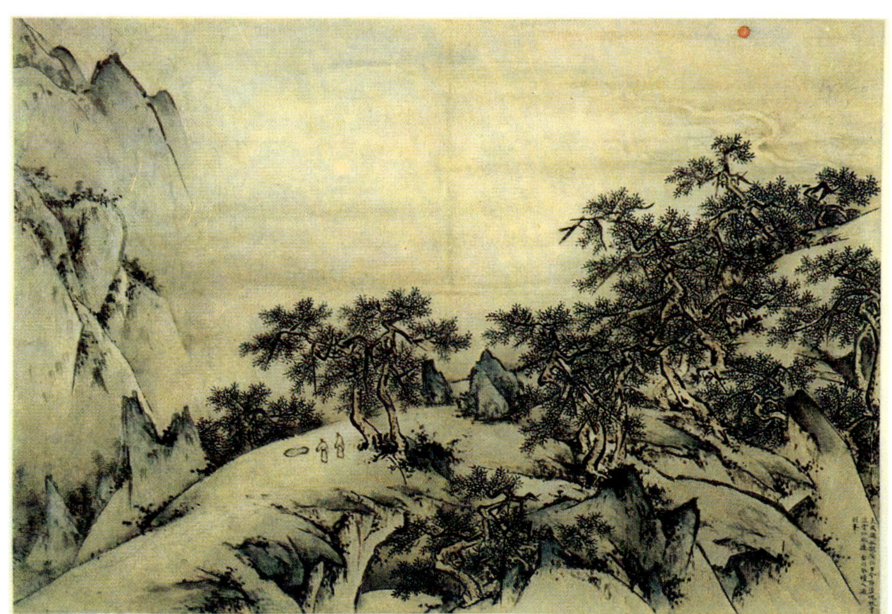

"Misty Jade Trees"
by Chen Lu (15th century)

Hanging scroll; ink on silk. 138.2 x 65.5cm
Gugong Museum, Peking

From the trunk of a plum tree which is just visible at the base of the scroll, a branch of flowering plum rises up the scroll, meandering in a seemingly casual manner as if it were smoke. The verticality of the composition is emphasised by the simple straight twigs which rise from the main lower branch with an extraordinary directness, rather like water weed quietly rising in placid water. It is a sombre, almost gloomy, painting not lightened by the addition of colour. The horizontal band of drifting mist, which for a moment all but obliterates a section of the branch, only serves to deepen the sense of mystery and provide the painting with an ethereal, unreal and timeless quality.

The plum, or prunus, as the traditional symbol of winter in China, and here particularly the flowering prunus which represents the passing of winter and the happy prospect of spring, was a much-favoured theme not only for painters but also as a decorative feature.

A native of Huiji, present-day Shaoxing, in Zhejiang province, Chen Lu became a noted painter of pine trees, bamboos, orchids and above all plum blossom, the subject of this painting.

Seals of the artist and collectors.
Recorded: **Xuzhai Minghua Xulu** (Lovell, no. 98).

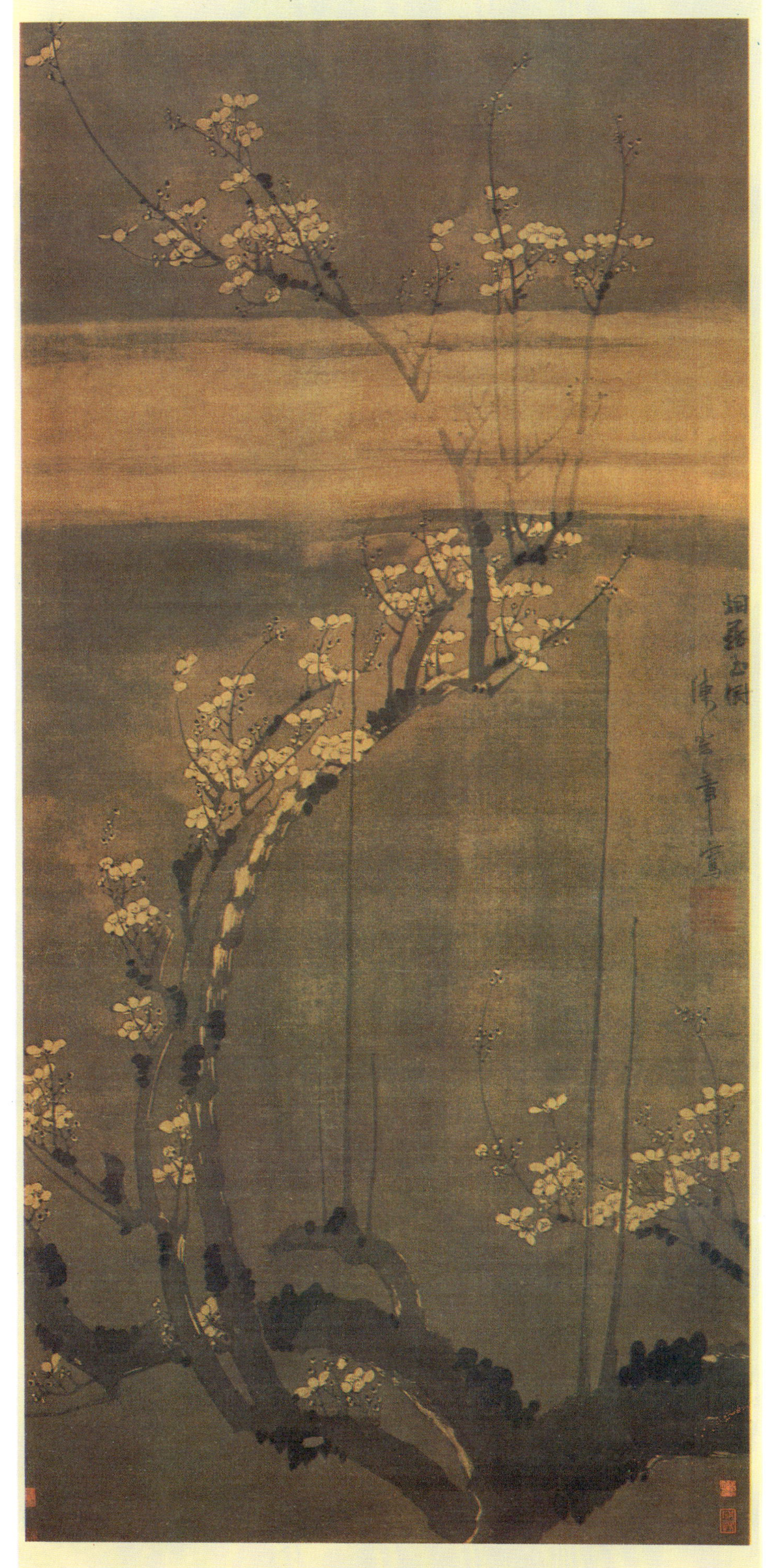

"Travellers in Snowy Mountains"
by Dai Jin (1388-1462)

Hanging scroll; ink and colour on silk. 144.2 x 78.1 cm
Gugong Museum, Peking

A tall snowy mountain, rising in fantastic shapes at the centre, is stabilized by a group of pine trees in the foreground. Buildings are found in misty gorges between the central mountain, and precipitous cliffs on the left. On the right is an expanse of calm water leading to distant hills. Travellers are crossing a bridge and approaching the gate of the mountain pass.

Dai Jin has painted a monumental landscape, possibly in the style of Guo Xi (early 11th century), a court academy artist of the Northern Song period (960-1127). But he reworked it in a creative way. Instead of being delineated in the usual mode of careful outline and texturing strokes as in a Song landscape, the central mountain, for example, is sketched in jagged, nervous lines, creating a rough impression of soft, drooping snow and its wind-swept movement. The mountain is activated into dynamic thrust and counter-thrust by the swift, running brush movement, which resembles in brush idiom the cursive script (**caoshu**) of calligraphy. With the sky and water darkened by a light ink wash, the snowscape is actually drawn (or written) with calligraphic strokes, rather than painted. In fact, Dai Jin signed his painting as having been written (**xie**) by him. Dai had experimented with the calligraphic **xieyi** (writing conception) manner of painting popular among scholar-amateur painters, and had used it in a Northern Song landscape of the court academy style. "**Xieyi**" is painting in a free and suggestive manner with calligraphic brushstrokes or ink wash to capture the essential characteristics of the object depicted. In spite of awkward passages of spatial ambiguity in the landscape, it is a dazzling performance of technical virtuosity in the mastery of the brush. It is a brilliant piece of calligraphy, executed with great exuberance, even though, for the refined taste of the scholar-amateur painters, it might appear too rough and lacking in restraint.

Dai Jin (1388-1460) was born in Qiantang, Zhejiang province. About 1425 he was recommended to serve at the court of the Xuande Emperor (r. 1426-1435). Dai fell victim to the jealousy of the other painters at court and lost the favour of the emperor. He was dismissed from the court and returned to Hangzhou where he tried to make a living as a professional painter. He died in poverty. He is, however, credited by later writers as having revitalized the court academic style of the Southern Song (1127-1279), particularly the styles of Ma Yuan and Xia Gui of the 13th century, and of having founded the Zhe school of painting.

The painting is inscribed by Dai Jin and bears his two seals.

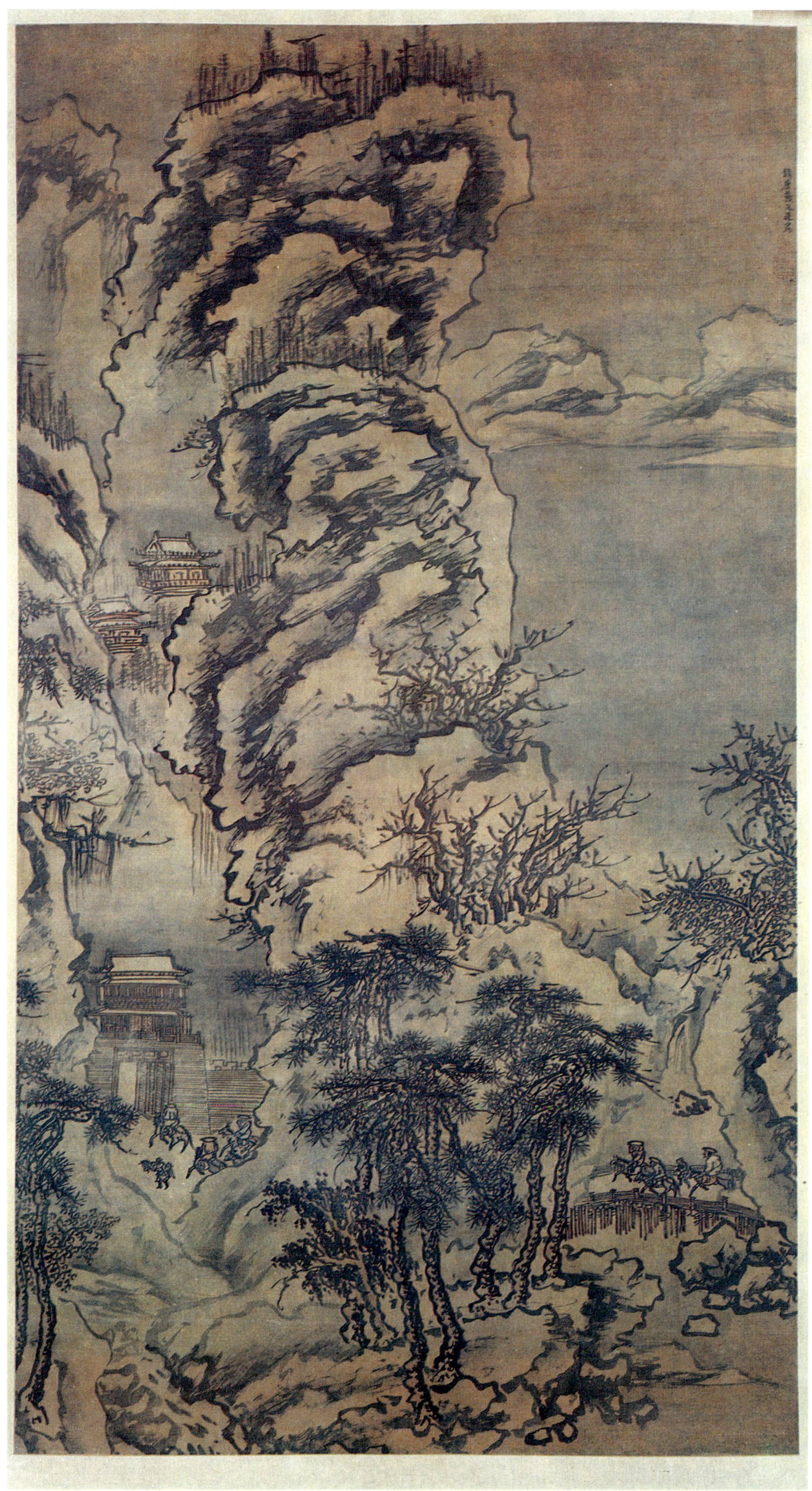

"Watching the Waterfall and Humming Poetry"
by Wu Wei (1459-1508)

Hanging scroll; ink and light colours on silk. 156.7 x 95.3cm
Shandong Provincial Cultural Relics Bureau

The subject of this painting, clearly described in the title, fully evokes the literati ideal of the sophisticated and learned scholar at one with nature. The scholar rests easily on one elbow, the right hand holding a book of poetry, his composure echoing the peace and tranquility of the scene. The simple landscape elements, rising mountains, waterfall and pine tree, balance perfectly and combine to provide a natural amphitheatre in which the scholar resides. In characteristic manner the natural elements are painted in a range of brush and texture strokes typical of the academic Zhe school and reminiscent of the Southern Song Ma-Xia school, whilst the scholar is carefully drawn with great linear clarity.

Wu Wei was born in Wuchang in Hubei province, the son of a distinguished and high-ranking official. The death of his father at a comparatively early age left the young Wu Wei an orphan to be raised by a provincial official in his home state. It is recorded that Wu received no formal training in the art of painting but learnt informally through studying his late father's collection. At the age of seventeen he settled in Nanking to pursue his career and success led to an invitation to Peking where he became painter-in-attendance at one of the Imperial Halls during the Chenghua period (1465-88). The late Ming dynasty historical compendium, the **Wushengshi Shi,** relates a famous meeting between the painter and the Emperor: "On one occasion when summoned by the Emperor, Wu was very drunk and came into the imperial presence with dishevelled and dirty hair, his shoes dragging and torn; he arrived staggering, supported under the arms by two court servants. The Emperor laughed and ordered him to paint on the spot a picture of 'Pines in Wind'. Wu knelt down and spilled the ink (on to the silk or paper provided), then began to rub and smear it freely, 'trusting his hand', making wind and clouds arise on the screen so appallingly strong that the two servants grew pale. The Emperor drew a deep breath and said: 'This is truly the brush of an Immortal'."

Signature and seal of the artist.

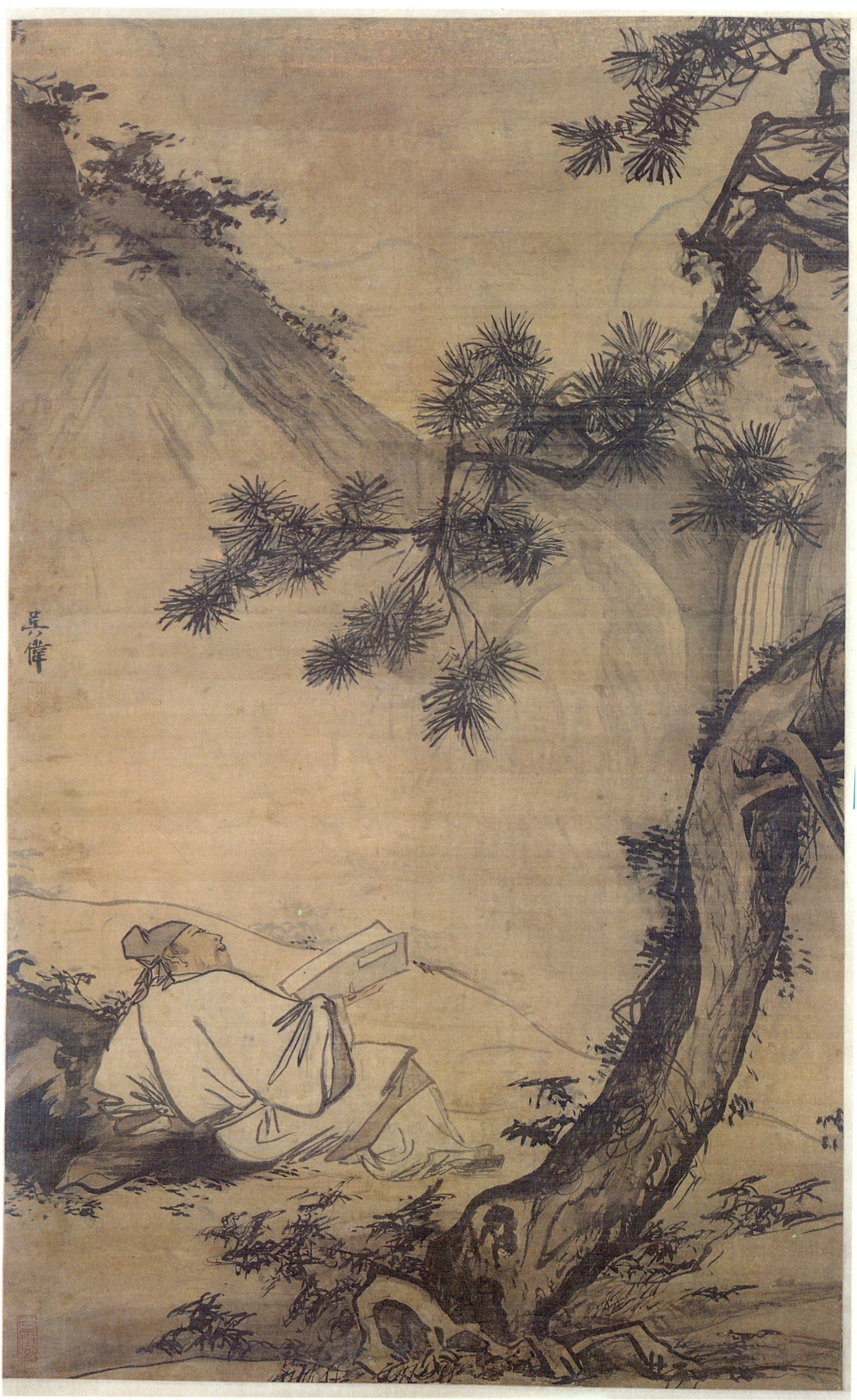
吳偉

"Playing the Flute in the Autumn Hall"
by Wang E (active late 15th century)

Hanging scroll; ink and light colours on silk. 184 x 98.2cm
Shandong Provincial Cultural Relics Bureau

This painting reflects the literati ideal of man pursuing a philosophical and cultured life in harmony with nature. On the balcony of a pavilion perched on a cliff two attendants listen to the scholar playing the flute and gazing into the misty void. The precision of the drawing of the pavilion and the figures contrasts with the broad and confident brushstrokes which define the elements of the natural world. The human presence in the setting is characteristically dwarfed by the overhanging rocks and towering peaks, and yet there is no feeling of tension, only peace and harmony between man and nature.

This distinctive composition, dominated by the rock masses and rising peaks on the right, reflects the 'one-sided' composition of the Southern Song Ma-Xia School which was so influential upon the Ming dynasty Zhe school of painting with which Wang E was associated.

Wang E was born in Fenghua, Zhejiang province and subsequently rose to become a prominent painter at the court during the Hongzhi period (1488-1506) where he was hailed as "the Ma Yuan of our time". The subsequent Zhengde Emperor (1506-22) honoured Wang further by appointing him to the rank of officer of the Imperial Guard. Throughout his career Wang confined himself to the literati theme of man and nature and this is a classic example of that tradition. Unlike the monumental and awe-inspiring landscapes of the Northern Song, in which man appeared subdued by nature, Wang sought to recreate the Southern Song ideal of man at peace with nature. The towering peaks may dwarf the human presence but they do not overwhelm.

Signature and seal of the artist.

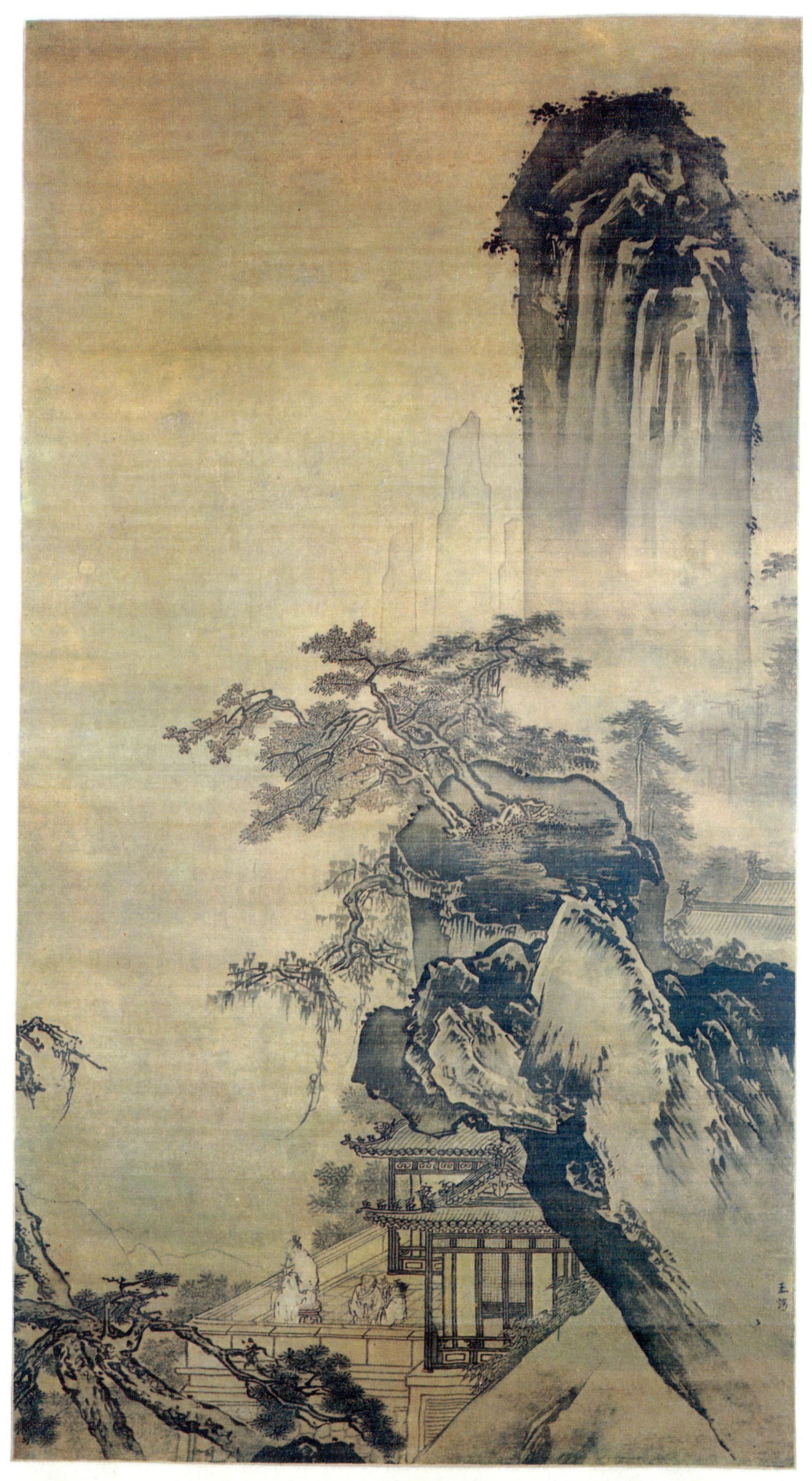

"Gazing at the Moon"
by Zhang Lu (1464-1538)

Hanging scroll; ink and light colours on silk. 151.5 x 103.2cm
Shandong Provincial Cultural Relics Bureau

Exemplifying the literati ideal the painting depicts a scholar gazing wistfully, but thoughtfully, at the moon through dappled trees, accompanied by an attentive servant. The scene is dominated by the trees whose mysterious presence is accentuated by the hanging foliage set against far distant mountains painted in a light colour wash. The contrast between the more densely painted foreground elements, rocks, trees and foliage, and the faint outlines of the distant mountain ranges implies the timeless and limitless qualities of nature. In the sky a pale moon casts a watery light on the scene. Once again the theme of harmony between man and nature is paramount.

Born in Kaifeng, in northerly Henan province, Zhang Lu was the most successful and famous of Wu Wei's (see cat. no. 4) followers. Like so many scholar gentleman painters Zhang showed great academic promise as a child, however, after attending the University at Nanking, he subsequently failed to obtain the necessary degree to enter the official hierarchy. It was then that he turned to painting, studying in particular the work of Dai Jin (see cat. no. 3) and then Wu Wei. Zhang became a popular figure among the Nanking hierarchy and it is recorded that "all the officials and gentlemen enjoyed going around with him". With an established clientele it seems that as his career progressed he became less innovative and his style increasingly stereotyped in order to satisfy that demand. As such an example, this painting echoes the refined and comfortable taste of the scholar-gentleman class in 15th-16th century Nanking.

Seal of the artist.

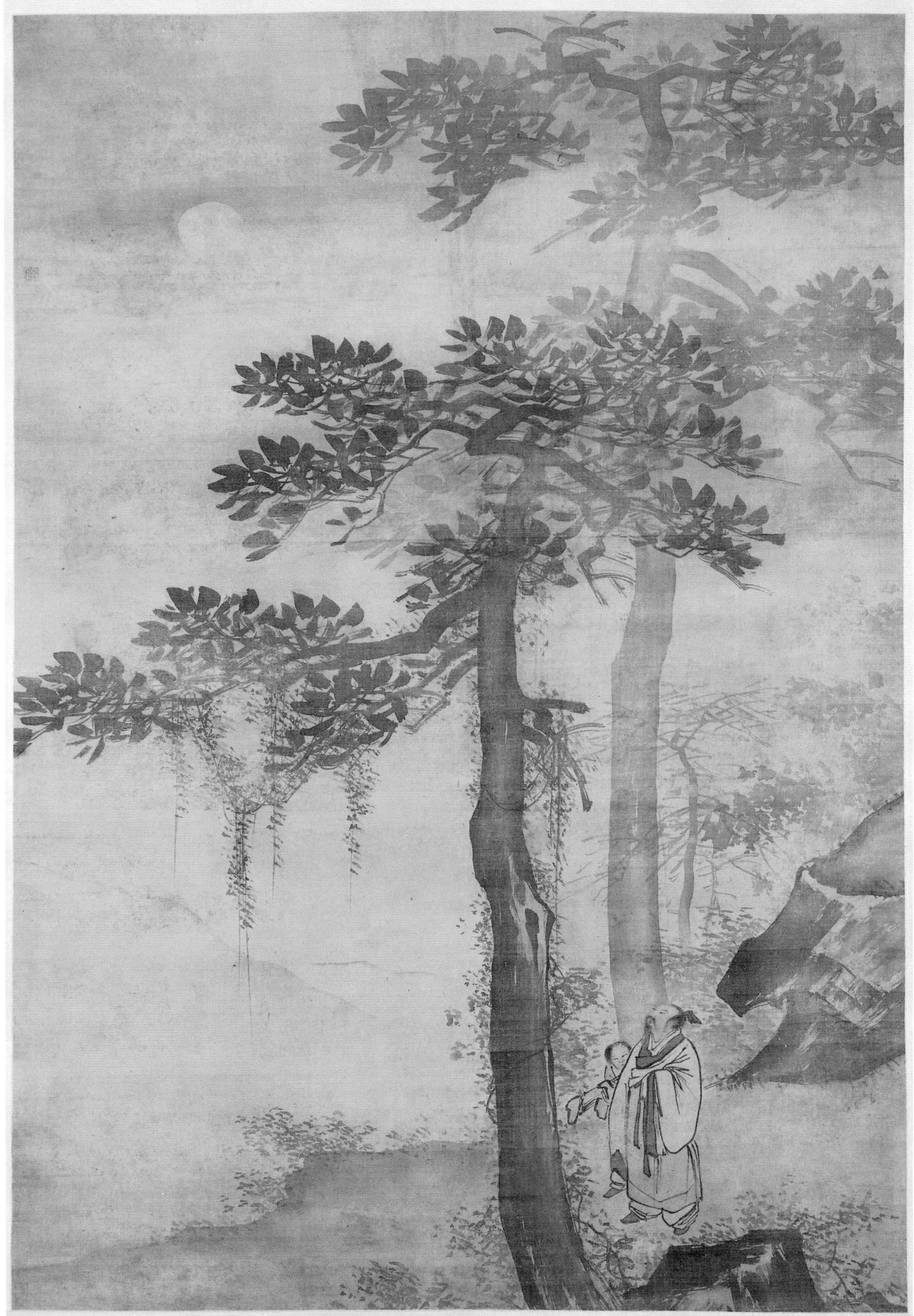

"Figures from daily life"
by Zhang Lu (1464-1538)

Handscroll; ink and light colours on silk. 25.8 x 161.3cm
Tianjin Arts Museum

This apparently random selection of human figures are nevertheless carefully composed so as to create both a structure and continuity for the scroll. The almost total absence of any kind of setting or context for the figures is at first disconcerting. For example, the two long-robed travellers on the right of the scroll have no ground line on which to stand and thus seem to be floating. However, the distinct relationship between the two conversing figures and the carefully placed load at their side, creates a context and environment within themselves. It is sufficient for them to exist in a reality without the elements of a natural setting in which we would expect to find such figures.

Our eye is then drawn, by the careful placing of the pole on which their load is carried, to the mere suggestion of a ground line which moves, sometimes uncertainly, to provide a base and context for the remaining figures. There is no doubt that the principal character in this composition is the large and portentous figure on the left who, by his aristocratic and determined demeanour, and his careful placement as our eye is drawn along the unfolding saga from right to left, eventually dominates. The seemingly casual disposition of the figures belies a very carefully constructed composition in which the artist deliberately draws our attention gradually along the scroll until we eventually reach this imposing figure.

The figures are characteristically drawn with a precise calligraphic line which lends forceful definition to contrast with the vagaries of the ground line and the softer brushwork of the rock and natural elements. This stylistic contrast between the rendering of natural and human elements was noted in the previous Zhang Lu painting.

Two seals of the artist.
For biographical details see catalogue number 6.
Reproduced: **Arts of China: vol. 111: Paintings in Chinese Museums**, pl. 64.

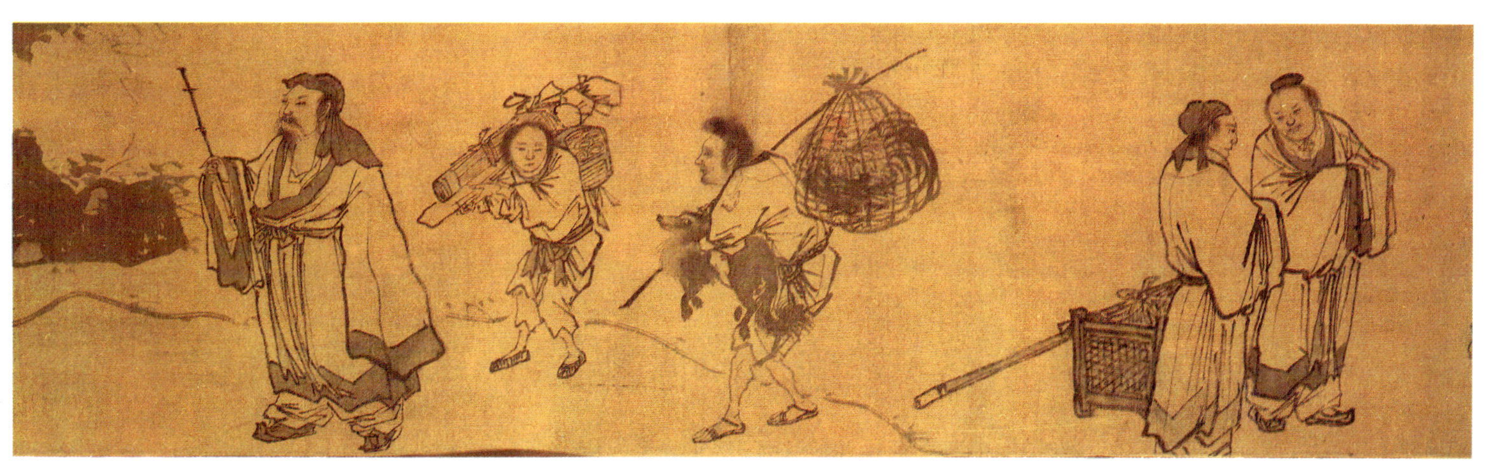

"Double Hawks"
by Lin Liang (15th century)

Hanging scroll; ink on silk. 172.5 x 104.5cm
Guangzhou Museum

A pair of proud hawks perch imperiously on a rocky peak and dominate the surrounding rocks and trees. The stark and often aggressive brushwork suggests a wintry flavour. The strong, uncompromising and broad brushstrokes which define the rocks and gnarled trees are typical of the early Ming academic style reflecting Southern Song traditions. The natural features rendered in this seemingly spontaneous style provide the perfect setting for the fearsome hawks, alert and on the lookout for their prey. Although far removed from the lyrical Southern Song landscapes, the brushwork and one-sided composition of this painting owe much to that earlier tradition.

Born in Guandong province Lin Liang is recorded as having served in the Provincial Administrations Office in Guangzhou (Canton) whilst learning the art of painting. Success as a painter overtook his official career and he eventually served at the Court in Peking during the Hongzhi period (1488-1506) where he attained the honorary rank of Commander in the Embroidered Uniform Guard. Although he also painted highly detailed and colourful pictures it was for his more dramatic ink paintings, particularly of birds, that Lin Liang is renowned.

Signature and seal of the artist.

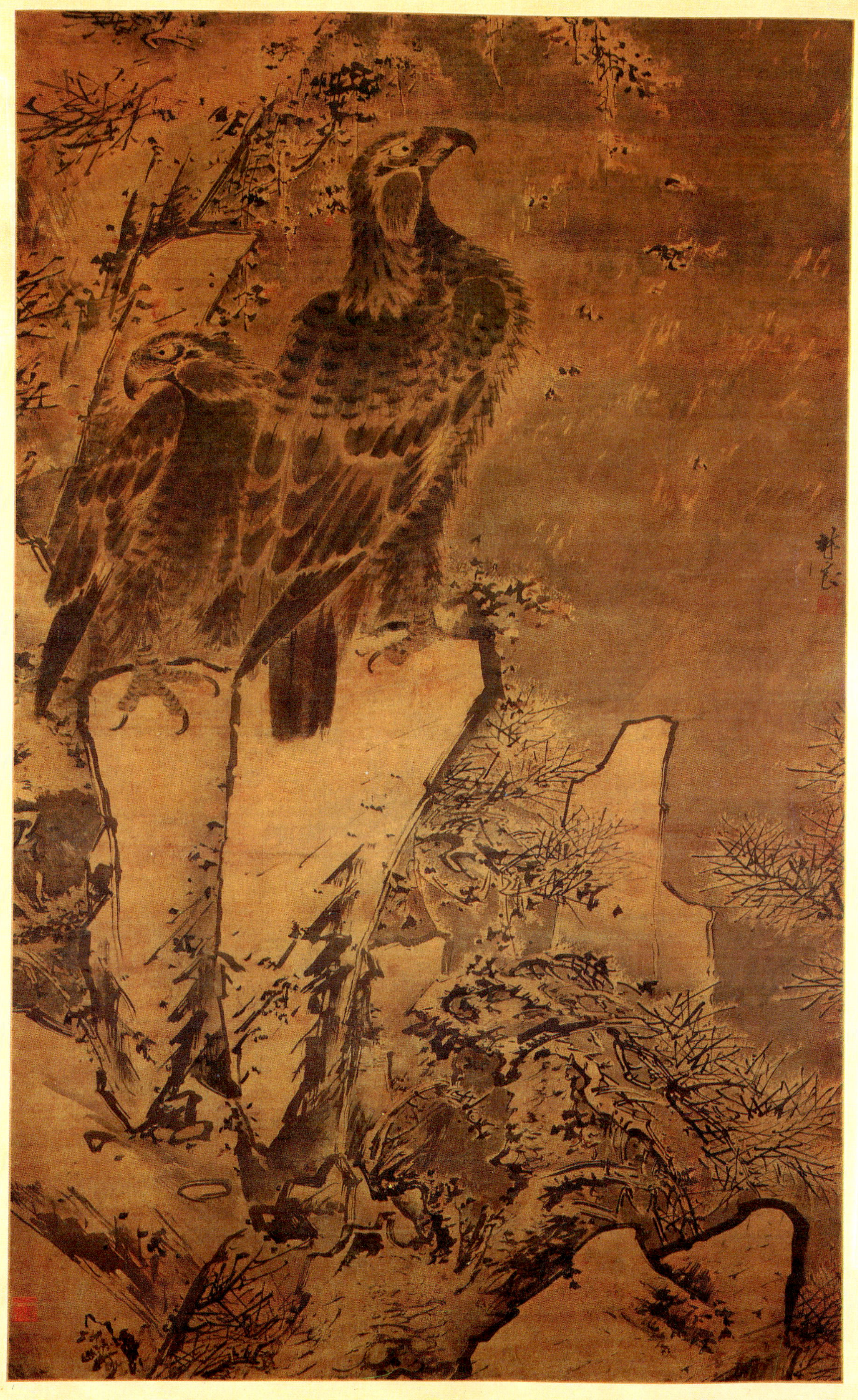

"Pomegranates Hollyhocks and Cock"
by Lu Ji (15th century)

Hanging scroll; ink and colours on silk. 170.5 x 105.7cm
Gugong Museum, Peking

A proud and colourful cockerel acts as the focal point for this decorative painting in a style so favoured in the conservative academic traditions of the Ming court. A rock outcrop, painted in the style of the Southern Song masters with definitive outlines and texture strokes, acts as a base for the floral elements. From behind the rocks appear hollyhocks, delicately drawn in black ink and coloured with light washes. Above, the branch of a tree overhangs to complete the deliberate and careful composition.

Lu Ji was a native of Ningpo in Zhejiang province who studied with another famous bird and flower painter in the academic tradition serving at the Ming court, Bian Wenjin. Lu Ji's studied and carefully executed, but conservative, decorative paintings were so favoured by the Emperor that during the Hongzhi period (1488-1506) he was appointed to the high honorific post, Commander of the Guard of the Gold Embroidered Robes. As well as studying the works of the Tang and Song bird and flower masters and those of his mentor, Bian Wenjin, Lu Ji is known to have also closely followed the style of the Guangzhou master, Lin Liang (see cat. no. 8).

Signature and seal of the artist.

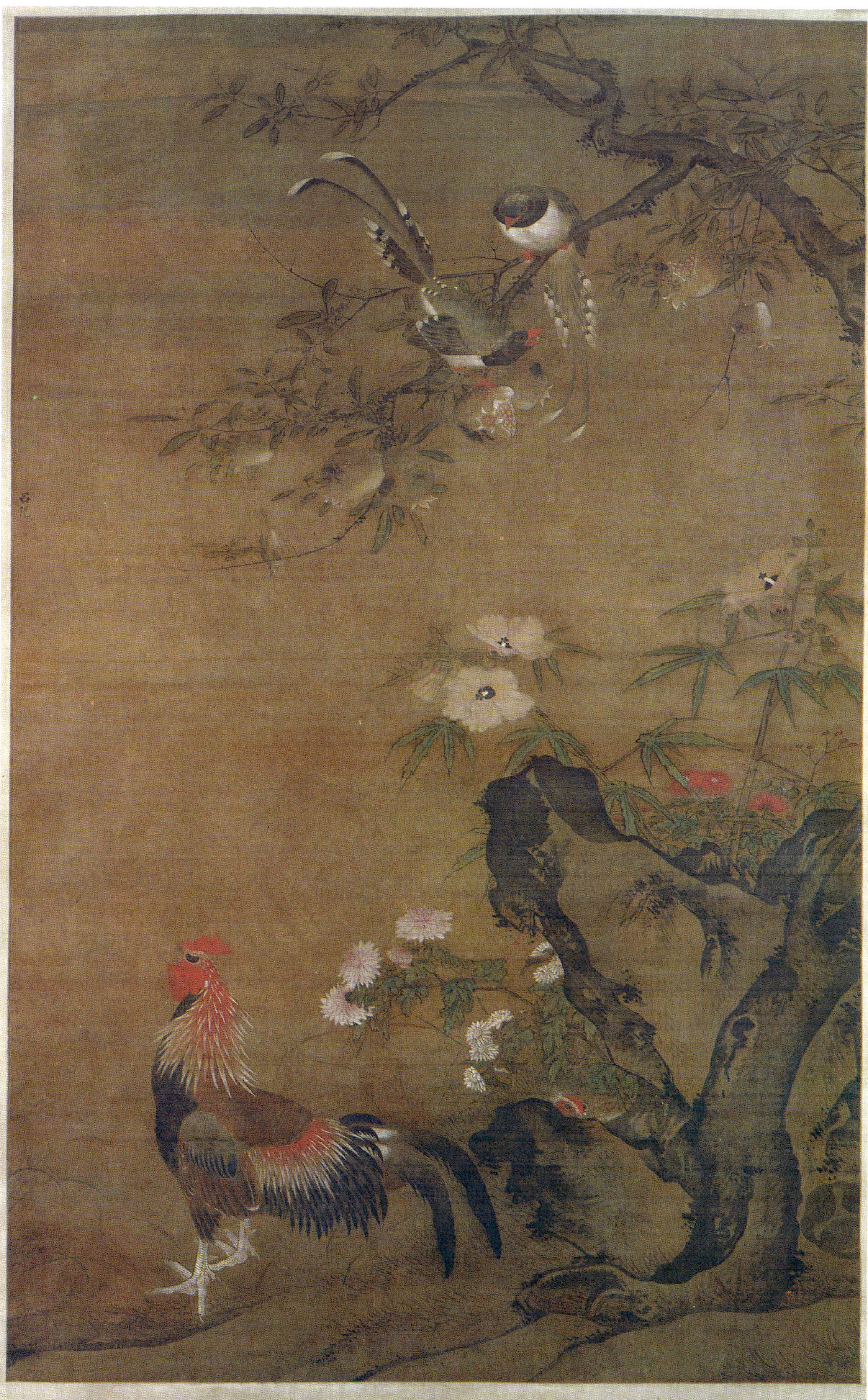

"White Rocks and Green Bamboo"
by Xia Chang (1388-1470)

Hanging scroll; ink on silk. 156.7 x 73.4cm
Gugong Museum, Peking

Two branches of bamboo spring from a rock outcrop in this simple but evocative painting. The eccentrically shaped rock is expressively painted with broad, often straggling, brushstrokes with no texturing of the surface to indicate volume and mass. The bamboo too is drawn with simple brushstrokes and washes with no linear definition. Variations in the density of the ink provide depth and variety, but the great sensitivity of the brushwork perfectly evokes the bamboo, perhaps gently swaying in the lightest of breezes but never buffeted by storms and high winds. The lightness of Xia's touch perfectly captures slight movement in the branches and the rustle of the leaves.

Xia Chang came from the picturesque town of Kunshan in Jiangsu province and entered the courtly world as a prominent official to be finally appointed President of the Court of Imperial Sacrifices at the beginning of the Tianxun period (1457-65). His fame was, however, as a painter of bamboo, the only subject he ever painted, and as a calligrapher. Such was his renown as a painter of bamboo that it was said at the time "a bamboo by Xia is worth ten taels of gold".

Inscriptions, one by the artist followed by his seals.

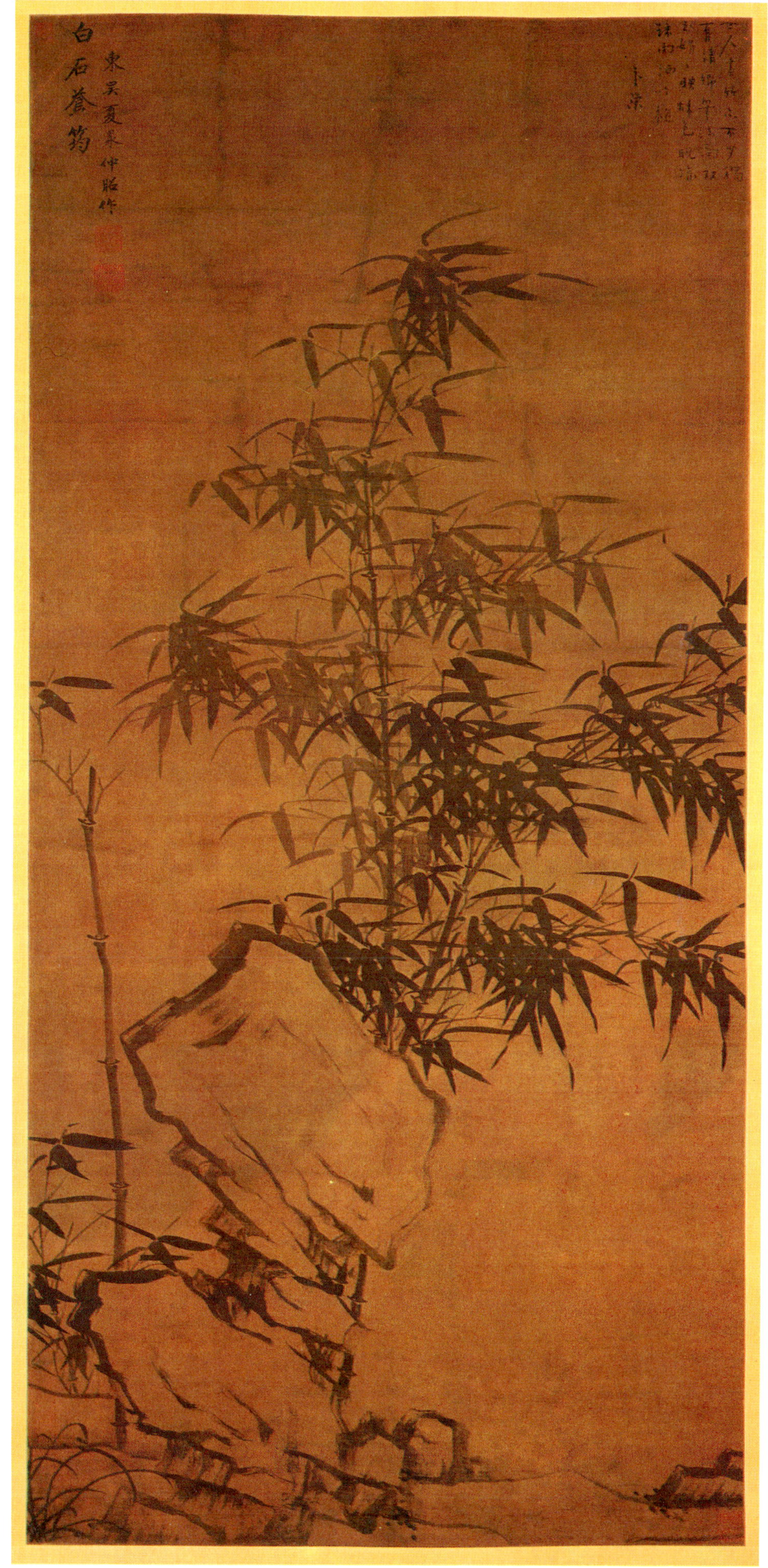
白石蒼筠
東吳夏㫤仲昭作

"Fishing in Solitude in an Autumn River" by Yao Shou (1423-1495)

Album leaf; ink and colour on paper. 31.3 x 48.3cm
Shanghai Museum

In this small, intimate landscape, Yao Shou is paying tribute to the impressionist style of Mi Fu (1051-1170), who was a scholar-amateur painter, calligrapher, and art collector of the Song dynasty. The central mountain and the surrounding peaks, immersed in clouds and mists, are painted in ink and colour washes with very little use of contour lines. The presence of mist is simply suggested by the blank areas of the painting. Trees are depicted with short, dabbing strokes of green and black (the so-called **mi dian** or **mi** dots). Echoing the distant blue hills, the marshland in the foreground, with its casually arranged trees, bridge, and a lonely fishing boat, is washed in pale green.

Yao Shou was from Jiaxing, Jiangsu province. He obtained his highest degree, the Jinshi degree, around 1464. He held various official positions until the early 1470's, when he retired from political life and devoted himself to painting.

The painting is signed by the artist and bears three of his seals.
Reproduced: **Shanghai Museum Catalogue of Paintings;** no. 42
       Arts of China: Paintings in Chinese Museums; pl. 11

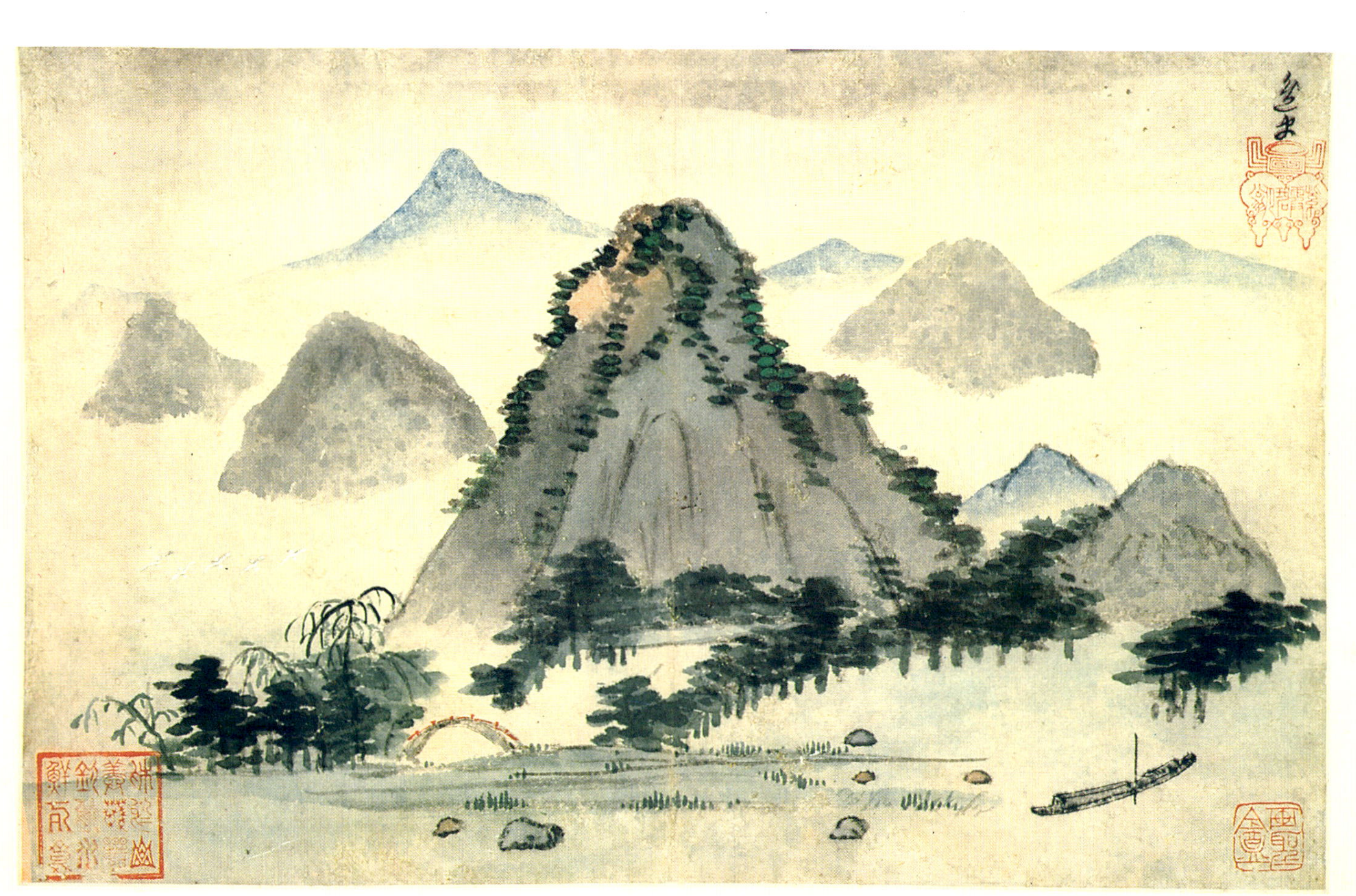

catalogue no. 12

"Playing the Qin under Tall Pines"
dated 1480 by Shen Zhou (1427-1509)

Hanging scroll; ink and colour on paper. 172 x 64.1 cm
Tianjin Arts Museum

A scholar sits on the foreground shore under tall pine trees, holding his **qin** (a plucked string instrument) and gazes across the river. A winding stream of a waterfall is seen through a screen of twisting pine branches. The dynamic thrust of the central mountain is stabilized by the tall trees in the foreground and the surrounding peaks. The dry, furry, undulating texture strokes that model the rocks and mountains, creating a quiet surface rhythm and a soft earthy texture, reveal the stylistic influence of the Yuan dynasty master, Wang Meng (c. 1309-1385). Within the bland flavour of the painting, subtlety and strength are found in the powerful composition and the rich tonal graduations of ink.

Shen Zhou was born into a distinguished and well-to-do scholar-gentry family of Suzhou. He did not seek an official career in government, but led a quiet life devoted to his interests in poetry, painting, and calligraphy, and to his mother, who lived to be almost 100 years old. Shen Zhou made friends with some of the most outstanding scholars, poets and artists of his time. He studied and followed the scholar-amateur paintings of the Yuan dynasty (1279-1368), from which he created a personal style of his own, regenerated the literati tradition of painting in Suzhou, and became the founder of the Wu school of painting.

An inscription by Shen Zhou records a farewell party given for his friend, Xu Zhongshan, at Tiger Hill, a scenic spot in Suzhou. The second inscription was written by Wu Kuan (1435-1504), a famous scholar and high official, and a childhood friend of Shen Zhou.

The painting bears several artist's and collectors' seals, including those of Bian Yongyu (1645-1702) and the Qianlong Emperor (r. 1736- 96).
Recorded: **Shigutang Shuhua Huikao** (Lovell, no. 47) and **Shiqu Baoji** (Lovell, no. 59a)

catalogue no. 13

"Fields of the Fungus of Longevity"
by Shen Zhou (1427-1509)

Handscroll, ink and colour on paper. 156 x 31.5 cm
Gugong Museum, Peking

The landscape begins with a gathering of friends and followed by fields of the "fungus of longevity". It is depicted with relaxed, broad brushstrokes and light washes of blue and pink.

The painting is signed by Shen Zhou and bears his seal. It also bears a seal of the Emperor Xuantong (r. 1908-12). The painting is followed by colophons of Shen Zhou, Yao Shou (1423-1495) and others.

Recorded: **Shigutang Shuhua Huikao**, by Pian Yongyu, dated 1682 (see Lovell, no. 47), **Jiangcun Xiaoxia Lu**, by Gao Shiqi, dated 1693 (see Lovell, no. 49).
For biographical details see catalogue number 12.

catalogue no. 12

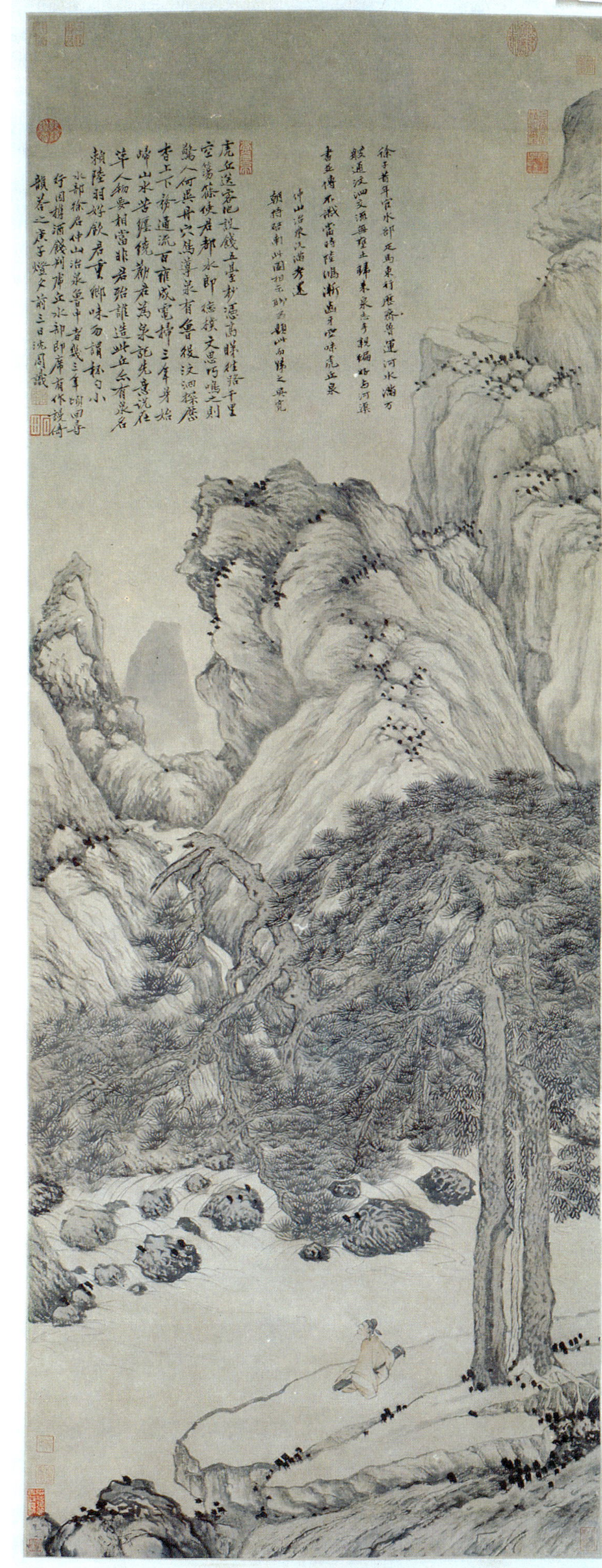

"Landscape in Snowy Scene"
by Wen Zhengming (1470-1559)

Hanging scroll; ink and colour on silk. 135 x 28.8cm
Gugong Museum, Peking

A quiet snowy landscape is sensitively rendered with soft, dry brushstrokes. Rocks and trees are gently outlined and shaded, leaving the blank areas of the silk to convey the colour of snow. A scholar in a red robe is riding a donkey and crossing a bridge and another traveller is approaching from a cave. Houses are hidden behind rocks and trees. The landscape was painted in the style of Li Cheng (died 967) of the Five dynasties period (906-960).

Complementing the painting is a poetic inscription by Wen Zhengming:
"Clouds burying trees on the mountain range and snows
everywhere, stretching far and wide.
Heaven has shaped [the landscape] into hibiscus flowers
and ten thousand frosty jades.
The little donkey does not seem to mind the long
journey home.
With a clear and lucid mind, I can compose
poetry while sitting in the saddle".

Wen Zhengming belonged to a family of scholar-officials who had distinguished themselves since the Song dynasty. In spite of having received the best education available, Wen tried and failed the examination for an official post at least ten times, the last time when he was fifty-two years old. In 1523, on the recommendation of a local governor, he was given a position in the Imperial Literary (Hanlin) Academy in Peking, serving as a compiler and editor of the official history of the preceding dynasty. He was so unhappy in the capital that he returned home after three years and devoted the rest of his long life to poetry, painting, and calligraphy. In his youth Wen studied painting with Shen Zhou (see cat. no. 12) and the paintings of the Song and Yuan dynasties, from which he created a style of painting that dominated Suzhou paintings of the 16th century.

The painting bears four seals of the artist.

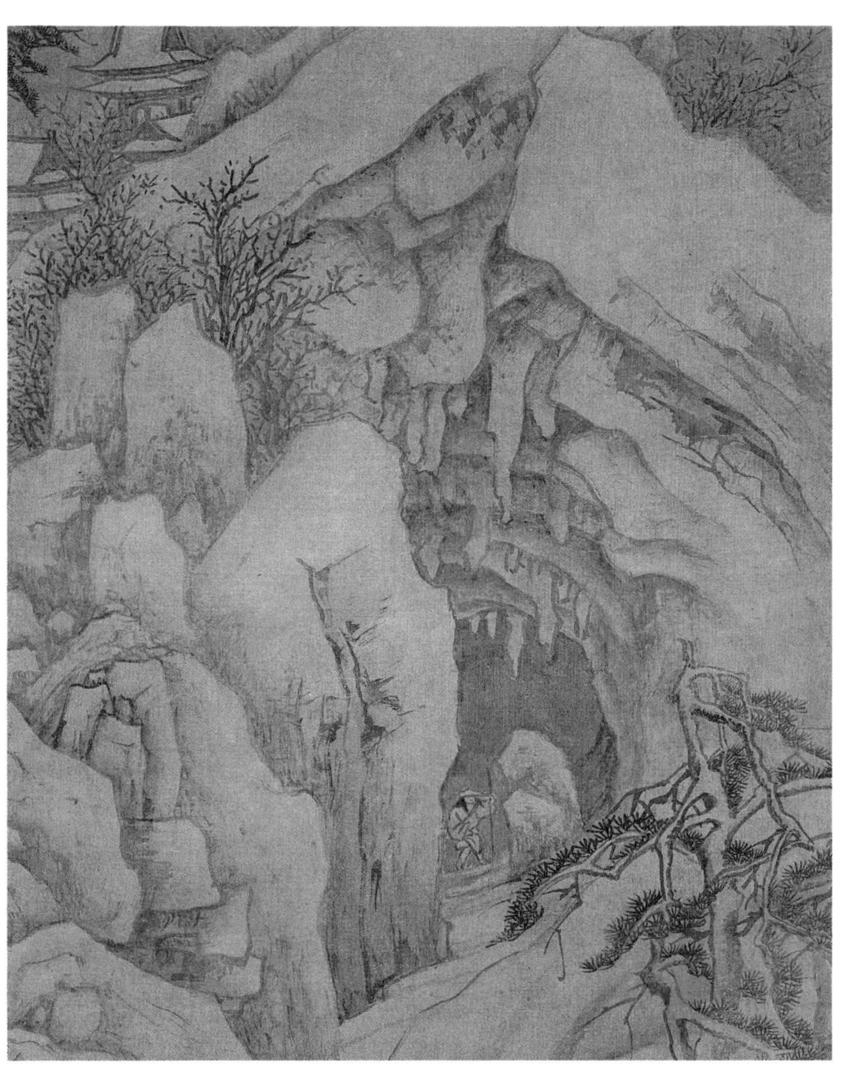

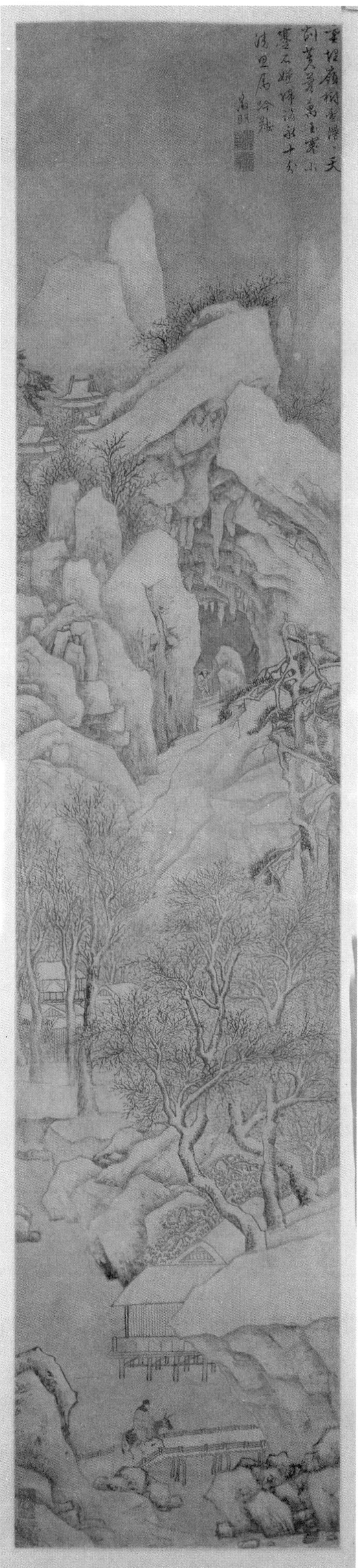

"Thatched Hut by a Stream"
by Wen Zhengming (1470-1559)

Handscroll; ink and colour on paper. 142.2 x 26.8cm
Liaoning Provincial Museum

The handscroll depicts the leisurely life of the scholar-gentry class living in retirement. It opens with a scene of two scholars engaged in conversation in a thatched house, while the servants are preparing tea. Another scholar, probably a friend, has just arrived by boat and is approaching the house, followed by a servant. Near the end of the river landscape, a farmer is returning home from the field. The painting is conceived with poetic sensitivity, reflecting Wen's reserved temperament and fastidious taste. It is delicately and carefully painted in cool colours, light washes of blue and green, with a slight touch of buff-pink. Tree foliage is depicted in small ink dots over blue washes, creating a misty effect and feeling of depth. The human figures and the geometric houses are very simply drawn. The lyricism of the painting lies in the softly graded ink and colour.

The painting is signed by the artist. It bears a seal of the artist, and several seals of the Qianlong Emperor (1736-1796). The painting is followed by a poetic inscription by Wen Zhengming, and colophons by Lu Can (1494-1551), Wang Zhideng (1535-1612), Wang Shimin (see cat. no. 41), Wen Nan (1596-1667), Jin Junming (1602-1675), his descendant Wen Dian (1633-1704), and others.

For biographical detail, see catalogue number 14.
Reproduced: **Liaoning Provincial Museum Catalogue of Paintings,** Vol. II, pp. 30-31.
Recorded: **Shigu Baoji** (Lovell, no. 59a)

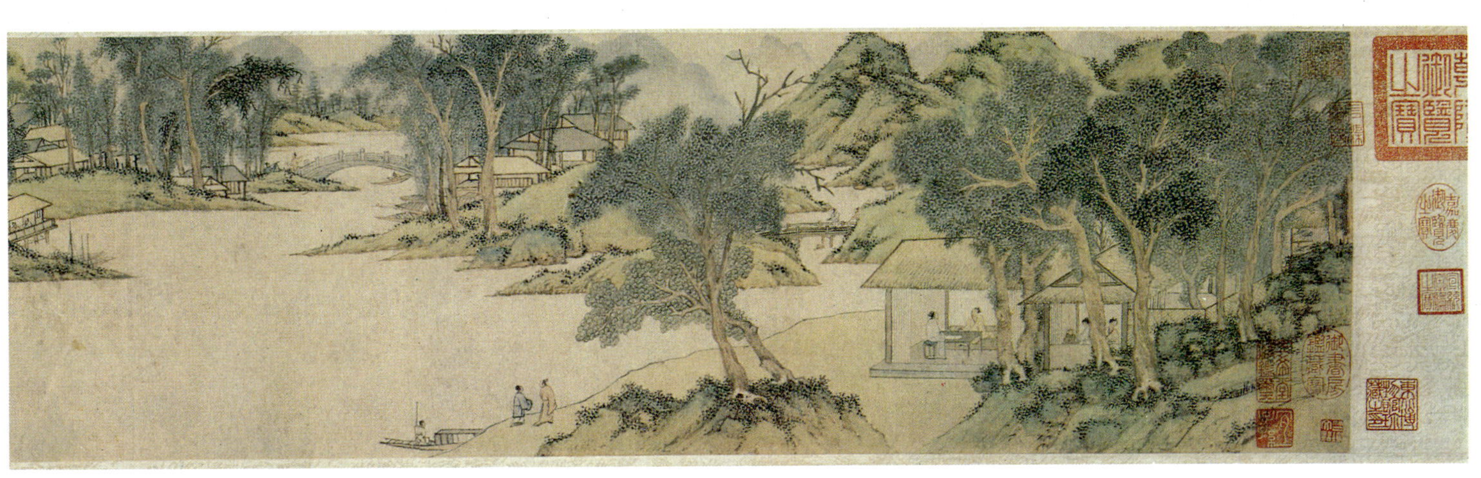

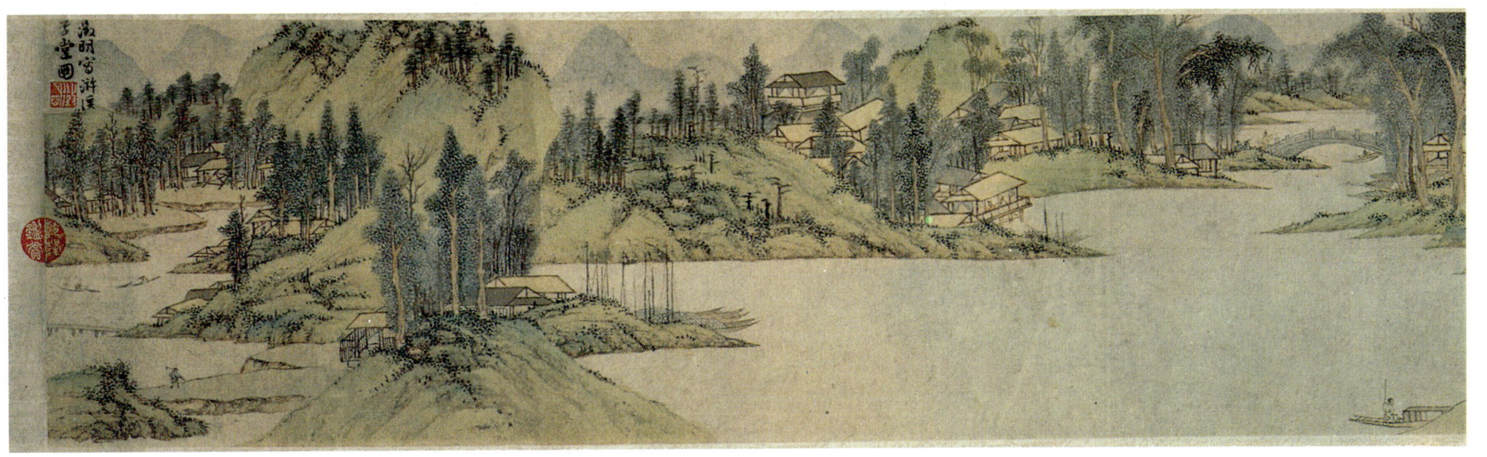

"Stop Playing the Qin and Start Listening to the Ruan" dated 1535 by Wen Jia (1501-1583)

Hanging scroll; ink and colour on silk. 50.5 x 27.7cm
Nanking Museum

In a secluded setting that creates a contemplative mood, two friends are communicating their thoughts through music. Behind them a waterfall is rushing from the top of the mountain. One friend has just finished playing the **qin** (a plucked string instrument resembling a zither) and is now listening to his friend playing the **ruan** (a plucked string instrument related to a lute). The theme of playing the **qin** for someone whose sensibility is tuned to one's own represents a perfect form of communication, a spiritual communion of minds. This intimate landscape is exquisite in colour. A warm glow comes from the colour of the silk surface. As washes of olive-green flow naturally into the yellow-ochre, the subtle colours of moss-covered rocks are achieved. Complementary are the soft, cool, misty blues and deep blues of the trees. The delicate drawing of trees, rocks, and especially that of the human figures, has a delightful, child-like quality, which illustrates what the scholar-amateur artist means by "awkwardness" in painting.

Wen Jia, second son of Wen Zhengming (see cat. no. 14), grew up in an environment of cultured and aesthetic refinement. This is demonstrated by his painting, in which the stylistic techniques he had inherited from his father have become even more cultivated and refined in taste. After teaching for a short time in a sub-prefectural school in Anhui province, Wen Jia seems to have spent most of his life in Suzhou. With experience as a connoisseur of painting, he was often asked to judge and authenticate paintings. He was employed in making a catalogue of the calligraphy and painting of the confiscated collection of the Grand Secretary Yan Song (1480-1565) who had fallen from power.

An inscription by the artist tells us that he painted it in 1535 as a parting gift for a friend of twenty years. The inscription also has the usual self-deprecatory remarks that his brushwork is not good and that his painting is awkward and out of practice.

The painting bears two seals of the artist.
Reproduced: **Nanking Museum Catalogue of Paintings;** Vol. I, page 46.

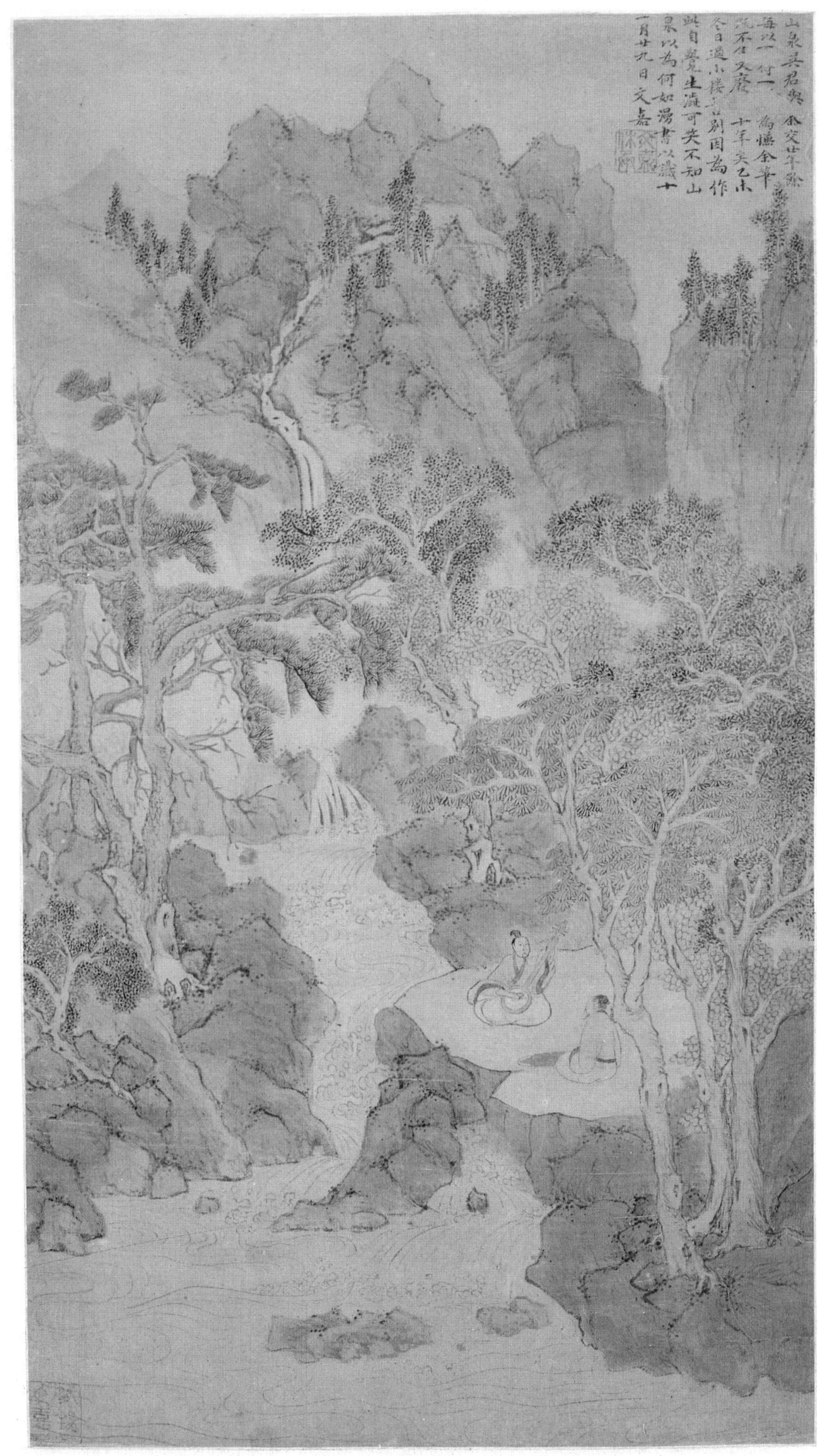

山泉吳君與余交廿年餘
每以一付一 為懷全年
況不住又廢 十年矣乙未
冬日過小樓 別固為作
此自覺生涯可笑不知山
泉以為何如湯書以識十
一月廿九日文嘉

"Fishing in Seclusion by a Clear Stream"
dated 1569 by Wen Boren (1502-1575)

Hanging scroll; ink and colour on paper. 126 x 33.2cm
Shanghai Museum

Hidden behind a group of rocks and tall trees in the foreground, a scholar is fishing from his boat. The winding stream is sheltered by trees growing on the river bank. In the mid-distance, a boy servant is calling a boatman, while his master is waiting inside the house. A poetic quality is evoked by the subtle nuances of ink, accomplished with a sensitive and delicate dry brush; the ink is soft and silvery in tone, enhanced by a slight suggestion of pale blue and pink.

The painting is signed by the artist and dated. An inscription by the Qianlong Emperor (1736-96), dated 1778, relates the poetic scene in the painting to the idyllic place described in the "Peach Blossom Spring" by Tao Yuanming (365-427). It was a hidden valley in which people had been dwelling in isolation for centuries. A fisherman discovered it by chance after following a stream through a peach blossom grove — and afterwards the place could never be found again.

Wen Boren, a nephew of Wen Zhengming (see cat. no. 14), learned painting from his uncle and became the next most distinguished painter of the Wen family. He was even acclaimed as the equal of Wen Zhengming himself, which seems quite justified by the excellence of this painting.

The painting bears seals of the artist and those of the Qianlong Emperor.
Reproduced: **Shanghai Museum Catalogue of Paintings;** no. 58.
       Arts of China: Paintings in Chinese Museums; pl. 77

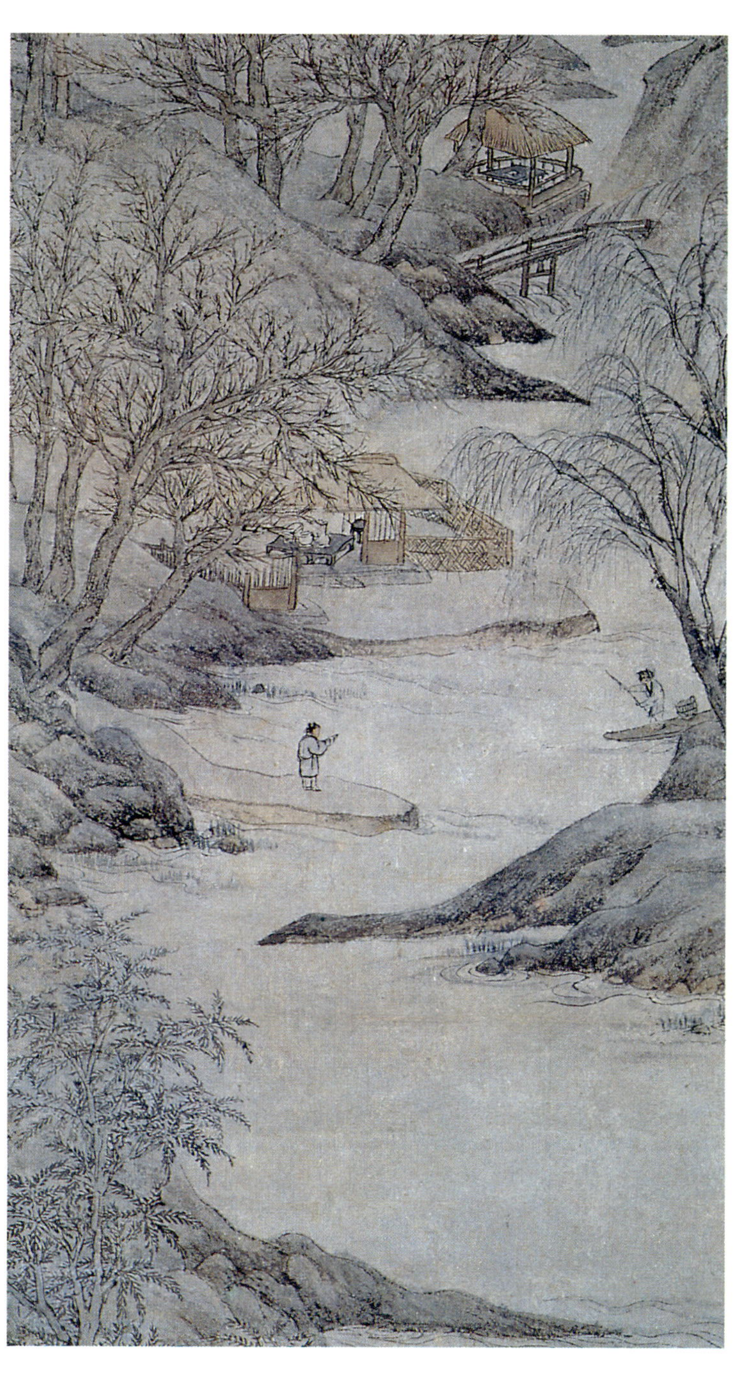

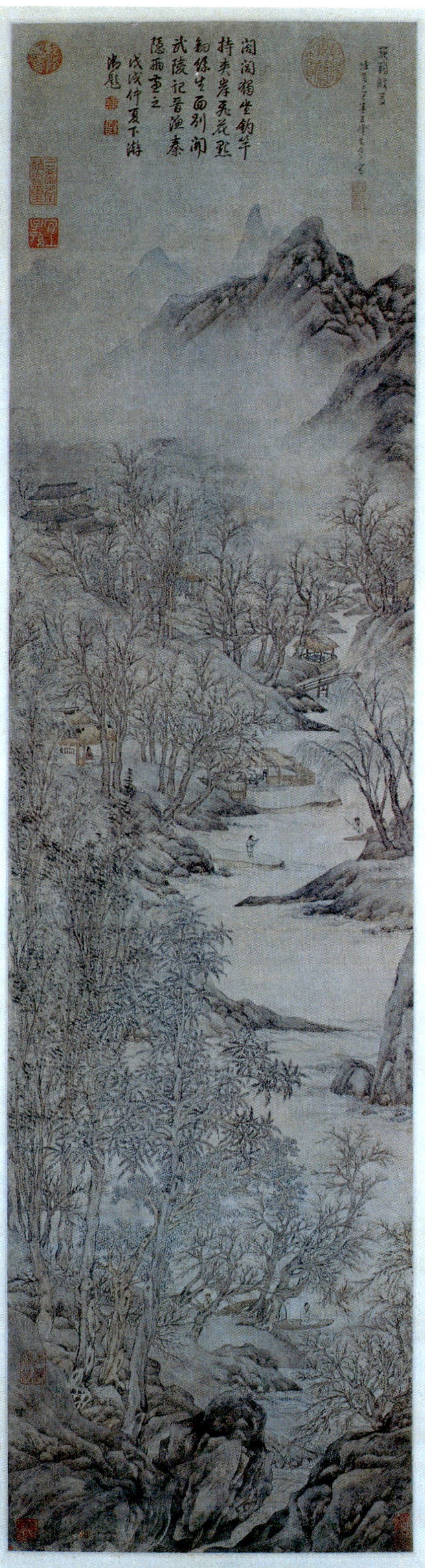
閬閬鴨塘釣舟
持來岸芷花嬌
細綠生面別渦
武陵記晉漁秦
隱而重之
戊戌仲夏下游
鴻飈

catalogue no. 18

"Cloudy Peaks and Wooded Valley"
dated 1552 by Lu Zhi (1496-1576)

Hanging scroll; ink and colour on paper. 85.5 x 46cm
Shanghai Museum

Secluded by an enclosure of rocks and overhanging cliffs, a scholar-recluse is sitting in quiet contemplation in front of a cave, from which flows a mountain stream. The foreground rocks seem to serve as gates to this sanctuary. A feeling of other-worldliness, associated with the realm of the immortals, is created by the stylised clouds, the chiselled, jade-like, multifaceted rocks and cliffs, formed by a network of dry, angular, bending brushstrokes applied over a light wash of blue-green and pink. Lu Zhi in this painting has adopted a recurring theme of the Wu school, which is concerned with seclusion and escape from the mundane world of everyday life. In spite of a reminiscence of the monumentality of Northern Song landscape, the dramatic effect of the cliffs and rocks engaged in dynamic thrust, the landscape remains cool and unimpassioned. In comparison to paintings by the three Wens (See cat. nos. 14-17), Lu Zhi's painting does not seem to have the same degree of sensitivity of touch and tonal range in colour and ink.

To accompany the landscape, Lu Zhi has inscribed a poem:
"Between the mountain walls, a waterfall is falling
like a snowy string, as if from the sky
Beyond the heavens, the cave of the distant cloudy peaks
is clear and bright
One often hears a clear and distinct chanting voice echoing
in the forested ravine
In the midst of the green cliffs, one suspects, there is
someone contemplating."

Lu Zhi came from a gentry family of Suzhou. He received the standard Confucian education, but did not seek an official position. He studied painting with Wen Zhengming (see cat. no. 14). His paintings were greatly sought after and were given away freely. In return, he was presented with gifts. Lu is said to have refused with indignation a direct cash payment for one of his paintings, saying: "I paint for my friends, not because I am poor". In the later years of his life, he became a recluse and lived in poverty in a house at the foot of a mountain near Suzhou, which was "surrounded by clouds and mists on all sides, with a running stream".

Lu Zhi signed his painting as having been made or manufactured **(zhi)** by him. ("Zhi" was a term generally used by professional or court academic painters to sign a painting on commission).

The painting bears several seals of the artist.
Reproduced: **Shanghai Museum Catalogue of Paintings:** no. 57
       Arts of China: Paintings in Chinese Museums: pl. 17

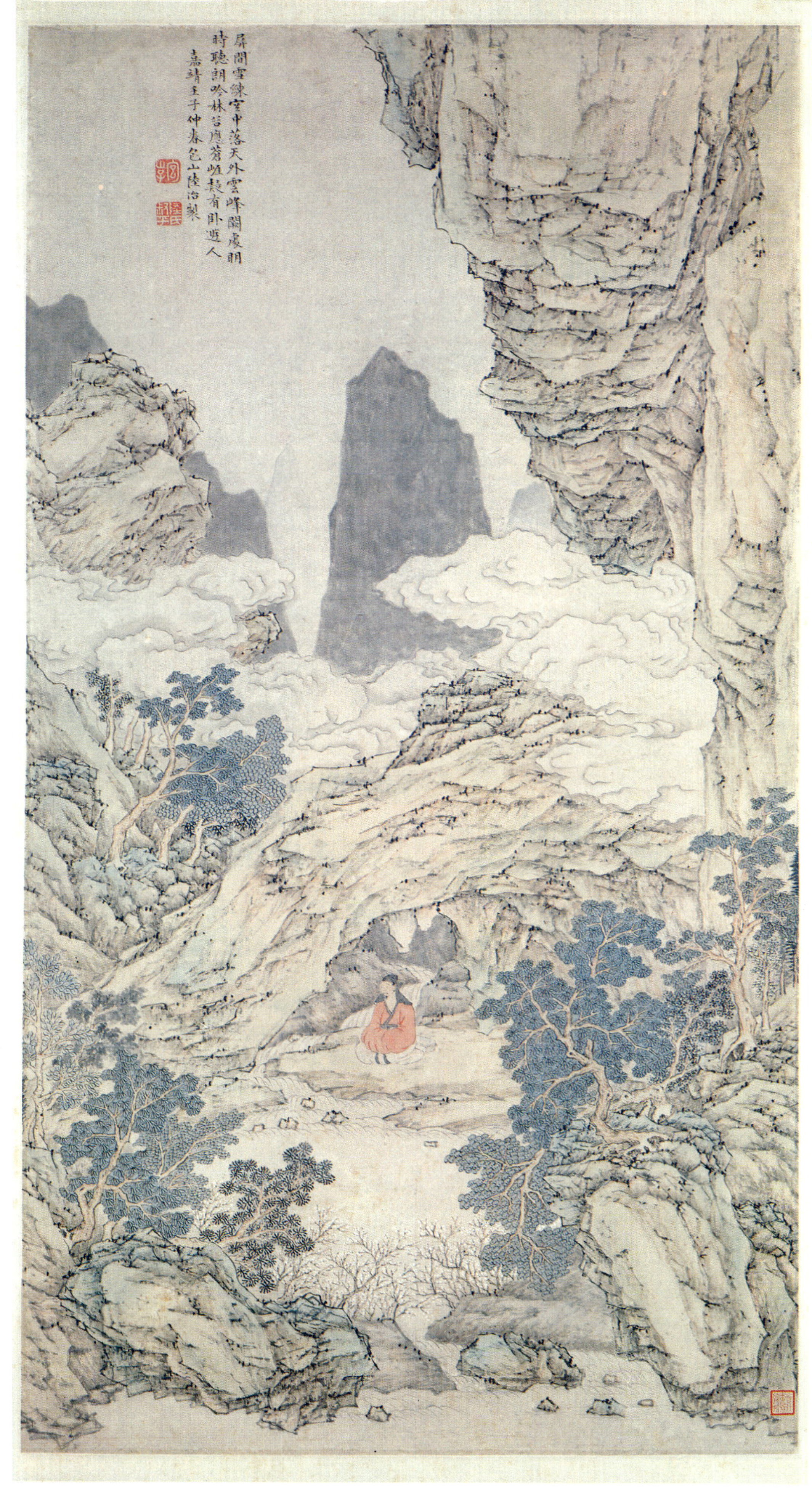

屏間雲練空中落天外雲峰閣處明
時聽朗吟林谷應蒼崖顥青有卧遊人
嘉靖壬子仲春色山陸治製

"Flowers"
dated 1537 by Chen Daofu (1483-1544)

Handscroll; ink on paper. 705 x 48.1 cm
Gugong Museum, Peking

Flowers and plants of the four seasons are depicted in ink monochrome and accompanied by poetic couplets written in beautiful calligraphy. The painting has an affinity with calligraphy in abstract design and expressive brushwork. The natural images are painted in calligraphic strokes, which are dynamic lines that fluctuate in thickness, vary in ink tonality, and move with a sense of direction and speed. The structural form, shape, and texture of a tree branch, for example, are all captured in one calligraphic brushstroke, and those of an entire leaf, in one single shaded stroke. In one such lyrical passage, the tapering leaves of a narcissus, "flower of autumn", are outlined in long, flowing lines that bend and move rhythmically, creating the impression of leaves turning in space and blown by the wind. Ink paintings of flowers and plants, based on the brush disciplines of calligraphy, were popular in the 11th century among the founders of scholar-amateur painting, Su Dongpo (1036-1101) and his friends, and eventually became the special province of the scholar-amateur painters. A scholar trained from childhood in writing with a brush found it relatively easy to transfer his calligraphic skill to paintings of this kind. Through the expressive movement of the brush, painting like calligraphy, serves as a means of self-expression. In this handscroll the three scholarly perfections of poetry, painting, and calligraphy are combined into one artistic form.

Chen Daofu was born in Suzhou and was the son of an official. Although he was well educated, he did not pursue an official career. He was one of Shen Zhou's (see cat. no. 12) young friends and may have learned painting from him. Wen Zhengming (see cat. no. 14) is often credited with having taught him.

The painting is signed by the artist, dating it to 1537, and bears seals of the artist. It is followed by a colophon by Li Rihua (c. 1522).

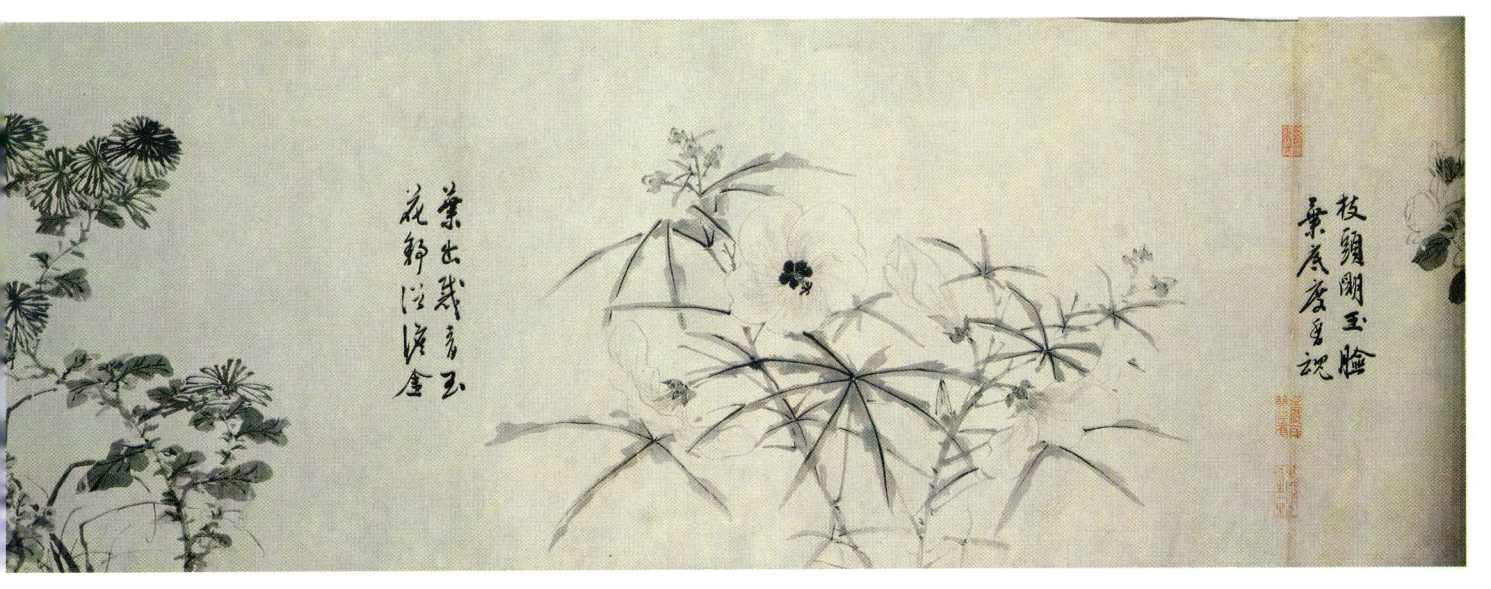
枝頭閒玉臉
葉底露金...
葉出殘書玉
花鈿注濃金

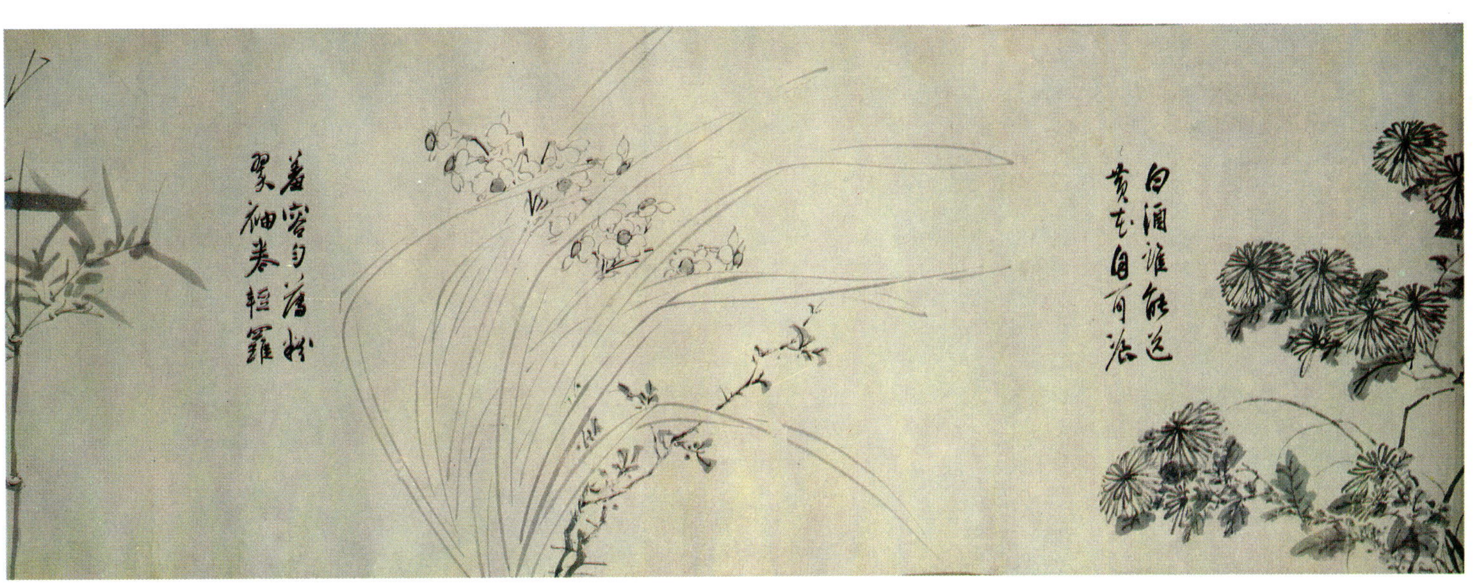
白酒誰能送
黃花自可憐
芳容句病枕
翠袖卷輕羅

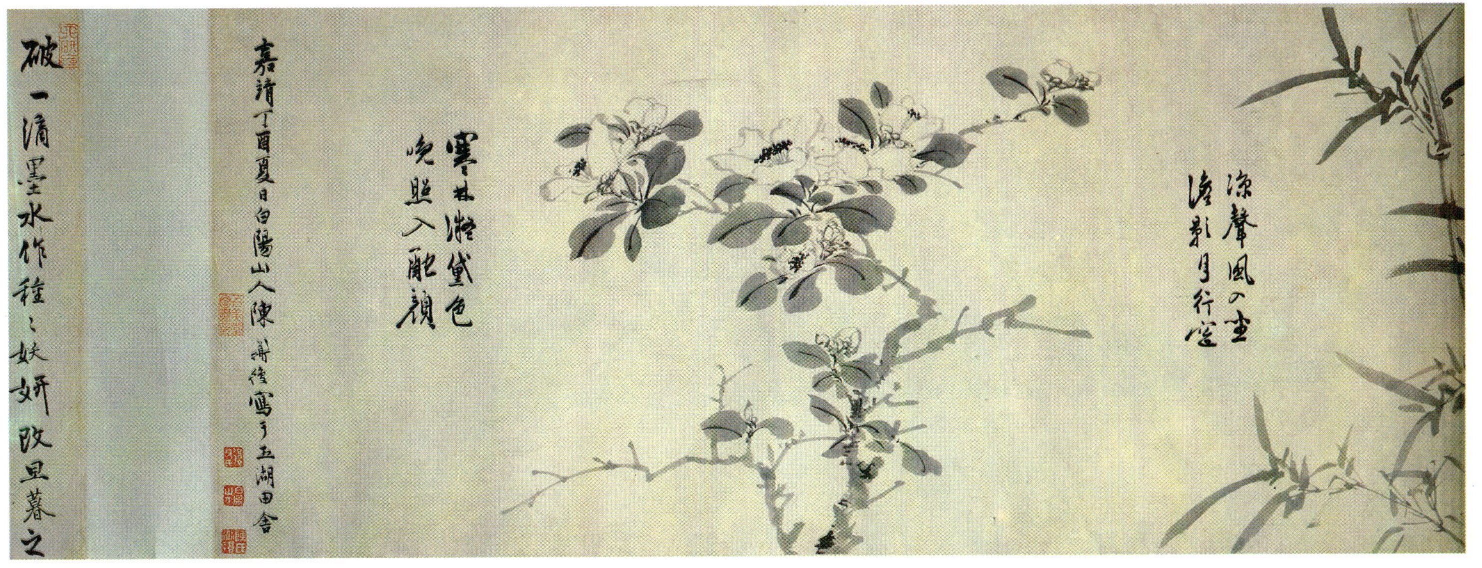
涼聲風外至
清影月行邊
寒林帶翠色
晚照入肌顏
嘉靖丁酉夏日白陽山人陳淳後寫于五湖田舍
破一溪墨水作種種妖妍政且暮之

"Calling on a Friend"
dated 1531 by Zhou Chen (late 15th-early 16th c.)

Hanging scroll; ink and colour on silk. 148 x 102.2cm
Shandong Provincial Cultural Relics Bureau

In a bleak landscape, a group of people are coming to visit a friend who is lying in bed, apparently sick. The sky and water are darkened with a light grey wash. The snowy mountains and trees are sharply outlined with fluent, calligraphic lines that turn suddenly at an angle. The mountains are shaded with short brushstrokes swiftly applied with a "squeezed brush" that resemble the "axe-cut" texture strokes in the manner of Li Tang (early 12th century), a court academy painter of the Northern Song (960-1127). The human figures, which are carefully executed in colour, present some human interest.

Zhou Chen was born in Suzhou, probably around the middle of the 15th century and died shortly after 1535. Zhou and his pupils, Tang Yin (see cat. no. 21) and Qiu Ying (see cat. no. 23), raised professional painting to a level of excellence from which the Zhe school had fallen. (This painting is stylistically related to the Zhe school of painting). However, Zhou was overshadowed by his pupils, especially by Tang Yin. The story goes that when Tang Yin was too busy to meet the great demands for his paintings, he asked Zhou Chen to paint for him; he then signed the painting and sold it as his own. Thirty years after Zhou's death, one of the Suzhou writers relegated Zhou to the status of an artisan-painter (artist-on-hire), competent in the technical skills of painting but lacking in the lofty sentiments of a scholar-amateur artist: "He [Zhou Chen] was praised by everybody in his time as an artisan-painter; the feelings of loneliness and solitude, the flavour of remoteness and reserve [i.e. qualities in a literary man's painting] were not within his reach".

The painting is signed by Zhou Chen, dating it to 1531.

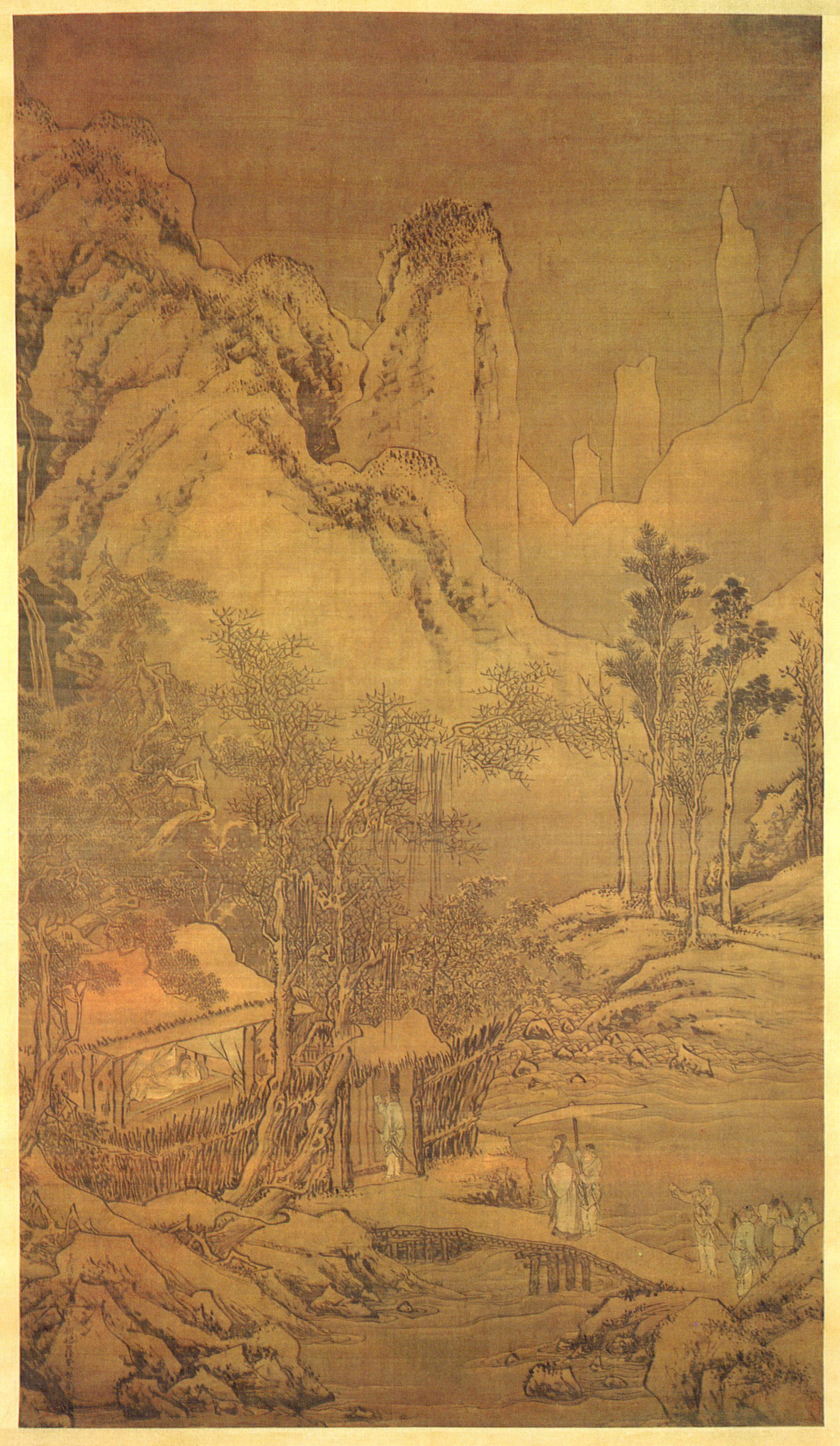

catalogue no. 21

"Travelling to the Frontier Pass"
dated 1506 by Tang Yin (1470-1523)

Hanging scroll; ink and colour on paper. 129.4 x 46.5cm
Gugong Museum, Peking

The gate tower of a frontier pass is seen behind a group of old, gnarled trees in a bleak landscape. A mood of desolation is evoked by the gusty, wind-swept movements of the bare branches. This feeling of isolation is relieved, however, by the presence of a traveller approaching the gate. At the same time, a sense of vital strength is conveyed by the tortuous movements of the trees. The leafless branches are engaged in an intricate, rhythmic flow of delicate brushstrokes. An illusion of space and the atmospheric effect of mist and frosty air is subtly created by depicting trees in progressively lighter tones as they recede into depth. Simply by means of a few pale brushstrokes, the artist has succeeded in giving the impression of distant trees emerging from the misty void.

A long inscription by Wu Yi comments on the arduous hardship of making a journey to the remote region of a frontier pass, where even the wild geese in their flight do not reach. He also comments on how the scenery of the wild plains could not match Tang Yin's painting in evoking the expansive feeling of vastness.

Tang Yin was the son of a Suzhou merchant, a restaurant owner, who was financially well off enough to start his son on a good education. Recognized for his early brilliance as a child, Tang continued his study under the direction of Wen Lin, the father of Wen Zhengming (see cat. no. 14), who introduced him to the gentry and scholar society of Suzhou. In 1498 he passed the provincial examination brilliantly, taking first place, and also in the following year the metropolitan examination in the capital which decided a scholar's official career. However, his chance of success in the last examination was ruined when it became known that a rich fellow-student and friend had obtained advanced information on one of the questions through bribery. Although probably innocent, Tang was involved in the scandal and had to give up his hope of a career in the bureaucracy. Back in Suzhou, Tang Yin took up painting for a living, began studying under Zhou Chen (see cat. no. 20), a professional painter, and became very successful. He turned to a bohemian way of life, drinking in the taverns and frequenting the pleasure quarters of Suzhou. This painting well illustrates Tang's artistic brilliance which combines the strength of both the styles of the scholar-amateur and of the professional.

The painting bears seals of the artist and an inscription by the artist dates the painting to 1506. Also with seals of the collector Xiang Yuanbian (1525-1590).

catalogue no. 22

"Watching the Stream and Listening to the Wind"
by Tang Yin (1470-1523)

Hanging scroll; ink and colour on silk. 72.5 x 34.6cm
Nanking Museum

In a quiet and peaceful setting, two friends are sitting in front of a waterfall and listening to the rustling of trees in the wind. This monumental landscape follows, in composition and in the use of "axe-cut" texture strokes, the tradition of Li Tang (early 12th century) which was revived in the landscape style of his teacher Zhou Chen (cat. no. 20). To this conservative and professional style of painting, however, Tang Yin injected new elements, such as the dynamic movements of rocks.

The painting is inscribed with a poem by Tang Yin and bears several of his seals.
Reproduced: **Nanking Museum Catalogue of Paintings,** vol. 1, page 30.

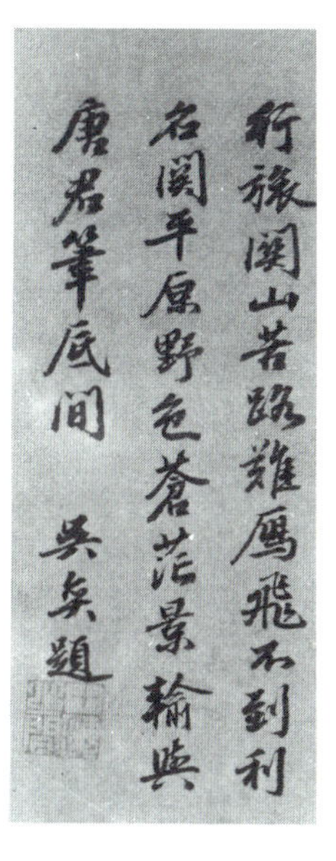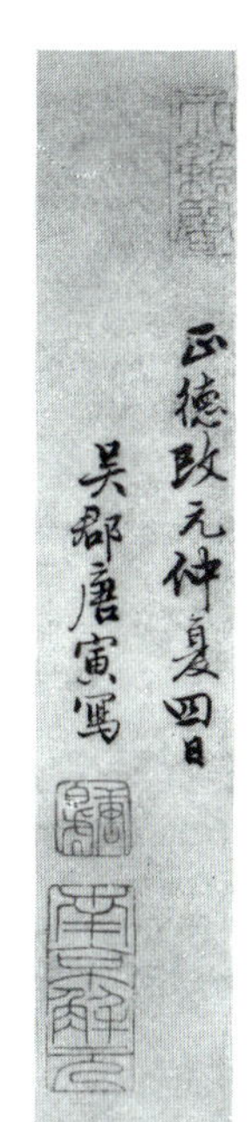

catalogue no. 21

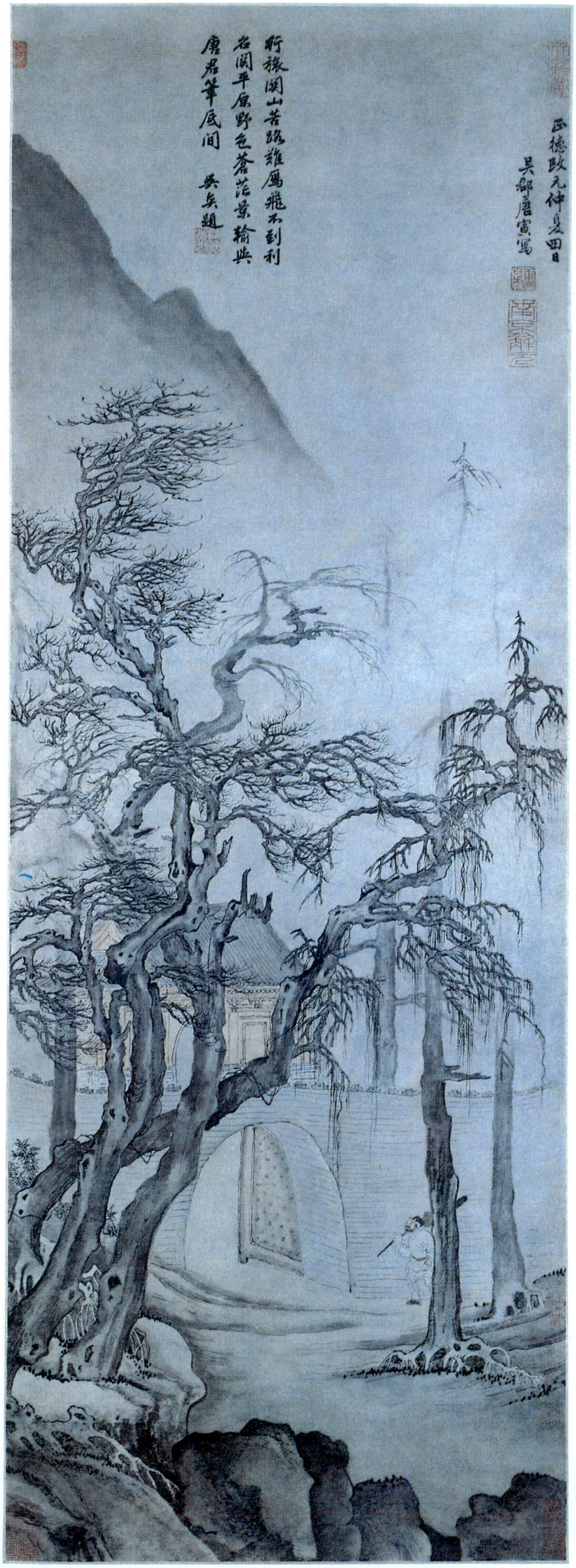

"Poetic Thoughts of Snowy Mountains"
dated 1560 by Xie Shichen (1487-after 1567)

Hanging scroll; ink and light colours on silk. 143.8 x 80.8cm
Tianjin Arts Museum

Jagged and serrated peaks overhang a quiet valley thereby creating an extraordinary contrast between the vast domains of endless mountains and the peaceful intimacy of the secluded house and the conversing figures. The rugged mountain rocks and peaks, with strong but strangely nervous outlines and abbreviated shading strokes, provide the terrain with an organic, almost evolving quality rather like heavy rumbling clouds. This particular manner of painting rocks and mountains is clearly derived from the style of Dai Jin (see cat. no. 3). The cold wintry effect is further heightened by the dense black strokes of barren trees outlining the mountain ridges, and the total cold effect almost denies our seeing the pavilions half hidden in a high valley in the upper right section of the scroll. The size of these buildings, compared with those in the foreground, lends emphasis to the scale and all-encompassing qualities of nature.

The house and figures in the foreground offer comfort and reality to the composition. The travellers with their mule are being greeted on the threshold of a small house surrounded by overhanging pine trees which seem to offer protection from the unforgiving mountains.

Xie Shichen came from a prosperous Suzhou family and, it is recorded, spent almost his entire life in that region, so renowned as a centre for painting. Contemporary and later critical writings confirm that Xie followed the styles of Dai Jin (cat. no. 3) and Wu Wei (cat. no. 4) having first studied the work of Shen Zhou (cat. nos. 12 and 13). The general style and tenor of his work clearly illustrates a dependence upon the early Ming Academy and the Zhe School which had their origins in the grand and awe-inspiring landscapes of the Northern Song. It is debatable as to whether Xie added much of significance to this already well-established tradition although there is no doubting that he was a most accomplished practitioner of the style. As the **Ming Hua Lu** states, Xie was "very competent in executing screens and large hanging scrolls which were bold and energetic in manner but did not escape the affliction of fussiness".

Inscription including the date by the artist.

"Returning to the Fen River"
by Qiu Ying (first half of the 16th c.)

Handscroll; ink and colour on silk. 123.7 x 26.7cm
Gugong Museum, Peking

The scroll opens with a mountain pass. The man in a red robe riding a horse and followed by servants carrying his luggage is probably a scholar-official who is returning home after retiring from an official post. Further on are horses running free near a pavilion in an empty area enclosed by rows of willow trees. We then encounter a winding river, probably the **Fen** river in Shanxi province. Next to the river are clusters of houses, possibly the home of the returning official. Scattered throughout the peaceful landscape are scenes of human activity.

The landscape is done in the archaistic-decorative mode of the "blue and green" landscapes of the Tang dynasty. Hills and rocks are softly modelled with green and blue washes. Technical competence is combined with a delicacy of touch that accords with the restrained and highly refined taste of Wen Zhengming (cat. no. 14), which had pervaded Suzhou painting of the 16th century. Qiu Ying signed the painting as having been "made" (zhi) by him, a term usually used for paintings that were made on commission by professional artists.

Qiu Ying came from a humble family in the Shanghai region. He moved to Suzhou to work as a painter's apprentice and was discovered by Zhou Chen (see cat. no. 20), who took him on as a pupil. Probably through Tang Yin (see cat. no. 21), he was introduced to the scholar-gentry of Suzhou, including Wen Zhengming (see cat. no. 14), and his circle of friends. A figure painter and illustrator, Qiu also excelled in imitating old paintings of the Tang and Song masters. He was therefore commissioned to make copies of old paintings by collectors. This landscape was probably done to satisfy the art-historical taste of a patron. In spite of the fact that he was considered an artisan-painter, Qiu enjoyed the appreciation of the educated gentry class, particularly the patronage of the collector Xiang Yuanbian (1525-1590).

The painting bears seals of the artist, and is followed by colophons by Fu Shan (1606-1683), Peng Nian (1505-1566) and others. catalogue no. 24

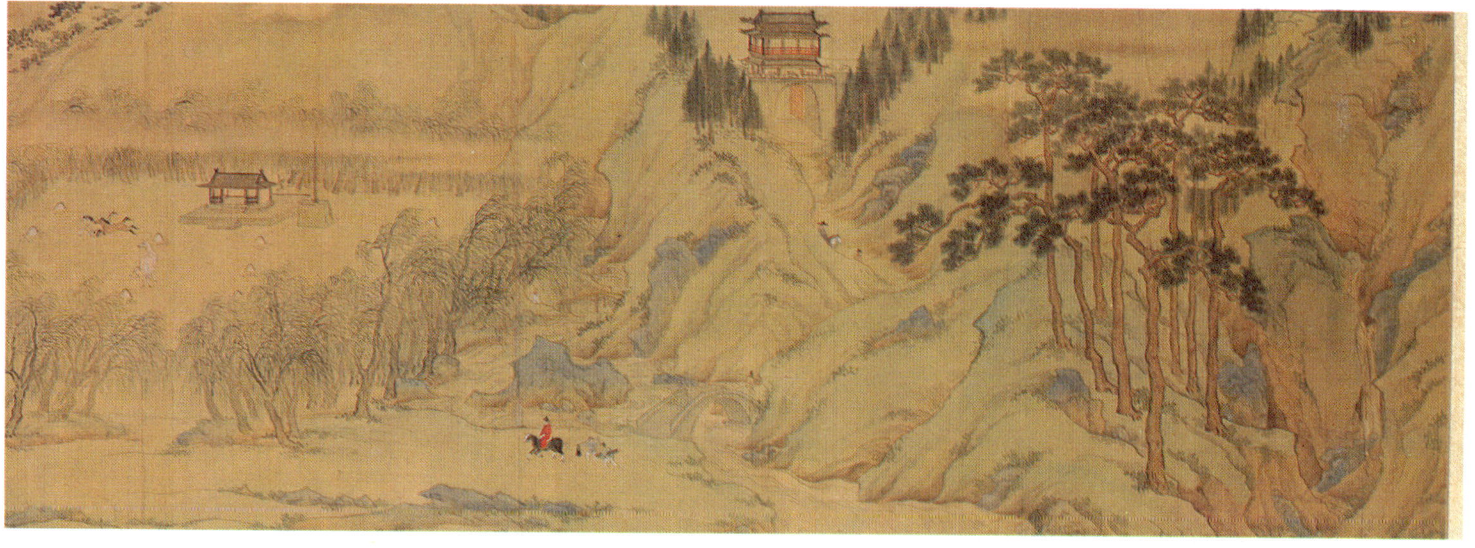

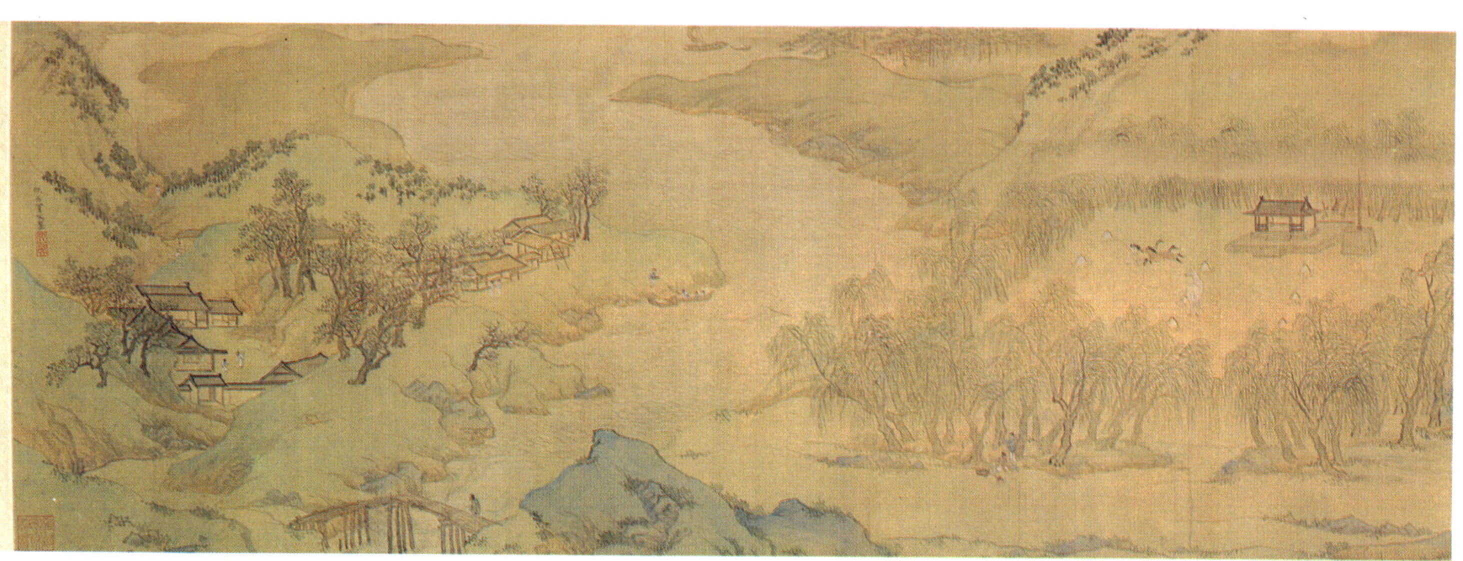

"Village Path and Humble Cottage"
dated 1643 by Zhang Hong (1577-after 1668)

Hanging scroll; ink and colour on silk. 205.7 x 86.7cm
Gugong Museum, Peking

From the tall pine forest in the foreground, the landscape recedes on a flat, continuous ground plane of rice paddies to a homestead among distant trees at the foot of the central mountain. The high viewpoint with typical Chinese spatial treatment is emphasised by the foreground receding to the village in the valley. The viewer's eye is then drawn to the different higher plane of the distant mountains. The varying levels and planes in this landscape combine to provide an unusual and strangely unsettling composition. Texture strokes in pale ink, which resemble those in the manner of Dong Yuan (10th century), appear weak and loose when viewed closely. But in the distance, they configurate into three-dimensional forms of solid, earthy mass, softly shaded with light and shadow. The clarity of vision and detail suggests this landscape may have been based on an actual place.

The painting is inscribed with a couplet by Zhang Hong:
"Village path, distant mountains, dark pine forest;
Humble cottage, flowing streams, rice fragrance".

Zhang Hong was a native and resident of Suzhou. He and a few other Suzhou painters managed to rise above the degenerate state of painting of the Suzhou school of their time and pointed a new direction in painting, which was unfortunately not followed by later artists. As could be seen in this painting, Zhang Hong still drew heavily on the Wu school tradition; it has a refinement of style and delicacy of mood that evoke reminiscences of the age of Wen Zhengming (see cat. no. 14) and his circle.

The painting is signed by the artist, dating it to 1643 and bears several seals of the artist.

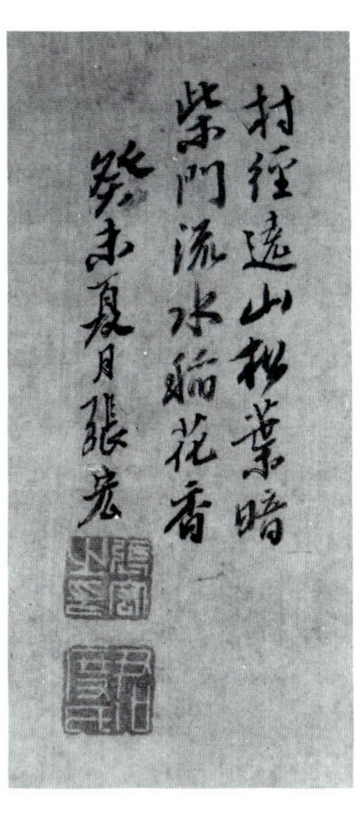

村徑遠山秋葉暗
柴門流水稻花香
癸未夏月張宏

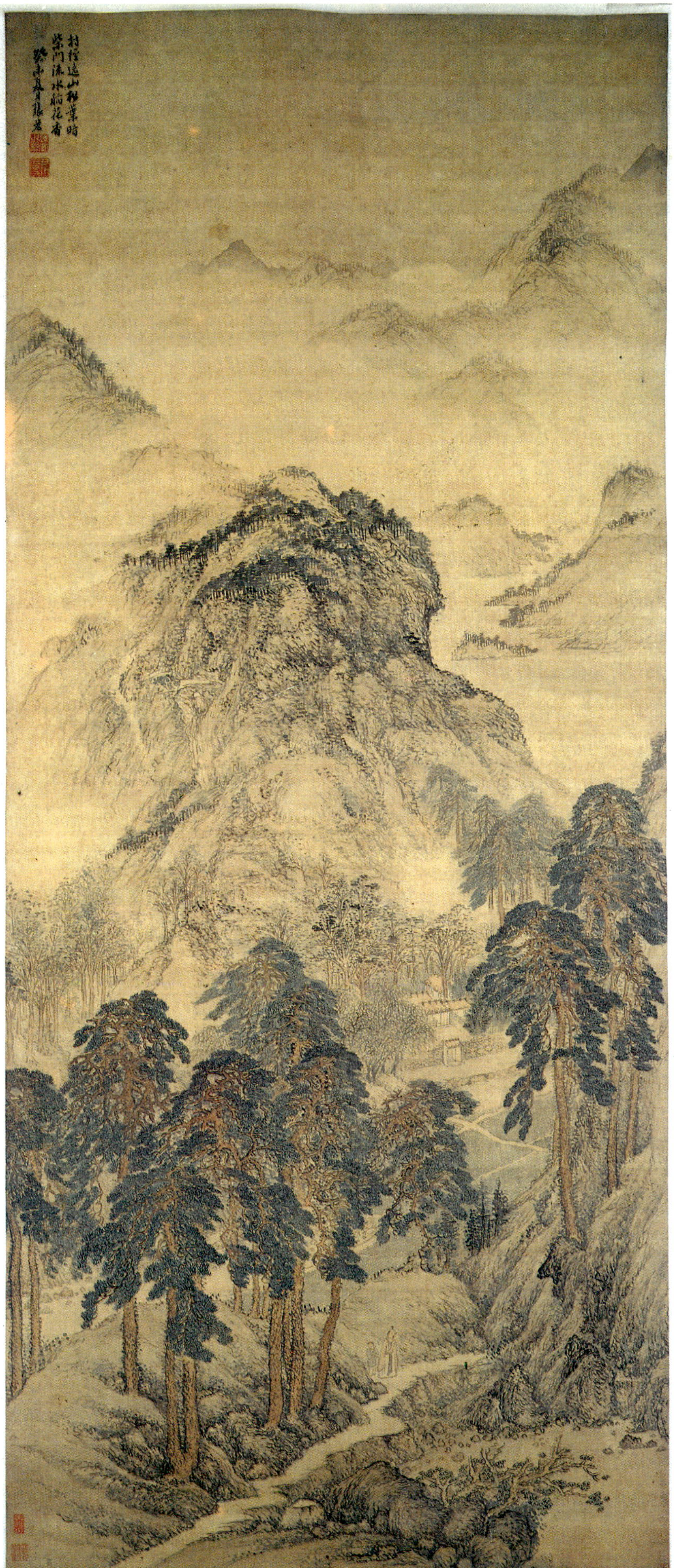

"Secluded Scenic Place with Pines and River Stream"
dated 1625 by Dong Qichang (1555-1636)

Hanging scroll; ink on paper. 134.4 x 46cm
Nanking Museum

A majestic river landscape begins with a screen of intertwining eccentric trees on the foreground river bank. Across a stretch of empty water, we encounter a rocky construction of trees, boulders, houses, and mountain peaks, which are carefully balanced and spaced.

Depicted is a cool, intellectual landscape, that epitomizes the literati ideal of "brilliance concealed under the appearance of blandness". The landscape appears stark and arid. Rocks are stripped of surface texture and reduced to basic structural form, with dry outlines and minimum shading. The drawing of houses, trees, rocks, and mountains, which are transformed into animated, expressive and individualistic forms, appears artless and awkward. Decorative elements of colour, technical skill, and narrative interest are all eliminated. These qualities, which are usually associated with paintings by professional (or artisan) painters, are considered by literati artists as being sweet, over-appealing, and hence vulgar. In the lofty and purified realm of the river landscape, no human beings are shown, a reminder that the banal and dusty world is excluded.

The inner richness of this austere landscape resides in the superb control of brush and ink, the strength and individuality of the brushstrokes, the great subtlety and sensitivity in the wide range of tonal and textural gradations of ink, and the tremendous creative power in the abstract manipulation and spacing of form. These formal qualities and the astringent flavour of the painting are the very qualities that a literati connoisseur would appreciate in a piece of calligraphy, which was regarded as the highest form of visual art.

In making a distinction between real scenery in nature and landscape painting, Dong stated the unique qualities of the latter in the following:
"Painting is no equal to mountains-and-water
[i.e. real scenery] for the wonder of scenery;
but mountains-and-water are no equal to painting
for the sheer marvels of brush and ink."

The fact that painting is not a counterpart of natural scenery and that natural scenery is not the reality behind painting is stated in another passage of his writing:
"Among the ancients, there are those who regarded painting
as simulations of natural landscape and regarded natural
landscape as real paintings [i.e. the reality behind
painting]. How they have inverted things in their
opinions [way of seeing]."

In these two statements, Dong reaffirms the literati attitude that painting goes beyond mere representation, which was first articulated several centuries earlier by the scholar-amateur painter Su Dongpo (1036-1101) when he said "Those who insisted [only] on formal likeness have the understanding of a child." Representation was therefore not the sole purpose of painting. Moreover, according to the scholar-amateur artists, artistic meaning comes not from the interest created by the subject matter of the painting, but from the artist himself. Landscape elements are merely used as vehicles for the self-expression of the artist. In his painting, rocks and trees are transformed into expressive forms, charged with vital force (qi) and activated into dynamic movements. The order of nature is also manipulated for expressive ends. This architectonic landscape is constructed from a system of established forms in accordance to an abstract order, that comes from the mind of the artist. It is an inner landscape, a painting of the mind.

In one of his inscriptions Dong tells us that he was inspired by the brush manner of a painting by Guo Zhongshu (10th century). However, as Xie Xizeng (18th century), one of the collectors of the painting, has pointed out in his colophon dated 1755, this painting seems to have been more influenced by the style of Huang Gongwang (1269-1354), a scholar-amateur

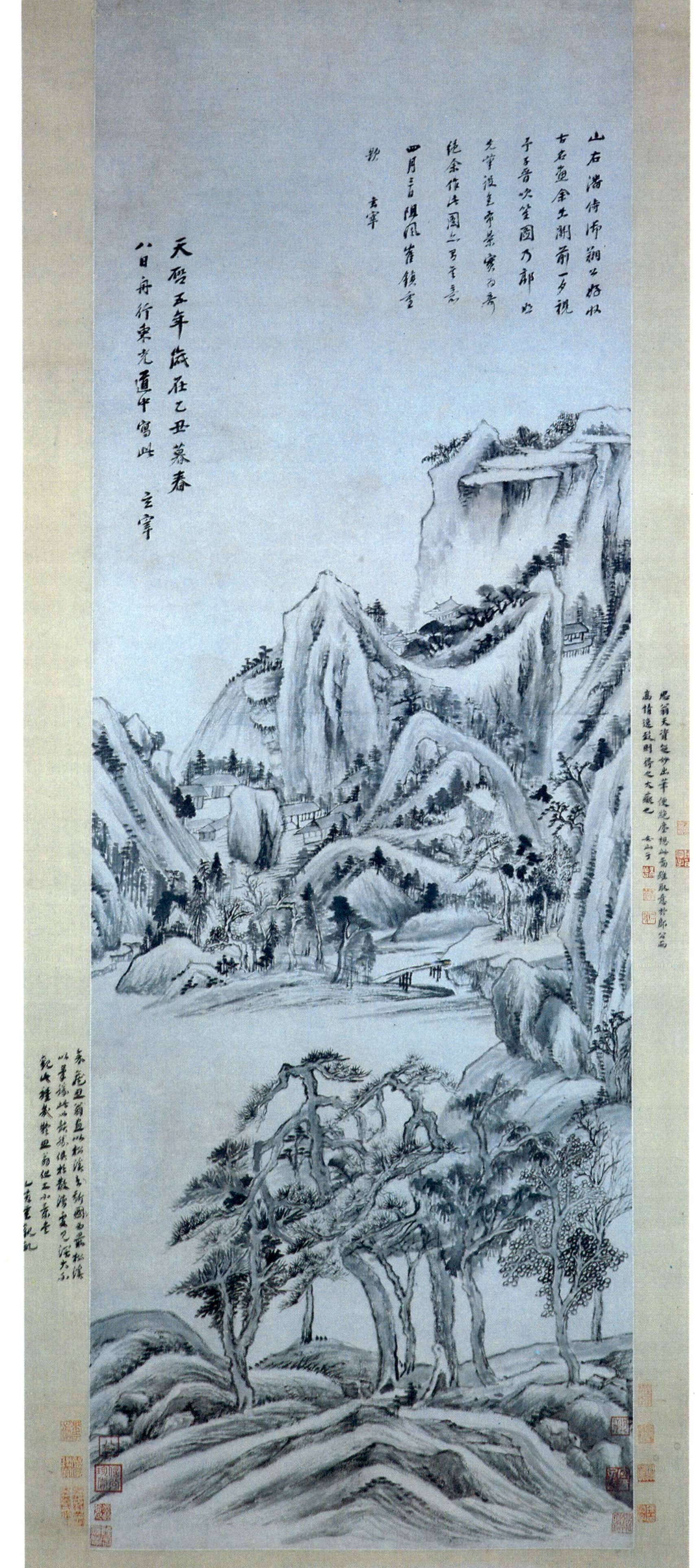
天啟五年歲在乙丑暮春
八日舟行東光道中寫此 玄宰
玄宰

painter of the Yuan dynasty (1279-1368). Probably in reaction to contemporary paintings by the professional painters of the Wu school, which were characterised by a lack of brushwork, structural form, and coherence in composition, Dong restored to landscape painting the purity of Yuan painting, the beauty of brush and ink. Dong also discovered in the paintings of Huang Gongwang three-dimensional structural form and the principles of formal construction (e.g. component forms constructed like modular units into larger composite forms) which he had manipulated to express the restlessness within himself. In transforming the style of Huang into a style of his own, Dong demonstrates his creative power. Dong signed his painting and dated it to 1625.

Dong Qichang (1555-1636) was born into a poor family in Shanghai, and later moved to live in Huating, Songjiang prefecture, Jiangsu province. He passed the civil examinations and rose to such high official positions as President of the Board of Rites and tutor to the heir apparent. His government service was interrupted, however, by long intervals of retirement in Huating. Escaping from the political turmoils at the court, he took a stand of non-involvement in politics. Instead, he played a dominant role in the world of art. A brilliant scholar, extremely talented and versatile, he assumed the various roles of connoisseur, collector, critic, historian and theoretician of art, as well as a very accomplished calligrapher and painter. Through both his paintings and writings on painting, in which he restated and elaborated the theory of the literary man's painting, he exerted great influence not only on paintings of the late Ming but also later Chinese paintings.

The painting bears seals of Wang Shimin (see cat. no. 41), Pang Yuanji (c. 1865-1949), and Xie Xizeng (18th century).
Recorded: **Xuzhai Minghualu,** dated 1909 (Lovell, no. 98)
Reproduced: **Nanking Museum Catalogue of Paintings;** vol. 1, p. 97.

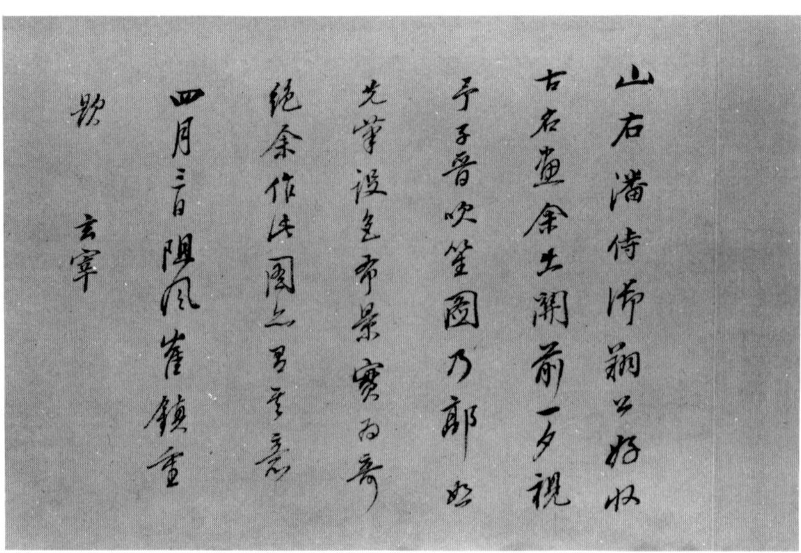

Opposite: Detail of cat. no. 26.

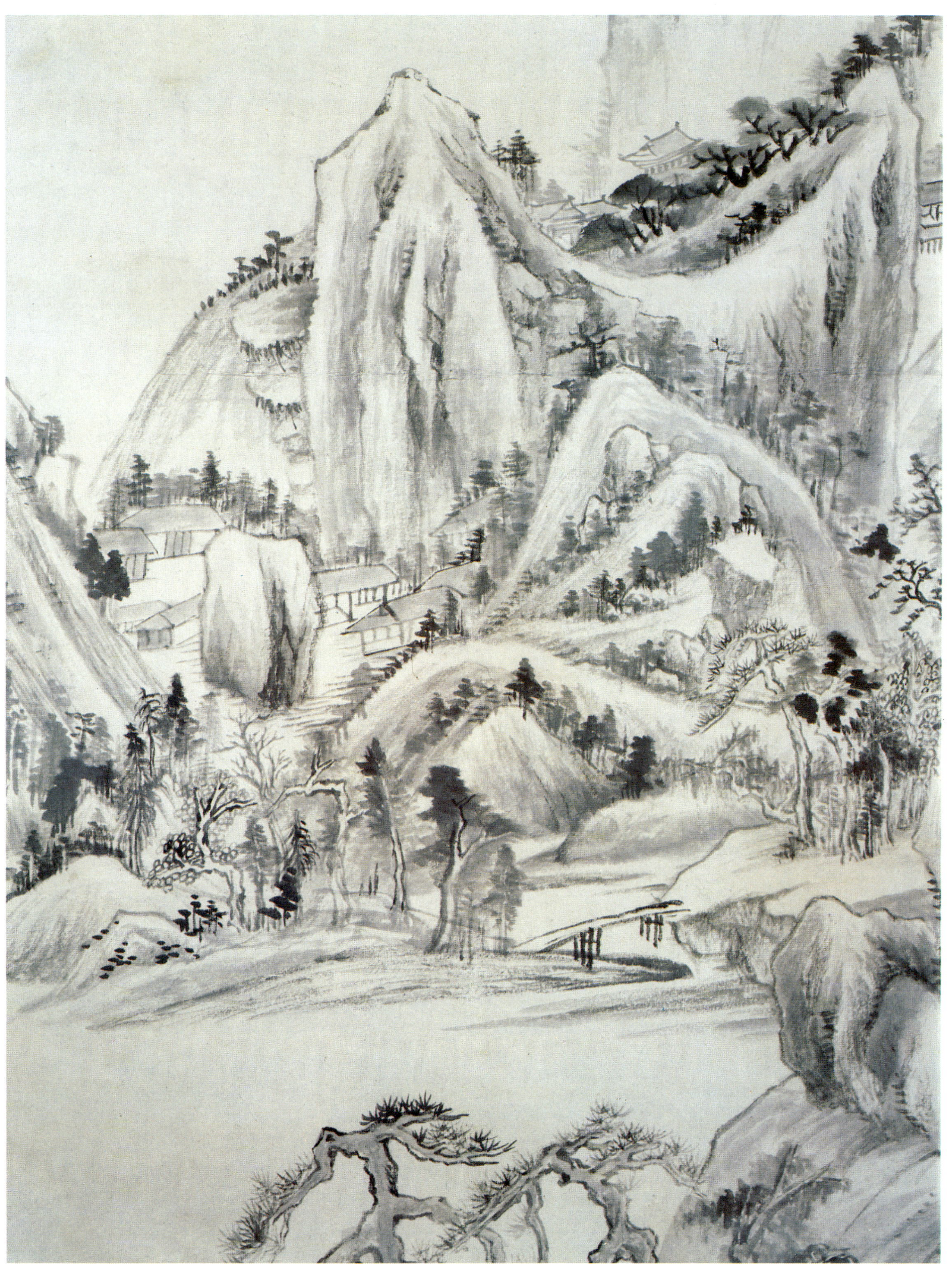

"Fishing Boat in Wintry Pond"
dated 1630 by Shen Shichong (17th century)
Hanging scroll; ink and colour on paper. 132 x 50.8cm
Gugong Museum, Peking

A scholar sitting in his boat seems to be enjoying the frosty winter air. He appears surrounded by mist and vapours rising from the river stream. The atmospheric effect of the landscape is created by short, dry brushstrokes softly applied on a slight wash of pink. These rich texturing strokes are accumulated and fused into crumbling three-dimensional forms, which are shaded with strong effects of light and dark.

Shen Shichong was born and lived in Huating in Songjiang prefecture, Jiangsu province, around 1610-1640. He studied painting under Song Moujin (active late 16th-early 17th century) and later under Zhao Zuo (active 1600-1630) of the Songjiang school of painting. The strong contrast of light and dark in the landscape is probably influenced by Zhao Zuo. Shen Shichong was also influenced by Dong Qichang (see cat. no. 26), for example, the cubic rocks, the composition of the multi-faceted mountain peak out of smaller forms, the diagonal thrust of the trees, and their finger-like branches extending in all directions. It was said that paintings by Shen were often signed by Dong Qichang.

The painting is signed by Shen, dated 1630, and bears his seals.

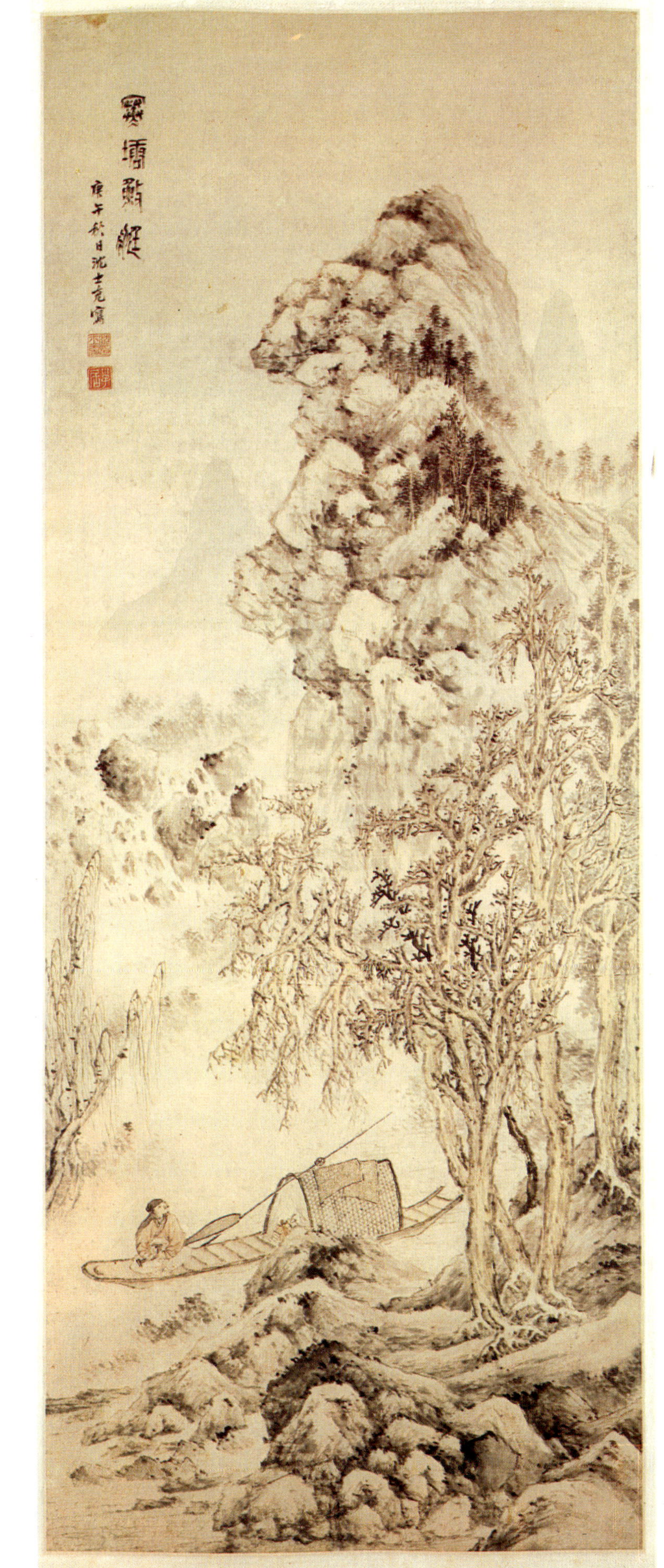
寒塘野艇
庚午秋日沈士充寫

"Myriad Peaks and Cliffs"
dated 1601 by Wu Bin (active c. 1568-1621)

Hanging scroll; ink and colour on paper. 223 x 49.8cm
Nanking Museum

The viewer is invited to enter the landscape from the bottom left corner and wander within it in imagination, climbing the ascending path that winds around a succession of rising peaks and disappears into the misty clouds. One is then brought down by the undulating flow of a river stream. A recluse's cottage is half-hidden among the foreground trees and rocks. A cowherd riding on an ox in the middle distance is playing his flute.

Based on a compositional formula popular among the scholar-amateur painters of Suzhou, the landscape is composed within a narrow vertical shape and organized in an episodic manner, as if in a vertical handscroll. It is constructed with distinct parts (e.g. rocks, cliffs, trees) which are repeated with variation and arranged around the winding mountain path and stream. The basic mode of composing a single large form of rock out of small ones may also have been derived from Wu school paintings. But the dense, furry, string-like, hemp-fibre texture strokes that construct the rocks, came ultimately from the paintings by Wang Meng (c. 1309-1385), one of the four great masters of the literati tradition of the Yuan dynasty. The child-like drawing of the houses and human figures also seem to have come from the style of Wang Meng.

The strong form-defining, dry texture strokes, well modulated in rich ink, are applied over a light grey wash, which glows with a slight bluish as well as pinkish tint. The density gradations of the brush strokes create a strong effect of light and shadow, and a feeling of solid mass, not usually found in the scholar-amateur paintings of Suzhou. The texture strokes also impart a twisting motion to the rock formation which appears to be churning with dynamic energy. Despite the exuberant richness of surface texture, accentuated by applications of scorched ink (**jiaomo**, dark, dry ink sparsely applied), the picture is clearly organized and unified by the rhythmic flow of the mountain stream. Repeated vertical trees stabilize the composition.

In this early work Wu Bin is trying to restore to landscape painting a feeling of substantial form and the majestic grandeur of nature, that was captured in the monumental landscapes of the Northern Song dynasty (960-1127). The awesomeness of nature and its solitude are expressed in Wu Bin's poetic inscription:

"Looking down are valleys a thousand **ren** (25,000 metre) deep
Looking up are lofty peaks ten thousand **xun** (27,000 metre) high
Misty clouds touch the rocks as they rise
Dark caverns emit extraordinary mists and vapours
Around the multitudinous peaks, small winding paths disappear [into the clouds]
The myriad cliffs cover the distant sky
One looks up to see the lofty trees in luxuriant growth
and scoops water from the murmuring stream
In the mountain lives a hidden recluse
Who takes delight in the absolute peacefulness of this place
He only responds to admiring the ancients
And enjoying the (pure) musical sounds produced by a single string".

Wu Bin came from Fukien province, and during the Wanli period (1573-1620) he served in an official position and also as a court painter. He began to paint in the style of the Suzhou school, then the dominant style of painting. During his stay in Nanking, he attempted to revive the awesome landscape of the Northern Song and created paintings of fantastic imagery.

The painting is signed by Wu Bin, dating it to 1601, and bears his seals.
Reproduced: **Nanking Museum Catalogue of Paintings,** vol. 1, page 87.

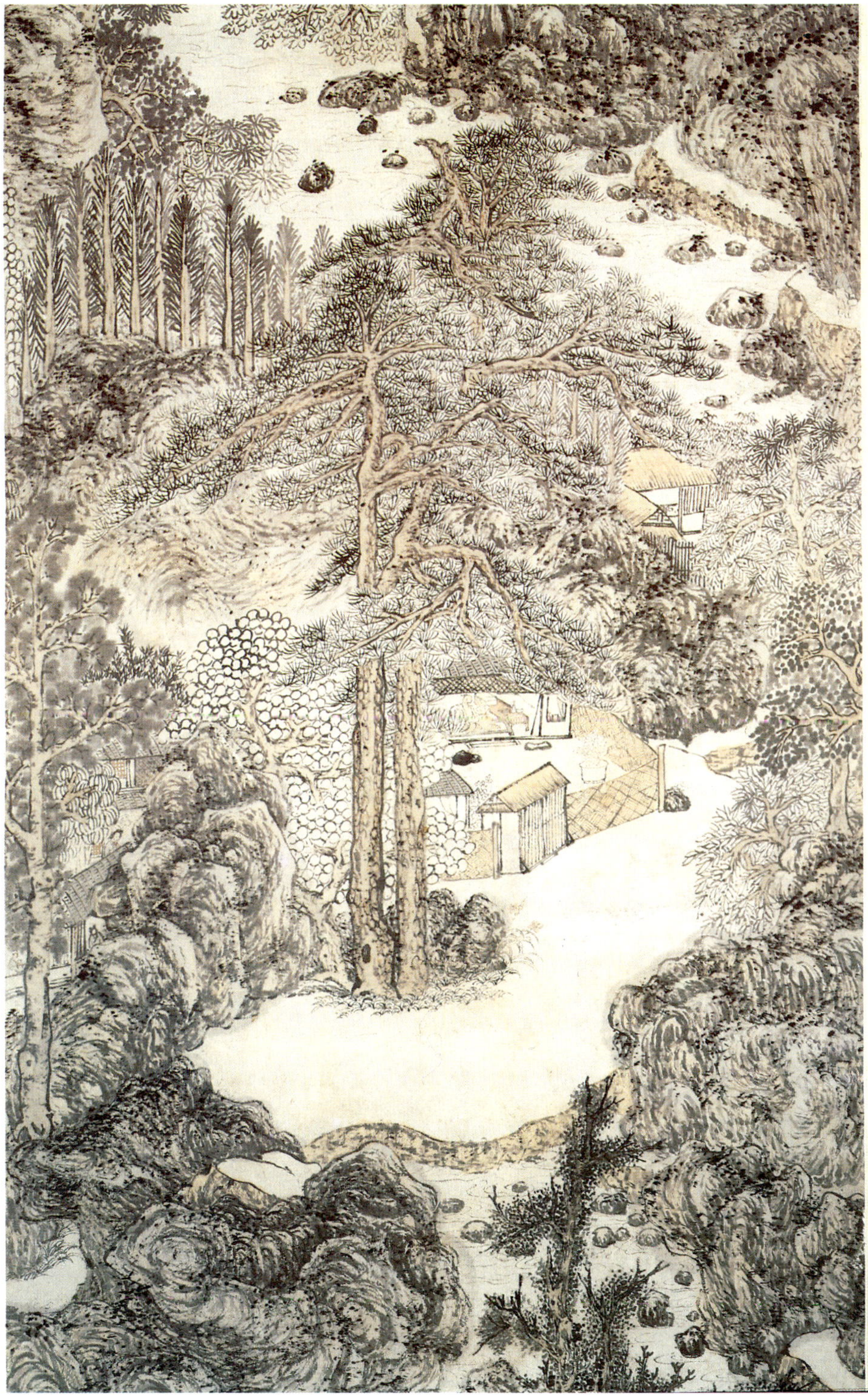

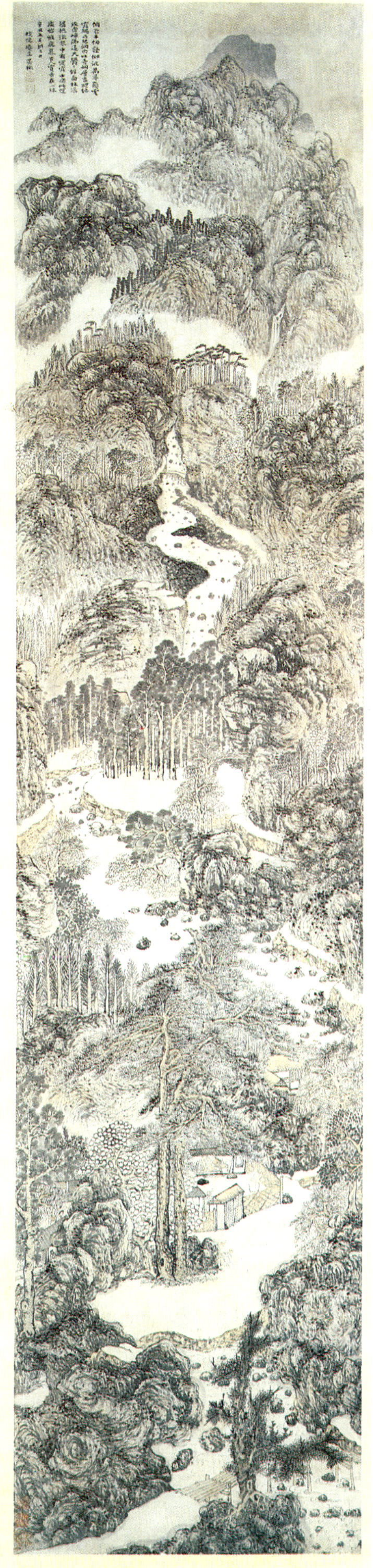

"Fishing in a Frosty River"
dated 1648 by Lan Ying (1585-after 1664)

Handscroll; ink on paper. 145.1 x 26cm
Tianjin Arts Museum

The fishermen in the river landscape appear to be scholar-recluses who are enjoying fishing as a pastime. The scroll begins with a group of friends feasting together, their boats anchored next to the riverbank. Across an expanse of empty water, a solitary figure is sitting in his boat. A flight of geese leads us to an empty pavilion and a group of trees. The handscroll concludes with an inscribed poem by Lan Ying, expressing the carefree life of the scholar-recluse; sharing the fish they have caught and three bottles of warm wine (bought on credit), and, while drunk, they forget all the cares of the world.

In his inscription, Lan Ying tells us that he modelled this painting on the style of a "fisherman-recluse" scroll by Wu Zhen (1280-1354), a scholar-amateur painter of the Yuan dynasty (1279-1368). From the style of Wu Zhen probably derived the blunt, thick brushstrokes and black dots, which are exaggerated and activated into swift, impulsive brush movements. By depicting an empty pavilion, Lan Ying also makes reference to the style of Ni Zan (1301-1374), another Yuan dynasty literati painter. Lan Ying seems to have given a dashing performance of a well-rehearsed Wu Zhen brush manner with great technical facility, but without capturing the contemplative and reserved quality of the scholar temperament. Even the three scholar-fishermen in the landscape seem to be very noisy, chattering away. Lan's brush manner would have been too showy and agitated for the quiet taste of a literary man. It is closer in spirit to the brush manner of the "fisherman" scrolls by both Dai Jin (see cat. no. 3) and Wu Wei (see cat. no. 4) of the Zhe school.

Lan Ying was born and lived in Qiantang, Zhejiang province. He worked as a professional painter and has always been considered as the last representative of the declining Zhe school. By Lan Ying's time scholar-amateur painting had become the dominant current in painting and was in popular demand. As a professional painter Lan had to paint in the scholar-amateur style and this painting follows that tradition by inscribing it with a poem and indicating the style he was following. Being a professional painter it is possible that Lan had restricted access to collections of old paintings, and he once complained that very few reliable works from the hands of the old masters were to be seen.

The painting is signed by Lan Ying and dated to 1643. It also bears seals of the artist.

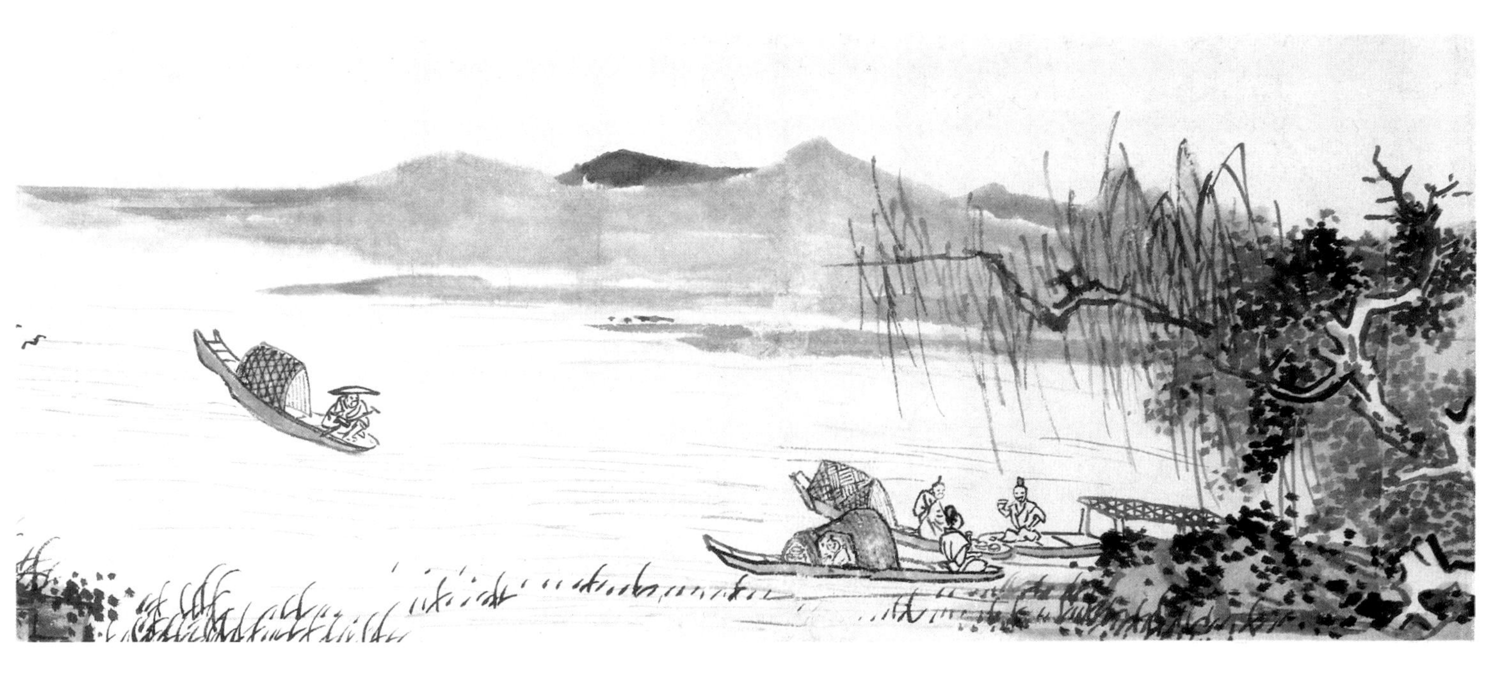

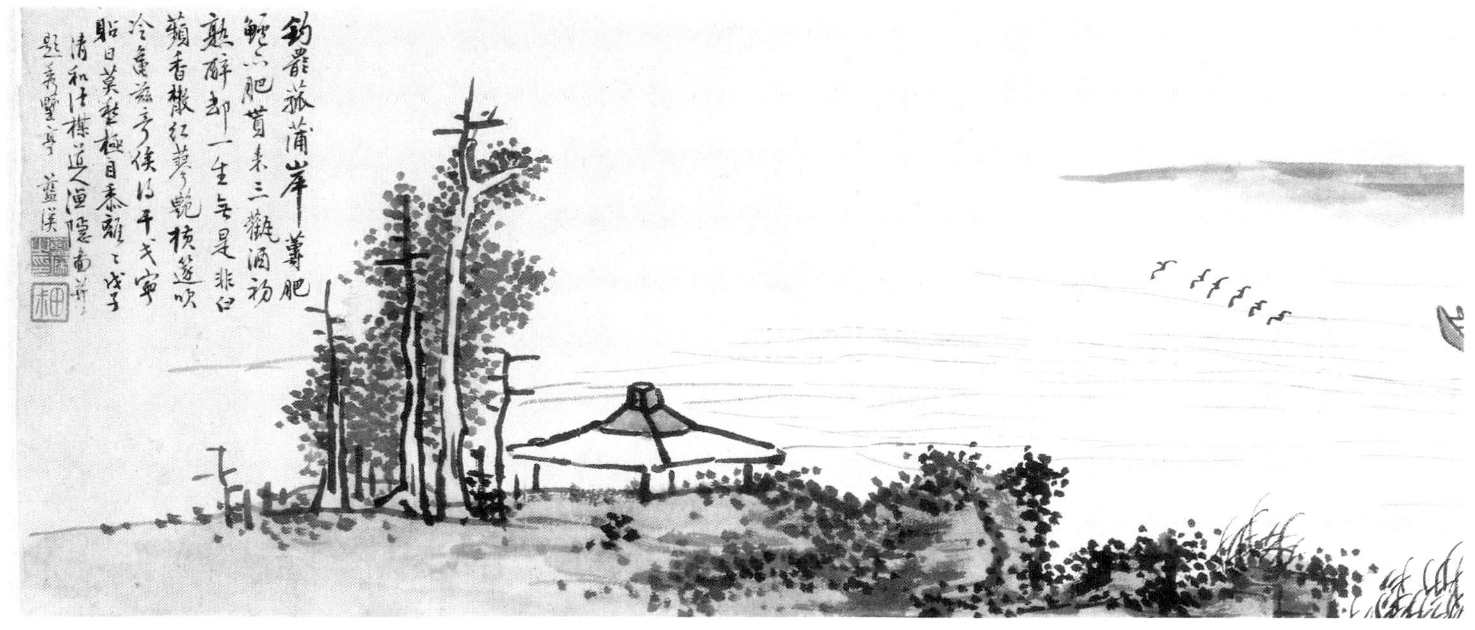

"Conversing on Antiquity"
dated 1651 by Lan Ying (1585-after 1664)

Hanging scroll; ink and colour on paper. 169.2 x 50cm
Gugong Museum, Peking

Two scholars are conversing on a riverbank behind tall trees and a perforated eccentric rock. Rocks and craggy trees are depicted with thick, spiky brushstrokes and dots that tend to appear rough. However, the execution of the distant hills is extremely sensitive, softly modulated in ink and colour. Lan Ying in his inscription tells us that he is following in conception the painting method of Guan Tong (10th century). It is, however, almost impossible for us to see any connection between this painting and the style of Guan Tong. It resembles rather a Yuan dynasty river landscape in composition.

The painting is signed by Lan Ying, dating it to 1651, and covered with seals of the artist.
For biographical details see catalogue no. 29.

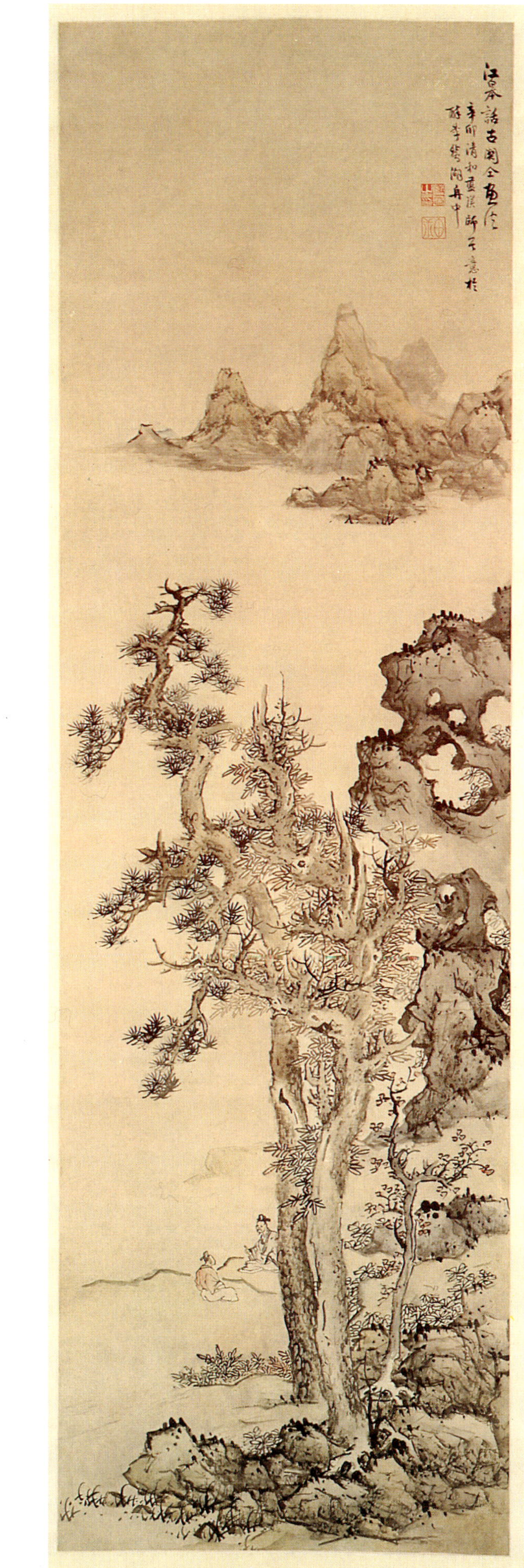
江峰話古圖仝畫﹐
辛卯清和重陽後一日寫於
松李堂陶舟中

catalogue no. 31

"Flowers in Four Seasons"
by Xu Wei (1521-1593)

Hanging scroll; ink on paper. 144.8 x 80.9 cm
Gugong Museum, Peking

Flowers and rocks are painted in a dynamic manner. Bold washes and broad strokes of ink and swift calligraphic lines not only capture the inherent nature of objects depicted, but also manifest the creative impulse of the artist. At the centre an eccentric rock is painted with patches of darker ink suffused in a larger area of diluted ink, creating an amorphous image with the underlying structure of the rock merely suggested. The peony (flower of spring), partly framed by the central rock, is depicted with dabs of dark, wet ink. Rising behind the rock is a banana tree, representing summer, done in powerful, broad strokes. The other plants, plum blossom (flower of winter), hibiscus (flower of autumn), orchid (flower of spring), bamboo (a winter plant), are rendered in animated brushstrokes that convey a feeling of life and growth. With apparent carelessness, the painting shows both discipline and freedom in the mastery of the brush, which transcends calligraphic conventions and embodies individuality.

To accompany the painting, Xu Wei composed a poem written in beautiful calligraphy:

"I, my old self, have been playing with ink dripping wet.

Painting flowers of the four seasons.

Please do not mind that I missed a brush or two.

After all, even the way of heaven has not been perfect lately".

Xu Wei was born to an official family from Shaoxing, Zhejiang province. He had a tragic life, suffering in the later years of his life severe mental breakdowns. The complex family situation in which he grew up must have been one of the contributing factors. He was known as a child prodigy; at a very early age, he mastered the arts of poetry, essays, music, swordsmanship, painting and calligraphy. Orphaned in his early teens, he went through a series of misfortunes. After passing the first degree examination in 1540, he failed repeatedly (seven times) the provincial examination for the second degree; his last attempt was in 1564. In his early twenties a lawsuit left him bankrupt. Living in semi-poverty, he was forced to make a living on his literary talent, writing essays and dramas. A major crisis in his life occurred when his patron, Hu Zongxian, was imprisoned in 1562 on extortion charges. Xu Wei feigned madness and thus escaped from being implicated. Probably disturbed by the setback of his career and the guilt feeling of not having come to the defence of his patron, Xu Wei attempted suicide three years later; he drove a nail into his ear, and also cracked his skull with an axe. In the following year, during one of his fitful attacks of derangement, he stabbed his third wife to death. Through the intervention of his friends, he was spared from a death sentence and was imprisoned for seven years. During the last two decades of his life, he lived in poverty, ill and mentally disturbed, and drunk much of the time. Friends came to his assistance with food and clothing, which he often repaid with a painting or a piece of calligraphy.

The painting is signed by Xu Wei and bears his seals.

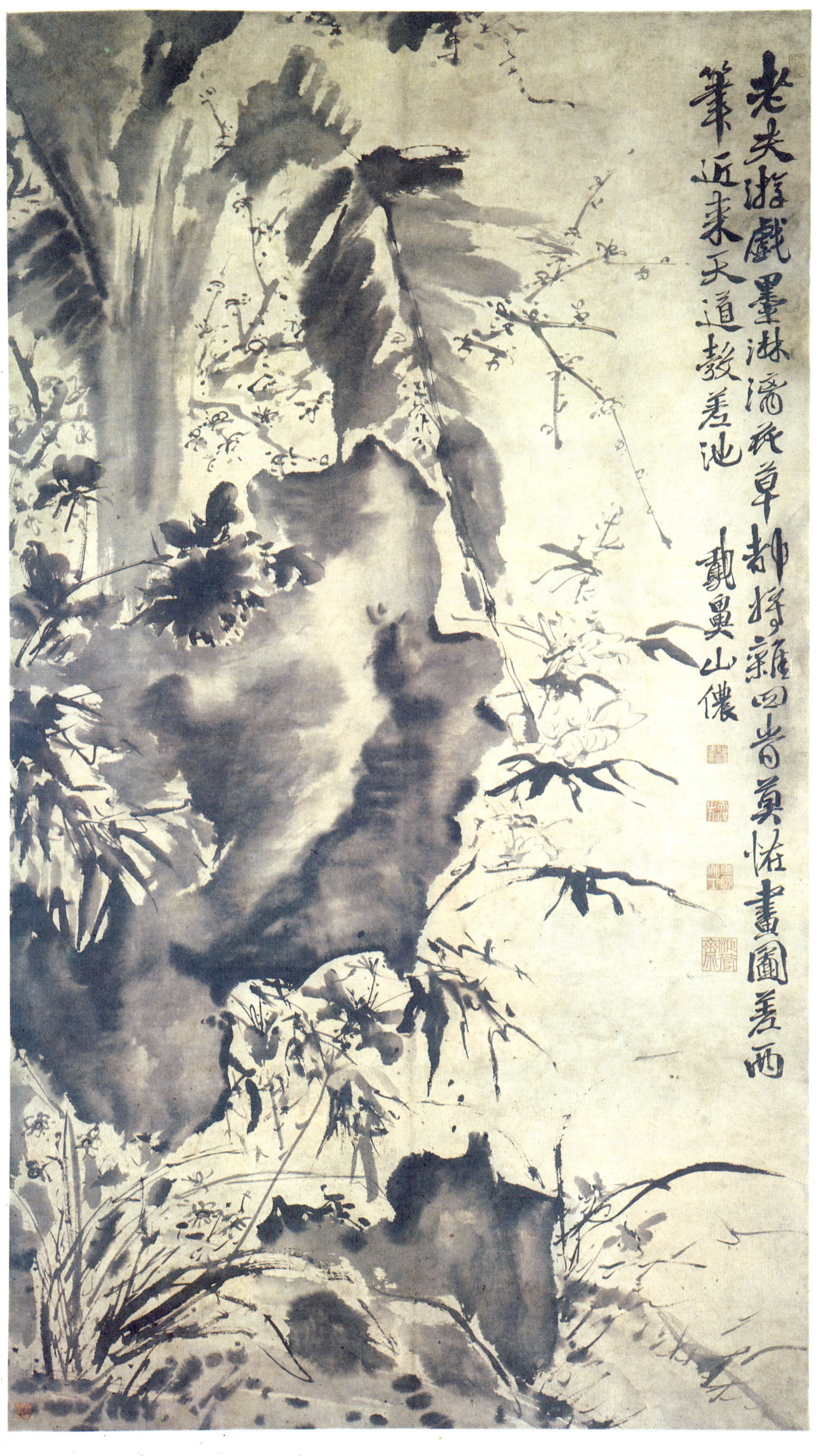

老夫遊戲墨淋漓花草都将雜四眥莫怪畫圖差西
筆近来天道教羞池
瓢翁山儂

catalogue no. 32

"Pear Blossom and Turtledove"
dated 1573 by Chen Jiayan (1539-after 1625)
Hanging scroll; ink and colours on paper. 121.8 x 49.5cm
Gugong Museum, Peking

A soft and lyrical painting composed around a colourful turtledove perched on a plunging bough of a full-blossomed pear tree. Painted in sensitive ink and colour washes without any definitive linear strokes the painting achieves the kind of tranquility and decorative beauty that is not found in the landscape tradition. The soft colouring in hues of pale blue and tan combine in a harmony that not even the more ominous grey washes above can disturb.

Chen Jiayan was born in Jiaxing in present-day Zhejiang province. Little detail of his life is known although the **Minghualu** records that he was noted for painting "flowers and birds in a free style imparting vigour and life to his works, which were excellent both in drawing and expression". Existing paintings of Chen Jiayan confirm that he was a painter who confined himself to bird and flower subjects always rendered in this sensitive, soft-coloured and almost impressionistic manner.

Inscription dated 1573 by the artist followed by his seals.

catalogue no. 33

"Bamboo Rock and Cockerel"
dated 1602 by Zhou Zhimian (active c. 1580-1610)
Hanging scroll; ink on paper. 157.2 x 47.5cm
Gugong Museum, Peking.

A classic, if academic, composition of a rocky outcrop with bamboo behind and in the foreground a resplendent cockerel, standing uncertainly on the steeply sloping ground. The rocks are drawn with broad ink washes which provide a craggy outline but a flat surface appearance, whilst the precisely painted bamboo leaves seem to hang in the air as if caught in a moment of suspense. The deliberate and contrived composition and studied brushwork clearly illustrate the more tasteful ideal of the Ming academic style.

Zhou Zhimian is frequently mentioned in connection with Lu Zhi (see cat. no. 18) as both hailed from the famed garden city of Suzhou, but Zhou gained his reputation as a painter of birds and flowers. Above all Zhou is renowned for his paintings of poultry and crows generally in combination with the exotic and eccentric rocks so familiar to the scholar's gardens of his home city.

Inscription by the artist dating the painting to 1602, followed by his seals.

"Goose"
by Shao Mi (circa 1594-1642)

Hanging scroll; ink and light colour on silk. 85.1 x 30.2 cm
Shanghai Museum

A single goose seated in an apparent void with the head turned in an enquiring manner. It is a precise, almost meticulous, rendering of a single bird totally unencumbered by the elements of an environment in which we might expect to find a goose. This isolation reflects the reserved and retiring nature which literary references generally accord Shao Mi. Similarly the lightly drawn dry ink brushlines and unexpected pink colour wash patches echo the isolation of the individual.

Shao Mi, a native of the painters' and scholars' mecca, Suzhou, was also known as a landscape painter, calligrapher, poet and litterateur. Unlike many of his colleagues and contemporaries Shao Mi did not gain access to the ranks of officialdom through the examination system, but his artistic standing nonetheless did assure him of a place in the elite of the late Ming scholar-gentleman class. He was a known associate of the doyen of this group, Dong Qichang (see cat. no. 26). Shao Mi's landscapes in particular reflect the literati ideal, for example his characteristic use of dry ink brushwork, although his use of pale and often unusual colour washes sets his style apart from the monochrome ink compositions of Dong Qichang.

Inscription and seals of the artists.
Reproduced: **Shanghai Museum Catalogue of Paintings;** no. 63.

"Miscellaneous Album Leaves"
by Chen Hongshou (1599-1652)

Set of four album leaves; ink and colours on paper. Each leaf measures: 31.6 x 25cm
Nanking Museum

Leaf 1: "Landscape"

Chen Hongshou's distinctive style of 'constructed'landscape elements is well illustrated in this small encapsulation of nature. Although clearly delineated into foreground, with rocks, trees and a promentory, middleground which is a river or lake, and the background of rocky mountains and a plunging waterfall, the scale is nonetheless intimate. The trees on the distant rocks are, for example, on the same scale as on the foreground promentory. The rocks are independently featured with strong linear outlines embracing wet brush washes, and it is these individual elements that are then built one upon the other to create the mass of the mountain.

Seals of the artist.

Leaf 2: "Butterflies and Flowers"

A mysterious, almost surrealist, painting of a large and exotic butterfly which hovers in the ominous manner of a praying mantis over colourful floating flowers and petals. The sense of movement in the flowing lines of the water is echoed in the rippling brushstrokes defining the rocks.

Seals of the artist.

Leaf 3: "Lake Rocks and lotus"

The unmistakable 'organic' rocks which are recognised as characteristic of Chen's style, are well illustrated in this leaf's loosely drawn brushstrokes which define the outlines, whilst others mould the form to provide a sense of volume as well as a sense of natural growth to the eccentric rocks. Stemming as it does from a small flowing stream, the combination of these elements gives the impression of a continuously evolving composition. In contrast the lotus flowers are drawn with a fine line and precision which, with the addition of delicate and even colour washes, offers a static and seemingly more permanent beauty.

On the opposite page facing the painting is a poetic inscription by Yun Shouping (see cat. no. 46). Seals of the artist.

Leaf 4: "Narcissus"

Chen Hongshou was particularly renowned for his flower paintings of which this finely drawn leaf of narcissus is a classic example. It is a very deliberate composition and the impression of contrivance is heightened by the carefully drawn overlapping leaves. These, like the flowers, appear caught and frozen as if to perpetuate a moment of beauty.

The literal translation of the characters for narcissus is 'water fairy' and the flowers were traditionally grown in jars filled with pebbles and water specially to blossom at the New Year to indicate good fortune for the ensuing twelve months.

Seals of the artist.
For biographical details see entry for catalogue number 38.
Reproduced: **Nanking Museum Catalogue of Paintings**, Vol 1, pages 130-1.

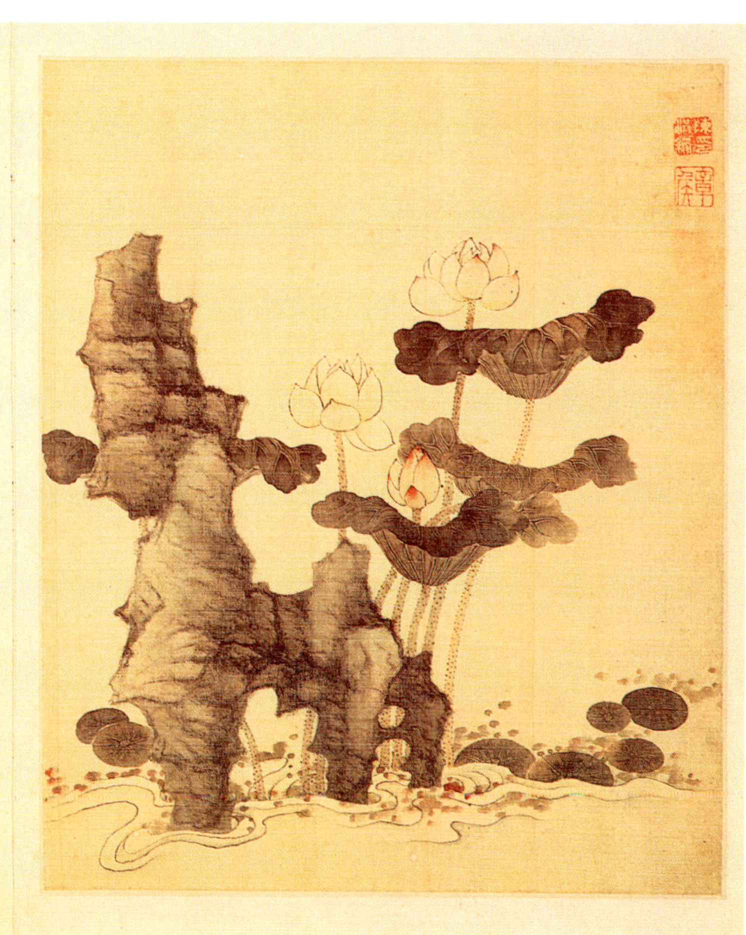

玉井殘煙未有枝綠雲空憶舊
琳池誰知吟客銷魂家寔是紅
衣欲墜時
　旅菴鈞岩壽

Leaf 3

"Millet and Crab"
dated 1651 by Xiang Shengmo (1597-1658)

Hanging scroll; ink and colours on paper. 105.8 x 38.5cm
Tianjin Arts Museum

In this unfamiliar combination of elements our eye is drawn to the darker ink washes of the crab which seems to emerge from the delicately drawn grasses and ground flora to threaten the swallows perched on the swaying millet plants. The composition, based on a steeply sloping ground and with the stalks of the millet sweeping into the scroll from beyond the confines of the picture, is a format familiar to many Chinese bird and flower paintings. The tension between the black monochrome ink crab and the tranquil birds and plants is heightened by the delicate brushwork and soft colouring.

Xiang Shengmo was a native of Jiaxing in northern Zhejiang province and thus close to Suzhou. There is no doubt that Xiang fell under the spell of the dominant coterie of artists and literary men of late Ming dynasty Suzhou. Born into an affluent and cultured family, his grandfather had assembled a noted collection of paintings and calligraphies, Xiang grew up in a profoundly cultured and sophisticated environment. Whilst still in his twenties he abandoned the security of home to lead a hermit's life dedicated to painting, poetry and calligraphy. Historical references record that after the fall of the Ming dynasty in 1644 his family's property was pillaged and the painting collection either destroyed or seized. It seems these dramatic events changed Xiang's outlook on life, for now he had no option but to lead the life of a hermit painter and to sell his paintings in order to survive. His early works were principally long landscape handscrolls which reflected his literati background and the qualities and richness of the scholar-hermit's existence. After the turmoil of the fall of the Ming his paintings adopted a more realistic approach, in which the theme of the idealised world of the scholar in nature is abandoned in favour of more intimate, objective and studied compositions, such as this example, which was executed in the early years of the Qing dynasty.

Inscription by artist dated 1651. Seals of artist.

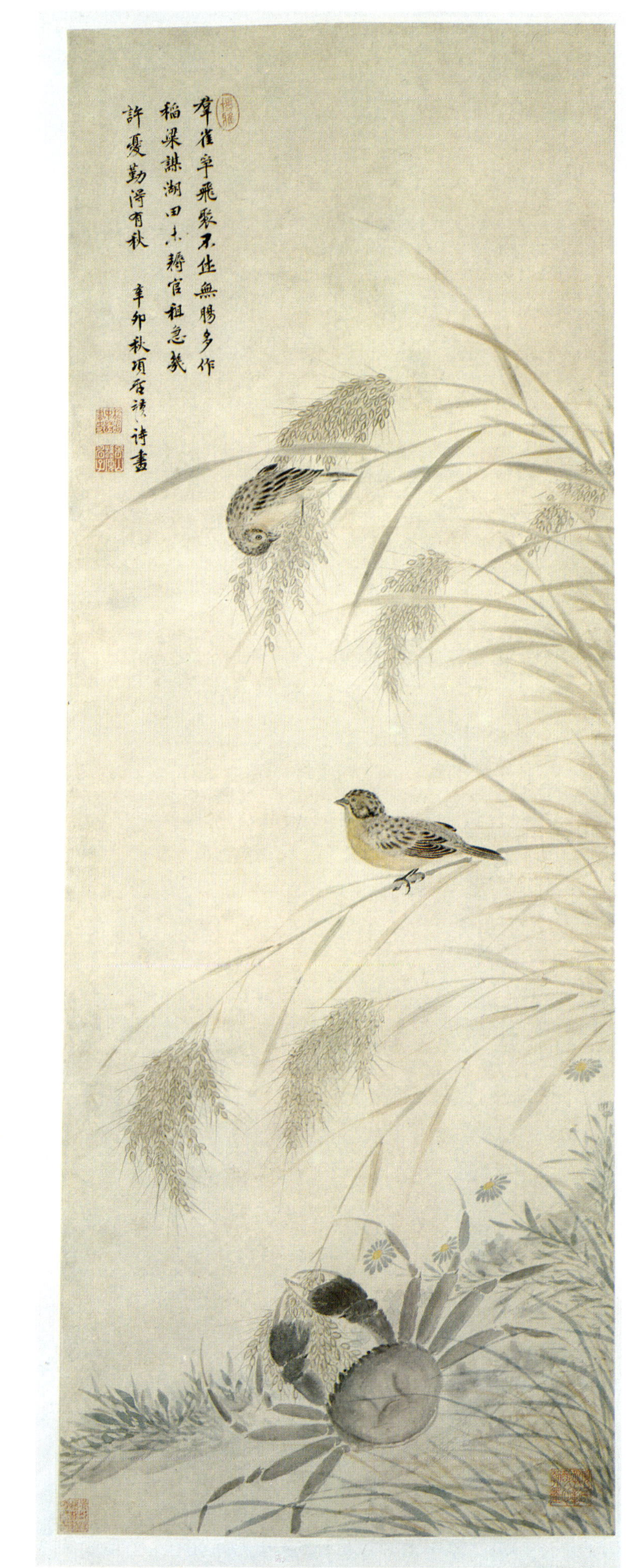
群雀率飛聚不住無賜多作
稻粱謀湖田木耧官租急歲
許憂勤浮有秋
辛卯秋項居禎詩畫

"Orchid and Bamboo"
dated 1642 by Yang Wencong (1597-1645)

Hanging scroll; ink on paper. 97 x 38cm
Guangzhou Museum

A classic literati composition of wistful orchids and bamboo sprouting from a sparsely drawn rock outcrop. The orchid is traditionally associated in China with the virtues of the scholar-gentleman. The simplicity of the composition belies the profound literati ideal which it represents. Executed in monochrome ink, the dry brushstrokes appear to have been dragged, almost reluctantly, across the paper, the painting fulfils the dictum of 'flavour with blandness'. The rocks are drawn with a broad dry brush producing a ragged outline which contrasts with the fluent calligraphic line of the reaching orchids, whilst the darker masses of the bamboo leaves provide contrast and points of emphasis. The painting is both sensitive and spontaneous; the perfect expression of the scholarly spirit.

Like so many of his colleague painters Yang Wencong, who although born in Guizhou province spent most of his life in Nanking, served in an official capacity. At the time of the fall of the Ming dynasty, shortly after this painting was executed and the writing was surely on the wall for the Ming, Yang was serving as a magistrate in Nanking. He was then appointed to organize the defence of the city in the face of the advancing Manchus. Upon the fall of the city Yang fled to Fujian province but his command was finally defeated and he was captured, to die a martyr to the cause of the fallen Ming.

Inscription dated 1642 and seals of the artist.
Published: **Wen Wu**, 1978, no. 10.

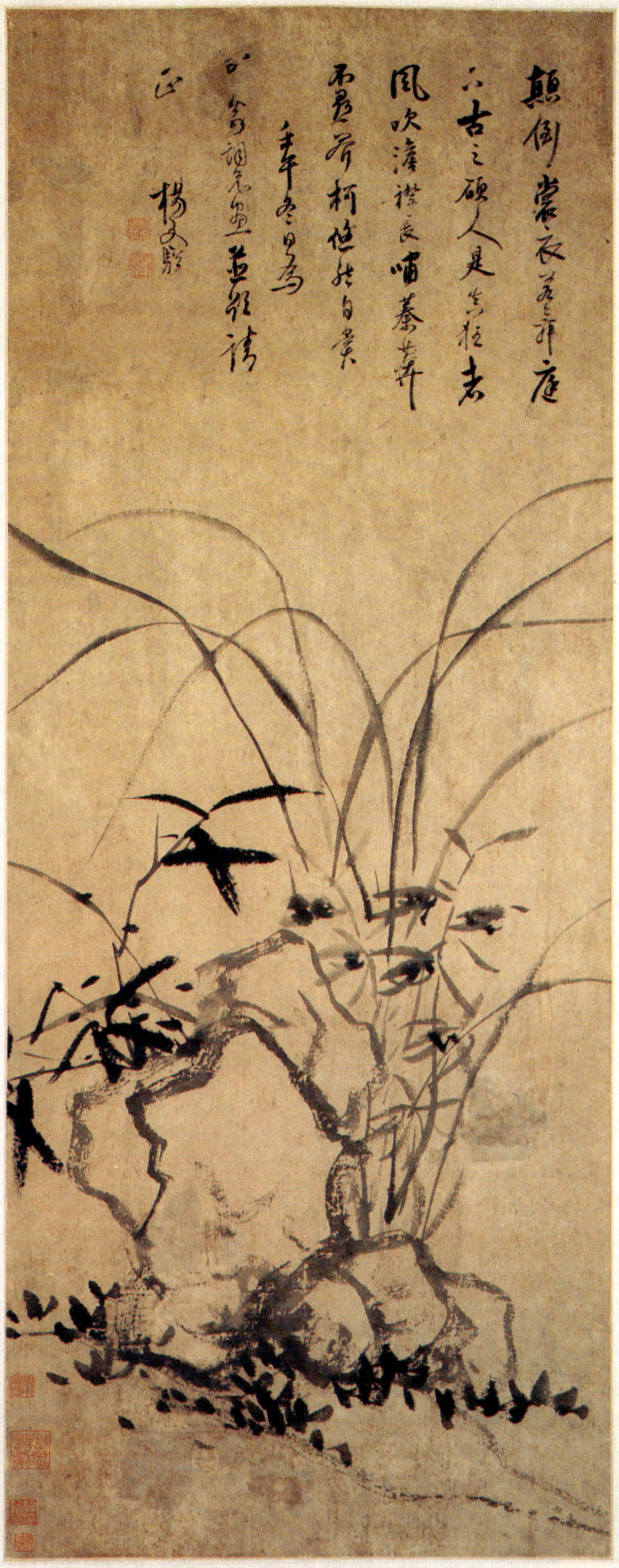

顛倒裳衣若拜庭
六古之碩人是無狂去
風吹漆襟長嘯蓁芋舞
不畏岸柯世共自賞
辛年冬日為
正 畫寄祖元先生一粲楊龍詩
楊文驄

"Enjoying a Painting"
by Chen Hongshou (1599-1652)

Hanging scroll; ink and colours on silk. 127 x 51 cm
Gugong Museum, Peking.

Over a typical Chen Hongshou 'organic' rock casually hangs a landscape painting which is being viewed by three figures. The absence of any form of ground on which the rock can settle is both strange and disconcerting but not untypical of the surrealist qualities often to be found in Chen's work.

The figure of the scholar is the undoubted focal point to the composition. The imposing demeanour is emphasised by the arrogant nose, exaggerated almost, but not quite, to the point of absurdity and caricature, and the finely manicured hand holding a green wine-cup aloft. He clearly is a man disdainful of all but the most lofty things in life. His robes and small Confucian hat are carefully drawn with dryish and oddly uninflected strokes and completed with pale modulated colour washes. The scholar is attended by a red-robed priest in the background and, in the foreground, a servant holding a large bowl, presumably containing ample supplies of wine. This latter figure's belted green robe and tight-fitting black cap are more reminiscent of European medieval costume than they are of traditional Chinese dress.

Chen Hongshou was born into a gentry family, in Zhejiang province, which although in decline nonetheless provided an appropriate environment for one seeking a scholarly and cultured life. At an early age Chen displayed a remarkable talent for figure painting and one apochryphal tale relates that at the tender age of four he painted a ten foot high portrait of Guang Zi. Later, at the age of ten, it is recorded in another biography that Chen met Lan Ying (see cat. nos. 29 and 30) who subsequently became his teacher for landscape painting. Chen Hongshou's figure painting style is characterised by the delicate, at times almost effete, line which along with his calligraphy was once described by the character **mei** meaning seductive, or alternatively, exaggerated femininity. It is an apt description and perhaps also reflects Chen's reported decadent life style. Chen was temporarily stirred by events when the Ming dynasty collapsed in 1644 and became a Buddhist monk rather than acknowledge Manchu rule. However, he himself admits that it was but a gesture of mere escapism as in an anthology of his writings, **Bao Lun Tang Ji,** he says "In the summer of 1646 I, the Repentant, ran into the mountains to save my life. At places where monkeys and birds gathered I then cut off my hair and put on monk's robe. How could I become a monk? It was only a matter of borrowing the monk's form for the sake of staying alive".

Inscription and seals of the artists.
Published: **Wen Wu** 1978, no. 11.

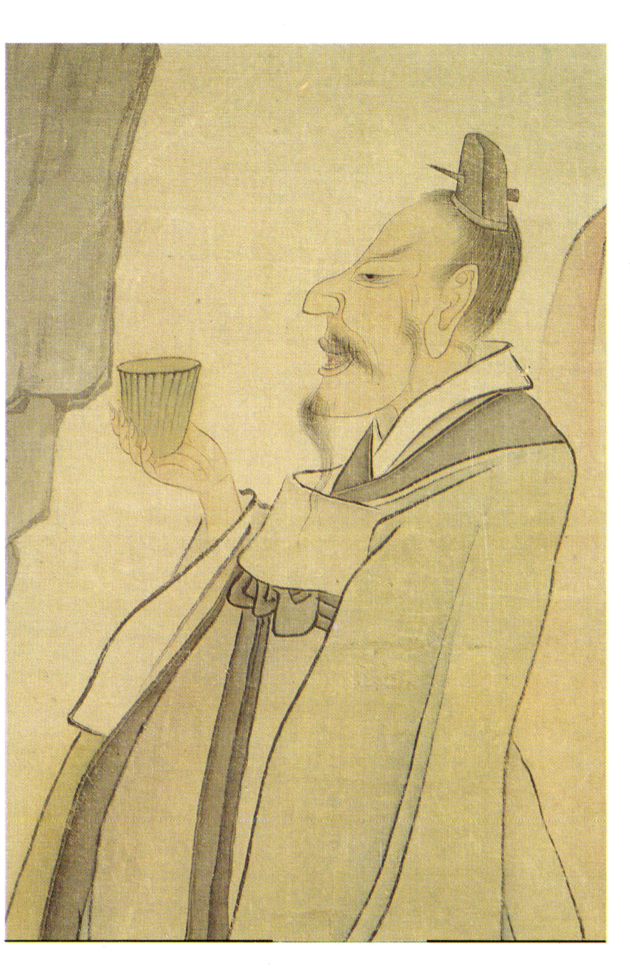

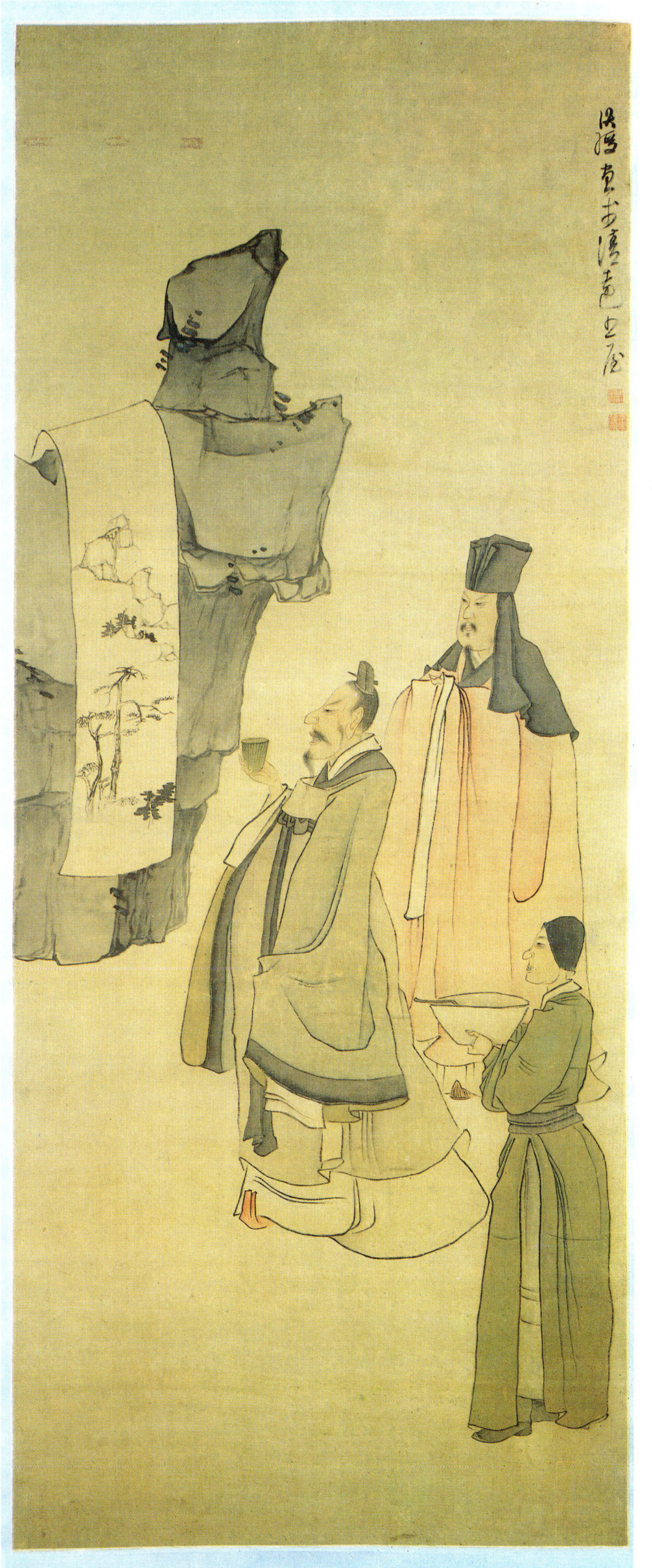

"Playing the Qin in the Shade of a Wutong Tree" dated 1581 by You Qiu (16th century)

Hanging scroll; ink and light colours on paper. 118.4 x 32.7cm
Gugong Museum, Peking.

Underneath a leafy Wutong tree, and surrounded by eccentric rocks and banana trees, sits the musician playing the **qin** and his two listening scholars. The **qin** is a traditional five or seven-stringed Chinese lute. In the foreground an attendant carrying the fungus of longevity in a pot crosses a bridge over a small stream. The composition reflects so many of the scholar-gentleman ideals in which the pleasures of the cultured life are harmoniously combined with nature. The effects of the influence of You's master, Qiu Ying (cat. no. 23), are clearly shown in this painting. Not only is the composition itself a reflection of Qiu Ying, there is a well known painting of a similar subject by Qiu in the National Palace Museum, Taipei, but so also is the detail brushwork of the eccentric rocks, banana trees and figures.

Born in Suzhou, You Qiu was brought up in the cultured and literary traditions of that city. His commitment to painting was confirmed by his marriage to the daughter of Qiu Ying, who was clearly the major influence in his development as a painter although it must be recognised that he never achieved the attainments of his master. Themes based on figures in landscapes were You's particular metier and he is known for his compositions illustrating popular and ancient legends and stories. Many of these he sought in still earlier paintings, such as those by Li Longmien (1040-1106) and Qian Xuan (circa. 1235-1300), tending to reproduce their works with the kind of strong linear clarity evident in this painting. It may be said that the distinctive literary content in You's paintings is better suited to the handscroll format where the gradual unrolling of the scroll parallels the succession of scenes illustrating the story. You's interest in historical legend is reflected in the strong traditionalism of his style and technique, both of which have their origins in early Song dynasty academic painting.

Inscription dated 1581 and seals of the artist.

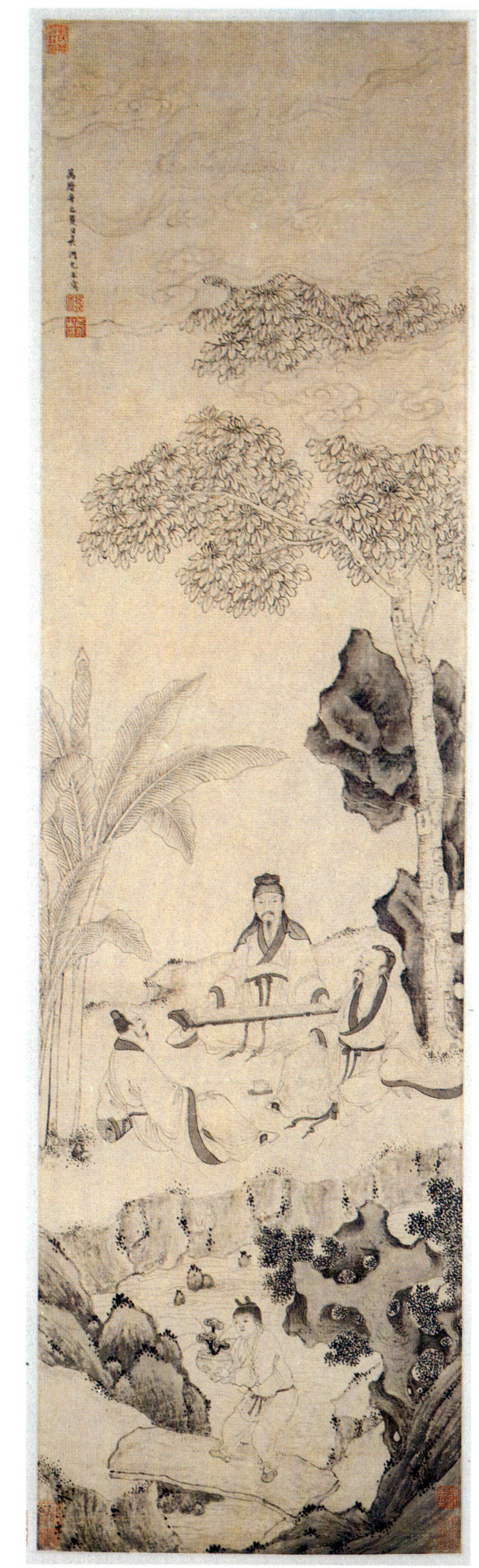

"Portrait of Hu Erzao"
dated 1627 by Zeng Jing (1568-1650)
Hanging scroll; ink and colours on silk. 162 x 81.3cm
Zhejiang Provincial Museum

The austere but scholarly figure of Hu Erzao, about whom nothing is unfortunately known, sits on a rock beneath gnarled pines beside a tumbling stream. Hu's attendant waits respectfully behind, half hidden by a pine tree, ready to serve his master. Beside Hu is placed a white incense burner. Once again the precision of the drawing of the figure and the delicate lines of the features contrast with the more robust and expressive style of the landscape. The so-called 'blue and green' style of landscape painting, employed by Zeng in this scroll, evolved during the Tang dynasty and was a convention adopted by many conservative painters during both Ming and Qing dynasties. Beyond the low horizon over which the stream appears no elements of the more distant landscape are shown: it is as though the world of Hu Erzao is confined to the small segment of the landscape in which he is seated.

Zeng Jing was a native of Fujian province but moved to Nanking where he was soon established as a portrait painter. He subsequently became the foremost portraitist of his age and rapidly achieved widespread fame in a field that was largely neglected by his fellow painters. Critics of the Ming and Qing dynasties were in agreement that Zeng brought a new realism to portraiture and it has been suggested that the shading and modelling of the faces in his portraits were techniques learnt from European missionaries active in the Nanking region during the 16th and 17th centuries. The **Wusheng Shishi** says of Zeng that "he painted portraits which looked exactly like reflections of the models in a mirror and grasped the spirit and emotions of the people in a marvellous way. His colouring was refined, and although the figures were simply on paper or silk, their eyes seemed to be moving and following the beholder as if they were the eyes of real beings . . . In his portraits he gave the noble countenance of the high officials, the elegance of the ladies, the refinement of the hermits, the character of monks and priests, rendering their ugly as well as their beautiful features in his search for likeness". Certainly in this portrait there is evidence to suggest that Zeng sought to achieve a real physical likeness, but in addition the expression captures the concentration, the solitude, the tranquility and perhaps a hint of melancholy in the subject.

Inscription dated 1627 and seal of the artist.

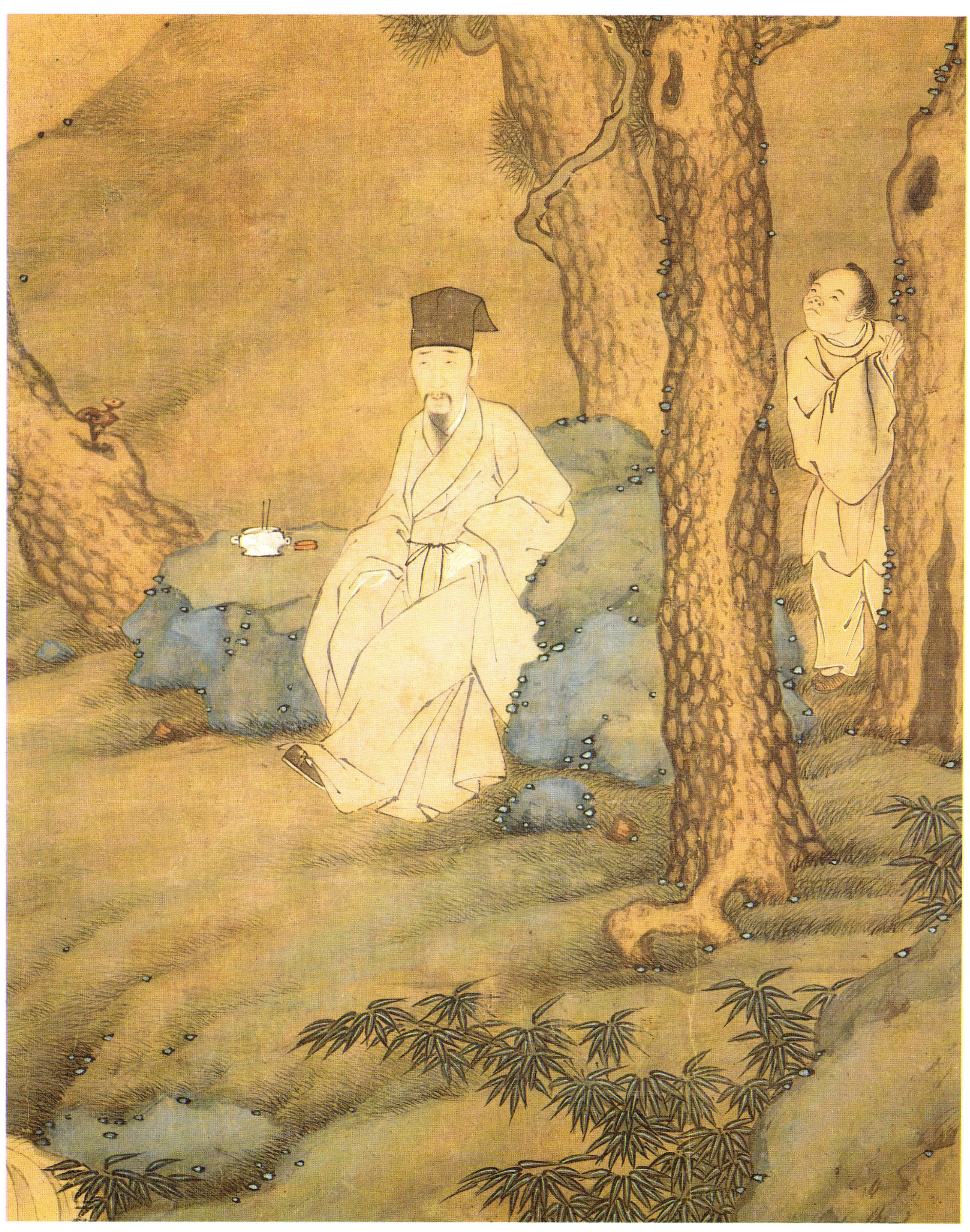

Painting in the Qing Dynasty

Mae Anna Pang

In 1644 the Ming dynasty was overthrown by the Manchus, who established the Qing dynasty (1644-1911). The early Qing was a period of great turbulence and social upheaval. Scholars, who were strongly disturbed by the fall of the Ming dynasty, were faced with the dilemma of whether to serve the Manchus, to resist the Manchus openly, or to protest in silence. Many scholars simply took the path of withdrawal from public service so as not to collaborate with the Manchus. They retreated into a quiet life of retirement; some even withdrew from society completely and became recluses.

Among the scholar-amateur painters who lived in retirement were Wang Shimin (1592-1680) (cat. no. 41) and Wang Jian (1598-1677) (cat. no. 44), regarded as the direct followers of Dong Qichang (1555-1636) (cat. no. 26) and leaders of the so-called Orthodox school of painting. Both Wang Shimin and Wang Jian came from prominent scholar-gentry families of Taicang, Jiangsu province. In his youth Wang Shimin had studied painting with Dong Qichang and served briefly as an official before the fall of the Ming dynasty. As followers of Dong Qichang, Wang Shimin and Wang Jian continued the conservative elements of his theory and style of painting. Being collectors and connoisseurs of art, they were more interested in recapturing and compiling the styles of the past masters than in creating an individual style of painting, which Dong had advocated. More as men of the brush than of art, they appreciated in painting, as in calligraphy, the fine brushstrokes and the antique flavours which they evoked. Thus, immersed in the styles of the past, their landscapes seem far removed from the visual reality of nature.

Some of the younger members of this group, Wang Yuanqi (1642-1715) (cat. no. 43) in particular, were more inventive and succeeded in creating a personal style of painting. However, by consciously carrying out Dong's concept of originality based on tradition, Wang intellectualised and formalised it into almost a ritual. The artist began by engaging in a "spiritual encounter" (**shenyu**) with the paintings of the ancient masters, during which he grasped the ideas and intentions behind the paintings. Then, by capturing and transforming the ancient styles in spirit, the artist succeeded in creating a style of his own. Wang Yuanqi usually accompanied his paintings with long inscriptions in which he discussed the style or styles he was following, his theories on painting, or the development of styles which demonstrated his own art-historical lineage and his role as a transmitter of tradition. Although Wang Yuanqi had succeeded in discovering new ideas both in actual painting and in theory, he nevertheless confined his creative activity within an art-historical framework of traditional styles.

A high official at the court of the Kangxi period (1662-1723), Wang Yuanqi dominated the Court Academy of painting during the latter decades of his life, although he was never a court painter in the true sense. His paintings and the Orthodox tradition of literati painting were personally patronized by the Emperor Kangxi, who was very fond of paintings by Dong Qichang. Scholar-amateur painting, which began in the 11th century as a means of self-expression practised by scholars outside the painting tradition of the court academy, had by now become part of the court establishment. Acclaimed as the "crown glory" of his time, Wang commanded an enormous following, said to have been more than a thousand, to raise the banner of the Loudong school, the name of which – "east of the River Lou" – came from his birthplace, Taicang.

Although the "Orthodox" masters were proclaimed as the direct followers of Dong Qichang, it was the so-called "Individualist" painters of the early Qing who were inspired by the revolutionary aspects of the style of Dong Qichang and who carried on his creative approach to painting in a truer sense. Most of the Individualist painters were recluses who withdrew not only from public life but also from society. Kun Can (1612-97) (cat. no. 51) joined the Buddhist monastic order before the fall of Ming, while Hong Ren (fl. c. 1603-1663) (cat. no. 47), Zhu Da (1626-1705) (cat. nos. 57, 58), and Dao Ji (1641-1707) (cat. nos. 59, 60) joined it after the fall of Ming. The latter two were descendants of the Ming Imperial line. They may well have taken religious orders for the sake of personal safety.

Deeply affected by the political and social turmoil of the time, some of these painters withdrew into a private world of eccentricities which were reflected in their behaviour as well as their paintings. Zhu Da, after the fall of the Ming dynasty and then the death of his father, became deranged and refused to speak. He only laughed and cried. In his paintings, one often finds birds standing on one leg and brooding with an enigmatic expression. Such eccentric behaviour as practiced by men who have dropped out of the mainstream of political and social life was tolerated in traditional Chinese society, for it was considered outside the conventional realm of social responsibilities and obligations.

The Individualist painters also returned to nature for refuge, as they spent their times roaming in the mountains, particularly the Huangshan ("Yellow Mountains") region in Anhui province. With their stylistic basis in the work of the ancients and the natural forms of nature, they created powerful "inner landscapes" and developed landscape painting to the highest artistic form.

As a champion of individualism, Dao Ji, one of the individualist painters, went further than Dong Qichang in artistic theory. At the invitation of his friend, Boerdu (act. 1680-1700), a member of the Manchu nobility, Dao Ji visited the court at Peking in 1689-1690, where he met the Orthodox master, Wang Yuanqi. Probably in reaction to Wang's formalized, art-historical method of painting which he must have found a hindrance to originality, Dao Ji advocated a return to the original state of painting, before any fixed methods were established and when the artist could create as spontaneously and naturally as nature. He called for a return to the "single brushstroke" (**yihua**), which he defined as the origin of all painting, just as the "primordial line" in the cosmological diagram is the symbol of the "origin of all existence, the root of the myriad phenomenon". Dao Ji also spoke of a "Method of No Method". "The Perfect Man", he wrote, "has no method, but it is not that he does not have method; he has the method that is no method". Based on its analogy to "non-being", which, according to the Taoist philosophy of creation, is "being" in an undifferentiated state with all the potentials for becoming and is therefore the origin of all things, "no-method" is the origin of all methods, encompassing all possibilities and free of any restrictions. Dao Ji's theories and paintings not only exerted a profound influence on later Chinese paintings, but also heralded a new, modern spirit in the undertaking of Chinese painting.

Against a background of conservative paintings produced by painters of the

Court Academy and artists who followed the Orthodox style of painting, a new kind of individualism emerged in Chinese painting of the 18th century. While expressions of individuality in the 17th century originated from deep-felt feelings, those of the 18th century came from a desire for novelty. Probably under compulsion to create a distinctive and original style of painting, Gao Qipei (1672-1732) (cat. nos. 69, 70), a Manchu by birth and a high official in the Imperial court, introduced an unusual method of painting with his fingers, the method of which was more fascinating than the actual paintings.

Under the long and stable reigns of the Kangxi (1662-1723) and Qianlong (1736-1796) emperors, China enjoyed a peaceful period of political stability and economic prosperity. Yangzhou, in particular, became a commercial centre. The salt merchants of Yangzhou, who made huge fortunes in a short time, became the new and enthusiastic patrons of the arts. Wealth enabled them to associate with men of the gentry and scholar class and to entertain lavishly men of talent, poets and artists. In emulating the taste of the scholar-gentry, they collected paintings in the literary style. Scholars who did not succeed in pursuing a successful career in the bureaucracy were attracted to Yangzhou and turned their talents to making a living. They were, however, not professional artists in the strict sense, in that they painted at will, and not upon demand. Theoretically, they were still painting as a means of self-expression, taking delight in painting, and never working on commission.

As an attribute of literati painting, "amateurishness" or technical awkwardness (**zhuo**), became a sought-after quality. "Eccentricities", both in the paintings and the behaviour of the artists, were not only tolerated, but were appreciated by the new patrons, who had a taste for novelty. They themselves also indulged in all kinds of capricious pursuits, which were becoming fashionable. Thus, a new mood entered into Chinese painting, that of a light-hearted playfulness, charm, and humour. Intimate subjects of birds and flowers overtook landscape in importance. Colours were more frequently used; soft, cool colours that were applied with great sensitivity and subtlety.

The great success of the Yangzhou artists brought strong reactions from the conservatives of the time. They were called the "Eight Eccentrics" (**baguai**) by a contemporary writer, and this later became a loose term that included nine, or even ten, different artists. The term "eccentric" (**guai**) was not used in the modern sense of being original and individualistic. It was a term of disapproval, having the meaning of being deviant from the correct (Orthodox) path of painting.

The 19th century was a period of political crisis, witnessing the decline of the Qing dynasty and the impact of the West. As a result of China's defeat in the Opium War with the British and the subsequent treaty of Nanking in 1842, Shanghai became one of the five treaty ports open to foreign trade and residence. With economic prosperity brought about by trade with the West, Shanghai became a centre of artistic activities. People like the Treaty Port Mandarins and Compradors, who rose to wealth and power quickly through their involvement with western trade, became the new patrons of the arts. These wealthy patrons, while competent in western languages and in dealing with westerners, were not educated in the traditional sense and therefore were not attracted to the tastes of the literati. They acquired paintings not so much for contemplation as to decorate their homes and business places and to exhibit their wealth. They tended to collect contemporary paintings that they could understand and relate to.

The artistic demands of the *nouveau riche* led to the rise of the Shanghai school ("**Haipai**", sea school) in the second half of the 19th century, which was dominated by the paintings of Ren Bonian (1840-1896) (cat. nos. 88, 89). "**Haipai**" was a deprecatory term used by Peking artists of the early 20th century, criticizing the commercial nature of the paintings of this school and their lack of adherence to traditional styles. Although they were decorative paintings produced for commercial consumption, the paintings of the Shanghai school were significant in that they drew inspirations from the folk tradition of woodblock illustrations in terms of subject matter and brush technique. They opened up new areas of subject matter that were not taken seriously by the literati, themes that had popular appeal, such as figure paintings of beautiful women and those based on mythology, birds and flowers, and paintings with auspicious symbols of longevity, happiness and wealth.

In the last decade of the 19th century, interest in the literati style of painting was revived in Shanghai. This was brought about by several factors. Art collectors in Shanghai had now become more sophisticated in taste. There was in Shanghai a concentration of collectors and artists from the scholar-gentry class who had been uprooted by the destruction brought about by the Taiping rebellion (1850-1864). An important factor was perhaps the "self-strengthening" (**ziqiang**) movement which came about as a response to the challenges of the West and culminated in the slogan of "Chinese learning as the basic substance, Western learning for practical use" (**Zong xue wei ti, xi xue wei yong**). In practice this doctrine meant that China should study Western science and technology in order to meet the military threats of the West. But, spiritually, China had to draw strength from her own cultural tradition and preserve her cultural identity. Painting in the literary style was part of this rich cultural tradition. As a result of all these factors, landscape became a popular theme again. Painters took great interest in mastering the other scholarly arts, particularly poetry, calligraphy, and seal carving. There was also a revival of interest in studying archaic bronze and stone inscriptions.

The Shanghai school of painting was absorbed into the literati style of painting, as seen in the works of Wu Changshuo (1844-1929) (cat. nos. 94, 95), who had studied painting with Ren Bonian after he had reached 50, and then overtook Ren in importance. As a member of the scholar-gentry class and a former minor official, versed in the Classics and competent in calligraphy, Wu and his paintings were seen as embodiments of traditional Chinese painting, which came to be called **guohua** ("National Style of Painting"). Paintings of this period, as exemplified by Wu's paintings, were characterised by a greater sense of directness, contrast, immediacy, and a more forceful kind of strength.

With the fall of the Qing dynasty in 1911, great political and social changes took place. The civil examination system and the bureaucracy were abolished and as a result, the scholar-gentry class lost their special privileges. However, paintings in the literati style were continued by artists who were born in the latter part of the 19th century and whose creative lives spanned well into the first half of the 20th century. As a new class of intellectuals, these artists held academic positions in the

Art Academies and the Universities. Huang Binhong (1863-1954) (cat. no. 98) continued to be very much a literati artist and painted traditional landscapes with great originality. One of a new generation of artists, Xu Beihong (1895-1953) (cat. no. 99) went to Paris to study Western painting in the early part of the 20th century. After experimenting with this style of painting, Xu returned to the traditional Chinese style which he enriched with the techniques of Western painting. Probably under the stimulus of Western art, Chinese artists of the 20th century and Xu Beihong in particular, returned to nature for direct observation. On the whole, the traditional style of Chinese painting was not affected by Western painting in any basic sense.

Of the artists working in the early part of the 20th century, however, it was Qi Baishi (1863-1957) (cat. no. 100) who gave traditional Chinese painting a Chinese character that transcends the distinctions between the professional and literati styles of painting, and that combines the spirits of both ancient and modern China.

Opposite: Detail of cat. no. 51, page 115.

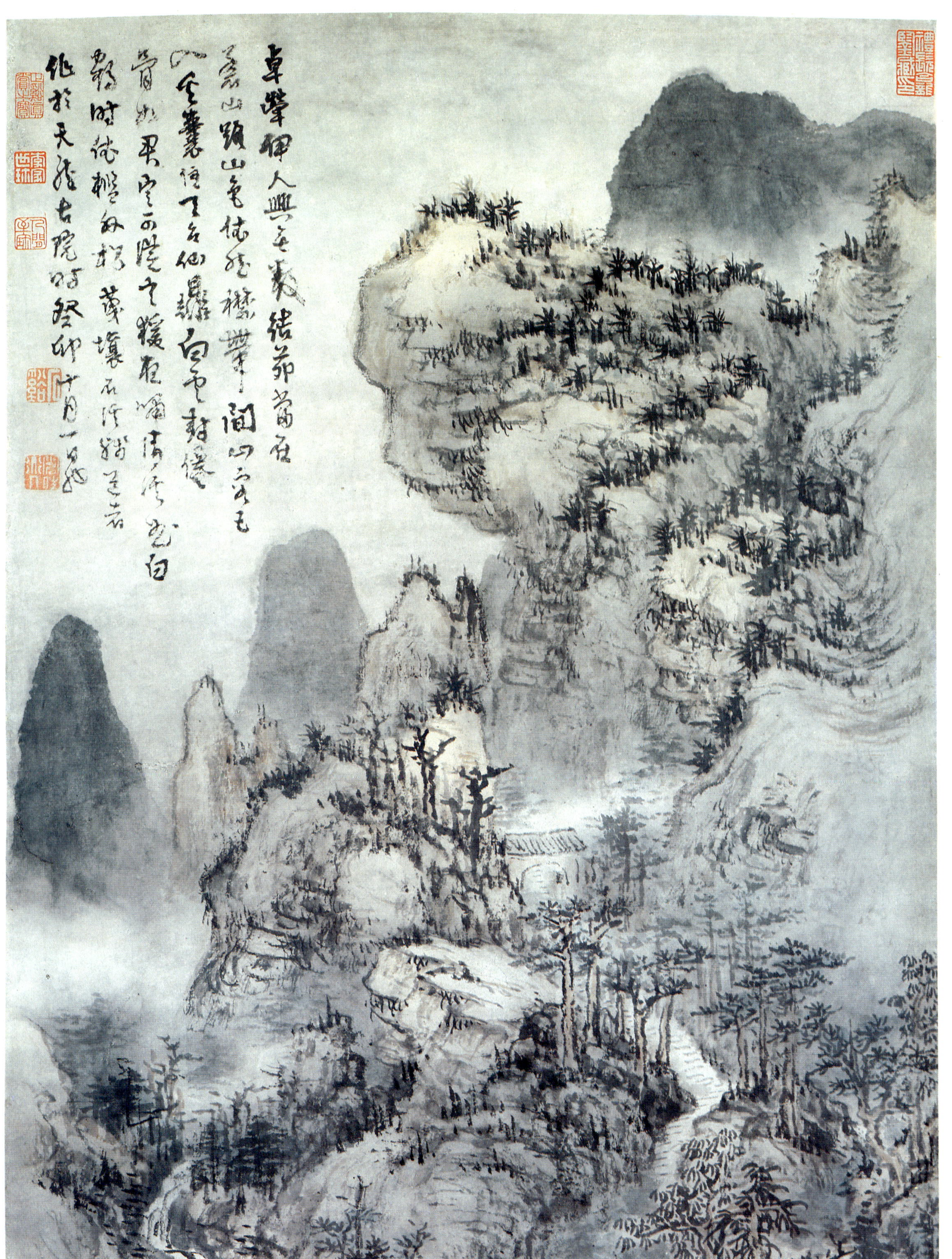

"Landscape"
dated 1669 by Wang Shimin (1592-1680)

Hanging scroll; ink on paper. 133.4 x 62.8cm
Gugong Museum, Peking.

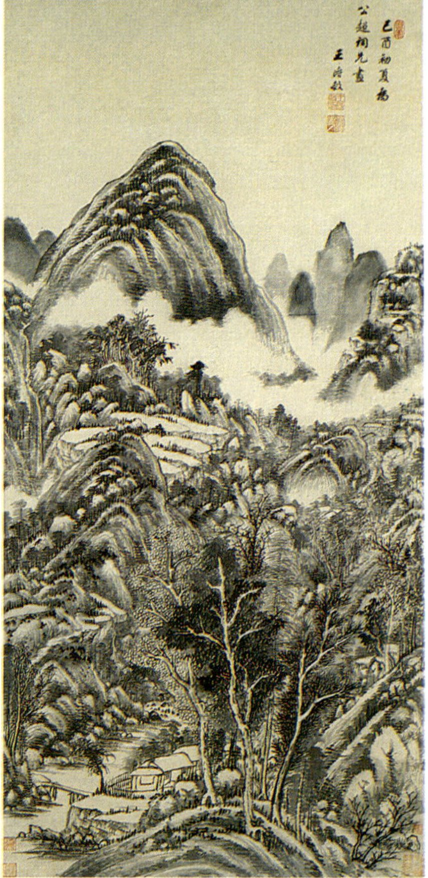

This dense, impenetrable landscape is over-crowded with boulders, trees, rocks, plateaux and mountain peaks, that are repeated and piled on each other without much structural support. As though taking Dong's distinction between real scenery and landscape painting literally (see cat. no. 26), Wang shows very little interest in representing the "wonder" of natural scenery. Landscape elements of rocks and trees are derived from paintings by the Yuan dynasty master, Huang Gongwang (1269-1354), which are composed without the abstract, formal relationship existing among them in Huang's landscape. It seems that in this bland landscape, Wang's main concern was to capture the "marvels of brush and ink". Throughout the painting, one finds sensitive passages of delicate brushstrokes, soft gradations of ink, rich tonal texture, which are achieved by a gradual accumulation of ink.

Wang Shimin (1592-1680), the oldest of the Orthodox masters, came from a prominent family of scholar-officials in Taicang, Jiangsu province. He studied painting with Dong Qichang while still young. After retiring from an official post in the Ming government several years before the fall of the dynasty, he devoted himself to his interest in art, painting and collecting. He followed Dong in his preference for the scholar-amateur artists of the Yuan dynasty (1279-1368), Huang Gongwang in particular. He once lamented how "from youth to white-headed old age, day and night" he had tried to capture Huang Gongwang's brush conception and failed to "resemble even one-thousandth part of it". In the usual self-deprecatory way of the scholar-gentleman, Wang admitted that his "natural endowment is blunt and limited" and that "it is easy to talk about the style of Huang Gongwang, but difficult to follow it".

An inscription by Wang Shimin tells us that he did the painting for a friend in 1669; it is followed by Wang's personal seals.

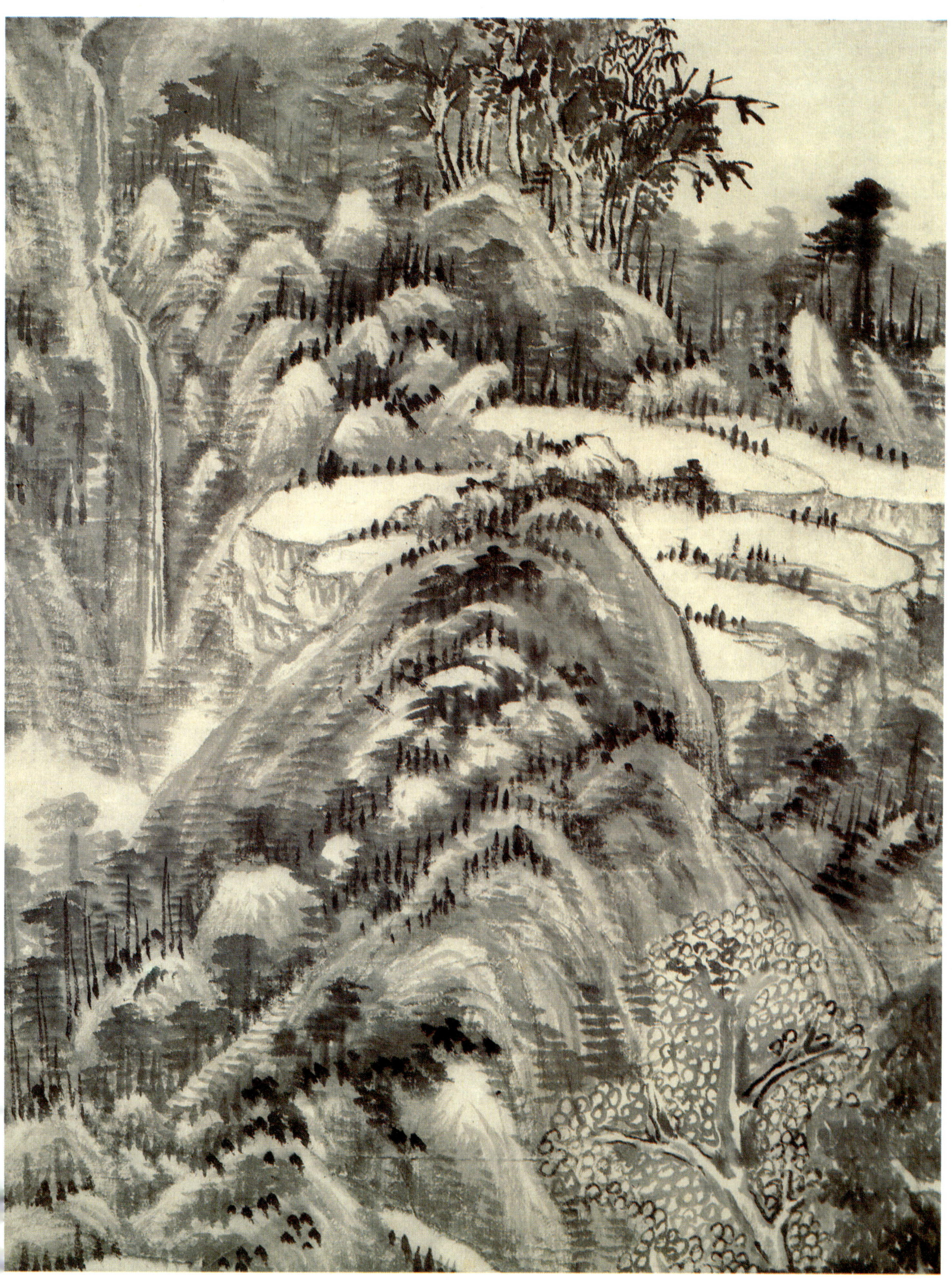

"Ode to the Plum Blossoms in the Summer Moon"
dated 1714 by Wang Hui (1632-1717)

Hanging scroll; ink and colour on paper. 90.8 x 60.2cm
Gugong Museum, Peking

A beautiful garden scene celebrating a poetic theme is depicted in a delicate and elegant manner. Surrounded by trees and eccentric rocks, a scholar sitting in a pavilion is gazing at a group of trees and bamboos across the river. Another scholar is standing on a bridge and contemplating the flowing stream. A cool, pleasant mood is created. In striking but exquisite colour combinations, blue is used throughout the landscape, depicting trees and grass. Silhouetted against the sky, which is partly darkened by a grey wash, blue pine needles and bamboo leaves are contrasted with those painted in rich black ink. Accenting the blue are the white and orange blossoms. The cool tonality is softened by warmer colours such as buff-pink applied on riverbanks, tree trunks and leaves. A soothing effect is created by a lulling, undulating rhythm that is echoed throughout the landscape, among the twisting pines, flowing water, misty rocks, and grass blown in a gentle breeze.

Wang Hui, in his inscription dated 1714, tells us that Mr Fang Zhou used to have, in front of his pavilion, an old prunus tree, which went into full bloom in the 5th month of every summer. Celebrities of the time who came to admire it composed poetry to celebrate the occasion. That was more than 50 years earlier. Mr Fang Zhou asked Wang Hui to do a painting (probably on commission) to recapture the beauty of such a scene, which Wang has certainly succeeded in doing. Technical skill is combined with a refinement of taste in the decorative sense.

Wang Hui (1632-1717), one of the Orthodox masters, came from a family of professional painters in Changshu, Jiangsu province. In his youth, his artistic talent was discovered by Wang Jian (1598-1677) (cat. no. 44) and Wang Shimin (1592-1680) (cat. no. 41), who took him on as their protégé and opened their collections of paintings for him to study. Wang Hui was admired by the two older Wangs for his ability to capture the styles of the ancient masters. In 1691, he was called to Peking by the Kangxi Emperor (r. 1662-1723) to supervise the project of depicting the emperor's visit to the south in 1689. As his fame grew, he began to have a large following of pupils, and became the founder of the Yushan school, named after a mountain near his birthplace.

Wang's inscription is followed by several of his personal seals. A colophon by the modern collector, Wu Hufan (1894-1970), is found beside the painting on the scroll.

For colour detail see frontispiece.

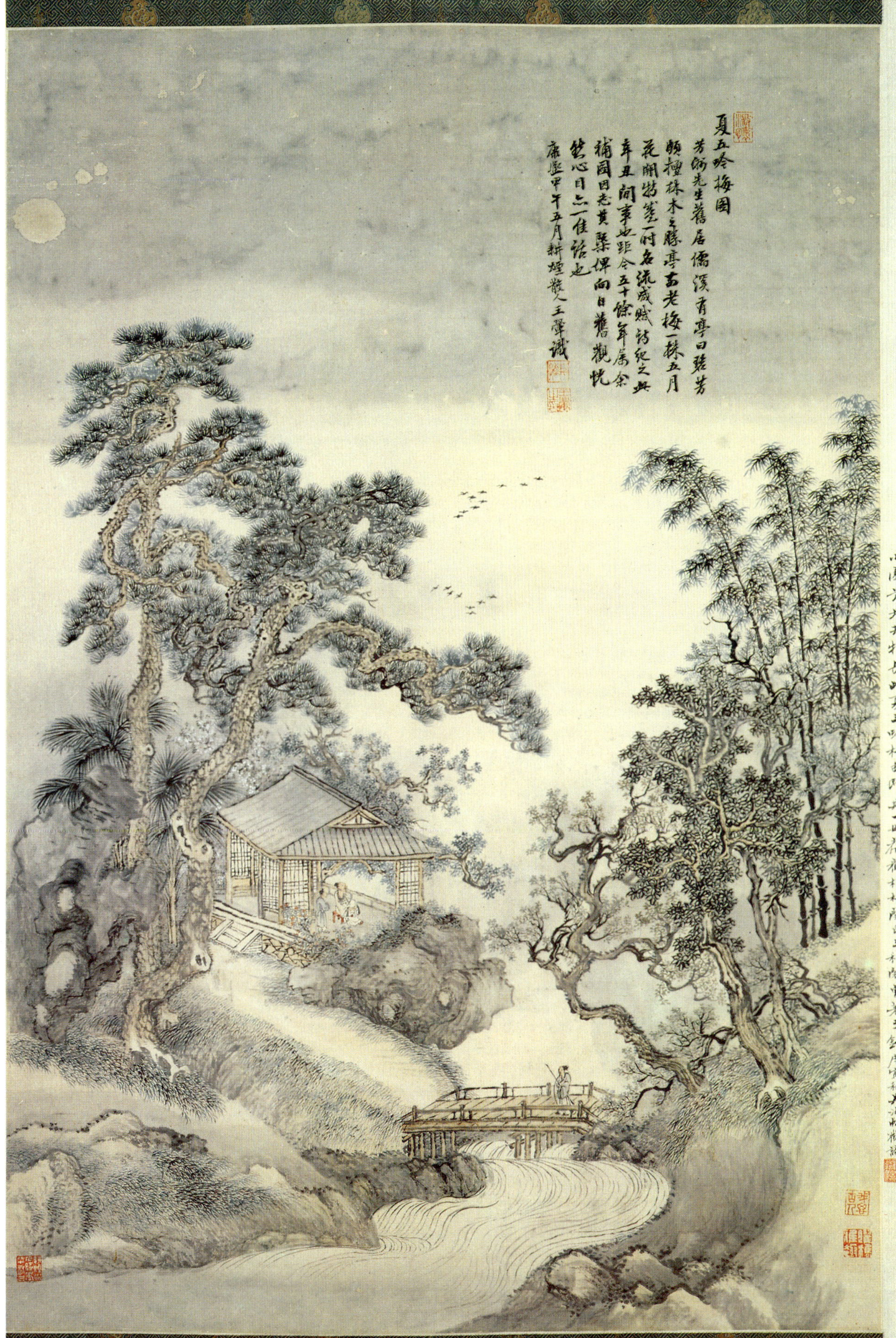

夏五吟梅圖
芳洲先生舊居儒溪有亭曰瑤芳
頗種株木之勝亭古老梅一株五月
花開物莖一冊名流咸賦詩紀之與
辛丑間事也距今五十餘年屬余
補園因志黃蘂俾向日舊觀恍
然心目之一佳話也
康熙甲午五月耕煙散人王翬識
石谷手晚年之作愈老愈
辣用筆拙樸具有所謂佃老遊絲
勁如屈鐵是也以大章法佛寫
小園景光共特長此夏五吟梅圖即其一此為
栽桂梧閣氏之秋閣嘗著于錄庚寅秋吳湖帆觀識
芳洲先生名天錦常熟人清初名補生工詩文與王石谷為友吾人松
蕭陽先生云翁文蓉當錄之外高祖也大寒卻俟花記

"Landscape"
by Wang Yuanqi (1642-1715)

Hanging scroll; ink and colour on paper. 94.2 x 45.3 cm
Hubei Provincial Museum

A cheerful landscape is painted in the vivid colours of red and green. Colour is used not so much for decorative effects as for enhancing the tonal richness of black ink. According to Wang Yuanqi, "applying colour is the same as using brush and ink. The intention of using colour is to supplement what is lacking in brush and ink as well as to bring out their marvels". In depicting rocks, pink and green washes are used structurally like ink washes. Three-dimensional forms are created by the overlaying of colour washes and dry brushstrokes in ink, which are also used in the shading and outlining of the rocks. Through such means, moreover, surface texture and a shimmering effect of light and shadow are created. The colours used are also infused with a sense of life and inherent beauty. Tree foliage is executed with spontaneous red and green brushstrokes, dabs, and patches. The fresh and brilliant colours are dynamic and animated, full of vital force (**qi**), whilst the trees themselves, as well as the defining brushstrokes, appear clumsy and almost lifeless (although imbued with hidden strength); it seems as if they were understated, so as not to compete with the dynamic use of colour. In the pure enjoyment of the colours (for example, the lush jade-green of the moss-covered rocks) and their subtle relationships (for example, soft green wash over pink), one tends to forget the landscape and the brushwork.

In his inscription Wang Yuanqi gives us the source of his stylistic reference. He tells us that he was inspired by the ideas in Dong Qichang's (1555-1636) (cat. no. 26) copy of Ni Zan's (1301-1374) "Pavilion by a River Stream in Autumn Colour" which was painted in colour, unusual for a painting by Ni. Dong also modelled on the styles of Jing Hao (900-960) and Guan Tong (10th century). Wang tells us that he found Dong's painting, which he had admired in secret, to be "subtle and seductive, lofty and elegant, transcending the mundane 'dusty' realm". He then says in the usual self-effacing manner that "with his childish hand in the learning stage, he could never dream of achieving those qualities".

In this painting, one finds stylistic references to the empty pavilion and the composition of Ni Zan's river landscape. From the style of Dong Qichang comes the principle of constructing larger forms out of smaller ones, which Dong had discovered in the paintings of Huang Gongwang (1269-1354), and the juxtaposition of spatial relationship. One could also see a stylistic allusion to the trees of Wang Shimin (cat. no. 41). Out of several layers of stylistic allusions, Wang Yuanqi succeeded in absorbing and transforming them into a style of his own; his originality lies in the creative use of colour.

In its art-historical approach, this painting reminds us of a research paper in art history in the way Wang enlightens us on the styles of painting and the origins of his ideas with proper acknowledgement and footnotes. Wang demonstrates his knowledge of art history, his connoisseurship in painting, his lineage and originality in art.

Wang Yuanqi (1642-1715), the youngest of the Orthodox masters, was the grandson and pupil of Wang Shimin (1592-1680). He pursued a successful official career, attaining, in 1712, the prominent position of Vice-President of the Board of Revenue. His paintings were highly appreciated by the Kangxi Emperor (1662-1723); he was put in charge of the imperial collection of calligraphy and painting, and the compilation of an encyclopedia on these disciplines. Being interested in the abstract theories of painting, which are elucidated in his writings and demonstrated in his paintings, Wang Yuanqi single-mindedly carried out Dong's theory of transforming the styles of the ancient masters into a style of one's own.

The inscription is signed and followed by several of Wang's seals. The painting also bears seals by the collector, Wu Hufan (1894-1970).

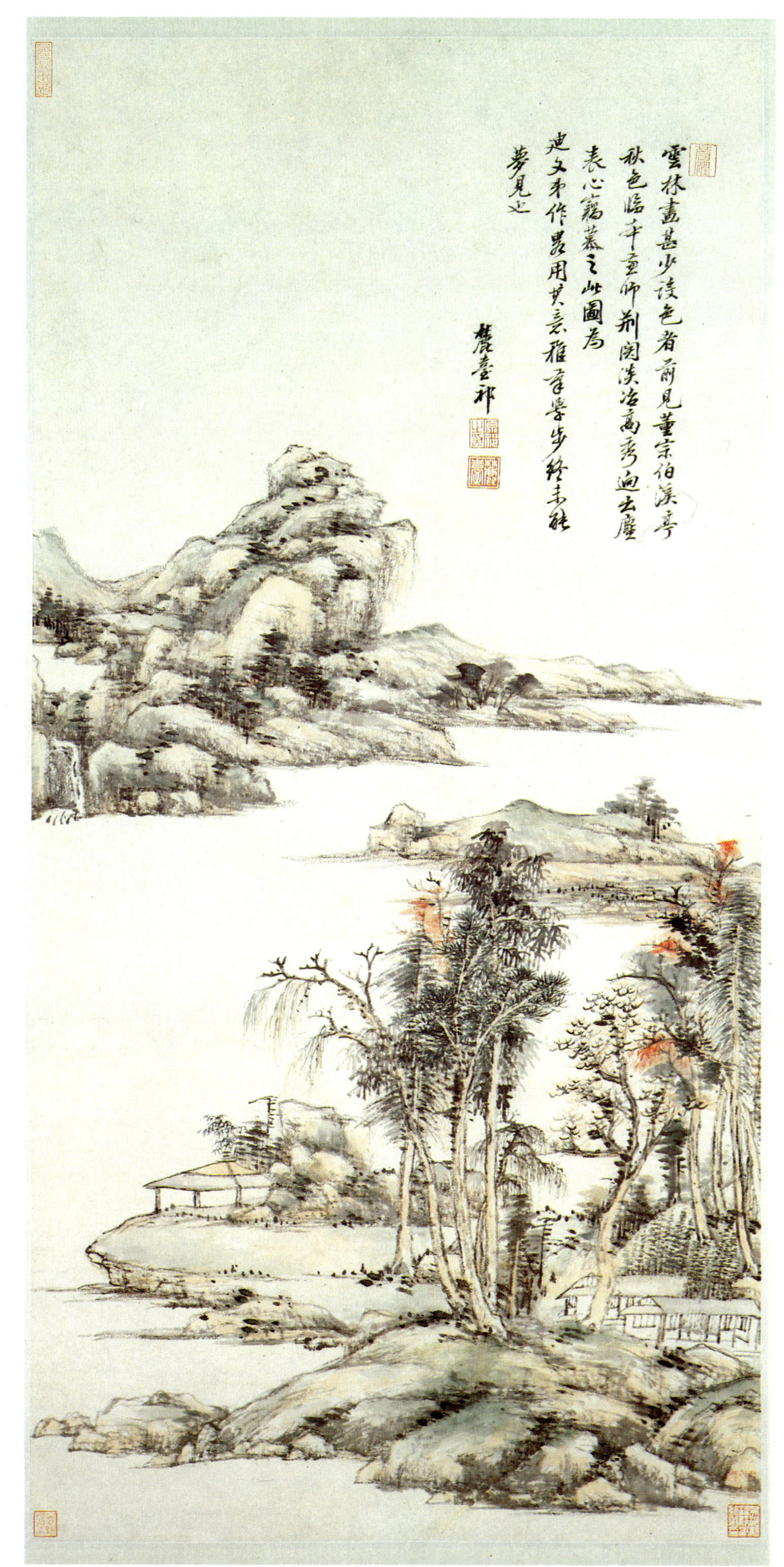

雲林畫甚少設色者前見董宗伯溪亭
秋色臨本董師荊關淡治高秀迥出塵
表心竊慕之此圖為
迪文年作畧用其意雅麗學步終未能
夢見之
麓臺祁

"Landscape in the Style of Huang Gongwang"
dated 1669 by Wang Jian (1598-1677)
Hanging scroll; ink and colour on silk. 126 x 61.1cm
Gugong Museum, Peking

The viewer is led from a group of pine trees in the foreground to a massive mountain spur rising at the centre of the landscape. It is repeated by a similar range in the background. Between the central mountain and the overhanging cliffs at the left is a ravine with a tumbling stream. Houses and trees are found in pockets formed by mountains and rocky outcrops.

In his inscription, Wang Jian tells us that he is following the brush manner of the Yuan dynasty master Huang Gongwang (1269-1354). Although landscape elements such as mountain spur and range, plateau, boulders and the use of the hemp-fibre texture strokes remind us of the landscape of Huang, it is in reality more influenced by the style of Dong Qichang (cat. no. 26). Stylistic features from the paintings of Dong are, however, reduced to a kind of mannerism that is devoid of the expressive power and dynamic impact of the original form. In the foreground, trees which resemble closely Dong's eccentric trees are portrayed without the contorted restlessness of the latter. As in Dong's landscapes, rocks are bare and stark. But Dong's structural and semi-abstract rocks are turned into massive solid forms with a surface patterning of light and dark. Moreover, diagonal movements of rocks, a device adopted from Dong's paintings, are not interrelated into a compositional network of dynamic movements, but remain static and isolated. On the whole, the landscape appears compartmentalised and disjointed; mountains, trees, and houses seem to be out of relative proportion.

To the Orthodox masters, this painting would have been appreciated for the special qualities of brush and ink, the antique flavour, the stylistic allusions to the works of Huang Gongwang and Dong Qichang. And probably most of all, it was appreciated for its blandness and monotony (**pingdan**), that is derived from the repetition of form, brush manner, and ink value. Without the subtle excitement of surprise and variation, that is present in works of other scholar-amateur painters such as Huang Gongwang and Dong Qichang, Wang Jian's painting is in danger of falling into dull monotony.

Wang Jian, one of the Orthodox masters of the Qing dynasty, belonged to a prominent scholar-gentry family of Taicang, Jiangsu province. His great grandfather was the well-known scholar Wang Shizhen (1526-1690) of the Ming dynasty. Wang Jian obtained his **jinshi** degree (the highest degree in the civil examinations) and served as a prefect in Guangdong province before the fall of the Ming dynasty. He later led a life of retirement and immersed himself in the world of art. He was a close friend of Wang Shimin (cat. no. 41), with whom he shared similar attitudes and interests in the art of painting. As direct followers of Dong Qichang, they were upholders of the Orthodox lineage of scholar-amateur painting that was formulated by Dong.

The painting has an inscription by the artist which dates the painting to 1669 and also bears his seal. It also has a colophon dated 1671, by the famous poet scholar Wu Weiye (1609-1671), praising Wang Jian's brush manner and the marvellous scenery that is captured in the painting. Wu Weiye wrote the descriptive poem called "The Nine Friends of Painting", referring to Dong Qichang, Li Liufang, Cheng Jiasui, Zhang Xuezeng, Bian Wenyu, Shao Mi (cat. no. 35), Wang Shimin and Wang Jian.

"Fishing Boat and Secluded Hills"
dated 1670 by Wu Li (1632-1718)

Hanging scroll; ink and light colours on silk. 119 x 61.3cm
Gugong Museum, Peking

It is generally asserted that Wu Li followed the landscape styles of the great masters of the Yuan dynasty and, in particular, Huang Gongwang (1269-1354). This painting, however, seems to look yet further into history, to the grandeur of the awe-inspiring landscapes of the Northern Song dynasty. The composition is dominated by the massive cliff-face on the right which overhangs, even threatens, the bridge and the boat on the placid river in the valley below. In the far distance lighter ink washes define seemingly endless ranges of mountains. The strength of the composition in directing our view up the scroll towards those distant peaks is such that the larger scale and more precisely drawn rocks and pine trees in the foreground seem almost incidental. The enormity of the vista, emphasised by the sweeping promontories into the river valley, is strongly reminiscent of the monumental landscapes of the great Song dynasty masters Dong Yuan and Guo Xi.

Wu Li was born in the same year as Wang Hui (cat. no. 43) and in the same place, Changsu in Jiangsu province. With a traditional literary family background Wu achieved the acceptable, and required, standards in poetry, calligraphy and music, as well as studying painting under Wang Shimin (cat. no. 41) and Wang Jian (cat. no. 44). In his early years as a painter Wu's career developed alongside that of Wang Hui. However, in middle-age, Wu Li's life took a dramatic turn occasioned by his conversion to Christianity, a most unusual occurrence for one so well trained in, and identified with, the cultural traditions of China. The latter years of his life were devoted to missionary work in and around Nanking and Shanghai but he did continue to paint. Interestingly his painting retained a totally Chinese identity and never succumbed to the Western influences which, in his life as a missionary, he must have been subject to. One of Wu Li's biographies records the epitaph reputedly inscribed on the stone at his tomb outside the south gate of Shanghai; it reads as follows: "His name was Li and his saint's name, after he had been baptised, Simon, from Changshu. He entered the Jesuit order in the 21st year of Kangxi (1682), and in the 27th year of Kangxi (1688) he became a priest and was sent to Shanghai and Jiading as a missionary. In the 57th year of Kangxi (1718) he fell ill and died on the day of the Holy Virgin. He was then 87 years old".

Signed and seals of the artist.

"Two Clear Streams"
dated 1686 by Yun Shouping (1633-1690)
Hanging scroll; ink and colours on silk. 88.2 x 54.4cm
Gugong Museum, Peking.

Straggling branches of flowering prunus reach across the scroll above a clump of narcissus. Neither the prunus nor the narcissus seem to be part of the real world, the branch of the prunus springs from a source unseen and the narcissus floats as if in thin air. The careful construction of the one-sided composition is perfectly balanced by the two colophons, the upper by Yun himself and the lower by his contemporary and close colleague Wang Hui (see cat. no. 42).

The clarity of the composition, emphasised in the sensitive but determined brushstrokes of the prunus, the fine linear qualities of the narcissus and the total absence of the expected contextual features echoes the purity of the subject: the flowering prunus symbolising the end of winter and the narcissus the new year. The first line of Yun's colophon too echoes the theme:
"Snow clearing in the face of spring
now see in the south the dawn frost melt".

And yet the faintest suggestion of a darker wash around the flowering tree and plant hints at depth, space and a mysterious reality.

Yun Shouping was born into an impoverished Jiangsu province gentry family in the declining years of the Ming dynasty. Clearly influenced by his father, a fervent supporter of the Ming, Yun declined to enter the world of officialdom and serve the Manchu rulers of the Qing dynasty. He studied painting, poetry and calligraphy and eked out a meagre living supported from time to time by his great friend, Wang Hui. Originally a landscapist it is said that Yun realised that he could not equal the paintings of Wang Hui and thus turned his attentions elsewhere. The **Guo Chao Hua Cheng Lu** records in what is probably the most comprehensive biography of Yun that: "he made it his aim to revive the old styles, but when he met Wang Shigu (Wang Hui) from Yushan he thought that his talent was not equal to that of Shigu and he said to the friend: 'I will leave you alone on your path, because it makes me humiliated to be only the second in the world'. Thenceforth he gave up landscape painting and devoted himself to the study of flowers". Certainly Yun is one of the most renowned flower painters of China. His compositions are characterised by the sensitive but confident line, evidence of his calligraphic ability, and delicate colour washes in which it seems, as Siren notes, the brush scarcely touches the paper.

Colophon by Wang Hui, inscription and seals of the artist.

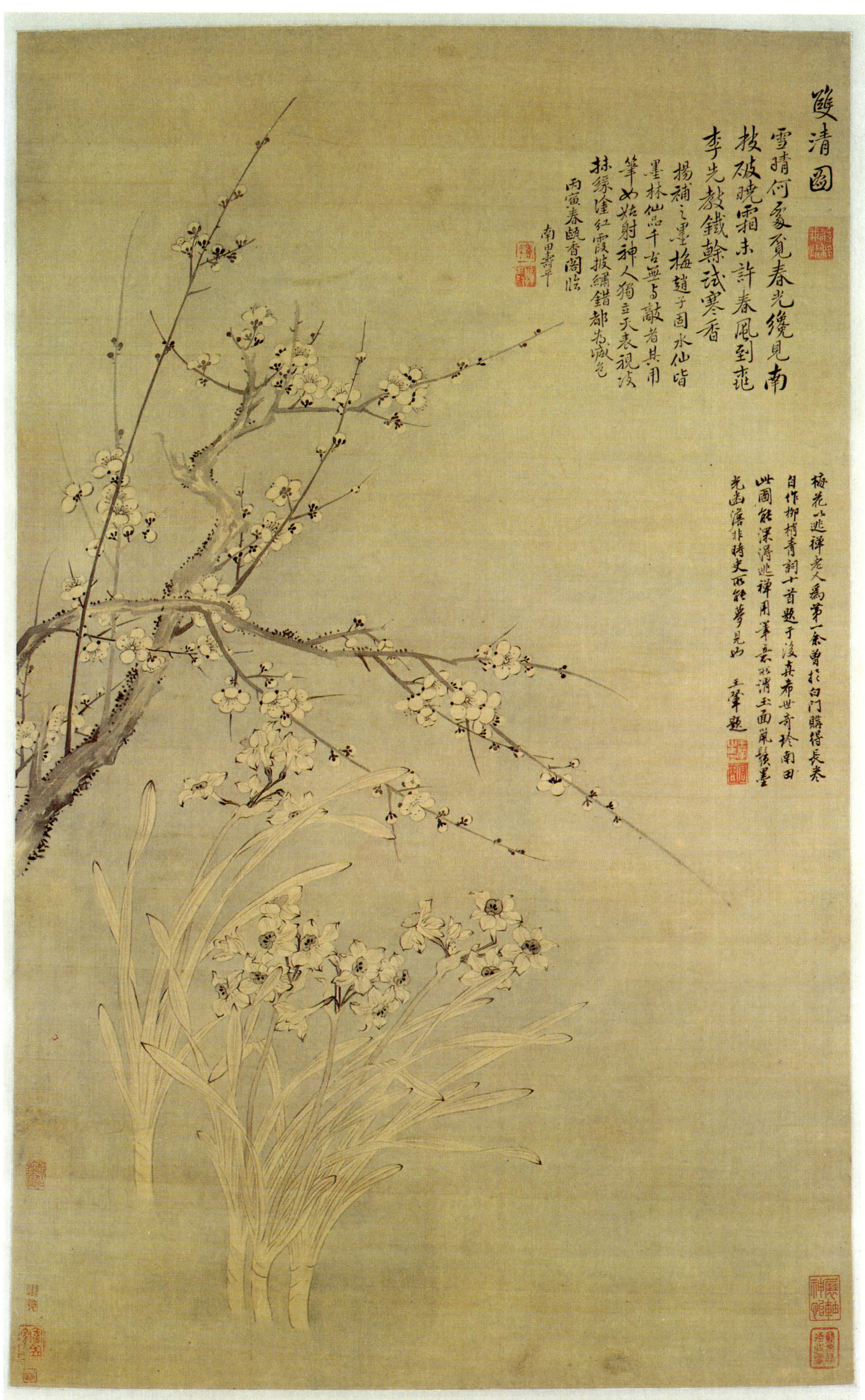

雙清圖

雪晴何處覓春光纔見南
枝破曉霜未許春風到處
李先教鐵幹試寒香
揚補之墨梅趙子固水仙皆
墨林仙品千古無与敵者其用
筆如妙射神人獨出天表視後
抹綠塗紅霞披繡錯都失嬌色
丙寅春颙香閣臨
南田壽平

梅花以逃禪老人為第一余曾於白門購得長春
自作柳梢青詞十首題于後真希世奇珍南田
此圖能深得逃禪用筆姿態形清玉面嚴頭墨
光曲浩非特史西能夢見山
王翬題

"Landscape in the style of Ni Zan"
dated 1661 by Hong Ren (1610-63)

Hanging scroll; ink on paper. 132.4 x 62.9cm
Gugong Museum, Peking.

In following the manner of the Yuan dynasty master, Ni Zan (1301-74), Hong Ren is making specific stylistic allusions to Ni's river landscape. He is making reference to Ni's cool, transparent, linear style of painting, his empty pavilion, trees, and distant hills. These stylistic references, which tend to be exaggerated and formalized, are transformed into Hong Ren's own pictorial images and artistic idioms. The thatched pavilion, which is identified with Ni's landscape, has become a wooden structure on a stone platform in Hong Ren's landscape. The group of tall trees in the foreground are more elongated in height and are executed with spontaneous brushstrokes, emphasising the "untrammelled" quality of Ni's brushwork. Ni Zan's use of bent, angular strokes to construct the multifaceted masses of three-dimensional rocks are now formalised into an interpenetrating network of angular, undulating lines. The subtle abstract manipulation of pure form in a Ni Zan landscape is more clearly articulated in this painting; it also extends to the formal relationship of tonal values. Probably based on the mountain scenery of Huangshan, Hong Ren introduces new landscape elements such as waterfalls, angular rocks and cliffs, which are constructed with a rectilinear formation of overlapping planes. On the whole, nature and the style of the past are organised by Hong Ren into a logical, abstract order that is underlying the river landscape.

Hong Ren inscribed the painting saying that in 1661, he was asked by Xiong You to do the painting for the recluse Dan Xian.

Hong Ren, an individualist painter, was from Xinan, Anhui province. After the fall of the Ming dynasty (1368-1644), he became a Buddhist monk and took the name of Hong Ren. Regarded as the greatest of the Anhui masters, Hong Ren was called one of the "Four Masters of Xinan".

The inscription is signed by Hong and followed by his seal.

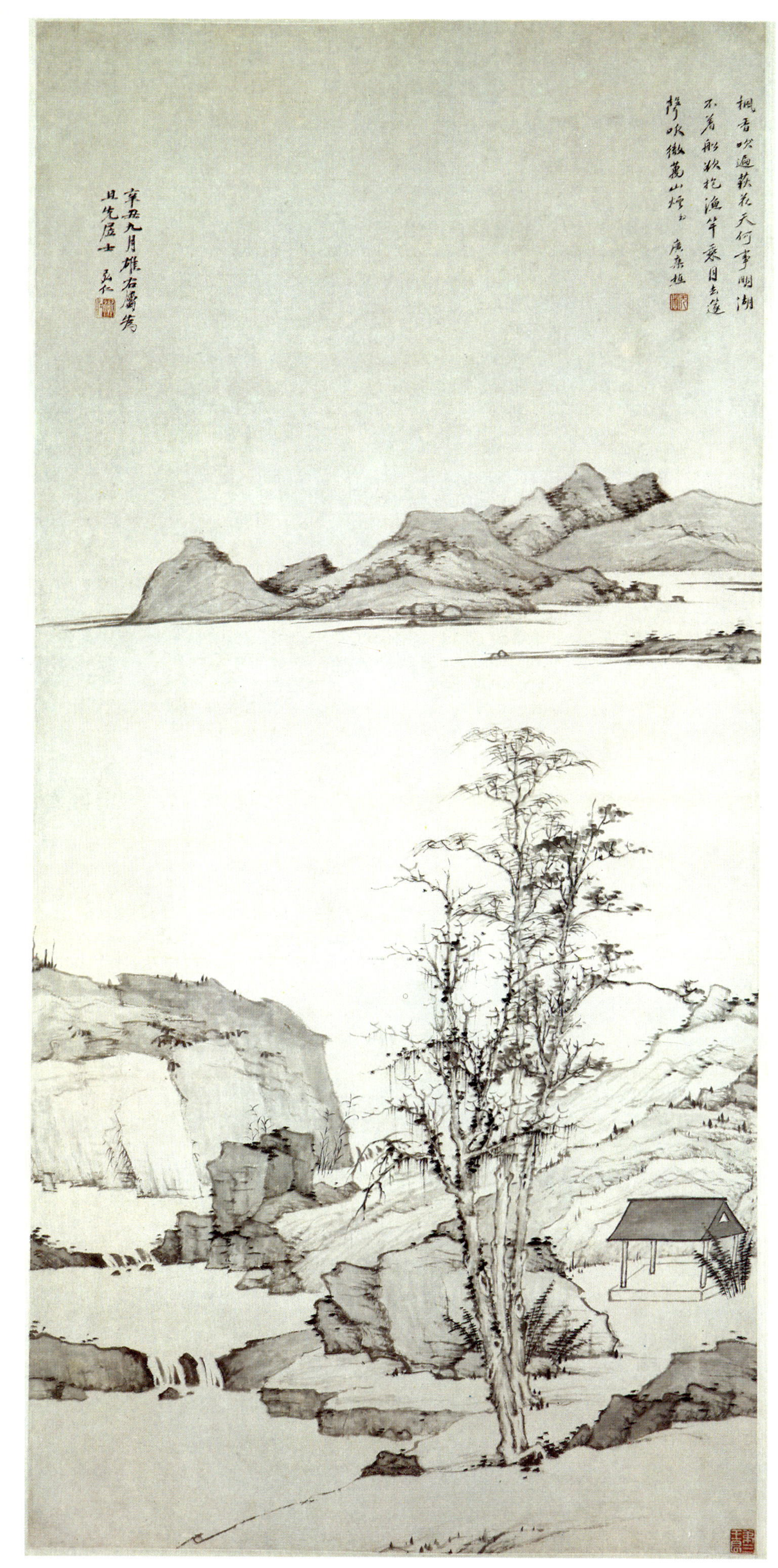

楓香吹遍荻花天何事明湖
不著船款把漁竿乘月去遠
橫吹徹萬山煙 廣東桓
辛丑九月雄右屬為
旦先居士
弘仁

"Waterfall and Bamboo in Deep Valley"
dated 1674 by Zha Shibiao (1615-1698)

Hanging scroll; ink on paper. 149 x 46.5cm
Nanking Museum

In a quiet, secluded river landscape, an empty hut, probably the abode of a scholar-recluse, is perched on a slope, overlooking a bamboo grove. Flanked by tall mountains, a stream flows from a narrow gorge into a widening stream. The languid, tall trees in the foreground add a lonely, melancholy air. This placid landscape is depicted with a very sensitive, delicate brush. Ink is sparsely used, creating subtle tonal values. With the paper surface shining through, the painting looks transparent. Rocks and mountains are softly drawn with a feathery, dry-brush line that is fluent and moves with ease in an undulating rhythm, suggesting three-dimensional earthy forms. The foreground trees, delineated in delicate, elegant lines, are arranged with an air of calculated casualness. Equally elegant are the misty bamboos; carefully drawn in stroke by stroke and separated by the joints of the bamboo that are left blank, the bamboo stem appears to have been accomplished in one continuous movement. On the whole, the painting evokes a subtle, bland flavour, which has a soothing and calming effect, meeting the quiet and refined taste of a scholar connoisseur. Like clear water, it reflects a state of spiritual calm, cleansed of vulgar emotions and free of all worldly concerns.

To accompany the painting, Zha has inscribed a poem:
"The bamboo grove is so dark, no sunlight can filter through.
The water in the spring sounds like falling rain.
In due course, when spring breezes come, peach and
plum blossoms will grow in profusion in the deep valley".

Zha tells us in his inscription that this poem was written by a Song dynasty (960-1279) monk by the name of Qing Shun; it became famous after being discovered on a wall by Su Dongbo, the great poet, scholar-official and amateur painter of the 11th century, during his trip to the Xihu (West Lake) region. A visitor recited the poem and presented it to Zha Shibiao. The poem was probably the inspiration for this painting. Zha also tells us that, in this landscape, he casually "writes" (**xie**) the "brush conception" (**biyi**) of the Yuan dynasty scholar-amateur painter Ni Zan (1301-1374); Zha is probably referring to the sparse, cool, linear style of Ni Zan that he has adopted. The landscape is also based on the bare mountain scenery of the Huangshan ("Yellow Mountain") region in Anhui province.

Zha Shibiao (1615-1698) came from a well-to-do family of Haiyang, Anhui province. After the fall of the Ming dynasty (1368-1644), he gave up further studies for examinations, and devoted himself to writing, painting, and studying his family's collection of paintings of the Song and Yuan dynasties. He was by nature somewhat of a recluse, carefree, leisurely, very fond of sleep, even-tempered; he never spoke an angry word about anyone, but did not care for visitors. These qualities are reflected in his paintings. As his fame grew, he became known as one of the "Four Masters of Xinan".

The inscription is signed by Zha and followed by his seals.

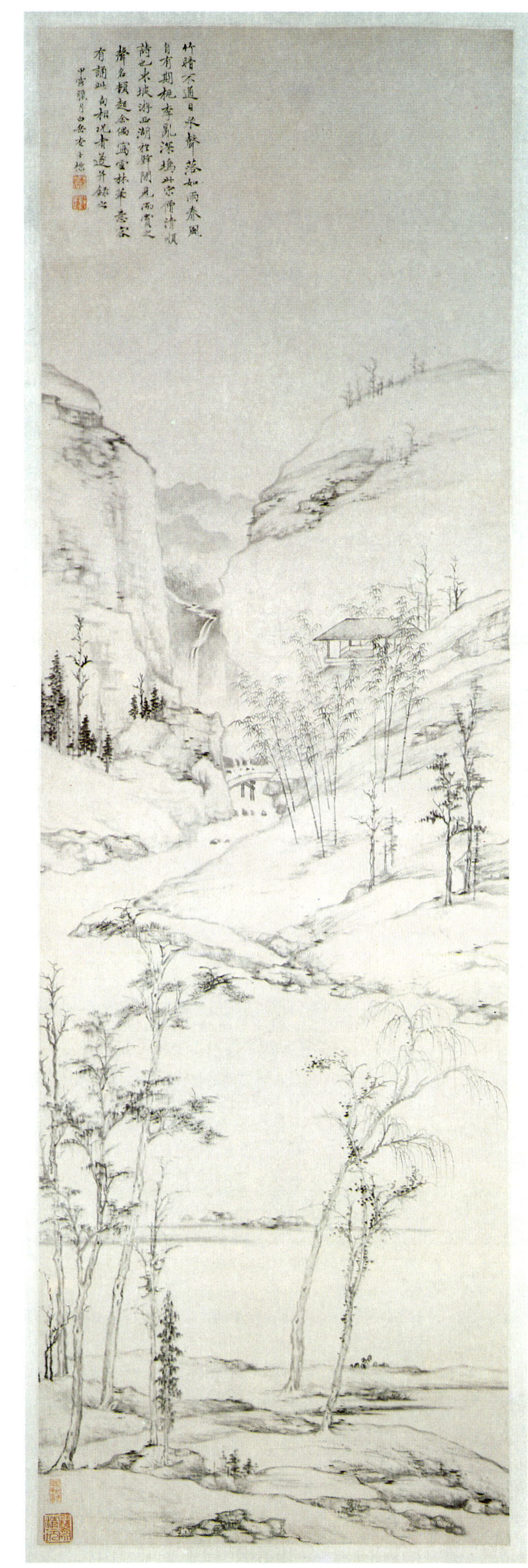
竹哇不過日求靜落如兩春風
自有期梅本氣深塢此家曾許頃
詩也東坡游西湖柱野開月而實之
静名頹起念偶寫雲林葉意宗
有誦此句相沈青逸并錄之
甲寅暮月白岳老士林

"The Heavenly Peak of Huangshan"
by Mei Qing (1623-1697)

Hanging scroll; ink on paper. 183.9 x 48.8cm
Gugong Museum, Peking.

A steep, arduous path leads from the bottom of the painting to a flat mountain top, where two tiny figures are conversing beside a temple-like building that is screened by a row of pine trees. Streams of clouds are descending from the right and flowing underneath this projecting cliff, emphasising its immense height. Partly veiled by clouds are three overhanging cliffs receding into the distance, and beyond them two floating mountain peaks. From the right corner another overhanging cliff soars to an extraordinary height, expanding and covering the sky like a perpendicular wall, all the way to the top of the painting.

The painting has a child-like simplicity and capriciousness. The composition is developed from a simple theme of projecting peaks into a complex and intricate abstract design. The striated formation of the cliffs is rendered by a repetition of parallel shaded folds which are varied and combined into new formal relationships. In its abstract construction this landscape evokes aesthetic feelings analogous to those of music. Prolonged contemplation of the painting tends to make us think in musical terms, reading its temporal arrangement of forms as rhythms, intervals, and movements, and viewing its compositional devices as repetition, variation, counterpoint, and crescendo.

The peaks appear child-like, bizarre, and fragile, and yet at the same time dynamic and monumental. The tiny human figures only accentuate their majestic grandeur. The fantastic cliff, which shoots up like a fungus expanding in all directions, is capricious in its extreme height and bold composition; dramatically cut off by the edge of the painting, it appears to rest with its entire weight on a point. It is, however, stabilised by the projecting cliff at the bottom of the painting. The white diagonal downward-moving strips that have been engraved by the weather throughout the ages, are stabilized by pine trees and boulders, and balanced by the cloud streams. Finally, the simple building anchors the entire landscape.

Mei Qing inscribed a poem which enlightens us on the theme of the painting. As the title indicates, it is in praise of the Tiendu (Heavenly) Peak of Huangshan, represented by the soaring peak in the painting, its immense height and grandeur accessible only to the immortals.

"For ten years, I have been dreaming of contacting Xuanyuan [Huangdi, Yellow Emperor].
Only after experiencing tier upon tier of cliffs did I come to know the highest peak.
In the sky, cloudy peaks are emitting and inhaling mists. Mountains south of the [Yangtze]
    river are all arranged like its children and grandchildren.
Rocky peaks soaring for a thousand **ren** [25,000 m.] are totally devoid of soil.
Where the roads disappear into thick clouds, only monkeys are found.
Who says the fire on the terrace where elixir was once made is now extinguished?
The cinnabar and spring water [ingredients of the elixir of life] are still warm".

This poem suggests that the extraordinarily tall peak in the painting, representing the Heavenly Peak of Huangshan (the tallest peak in the south of the Yangtze river region), was once inhabited by the legendary Yellow Emperor who was there refining pills of immortality. The Yellow Emperor is treated here as a Taoist immortal. Mei Qing, in his inscription, also tells us that he was following the brush manner of Jing Hao (900-960) and Guan Tong (10th century), by which he is probably referring to the method of depicting rock formation in parallel shaded folds.

Inscription and seals of the artist
Reproduced: **Peking Museum Catalogue**; no. 54

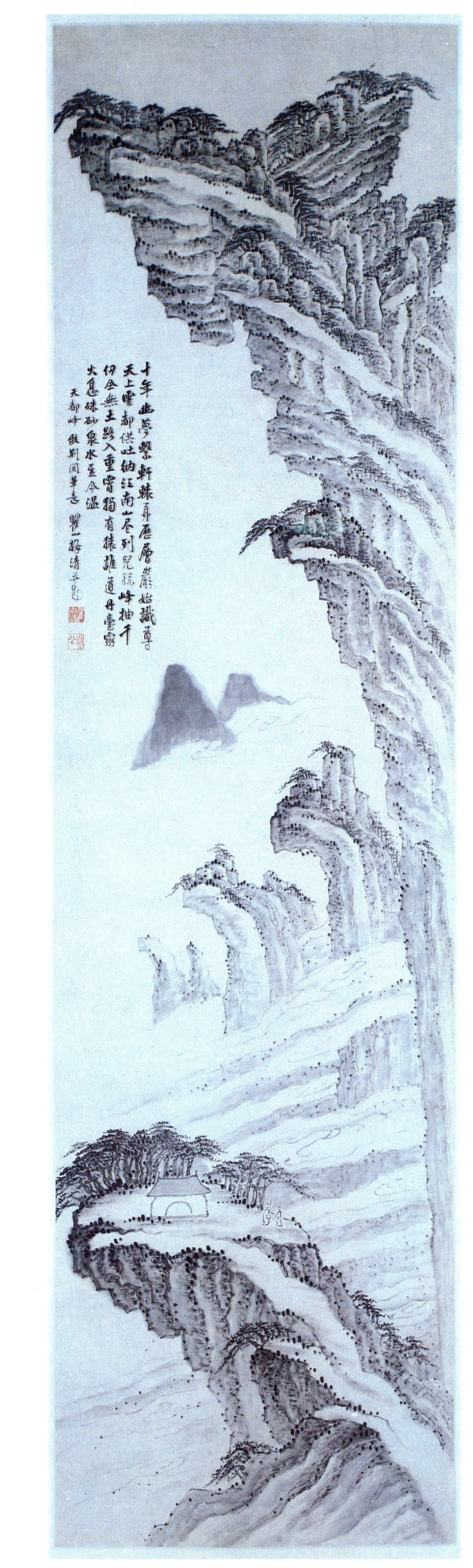

十年蠟屐夢攀躋軒轅身歷層巖始識尊
天上雲都供吐納江南一盡列兒孫峰抽干
仍念無主猿入重霄猶有樣誰道丹臺窮
火毫硃砂泉水至今溫
天都峰 傲荊門華志
塑梅清平山

"Two Album Leaves"
by Mei Qing (1623-1697)

Album leaves, ink and colour on paper, each leaf measures 33.8 x 44.1cm
Shanghai Museum

Leaf 1: "Making Pills of Immortality at a Terrace in Huangshan"

A powerful vision of dark, foreboding clouds is evoked by this small painting. A lonely house is perched on top of an overhanging cliff which, partly concealed by mist, appears to be floating in the clouds. The visual and tactile impact of the vaporous clouds are simply achieved by washes of rich, deep, black ink suffused in diluted ink. According to Mei Qing's poetic inscription, this ethereal scene belongs to the mysterious, transcendental realm of the immortals:

"The immortal Huangdi [Yellow Emperor] once lived here.
The abandoned terrace with its old remains is now desolate.
In which year will the elixir of immortality be collected and the fire in the refining-furnace be lit again?"

The painting bears seals of the artist.
Reproduced: **Shanghai Museum Catalogue of Paintings;** no. 72
     Arts of China Vol III: Paintings in Chinese Museums; pl. 106

Leaf 2: "Landscape"

A poetic scene of pointed peaks and rows of pines in the Huangshan region is depicted in pale ink and soft, light blue, with childlike fantasy.

Mei Qing (1625-1697) was a native of Xuancheng, Anhui province. He spent a great deal of his time roaming the Yellow Mountain (Huangshan) and depicting the famous sights of that region. As in these paintings, the lofty scenes of Huangshan are transformed by his poetic imagination into a fantastic notion. His close friend, Dao Ji (cat. no. 59), the greatest of the individualist painters, visited the Huangshan area several times.

The painting is signed by Mei Qing and bears several of his seals.

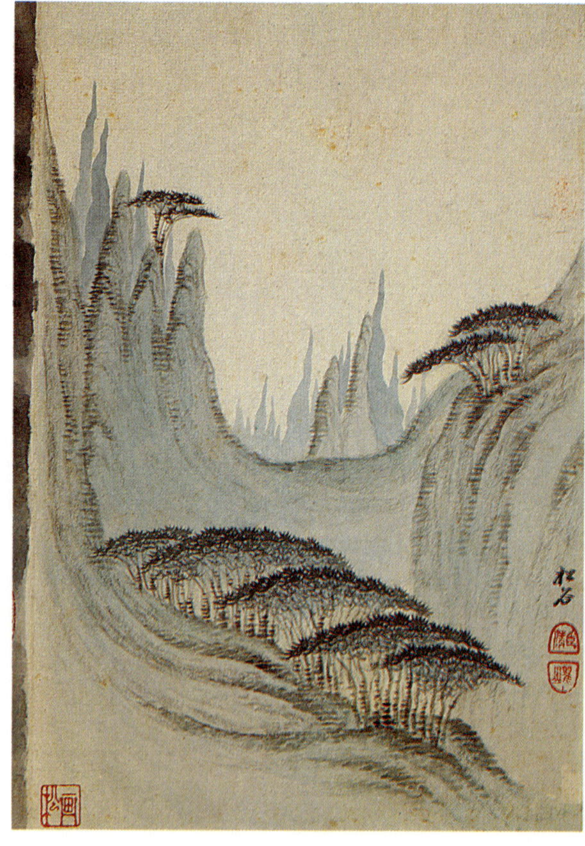

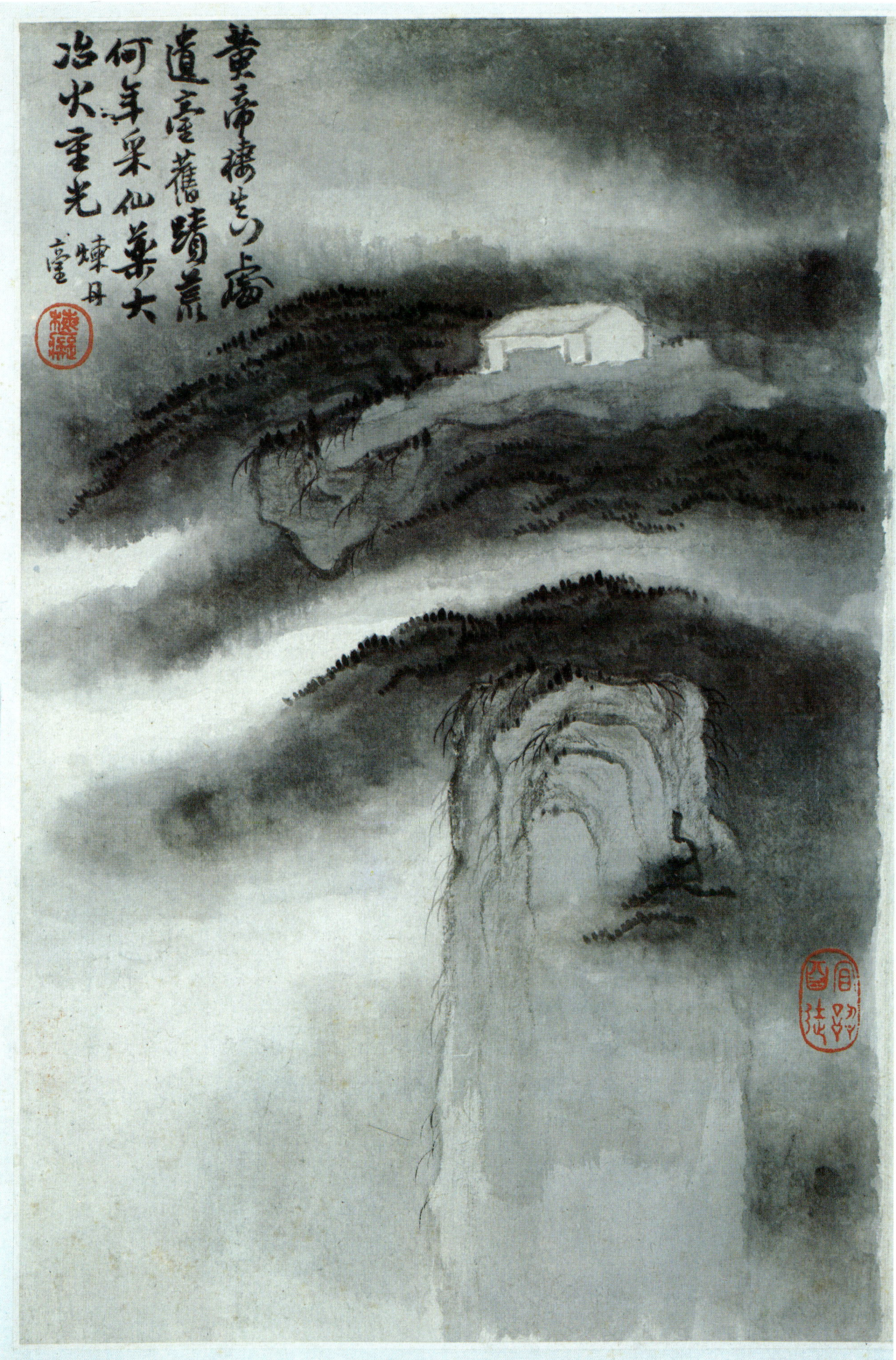

黃帝樓臺鳥上虛
遺臺舊靖荒
何年采仙藥大
治火重光
煉丹
臺

catalogue no. 51

"Thatched Hut in Green Mountain"
dated 1663 by Kun Can (1612-after 1671)

Hanging scroll; ink and colour on paper. 89.6 x 33.9cm
Shanghai Museum

A path from the left corner of the painting introduces us to an idyllic mountain retreat, hidden beside a river stream, surrounded by trees, and shrouded by a rushing current of vaporous mist. A scholar is sitting quietly studying inside one of the houses and another scholar is looking out of a window. A crane is strolling on the terrace. A winding path overlooking a waterfall and misty ravines leads us towards a gate entrance near the top of the mountain. In this densely crowded landscape, nature is portrayed in its natural state of profuse growth and visual richness. Craggy rocks are painted in a light pinkish-brown wash and then shaded by ink wash, together with a spontaneous and rich application of wet and crumbly dry brushstrokes in ink. Three-dimensional forms with substantial mass are created. Trees, mostly pines and bare old trees are also covered with a pink wash and then outlined with animated, vigorous brushstrokes. Reminding us very much of a monumental landscape of the Northern Song period (960-1127), Kun Can's landscape, enveloped in mist and bathed in light, evokes a feeling of air and space, allowing the viewer to wander in imagination within the landscape. Also like a Northern Song landscape, rocks, trees, waterfall, and mists are portrayed in dynamic movements, as though activated by the creative vital force (qi), which, according to Taoist philosophy, permeates and animates all phenomena of the universe.

With symbols of longevity, such as the crane and the pine trees, and the extraordinary stream of mist which suggests mystery and impenetrable depth, this landscape belongs to the unearthly realm of the immortals. This is substantiated by Kun's inscription:

"This extraordinarily talented person with a diverse interest in many things built a
thatched hut on a green mountain path.
The mountain scenery is still lingering within me, [Although] it has already entered my
painter's bag [in the form of sketches].
The heavenly terrace and the immortal's **ding** tripod are concealed in white clouds.
With an immortal's framework like yours, one can definitely reach immortality.
Monkeys are howling in the cold night, in a tune as clear as the sound of a stream.
Frequently, a white crane leans against the pine outside the window."

Kun Can was from Wuling, Hunan province. He became a Chan Buddhist monk at an early age, and spent most of his life as a recluse, living and roaming in the mountains. Often ill, he passed months and years without seeing anyone, and whole days passed without his speaking a single word. After some years of wandering, he settled near Nanking as abbot of a Chan Buddhist temple. Occasionally he painted for his own enjoyment. Through painting, mainly landscapes, he re-experienced his wild ramblings in the mountains.

The inscription is signed and dated by Kun Can to 1663, and followed by his seals.
Reproduced: **Shanghai Museum Catalogue of Paintings;** no. 70
Arts of China Vol III: Paintings in Chinese Museum; pl. 104

For colour detail see page 95.

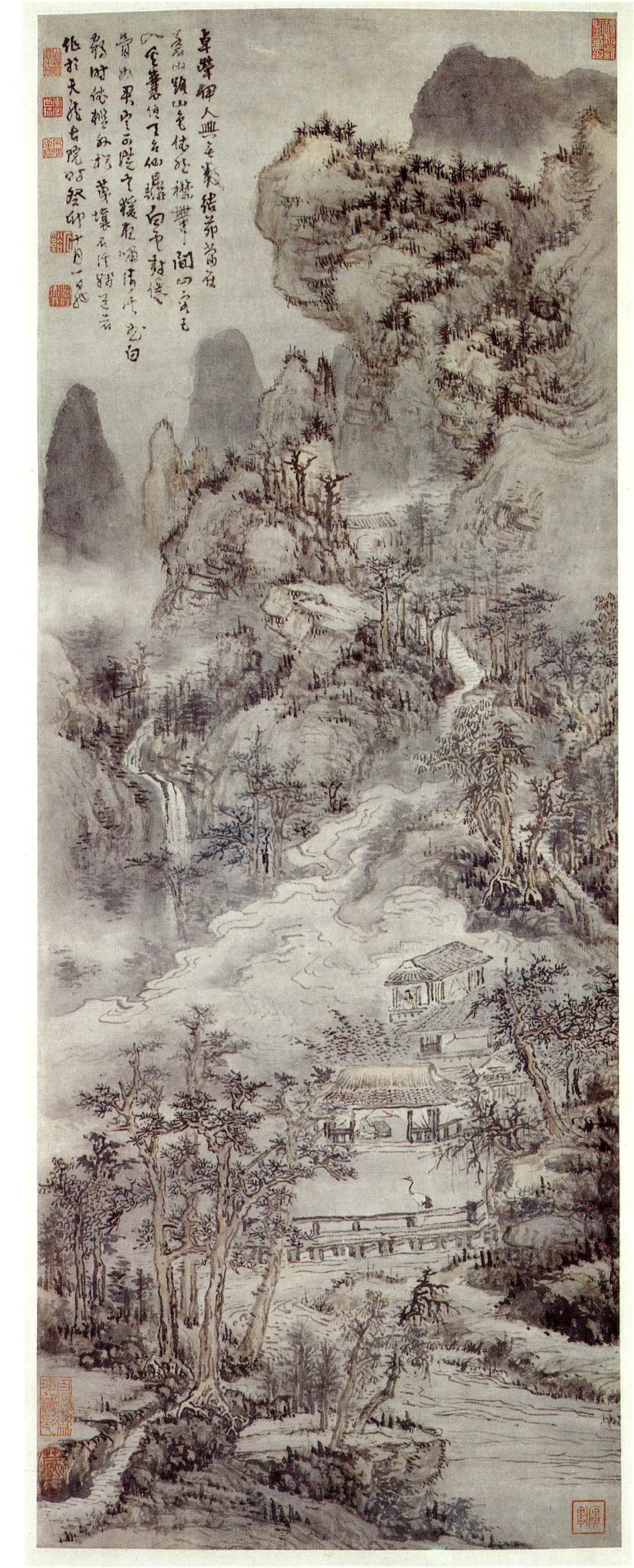

"Conversing with a Monk in a Pine Forest" dated 1647 by Zou Zhe (active c. 1647-79)

Hanging scroll; ink and colour on paper. 80 x 43.5cm
Shanghai Museum

Based on a conventional theme of a scholar's rustic retreat, this intimate landscape has stylistic features that are unusual to the Chinese tradition of painting. It has a low horizon and a sense of spatial depth, moving along the winding path from the foreground to the houses in the middle ground, which are sheltered by rising mountains. With the sky, river, and land-mass darkened by a grey wash of ink, together with a warm glow emitted by the pink wash, the landscape not only evokes an autumnal mood, but also resembles an evening scene. In contrast to its darkened surrounding, the houses with pink roofs are left in white, serving as the focal point of the painting. Two human figures, a scholar and a monk, are engaged in conversation, while the scholar's wife appears to be weaving in another room. The tall, dark pine trees, spreading out at the top like an umbrella and silhouetting against the mountain and the houses, are also unusual in having their stems depicted in one broad, continuous, undulating brushstroke in even, black ink.

This painting also reminds us of the style of Shen Zhou (1427-1509) of the Suzhou (Wu) school of painting in the mild, relaxed, and secure atmosphere that is created, and the formation of rocks which are washed with a soft pink colour and then outlined with broad, even brushstrokes. However, Zou's painting is more direct, forthright, and immediate in its approach and is imbued with greater spontaneity and vigour. Rocks, which are modelled with sweeping, restless brushstrokes, are more dynamic.

Born in Suzhou, Kiangsu province, Zou Zhe was the son of the painter Zou Dian. He later moved to Nanking where he worked most of his life and was regarded as one of the "Eight Masters of Nanking".

The painting is signed and dated by Zou Zhe to 1647 and bears his seal. It also bears a seal of the modern collector Wang Jiqian (b. 1907), saying "having been seen by Wang Jiqian". On the mounted surface of the scroll and beside the painting are colophons by the modern painter Liu Haisu (b. 1895).

Reproduced: **Shanghai Museum Catalogue of Paintings;** no. 69
Arts of China Vol III: Paintings in Chinese Museum; pl. 103

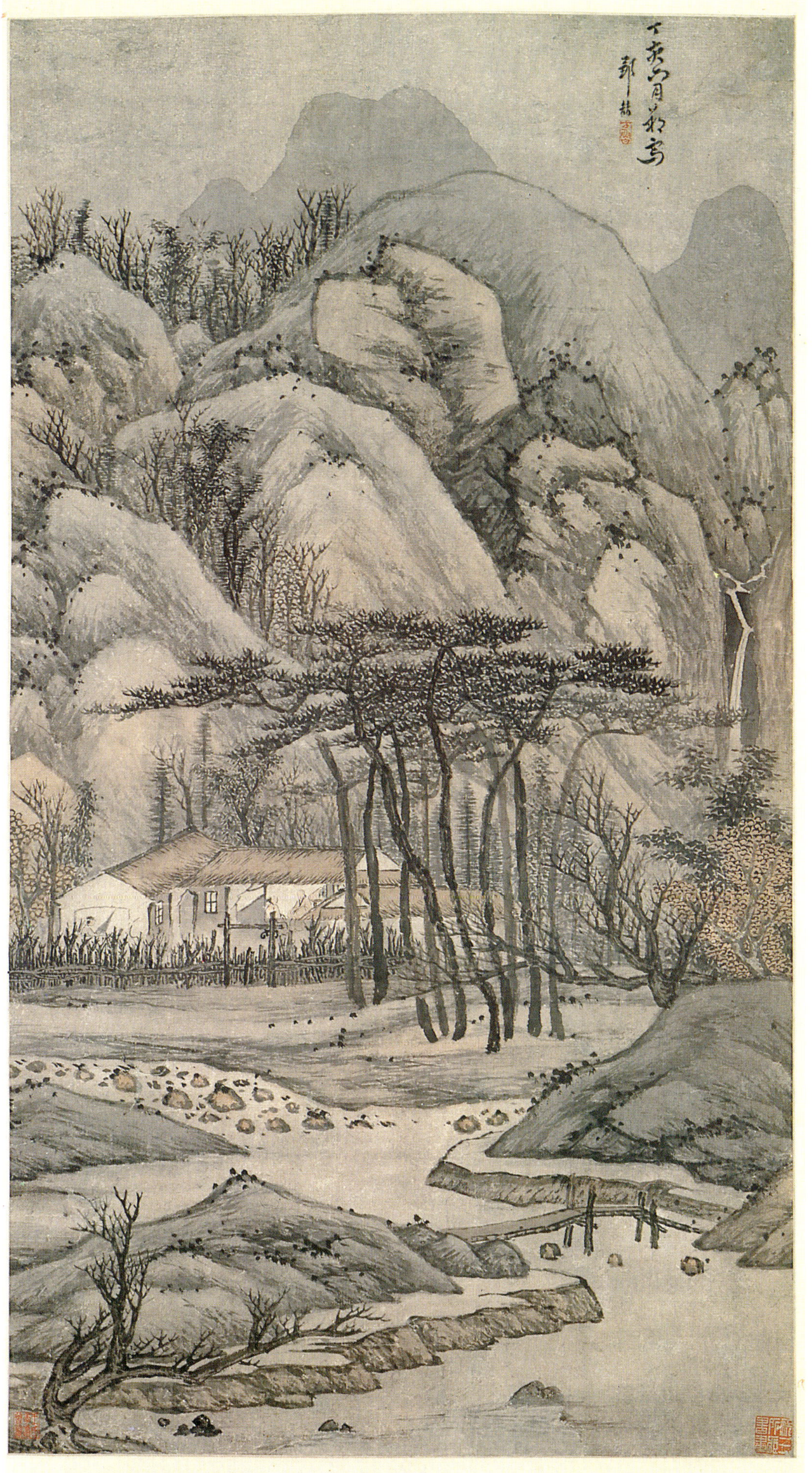

丁亥六月為柏寫
郭𡶳

"Sailboats Homeward Bound"
dated 1657 by Fan Qi (1616-92)

Handscroll; ink and colour on paper. 318 x 29cm
Liaoning Provincial Museum

The handscroll introduces us to a peaceful, leisurely river landscape that depicts the beautiful scenery of the Jiangnan (south of the Yangtze river) region; hills and cliffs are surrounded by water and enveloped in mist. Scattered throughout the landscape are scenic spots and lookouts, such as temples, pagoda, and an empty pavilion. A summer house perched on a rock is overlooking the sailboats in the distance. Houses on top of mountain cliffs obscured by mist, appear to be floating in mid-air. Human figures are engaged in leisurely activities. Two friends are conversing on top of a promontory, enjoying the river view. A scholar with a staff is crossing a bridge, and near the conclusion of the landscape another scholar is returning from his walk.

This painting shows stylistic influences from works by masters of the past, which are however transformed into a personal style that suggests new directions. Like paintings by Shen Zhou (1427-1509) of the Wu school, it is painted in the warm-and-cool colour washes of buff-pink and blue, and is also cool and mild, imbued with a general feeling of well-being and contentment. The misty trees depicted in ink dots over a light green wash remind us of trees in Wen Zhengming's (1470-1559) landscapes (cat. no. 14, 15); the careful and meticulous execution of the painting also recalls the fastidious approach of Wen Zhengming. Over light washes of ink and colour, rocks are modelled by a graded accumulation of small flicks of diluted ink that resemble somewhat the "rain-drop" texture strokes of the Northern Song landscapist Fan Guan (early 11th century). Out of all these emerges a painting with new possibilities. It has a clear, luminous quality. As though illuminated by an intense light, rocks are sharply delineated with hard edges, and appear to have been carved and chiselled into smooth round, cubic forms. The monotonous, angular repetition of hard-edged shapes (which shows the influence of Dong Qichang's abstract manipulation of forms) is, however, softened by subtle changes in the tonality of ink and (subdued) colour washes, ranging from buff-pink to silvery grey to light blue.

Fan Qi in his inscription tells us that he painted the landscape in 1657 with the intention of asking his friend, Zhou Lianggong (1612-1672), for instruction and correction. Zhou Lianggong was a scholar-official and a collector of paintings, who attracted around him a coterie of artists and intellectuals living in and around Nanking. Zhou was the author of a series of brief notes on artists of his acquaintance, the **Tuhua Lu.** There are a number of collective albums dedicated to him, with leaves contributed by various painters.

Little is known of Fan Qi's life except that he was born and lived in the Nanking area, and made his living as a professional painter. Acclaimed as one of the "Eight Masters of Nanking", he worked in a variety of styles, and was receptive to new ideas.

The painting is signed and dated to 1657 by Fan Qi and bears his seal.
Reproduced: **Liaoning Museum Catalogue of Paintings;** vol. II, pp. 91-2.

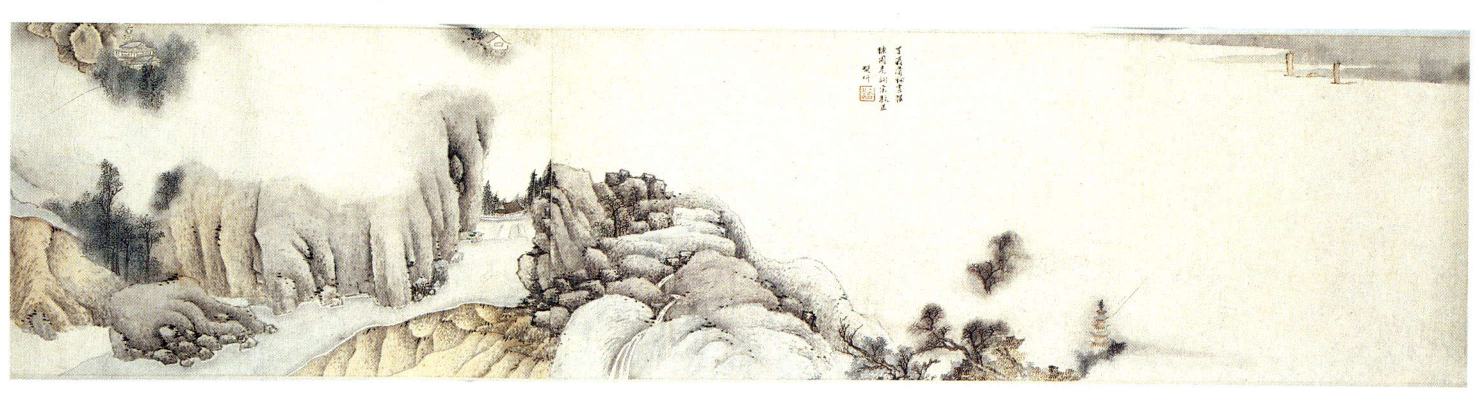
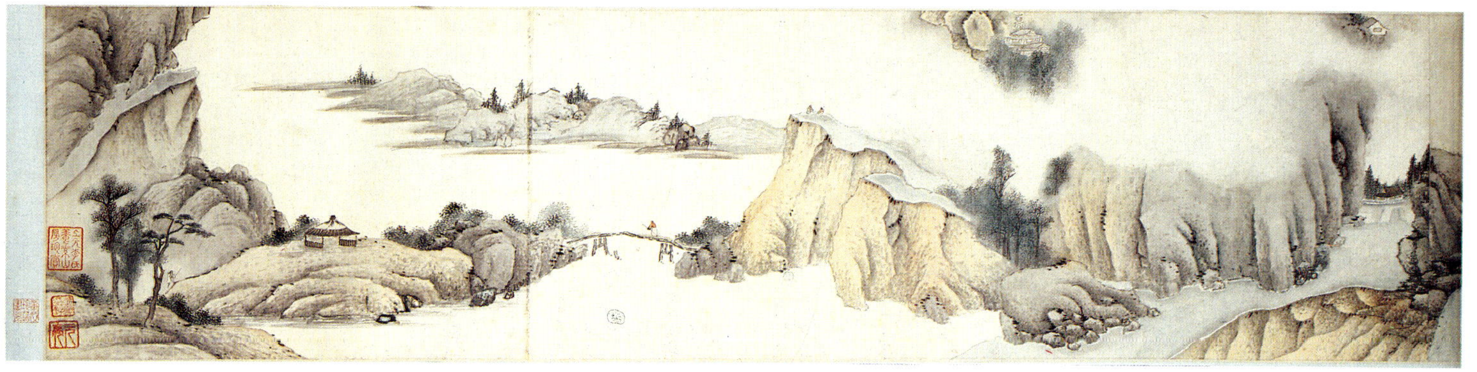

"One Thousand Peaks and Ten Thousand Valleys"
dated 1673 by Gong Xian (c. 1619-89)

Handscroll; ink on paper. 979.4 x 27cm
Nanking Museum

Depicted is a panoramic view of mountains and ravines, cliffs and caverns, rivers and waterfalls, which are enveloped in light and mist, and constructed in accordance to an underlying abstract order. Rocks are carefully shaded with soft, dry texture strokes resembling charcoal drawing, and accented by black dots (**dian**, representing moss), creating a strong contrast of light and shadow. Some misty passages of very sensitive tonal gradations are introduced. Stylised brush conventions such as dots, vertical and horizontal strokes, undulating zigzag lines, configurate into dynamic trees with delicate foliage. The landscape moves from a softer and gentler to a more sombre and melancholy mood. The earlier section of the landscape is shown with some signs of life, such as groups of trees and houses, misty hollows and mountain tops, waterfalls and streams. The mood begins to change as we encounter a lonely river scene, punctuated with a few isolated bare trees and empty fishing boats. A drier passage of rocky cliffs follows and concludes the scroll with a lonely house perched on top of a rock. Throughout the painting, no human beings are depicted, although there are houses and fishing boats.

The individualist painter Gong Xian was born in Kunshan, Jiangsu province, but lived in Nanking most of his life. He was highly educated and very talented in poetry, calligraphy, music and painting. Deeply disturbed by the fall of the Ming dynasty (1368-1644), he joined the other scholars loyal to the fallen dynasty, known as **yimin** ("left-over people"), in refusing to serve in the new Manchu government. Being a staunch loyalist, he was said to associate only with those who shared his loyalty to the past. Probably because of this, he was described by others as "eccentric" and "difficult to get along with". In the latter years of his life, Gong Xian retreated to a life of self-imposed isolation and semi-retirement, earning a humble living through the sale of his poems and paintings.

By adopting from the style of Dong Qichang (1555-1636) (cat. no. 26), the constructive mode of building forms, which are then enriched by heavy illusionistic shading, Gong Xian created a highly individualistic style which captured the atmospheric effects of nature and at the same time expressed his inner world. Acclaimed as the foremost master of the "Eight Masters of Nanking", Gong Xian actually said of himself, "There has been no one before me, and will be no one after me".

On his method of illusionistic shading, it is now generally agreed that Gong Xian was influenced by the chiaroscuro method of shading in Western prints. The Italian Jesuit Matteo Ricci (1552-1610) was in Nanking in 1595 and 1599; it is recorded that he brought with him many European engravings and paintings and that the Chinese were fascinated by them. Gong was probably also influenced by early paintings in the Chinese tradition, such as landscapes of the Northern Song period (960-1127) and the paintings of Mi Youren (before 1135), which he claimed to have studied for more than 40 years.

The painting is signed and dated by Gong Xian to 1673 and bears his seal.
Reproduced: **Nanking Museum Catalogue of Paintings:** Vol. II, p. 8-13.

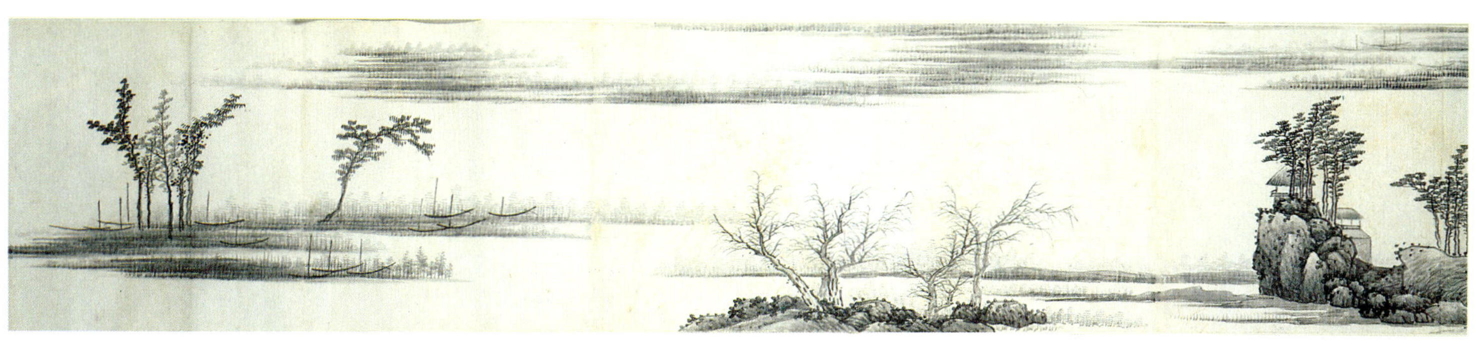

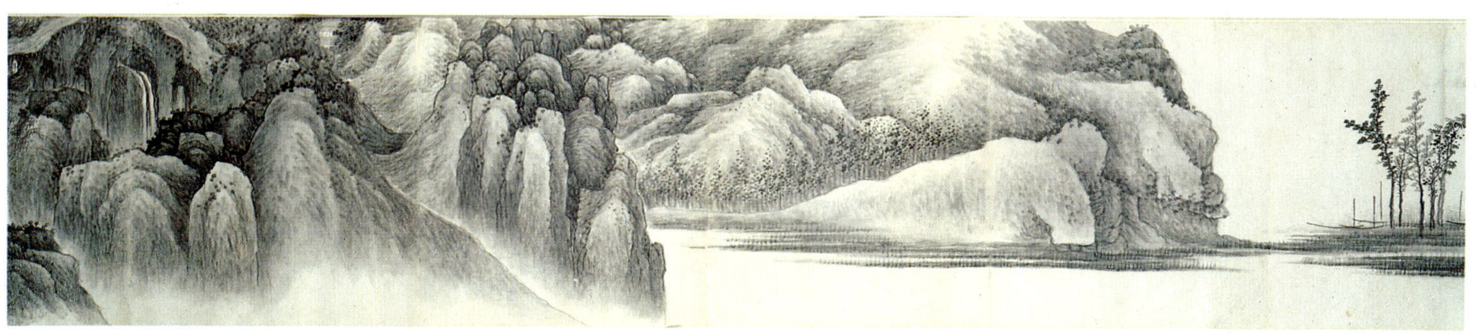

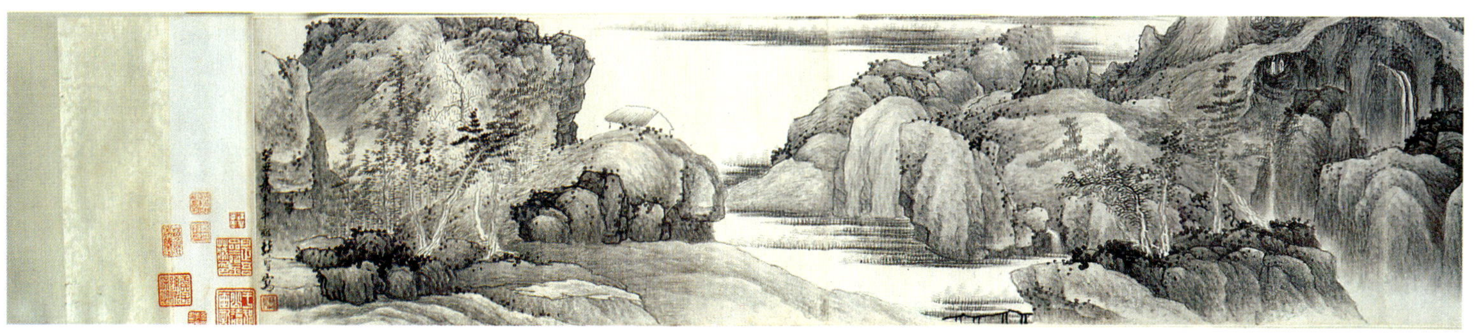

"Leaves in Red and Yellow"
dated 1685 by Gong Xian (c. 1619-89)

Hanging scroll; ink on paper. 99.7 x 33.9cm
Shanghai Museum

This bleak, desolate landscape has an overall feeling of greyness. The land appears eroded of soil and scorched of vegetation. Constructed like "building blocks", rocks are shaded with spiking texture strokes in a stippling manner that resembles charcoal drawing. The screen of tall spiky trees, which form an intricate abstract pattern, look dry and withered, as though in a state of decline. The brittle branches and a few dangling leaves evoke a melancholy and nostalgic mood. The empty areas of water in this marshland appear stagnant. What is depicted is an ominous, forbidding "inner vision", expressed by a powerful pictorial language.

To accompany the painting, Gong Xian inscribed a poem and dated the painting to 1685, four years before he died:

"Leaves in red and yellow, where does it all end?
Sitting high in a tower, one feels almost like an immortal.
The jade palace (heaven) seems so close, I begin to ask.
At the horizon the wind begins to rise, is that the sound of (heavenly) music?"

The painting also has a 1698 colophon by Gao Shiqi (1645-1704) which describes the landscape. Gao Shiqi was a scholar, collector and a personal secretary to the Kangxi Emperor (r. 1622-1722).

The painting bears seals of the artist and seals of the collector Pang Yuanji (ca. 1865-1949).
Reproduced: **Shanghai Museum Catalogue of Paintings**, no. 68
       Arts of China Vol III: Paintings in Chinese Museum; pl. 98
Recorded: **Xuzhai Minghua Lu** (see Lovell, no. 98).

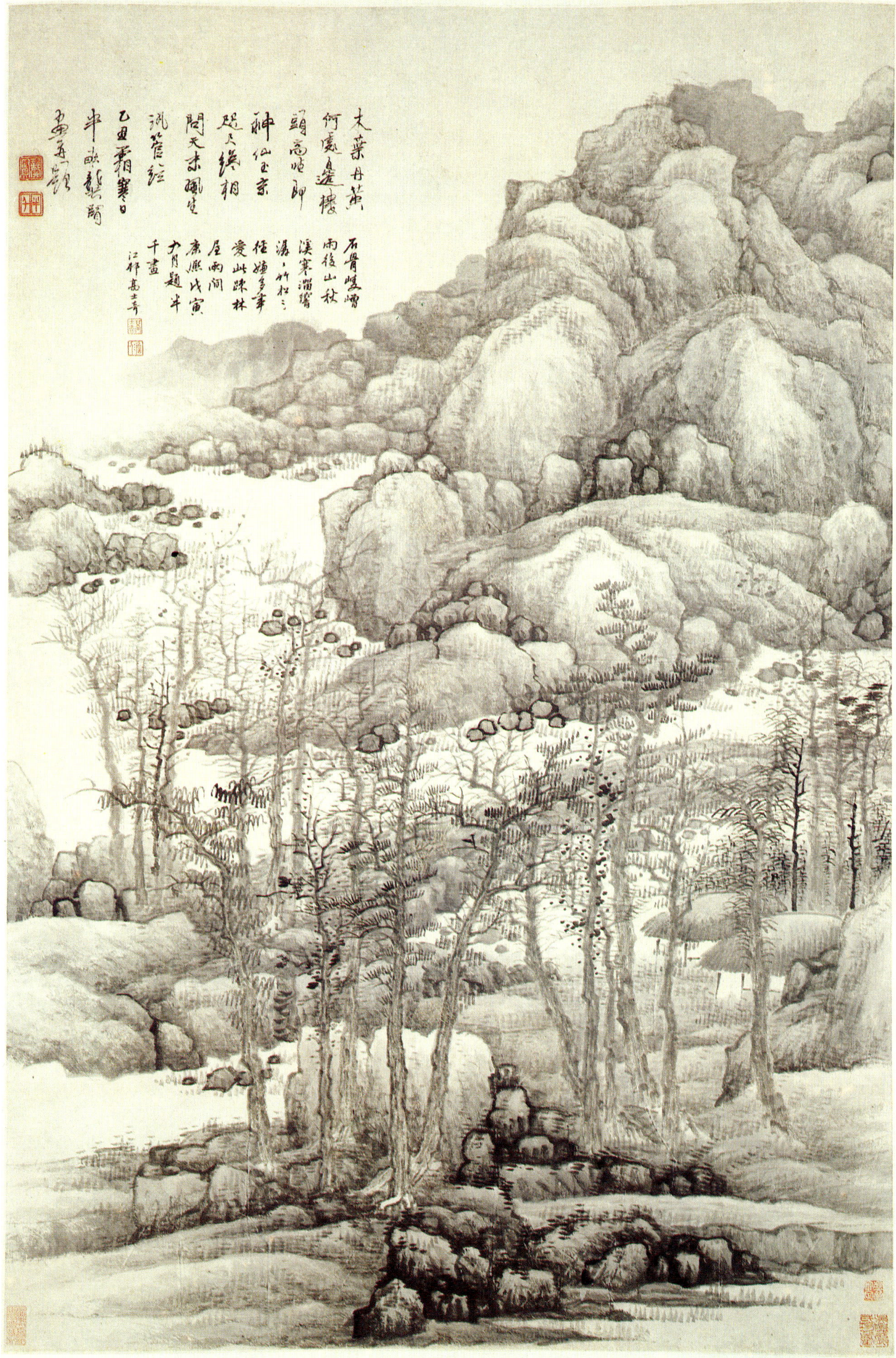

木葉丹黃
何處邊樓
頭高晰師
神仙世宗
超人樂相
問天来佩建
汎舊經
石骨崚嶒
雨後山秋
溪寒淄礀
湯湯竹松之
任娷多事
愛山踈林
屋雨間
康熙戊寅
九月題半
千畫
江邨高青
乙丑看寶日
中啟龍蘭
嵩丘題

"Set of 8 Album Leaves"
by Wang Gai (late 16th-early 17th century)
Album leaves; ink and colour on paper. Each leaf measures 21.6 x 17.8cm
Tianjin Arts Museum

Leaf 1: "Old Tree and Thatched Huts"
Two seals of Wang Gai. Inscription by Gao Shiqi (1645-1704) dated 1702:
"Old tree, thatched huts.
Deep mountain, flowing stream.
There must be people here".

Leaf 2: "Lonely Pavilion and Sailboats in the Distance"
In a simple, lyrical landscape, a pavilion accompanied by two pine trees is perched on an overhanging cliff. In the misty distance are sailboats and two fishing boats are anchored underneath the cliff. Seals of Wang Gai.

Leaf 3: "Soundly Asleep Under a Tree in Summer"
Seals of Wang Gai. Inscription by Gao Shiqi:
"In the shades of summer trees
Holding a book and sleeping without a care in the world.
[Such pleasure] is no less than those enjoyed by people of High Antiquity
Recently I have deep within me this wonderful feeling".
The inscription is dated in the summer (6th month) of 1702.

Leaf 4: "Thatched Hut in a Frosty Forest"
A soft, wintry landscape of bare trees sensitively depicted with faint touches of the brush and ink. Seal of the artist.

Leaf 5: "Three Mountains of the Immortals"
Lonely peaks jut out of a sea of mist created by the blank surface of the paper and the surrounding ink wash. Seals of Wang Gai.

Leaf 6: "Banana and Wutong Tree in Deep Autumn"
Seal of Wang Gai. Inscribed by Gao Shiqi in 1702:
"[Covered with] frosty dew in deep autumn, the banana and
the Wutong trees are gradually acquiring a melancholy air.
Today, the summer rain rises like steam.
Whenever I look at this painting, I feel happy [gratified]".

Leaf 7: "Gazing at the Waterfall in Wintry Forest"
In a wintry landscape, a scholar is gazing at a waterfall. Seal of Wang Gai.

Leaf 8: "Boats Anchored Under Snowy Pines"
Signed by Wang Gai with his seal. Inscribed by Gao Shiqi in 1702:
"A solitary pine under a precipitous cliff.
Snow is accumulated at the head-waters of the stream.
A small boat is moored near the bank.
Where can we buy wine?
Looking at this painting in a summer day like today,
I am shivering with cold".
Wang Gai was a native of Xiushui, Zhejiang province, but lived in Nanking for the most part of his life. He was said to have studied painting with Gong Xian (c. 1619-1689). He became well-known for having compiled the **Qieciyuan Huajuan** ("Painting Manual of the Mustard Seed Gardens") which became very popular and was widely used throughout China and Japan as well.

Leaf 1

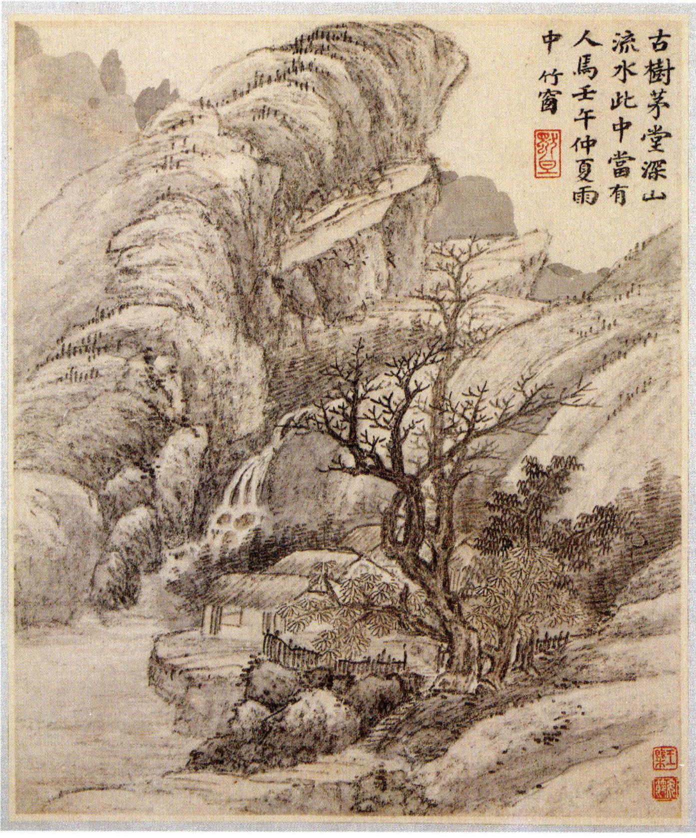

Leaf 3

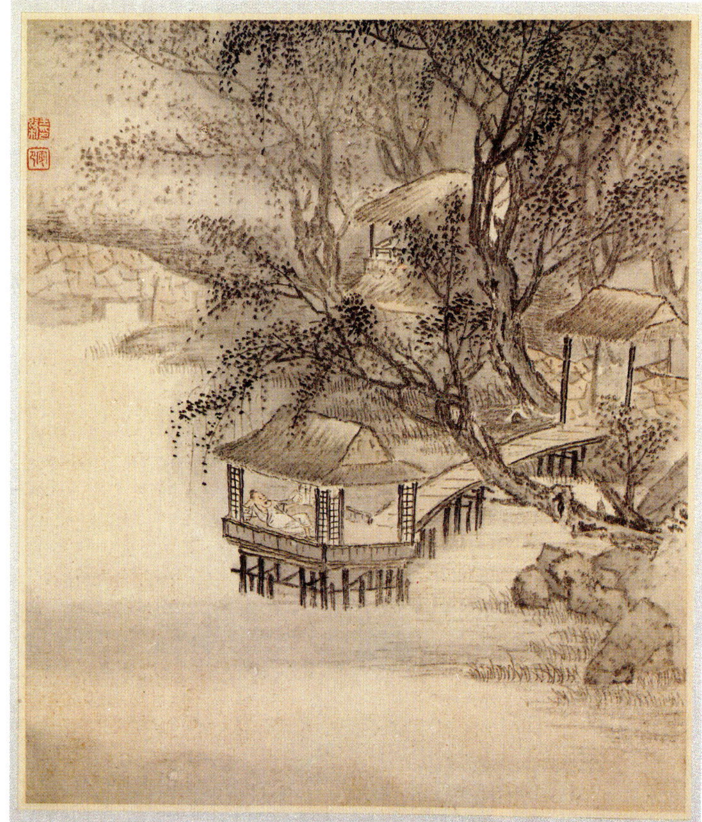

Leaf 6

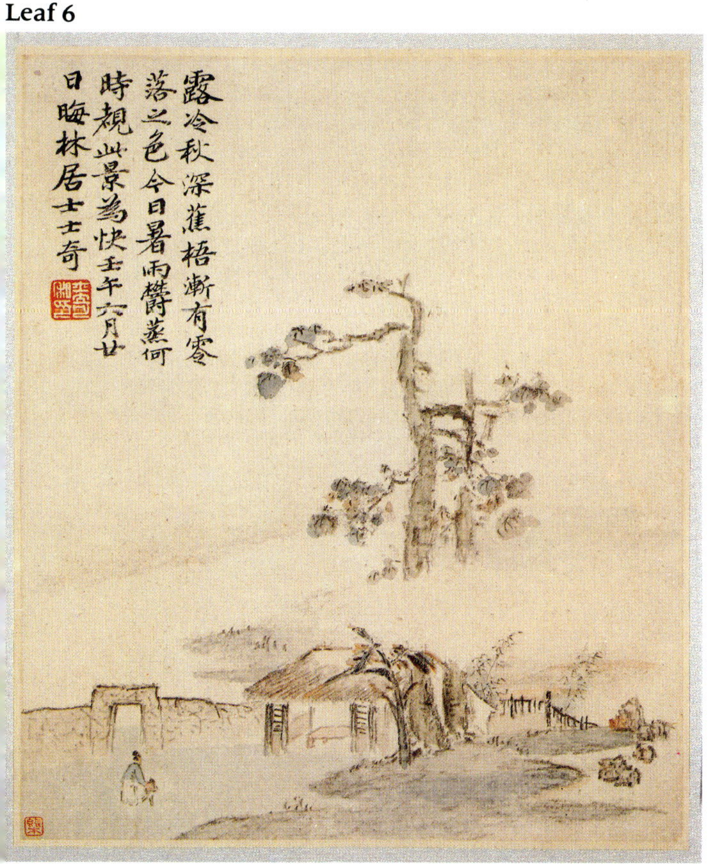

Leaf 8

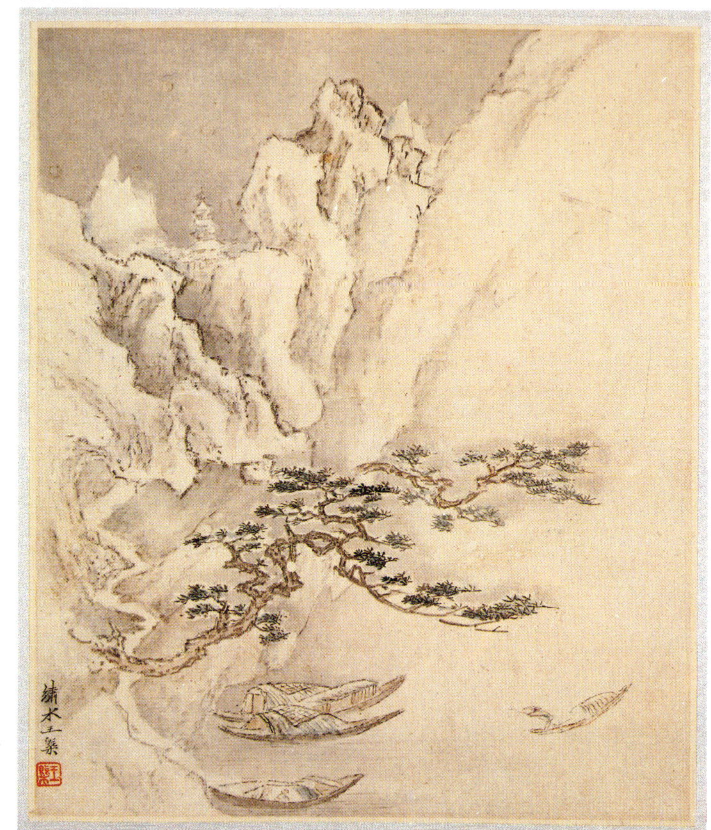

"Lotus"
dated 1694 by Zhu Da (Bada shanren) (1626-after 1705)
Hanging scroll; ink on paper. 120.5 x 50.5 cm
Nanking Museum

In this contemplative painting of great spiritual beauty and purity, Zhu Da reveals his genius as a master of composition and of brush and ink. A familiar subject matter is treated in a totally new way, with great freshness. Brushstrokes and ink washes, which are suggestive of natural images (e.g. rocks, lotus, chrysanthemums), are imbued with independent, expressive qualities and structural, compositional meanings. Endowed with an almost ethereal beauty, the long, elegant lines representing lotus stems are accomplished effortlessly in one continuous brush movement that turns and flows in a quiet rhythm. Old, withering lotus leaves are suggested by energetic brushstrokes of wet and dry ink, applied in a dynamic and spontaneous manner. Created are rich tonal textures evoking the different shades of colour, the shimmering effects of light and dark, and a tactile feeling of surface texture and substantial form. Spots of deep black ink with blurred edges are arranged into an attractive design evocative of a young lotus leaf. The ink spots were applied so wet that the edges blur as the ink suffuses outward.

The overhanging rocks covered with chrysanthemums are balanced by dark patches of lotus leaves and at the same time stabilised by the repeated, graceful movements of the lotus stems that enclose empty areas and seem to form a structural framework arching over a prominent empty space at the centre of the painting. Uncluttered and empty, this central void has a mind-cleansing effect. It is enigmatic in its silence.

A descendant of one branch of the Ming imperial family, the Individualist master Zhu Da was born in Nanchang, Jiangsi province. When he was barely twenty, the Ming dynasty fell, followed closely by the death of his father. These tragic events must have disturbed him greatly. He then retired to the Fengxin mountain and became a Chan Buddhist monk. He later left the temple and began to behave like a madman in the market place "dancing and waving his sleeves"; he spent days "laughing loudly and crying out in pain". One day, he simply pasted on his door a sign bearing the single character "**ya**" (dumb) and from then on, never spoke a word to anyone. He communicated with others by laughing, crying, gesticulating with his hands, writing and painting. He was very fond of drinking wine and most of his paintings were done while he was drunk. To people holding high positions in the government, he was proud and unapproachable, refusing to paint for them. One of his contemporaries recounts: "Shanren [Zhu Da] was crazy! But how then can the productions of his brush have such strength?...I have asked people from his home, and they all said: 'He accomplished it all while he was drunk'. Alas! Alas! One can get as drunk as he did, but not crazy as he was!"

The painting is inscribed by the artist dating it to 1694 and bears his seals.
Reproduced: **Nanking Museum Catalogue of Paintings;** vol. 2, p. 2.

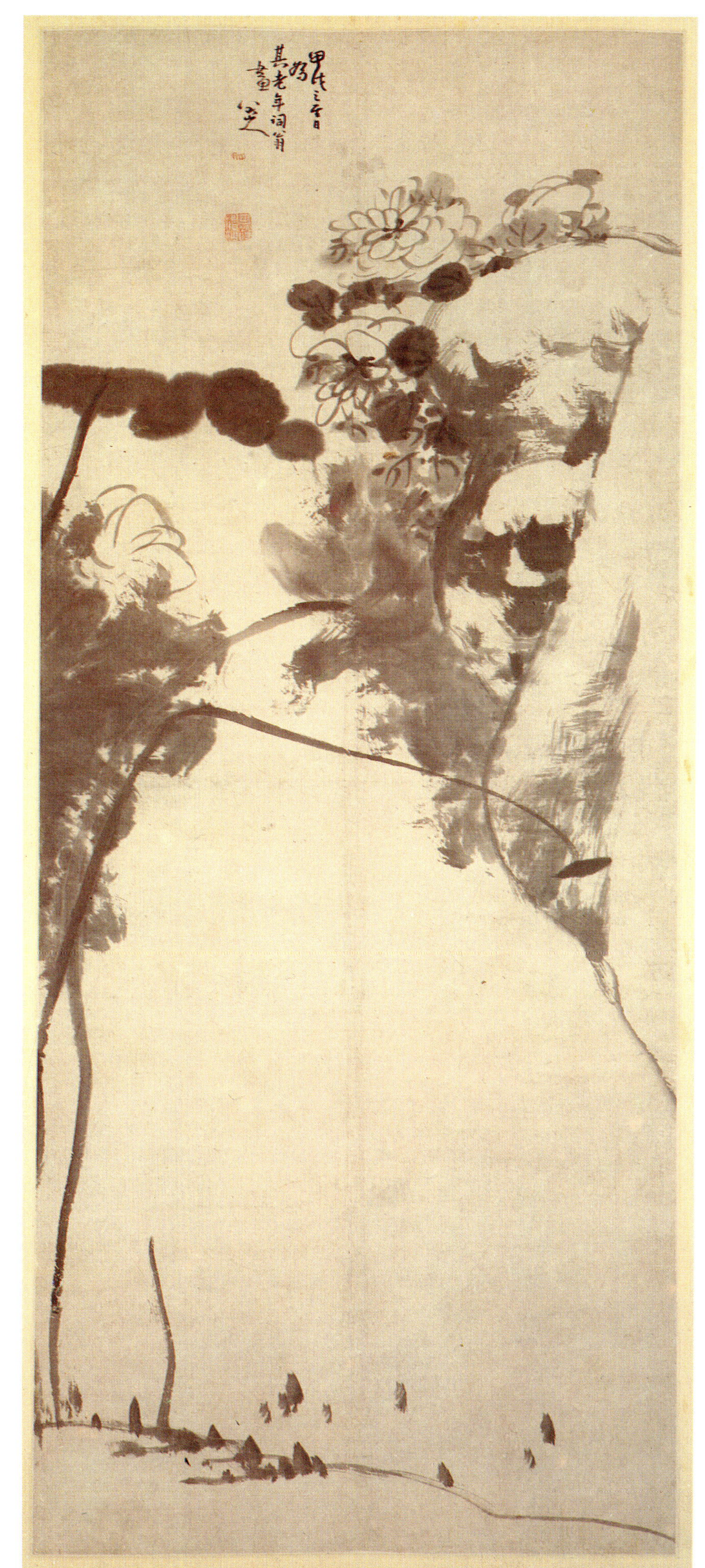

甲辰三月日
為其老年詞翁畫
定

"Rocks and Birds"
by Zhu Da (1626-after 1705)

Hanging scroll; ink on paper. 107.5 x 64.8cm
Shandong Provincial Cultural Relics Bureau

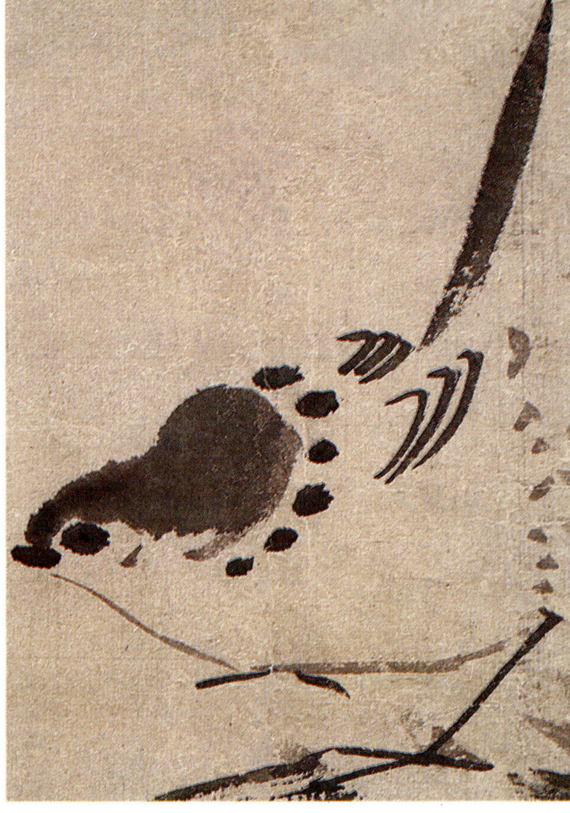

An enigmatic and unsettling picture of a pair pair of birds each balanced on one leg on a tapering eccentric rock, is depicted in an impressionistic manner with powerful and evocative calligraphic brushstrokes. Objects from nature (birds, rock, and tree) are succinctly suggested in abbreviated images that stop short of full revelation. The viewer is required to use his imagination and interpret what he sees. As in calligraphy, brushstrokes have expressive qualities, formal and structural properties, that are independent of the objects represented. Long undulating lines that move slowly and turn with a twisting motion, not only outline the arbitrary contour of the bizarre rock but also the surrounding space, creating spatial ambiguity between solid and void. These brushlines are characterized by a marked variation in ink tonality, varying from wet even ink to dry, scratchy passages that contain white streaks within the stroke (the so-called **"feibai"** or "flying-white" brushstroke). The unevenly inked brushstrokes may appear lax and loose in brush movement, and impoverished in ink. But in actuality, they are full of tensile strength and charged with dynamic tension. Repeated movements of short, vigorous brushstrokes, that appear to be slashing against the paper surface in a frenzy, create a feeling of surface excitement as well as suggesting the three dimensional form of the rock. These swift, short brushstrokes also impart to the painting a feeling of life and vitality. The rock appears organic and dynamic. Clusters of deep black strokes also tend to stabilise the precarious compositional framework formed by the contour-lines. Also balancing it is the diagonal thrust of what appears to be an abbreviated image of a tree, without roots, in deep black ink. Finally, each bird is balanced tensely with full concentration on one leg, as though on a tightrope. Made up of a few dots, lines, and brushstrokes, these birds are actually images invented by Zhu Da. It is uncertain if the bird at the middle is standing on a tree branch or on top of the rock. The bird at the top is standing on the tip of the rock outlined by a broken brushstroke. Most disturbing of all, the birds do not seem to be standing on anything, as their claws fill in the gap in the contour-lines. A feeling of tension and instability is thus created.

The painting is signed by the artist and bears his seals.

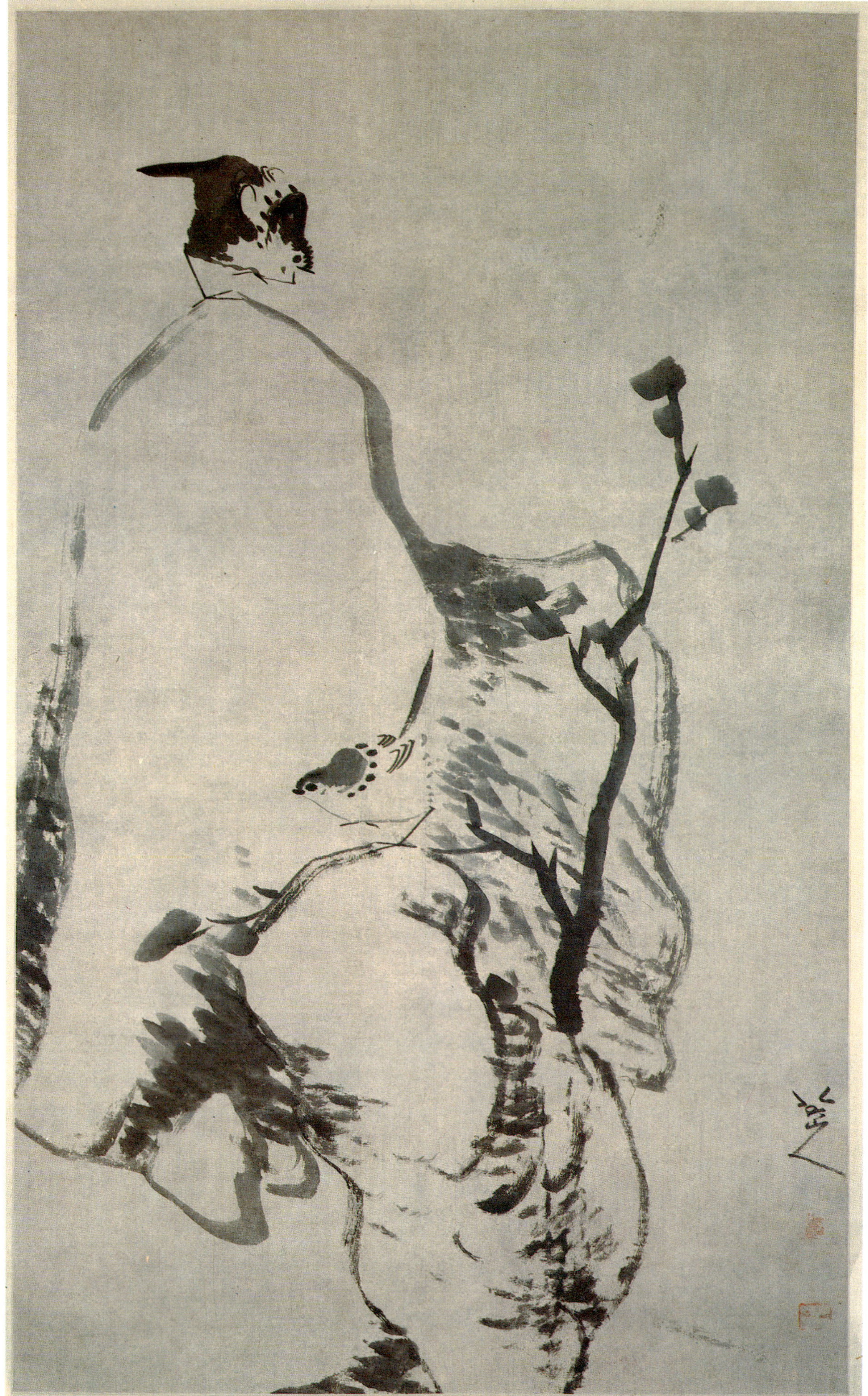

catalogue no. 59

"Landscape"
dated 1685 by Dao Ji (Shi Tao) (1642-c. 1707)

Handscroll; ink on paper. 115.2 x 33.2cm
Suzhou Museum

Executed in a bold and spontaneous manner, the painting is dominated by a surface excitement of spattering ink dots and long straggling lines. A landscape gradually emerges: a group of pine and other assorted trees entangled in a profusion of vegetal growth leads us to a pocket of houses and trees, followed by the dynamic movement of a rocky cliff that moves out of the painting and then re-enters to enclose a hollow space. Hardly noticed at first, in the midst of all this excitement, a scholar is gazing calmly out of the window of his country retreat.

On the surface, the painting may appear confusingly crowded with dense overlayings of wet and dry ink, as though rendered in a careless and haphazard manner. Pictorial images evocative of landscape elements seem to have been created by the chance configuration of brush and ink. Trees and rocks and houses look awkward and clumsy in execution. The dry, streaky, wavering brushstrokes (the so-called "feibai" or "flying-white" brushstroke), in particular, appear rough, scribbly, and impoverished of ink. But underneath all these, there is strength and discipline, and an underlying structural and abstract order. The apparent child-like amateurishness and awkwardness, qualities valued by the scholar-amateur artists, were intended by the artist rather than the direct results of a lack of skill. On the other hand, it was recognised that it took a greater mastery of the technical skills of brush and ink to achieve the appearance of these qualities. One had to transcend the conventions of the brush first, before one could obtain the spontaneous effect of effortless ease, and the natural state of child-like naïveté. Thus, as a brilliant performance of "ink-play", the painting is full of life and vitality, which is manifested in the dancing movements of ink and the rhythmic flow of line, evoking the creative forces of nature and expressing the exhilaration of the artist.

Completing the painting are the dynamic movements of an inscription dated 1685 written by Dao Ji in the cursive script of calligraphy. The inscription enlightens us on Dao Ji's attitude toward painting and his artistic intentions behind this painting. It is written in a humorous and self-effacing mood:

"The ten-thousand ugly ink dots will really annoy crazy Mi [Mi Fu] to death.

A few threads of gentle traces [of the brush] will throw Bei Yuan [Dong Yuan] off into laughter.

The distant passages are not in accord [with each other]; they do not show the turning and winding movements of mountains and streams.

The closer passages are dense and crowded; one can see only the humble village dwellings. When the mind breaks away completely from the restricting framework of established conventions and methods of painting, one's painting will naturally be like an immortal gliding in the wind [i.e. imbued with a free, untrammelled spirit].

The skin [i.e. brush and ink] and bone [i.e. composition] will become manifest in a compelling manner an unearthly spirit [i.e. signs of inspiration]."

Dao Ji concludes the inscription by saying that he "splashed the ink" (pomo) to get a laugh from his friend, a Chan Buddhist monk.

In the inscription Dao Ji appears to be laughing at himself. But, in actuality, he is criticizing people who look and judge a landscape painting in terms of the stylistic conventions of the ancient masters, and of the appearance of nature. For those people, they would compare his ink dots to those in the paintings of Mi Fu (1051-1107), his brushlines to the "hemp-fibre" texture strokes (mapi cun) of Dong Yuan (ca. 950), and his landscape to natural scenery. They would find faults in his painting, like the ones that are stated in the inscription. He then points out that it is not his intention to imitate these conventions at all, for he has already transcended them. The merit of his painting lies in the "untrammelled spirit", a spontaneity that is totally free of all kinds of restraints, and the inspired creativity in the formal aspects of composition and of brush and ink.

130

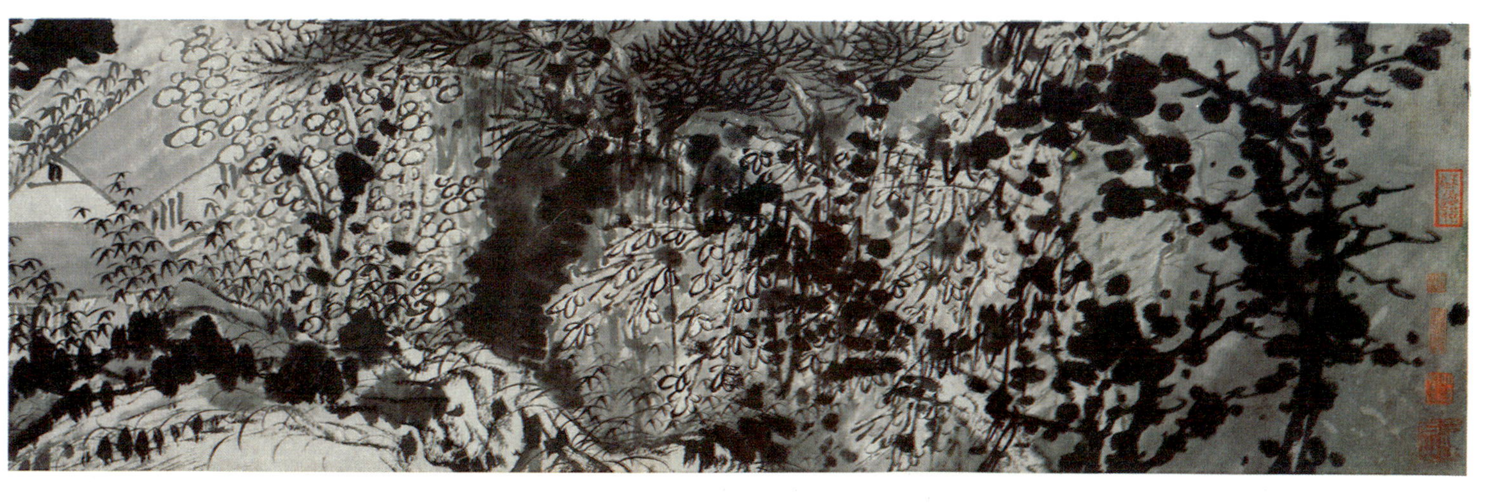

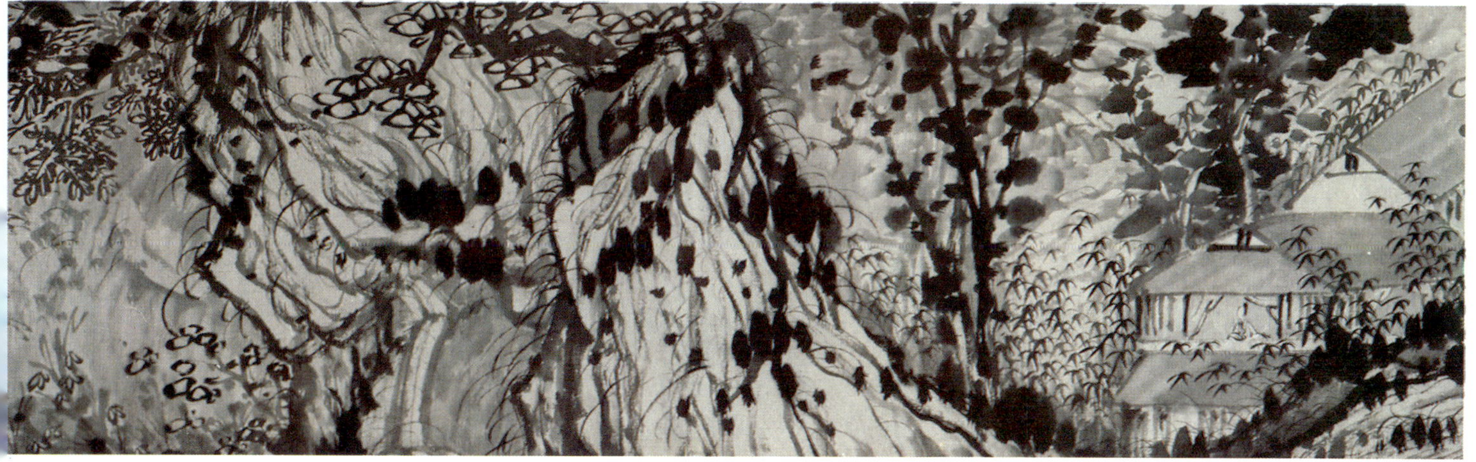

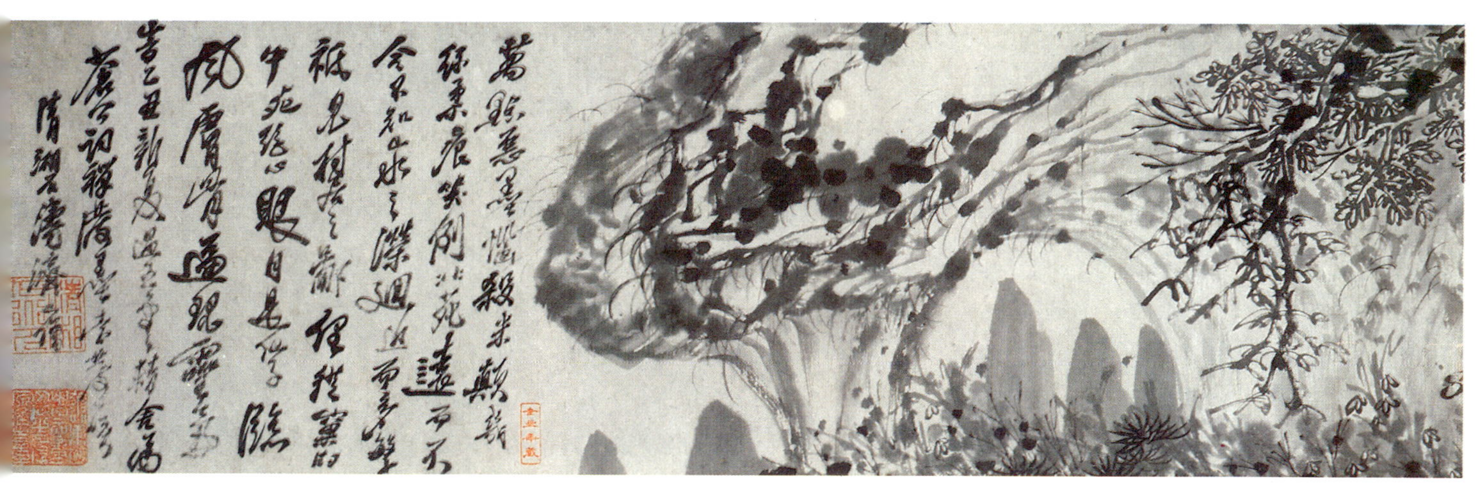

catalogue no. 59 continued

Dao Ji was a descendant of a distant branch of the Ming imperial family and was born in the remote area of Guilin, Guangxi province. After the fall of the Ming dynasty in 1644, he became a Buddhist monk and adopted the Buddhist name Dao Ji. Until the later years of his life when he settled in Yangzhou, he spent most of his life travelling, visiting scenic places, climbing famous mountains, living in different artistic centres, mixing with scholars and artists. He came to know and became friends with other artists like Mei Qing (cat. no. 49), Zha Shibiao (cat. no. 48), Gong Xian (cat. no. 54), Kun Can (cat. no. 51) and Wang Gai (cat. no. 56). Among all the Individualist masters, Dao Ji is recognised as the most original and creative. His views on painting are expressed in the **Huayu Lu (Record of Sayings on Paintings)**, which was written in about 1704.

The painting is signed by the artist and bears his seals.
Reproduced: **Suzhou Museum Catalogue of Paintings**, pp. 51-54.
Published: **Yiyuan Duoying**, 1978, no. 1, pp. 14-19.
        R. Edwards: **The Painting of Tao-chi**, pp. 34-37.
        S. and M. Fu: **Studies in Connoisseurship**, pp. 174-179.

catalogue no. 60

"Plum and Blossom"
by Dao Ji (Shi Tao) (1642-c. 1717)
Hanging scroll; ink and colour on paper. 115.2 x 33.2cm
Gugong Museum, Peking

Against a background of shadowy bamboo leaves painted in pale blue, a prunus with clusters of white blossoms is portrayed with contorted trunk and branches shooting in all directions. Accenting the painting are strong patterns of bamboo leaves painted in deep black brush strokes.

The painting is signed by the artist and bears his seal.

catalogue no. 59

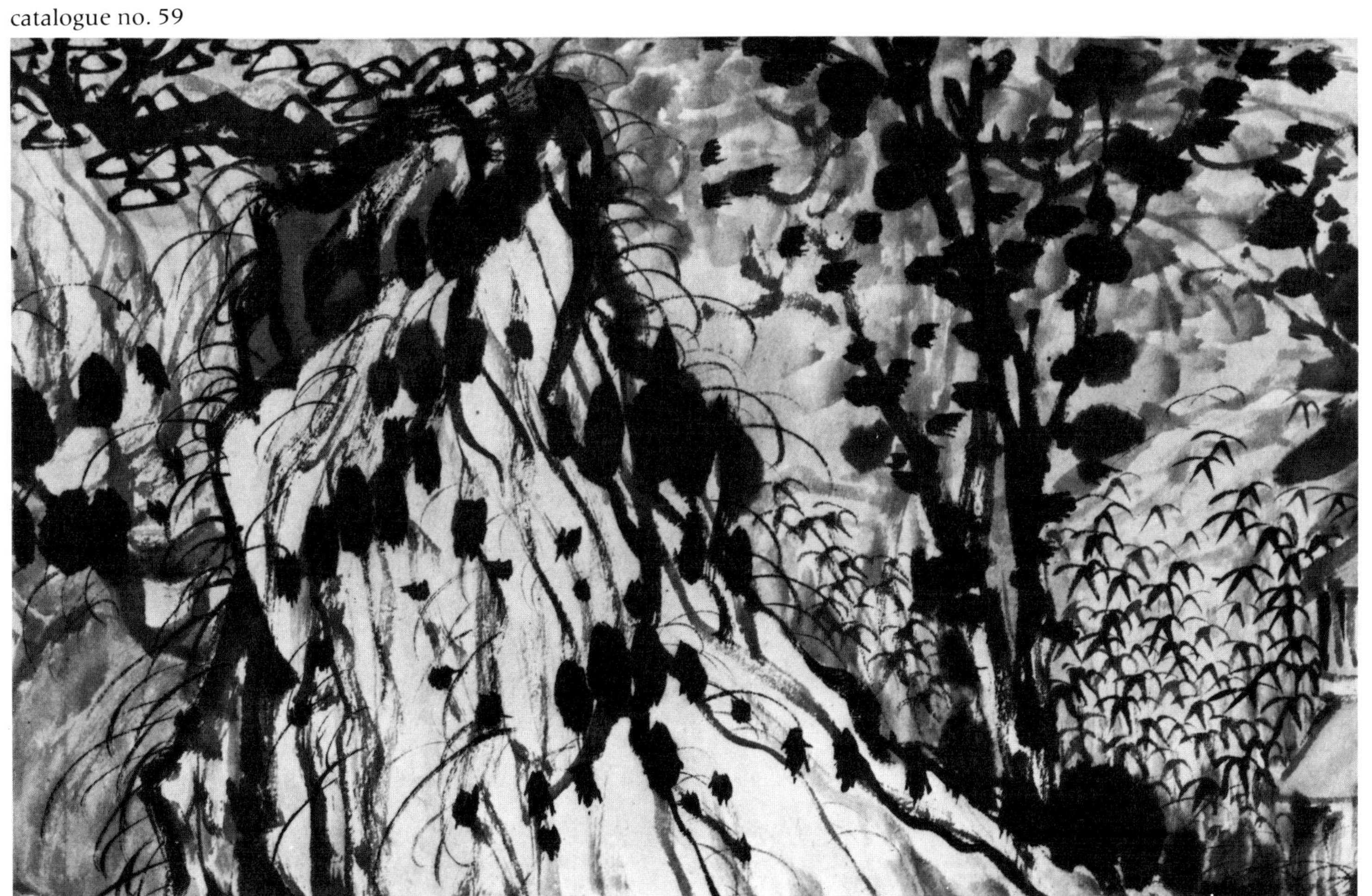

"Fishing Terrace"
by Zhang Duhang (17th century)

Handscroll; ink and colour on paper. 220.5 x 28.2cm
Nanking Museum

The handscroll opens with a panoramic view of soft folded hills and winding rivers enveloped in mist. Fishing boats are seen along the river. Painted in a modulated milky jade-green colour, the hills seem to have been carved by the wind. A dreamy, alluring feeling is created by the fluid movement of the hills and the careful toning of colour.

Little is known of Zhang Duhang and this is the only known painting attributed to the artist.

Reproduced: **Nanking Museum Catalogue of Painting**, vol. 2, pp. 72-5.

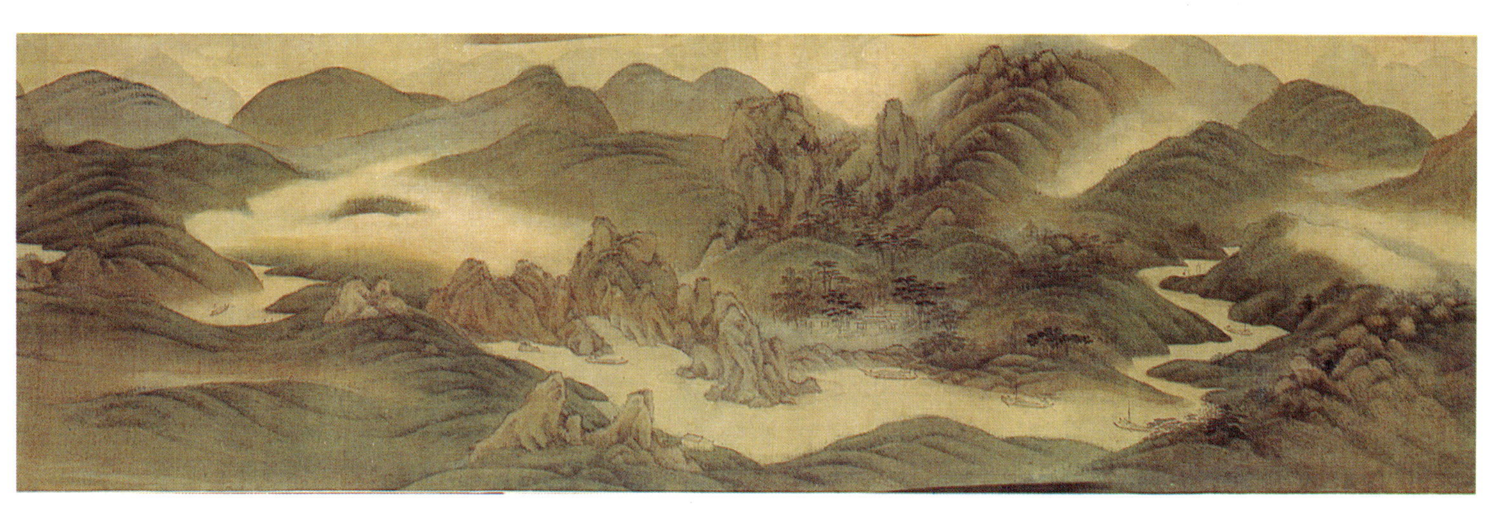

"Playing the Flute by Moonlight"
dated 1688 by Yu Zhiding (1647-1709)

Handscroll; ink and light colours on silk. 29.5 x 144.5 cm
Gugong Museum, Peking.

In a painting which resounds with silence, peace and tranquility it is almost as if the viewer could hear the muted tones of the flute being played by the figure seated in his boat. The very simplicity of the composition is evocative of the peaceful solace of the contented scholar-musician. There is no hint of threat or subterfuge in the painting; even the tiny moon surrounded by a faint dark wash to suggest the night is pale and insignificant. The delicate brushstrokes and light colour washes echo against the infinity of nature implied by the virtually untouched background. Emphatic but graceful brushstrokes, such as those defining the languid willows, and the occasional ripples in the water which gradually dissolve into the night mist combine to heighten this effect.

Yu Zhiding came from the Yangzhou region of Jiangsu province, the natural home for so many Chinese painters. He served for some time at the Court of the Kangxi Emperor (1662-1723) in the Board of Rites, a ministry concerned with the administration of Ritual, Ceremony and the official examination system. It seems, however, that official life at the capital (Peking) did not suit Yu and he returned to his favoured Dongting island in Lake Tai, a theme on which this painting is perhaps based, to resume his career as a painter. He is known not only for his landscapes, but also for his bamboo and, particularly, portrait paintings. In spite of this range his style was consistent in the use of fine and precise linear brushwork with light colour washes.

Inscription dated 1688 and seals of the artist.
Two colophons on the painting and a long list of colophons following the painting.

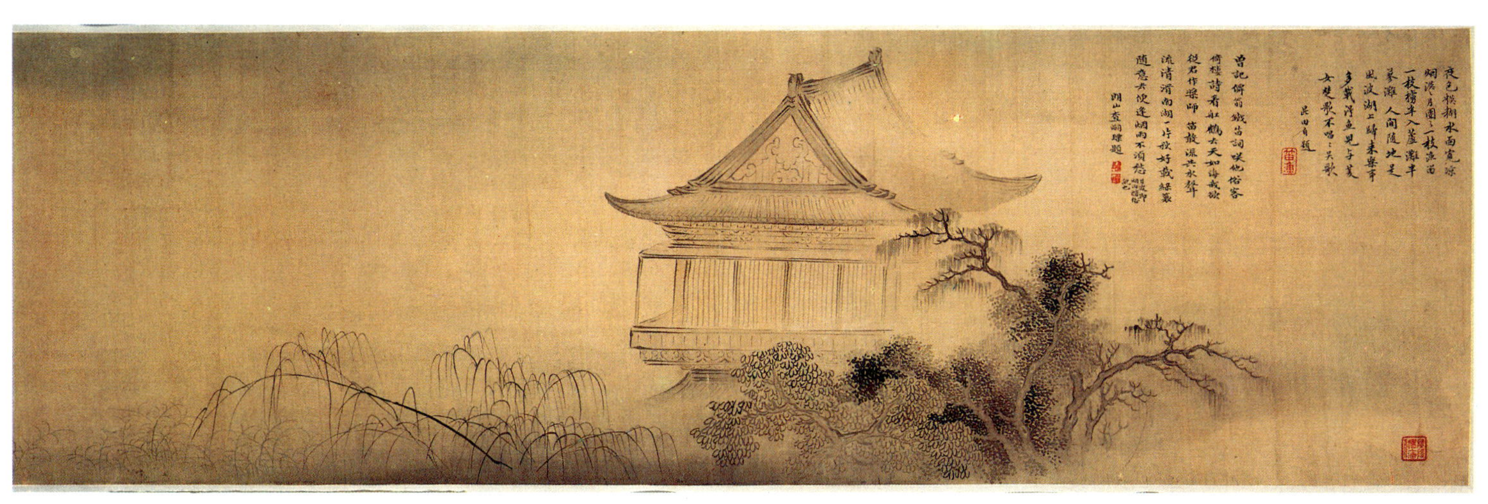
曾記餅師蛾苗詞咲他俗客
倚樓詩看紅鶴去天如海戟破
從君作樂師 苗龍渌共水聲
流清滑雨湖一片秋好藏綠叢
隨意且使連湖兩不須愁
閑山查嗣瑮題

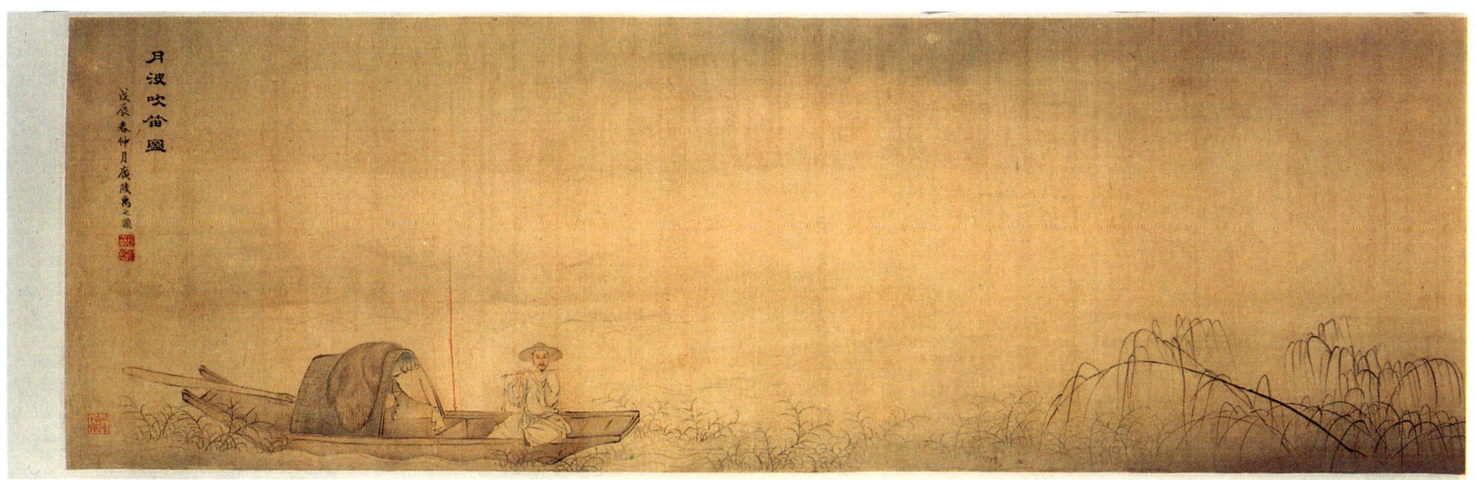
月波吹笛圖
戊辰春仲月廬陵禹之鼎畫

"Landscape with Pavilion"
dated 1722 by Yuan Jiang (late 17th-early 18th century)

Hanging scroll; ink and light colour on silk. 210.5 x 111cm
Gugong Museum, Peking.

The grand designs of the Northern Song landscapists are reflected in this large scale composition. It is unashamedly an attempt to recall those momentous paintings of the 11th and 12th centuries in which nature is portrayed in all her vast domains and the presence of man kept to a humble and insignificant level. The sense of scale is captured in this painting by the very deliberate division of the composition into foreground, with rocks, trees and the pavilion, the middle ground, a spacious river and valley, and in the distance, mountain ranges. The closer of these are outlined with strong ink brushlines and those beyond defined by ink washes. The painting represents that tradition of conventional archaism that was present in academic painting circles in the 18th century, when painters attempted to recreate the grandiose schemes of such masters as, in Yuan Jiang's case, Guo Xi (Northern Song dynasty).

Yuan Jiang was born in Jiangsu province and although little is recorded of the detail of his life, he is known to have served as a Court painter in the Yongzheng period (1723-36). Biographies confirm his interest in Song landscapes and the representation of the legendary palaces of the rulers of the Han and Tang dynasties. Ideologically, stylistically and technically Yuan Jiang was a painter seeking to re-present ancient ideals.

Inscription dated 1722 and seal of artist.

"Landscape"
by Yuan Yao (18th century)
Hanging scroll; ink and colours on silk. 233 x 100.8cm
Gugong Museum, Peking

Yuan Yao was a nephew of Yuang Jiang and like his uncle he sought to recreate the grandeur of the Northern Song landscape. The composition is carefully constructed to lead the viewer through the rocky foreground by such devices as paths, bridges and streams, through the village courtyard and up to a lofty pavilion. This overlooks a deep valley from which rises a soaring mist shrouded peak. The impression of infinite space and scale is provided by the valley on the right which gradually recedes to far distant mountains defined by a light blue colour wash. The painting again reflects the conventional archaism of academic painting circles working at the Court in the 18th century.

Yuan Yao, like his uncle, from Jiangsu province, followed the traditional path to serve as a painter at the Court of the Qianlong Emperor (1736-96). Specialising in grandiose landscapes, such as this example, he too was noted for his paintings of ancient palaces and pavilions.

Seals and inscription of the artist saying that he was following the brush manner of the Yuan dynasty master Wang Meng.

"One Hundred Flowers"
by Zou Yigui (1686-1772)

Handscroll; ink and colours on silk. 32.8 x 775.8cm
Museum of Chinese History, Peking

This long handscroll reflects the appreciation at the Qianlong court for works of art of great virtuosity and technical excellence. It is in complete contrast to the intellectual landscapes of the literati tradition. The precise and delicate brushlines which so studiously define the one hundred flowers are a far cry from the varied and expressive strokes of landscapes in the scholarly tradition. Nevertheless it is still the essentials of brushwork and line which determine quality. Technical excellence and rigid composition combine in this scroll to make for great decorative impact but we must acknowledge that such precision renders the flowers stylised. Zou Yigui developed a distinctive technique employing powder colour, perhaps reflecting influences of Western painting, and which is in some contrast to the more traditional styles of light brushwork and subtle colour washes. The 18th century collector and connoisseur, Qin Zuyang, summarises Zou's work: "I have a few pictures by this artist in my collection, representing chrysanthemum flowers in colour. In painting these he first used thick powder for the petals and then washed them over with light colour. The powder made them stand out in relief on the silk. They are skilfully executed and beautiful, but after all rather stiff and deficient in elegant design". Qin refers to 'elegant design' and certainly each individual section is carefully composed, but maintaining a sense of continuity in a long scroll composed of such individual floral groupings was not successfully achieved by Zou in this example. The scroll is more a series of independent elements than it is a single evolving and coherent composition.

Zou Yigui followed a traditional and predictable career after passing his jinshi examination in 1727. He became a member of the Hanlin Academy, a censor, a Secretary in the Grand Council and finally Vice-President of the Board of Rites. He enjoyed a high reputation during the Qianlong period and his work was greatly admired by the Emperor who, as an avid collector and commentator, frequently appended colophons to Zou's paintings in praise of their 'unequalled quality and beauty'.

Zou Yigui signed the painting as having been "written respectfully by your subject Zou Yigui"; the painting was probably painted for the Qianlong Emperor (1736-1796).
It bears seals of the artist and seals of the Qianlong Emperor.
Recorded: **Shigu Baoji** (Lovell no. 59a).

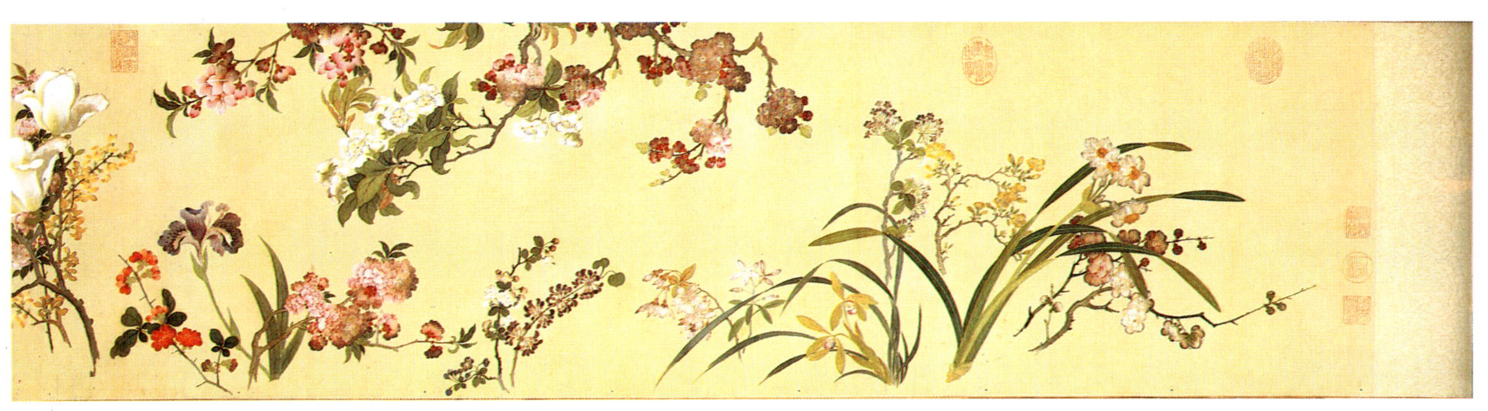

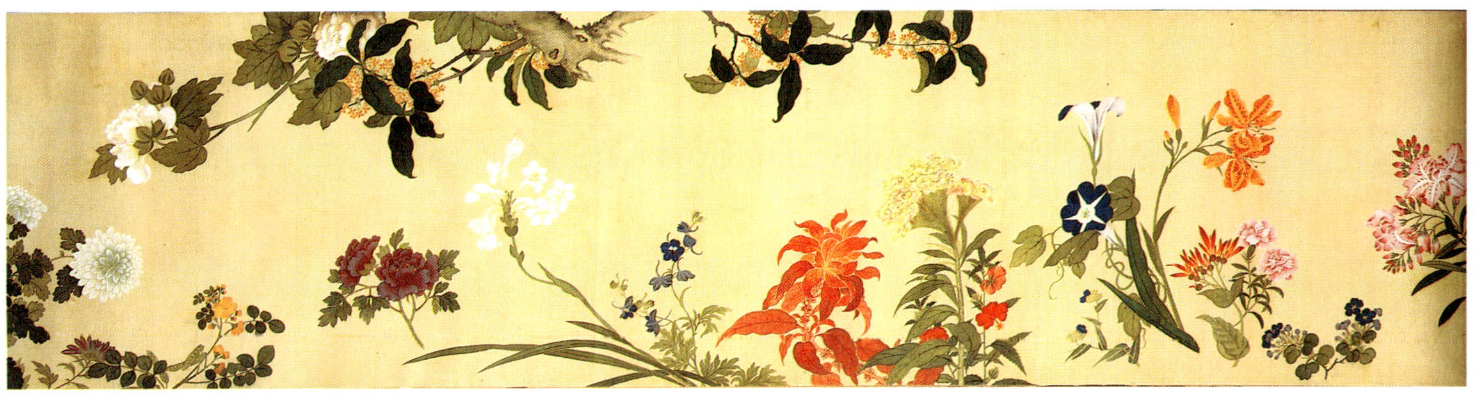

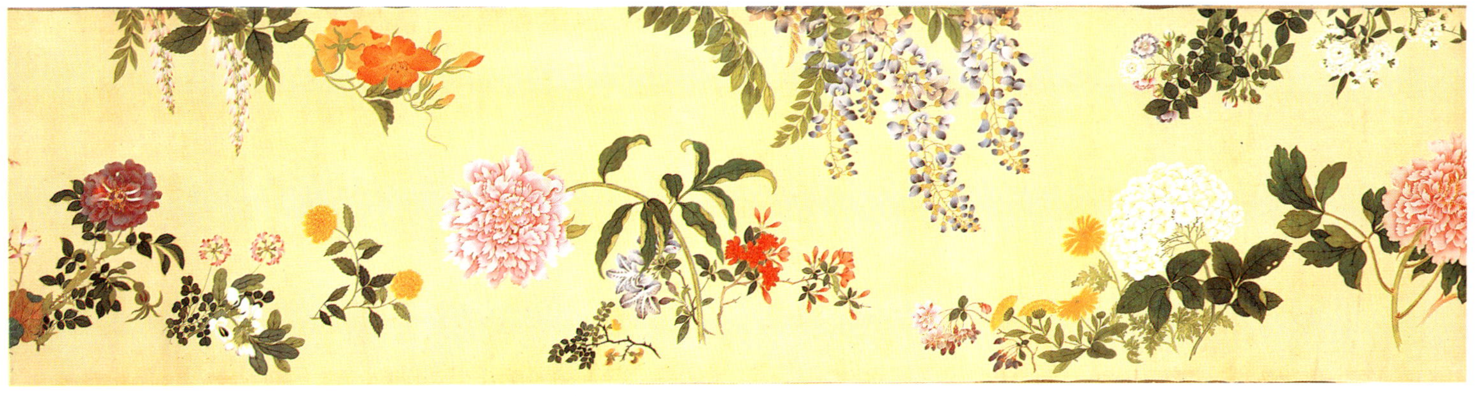

"Pine and Crane"
dated 1759 by Shen Quan (1682-1760)

Hanging scroll; ink and colour on silk. 191 x 98cm
Gugong Museum, Peking

This painting embodied many of the ideals of the conservative traditions prevalent at the Court in 18th century China. It is carefully composed with landscape elements which stylistically echo the early Ming Zhe school whilst the birds and flowers echo auspicious symbolism. Beneath overhanging pine and blossoming plum trees stand two cranes beside a rippling stream. The bright colours of the birds and floral elements not only provide decorative effect but also stand in contrast to the more sombre, but evocative, landscape elements. The painting is, therefore, a combination of the more reserved monochrome landscape in a traditional manner and the decorative colourful naturalistic style so favoured at the Qianlong Court. Shen Quan was a contemporary of Lang Shining (Castiglione: see cat. no. 67) and there seems little doubt that he was influenced by the Western sense of naturalism promoted by Lang. Shen Quan was highly praised by critics and connoisseurs for his brilliant colouring and facility for grasping and expressing the particular qualities of the birds and animals he painted. The cranes in this painting, along with pine trees, traditional symbols of longevity, are, for example, precisely drawn but exotic and with a hint of imperious splendour.

Shen Quan hailed from Wuxing in Zhejiang province but strangely did not follow the usual path to the Court. Instead, in 1731, he accepted an invitation issued by a Japanese patron to visit Nagasaki where he worked for three years and exercised some influence upon local painting styles. Throughout his life Shen confined himself to painting birds, flowers and animals in the Chinese taste.

Seals and inscription of the artist stating that the painting was executed in 1759 when he was 78 years old.

"The Nine Songs"
by Yao Wenhan (18th century)

Handscroll; ink and colours on paper. 41.8 x 729.5 cm
Museum of Chinese History, Peking

A colourful and lively rendering of the 'Nine Songs'; a composition of shamanistic poems dedicated to the nine classes of deities worshipped by the people of the State of Chu, a powerful late Bronze Age State in the Yangtze valley, in the 4th to 3rd centuries BC. The original text comprised eleven songs dedicated to the following deities:

1. The Eastern Emperor of Heaven
2. The Lord of the Clouds
3. Lady of Xiang
4. Mistress of Xiang
5. The Senior Lord of Lives
6. The Junior Lord of Lives
7. The Lord of the East
8. The River Spirit
9. The Mountain Spirit
10. The War Dead
11. The Soul of Ritual

This array of historical and legendary figures are painted in a precise and colourful style which was favoured for the portrayal of ancient mythological themes. The precision of the drawing renders a stiffness to the composition which allied to the bright colours employed, provides for strong decorative effect.

Yao Wenhan, about whom little is recorded, was a painter at the Court of the Qianlong Emperor in the second half of the 18th century.

Signed by the artist as "respectfully painted by the subject Yao Wenhan" followed by his seal. Seals of the Qianlong Emperor.
Recorded: **Shigu Baoji** (Lovell no. 59a).

"Eight Noble Horses"
by Lang Shining (Giuseppe Castiglione) 1688-1766

Handscroll; ink and colours on silk. 52.7 x 92.5 cm
Jiangxi Provincial Museum

Eight noble horses are portrayed in a range of poses, standing, romping, rolling and lying, which are reminiscent both compositionally and stylistically of European Old Master study drawings. In both concept and style the painting does of course reflect the European artistic traditions which Castiglione brought to China early in the 18th century. The fine, detailed and realistic drawing, the sense of volume described through light, shadow and shading and the accurate rendition of colour all betray that European heritage. Perhaps the absence of the natural features of the environment, the sense of space and the delicate brushwork may be regarded as concessions to the Chinese concept of such studies, but in other respects it is very much a European painting. Although a studied and contrived composition the theme of eight horses was a well-established one in Chinese mythology. The Eight Horses of Mu Wang (King Mu) were traditionally thought to have been in the service of King Mu of the Zhou dynasty (circa 950 BC) and used in his expeditions to quell barbarian uprisings and incursions. They thereby acquired a virtually legendary status and even, it is said, transported the King on his mythical visit to Xi Wangmu (the Queen Mother of the West). The theme of the Eight Horses appears constantly as a decorative motif in Chinese art and furthermore they were a favoured subject for many of the renowned painters of horses, including Han Gan (Tang dynasty) and Zhao Mengfu (Yuan dynasty).

There is no doubt that Italian born Castiglione was one of the most interesting, unusual and, in a sense, revolutionary figures, in 18th century China. He arrived in Peking, where he was to spend the remainder of his life, in 1715 as a Jesuit missionary but his claim to fame is not as a successful emissary for the Catholic church but as a painter at the Court of the Emperor of China. Castiglione was in fact one of a number of European missionary painters, decorators, architects and instrument-makers working at the Court in extraordinary and rarified conditions. An excerpt from a letter, written in 1743, from the Old Summer Palace by a colleague of Castiglione, Père Attiret, gives some clue to their circumstances: "Of all the Europeans staying here (in the Summer Palace) it is only the painters and watch-makers who have access everywhere on account of their work. The rooms in which we paint are situated in one of the little palaces that I have mentioned. The Emperor comes nearly every day to see how we are working, so it is scarcely possible to go away. We no longer go out to paint, unless the object to be represented is such that it cannot be transported; in that case we are taken under escort of eunuchs to the palace where it is situated. One must then walk very quickly and noiselessly on tiptoe, almost as if one were about to commit some heinous act".

Of all the Europeans serving at the Court it was only Castiglione who won an established place in history. He assimilated to some extent the methods and techniques of Chinese painting, and used traditional Chinese ink and brushes, which of course gained for him Imperial approval and ever-increasing status. In the Qianlong period he was uniquely honoured on his appointment as a senior member of the Imperial Painting Bureau. The Qianlong Emperor was particularly fond of his work and records indicate that no less than fifty-six works by Castiglione were in the Imperial collections at that time. Many of these bear colophons by the Emperor expressing his unsurpassed admiration for the vivacious and lifelike qualities of his art.

The painting is signed by the artist as "respectfully painted by Lang Shining" and bears his seals, one of which says "writing (or painting) from life".

The inscription was written by Prince Guo (1697-1738), the sixth son of the Yongzheng Emperor, and states that the scroll was painted for Prince Shen (1711-1758), the 21st son of the Kangxi Emperor. The death of Prince Shen in 1758 provides a **terminus ad quem** for the painting.
Seals of Prince Guo and Prince Shen. Published: **Wen Wu**, 1980 no. 11, p. 93.

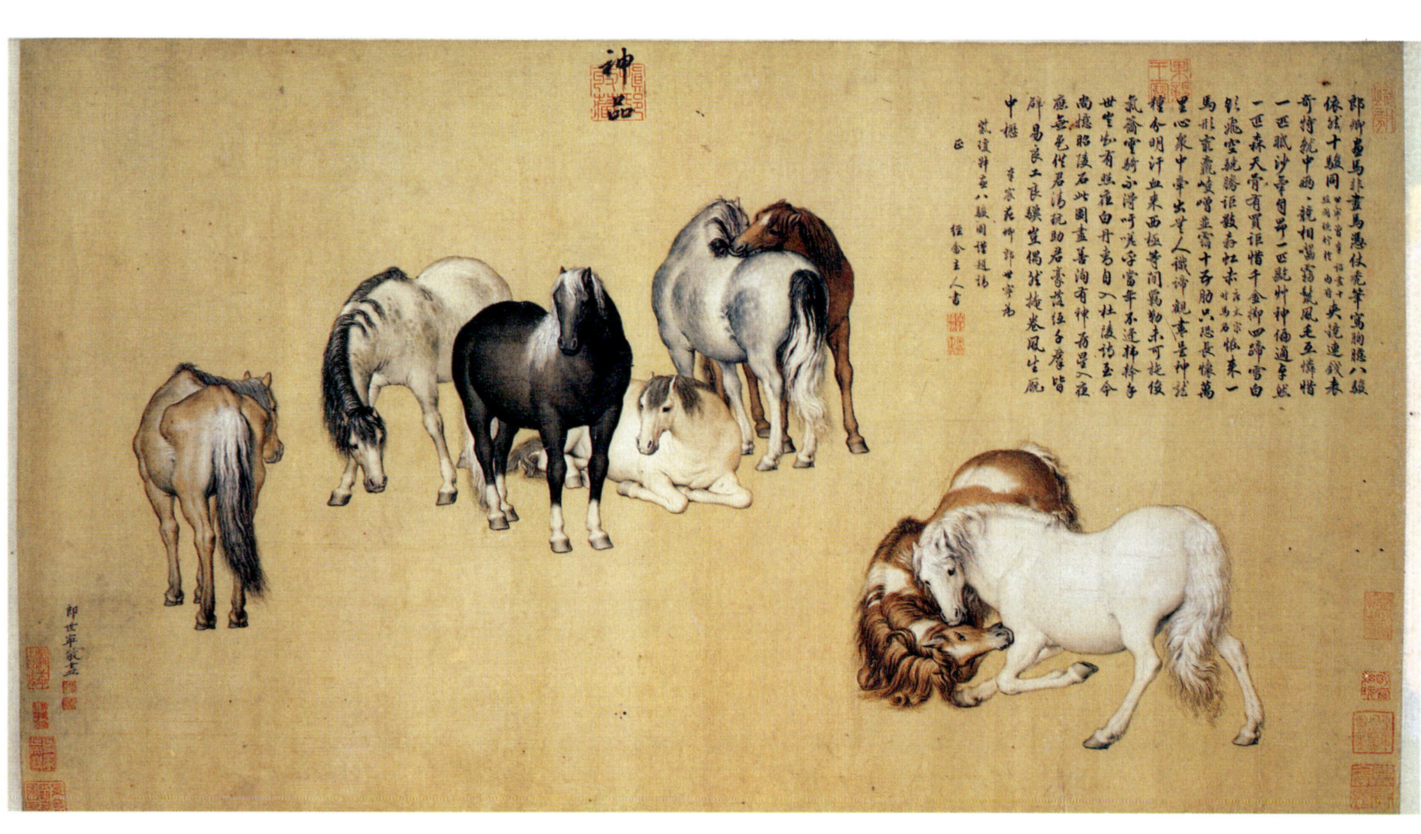

"Lofty Ridge"
by Gao Qipei (1672-1734)
Hanging scroll; ink on paper. 70.5 x 38.4cm
Gugong Museum, Peking

A lone windswept scholar stands thoughtfully, almost forlornly, atop a mountain ridge. The composition is simple, the painting style calligraphic in its expressiveness and spontaneity. Quick decisive strokes describe the scholar's robes blowing in the wind; there is neither time nor need for attention to detail. The mountain ridge on which the scholar stands is painted in broad wet strokes which contrast with the strong linear qualities of the figure. Yet there is still a sense of spontaneity and urgency in this ink work which complements the drama and the simplicity of the solitary figure silhouetted against an infinite void.

There are a number of features about Gao Qipei which distinguish him from the general traditions of Chinese painters. He was a Manchu, born in present-day Liaoning, and thus far removed from the regions traditionally favoured by Chinese painters with whom, it seems, he had little connection. However, as a Manchu he did serve at the Court in both the Kangxi and Yongzheng periods where he enjoyed a highly successful official career attaining the post of Vice-President of the Board of Rites. Official duties did not deter him from painting, but far from following any academic or established style Gao displayed a marked originality and virtuosity in his work. New and inventive techniques, such as finger painting for which Gao was renowned, at times outweight genuine creativity and the charge of 'forced originality' is often laid at Gao. The style of this painting strongly suggests, in the abbreviated and energetic strokes, that it is a finger painting. In the early 18th century when painting in China was so strongly institutionalised there was a certain compulsion among painters to create something new. Gao is recorded early in his career to have recognised this: he was "already anxious that he might not form his own style. He was constantly depressed and took to his bed with exhaustion". Nonetheless his successful search for a unique expression was acknowledged by his peers and contemporaries; Zhang Geng in **Guochao Luazheng lu** notes: "Gao Qipei's natural gifts were extraordinary; his conceptions were strange and he expressed them in painting with great ease…people usually praise him simply for his finger-paintings; they have no idea of the beauty of his paintings with the brush. Since his finger-painting met with such success, and as he found it easier, with increasing years, to work with the fingers, he abandoned the brush completely and consequently such works of his are very rare".

Technically inventive, perhaps to the point of glibness, though he was, Gao Qipei was a genuinely innovative and eccentric painter. Apart from the figure and animal (cat. no. 70) studies shown here he was probably best known as a landscapist, creating moody, surrealist and fugitive impressions in the simple but evocative style so well expressed in this scroll.

Seals of the artist one of which says "finger-painting".

萬緣淫重意如何　怩九熊燈中拉飄食　破儻諂來山細膽　空天驚見一人長

"Eight Scenes in Water"
by Gao Qipei (1672-1734)

Two album leaves from a set of eight; ink on paper, each leaf measures: 31.6 x 41cm
Nanking Museum

Leaf 1: "Water Buffalo"

With extraordinary economy Gao Qipei illustrates an almost totally submerged water buffalo; only part of the head and rump show above the water. The water is represented by blank paper but we are in no doubt as to the subject for the careful expression of the buffalo and the pose of the head clearly indicate the animal's striving to keep his head above water.
Signed at the top of the leaf with **zi** 'Wei Zhi' and the seal "finger painting".

Leaf 2: "Duckweed and Prawns"

An album leaf of simplicity but great vivacity. The prawns encircle and advance upon the duckweed attracting and harbouring shoals of tiny minnows which seem to reverberate with frenzied activity. Again the economy of the style, the simple but effective ink play and the colour spots of the duckweed combine in beauty, humour and liveliness.
Seals of 'Qi' and 'Pei' and "finger painting".

For biographical details see catalogue no. 69.
Reproduced: **Nanking Museum Catalogue of Paintings;** vol. 2, pp. 84-85.

Leaf 1

Leaf 2

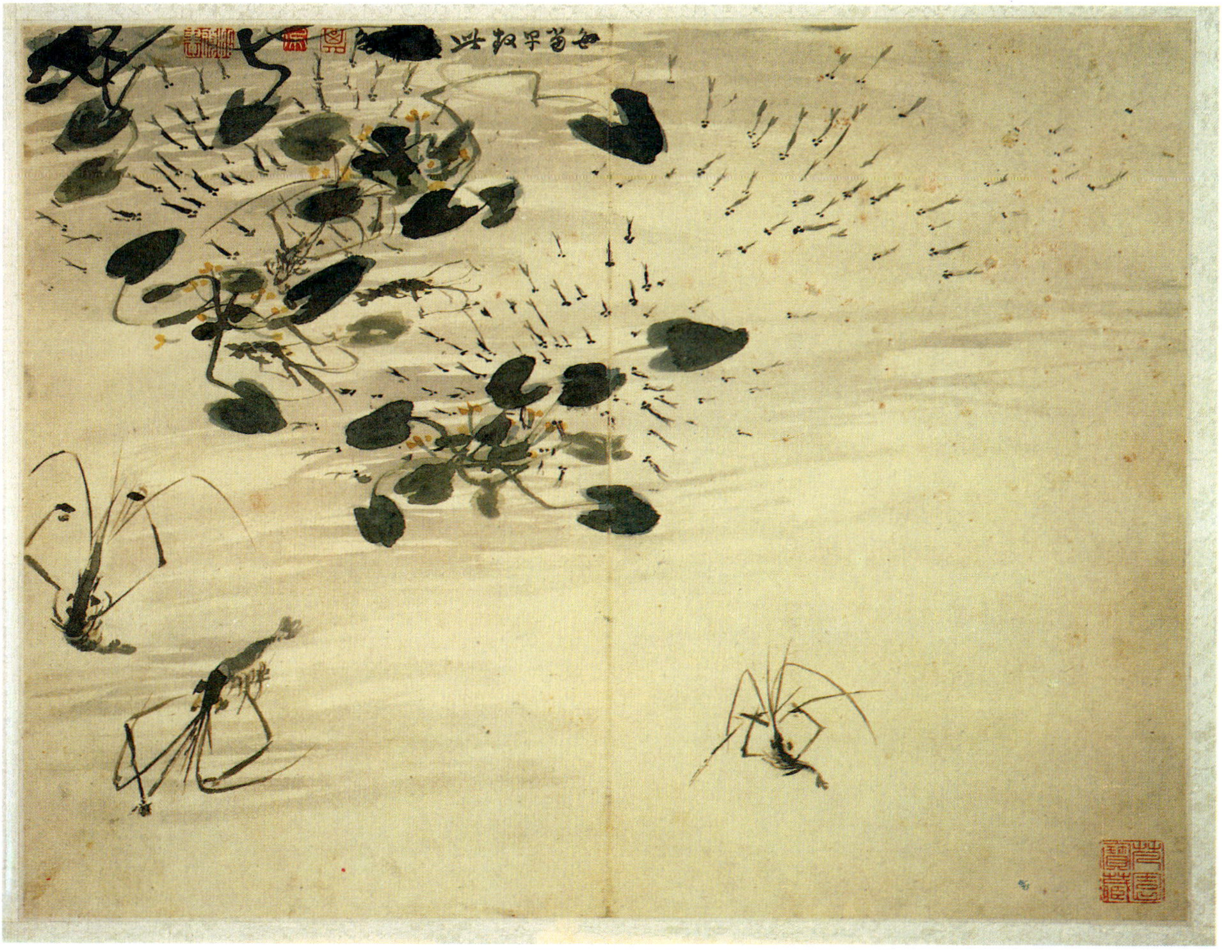

catalogue no. 71

"Wutong Tree and Squirrel"
by Hua Yan (1682-1756)

Hanging scroll; ink and colour on paper. 164 x 55 cm.
Gugong Museum, Peking

A pair of squirrels are playing on the branches of a **Wutong (Firmiana Simplex)** tree. Their delightful movements are caught with great spontaneity. The squirrel on the upper branch is watching the antics of the squirrel dangling on the lower branch. These sweet, agile creatures, portrayed from careful observation, are very life-like; their fur is realistically depicted with minute dry brushstrokes. The branches are bouncing gracefully with the weight of the squirrels. Blowing in the wind are the soft, drooping leaves painted in a tonal pattern of flat even ink. Balancing the tree branches in the lower right corner is a perforated eccentric rock, sketched in broad, sweeping wet brushstrokes of ink. Beside it is a delicate flower painted in cool colours; the blossoms are painted in white accented with pink and the leaves in pale blue. Just behind the hole in the rock is a glimpse of another flower, reminding one of a shy young girl peeping through a half closed door.

The painting also bears an inscription by the artist:
"Leisurely gazing out of my window at the inn,
By chance, I saw something [that happened to interest me].
With a playful brush I did this painting".

A native of Fujian province, Hua Yan lived mainly in Hangzhou, Zhejiang province and spent some years in Yangzhou. He is generally counted as one of the "Eight Yangzhou Masters" and regarded as the most versatile and technically accomplished of them. He was best known in his day for pictures of birds and flowers, insects and animals, but also excelled in figure and landscape paintings.

The painting is signed by the artist and bears his seal.

catalogue no. 72

"Ducks in Spring Water"
by Hua Yan (1682-1756)

Hanging scroll; ink and colour on satin. 55.6 x 37.8 cm
Nanking Museum

An interesting and unusual scene is depicted. A pair of ducks are shown swimming in the water. One of the ducks playfully dives into the water. It is as though the pond is seen in a cross-section, showing the head of the duck submerged in the water. The illusion of underwater is created by the misty effect of the duck, achieved by the soft, subtle shading of dry ink rubbed on top of the satin surface. A few rhythmic lines suggest ripples on the water surface.

The painting is inscribed by the artist: "Ducks bathing in spring water", and bears his seal.
Reproduced: **Nanking Museum Catalogue of Paintings,** vol. 2, p. 111.
Yiyuan Duoying, no. 5 (1979). p. 33.

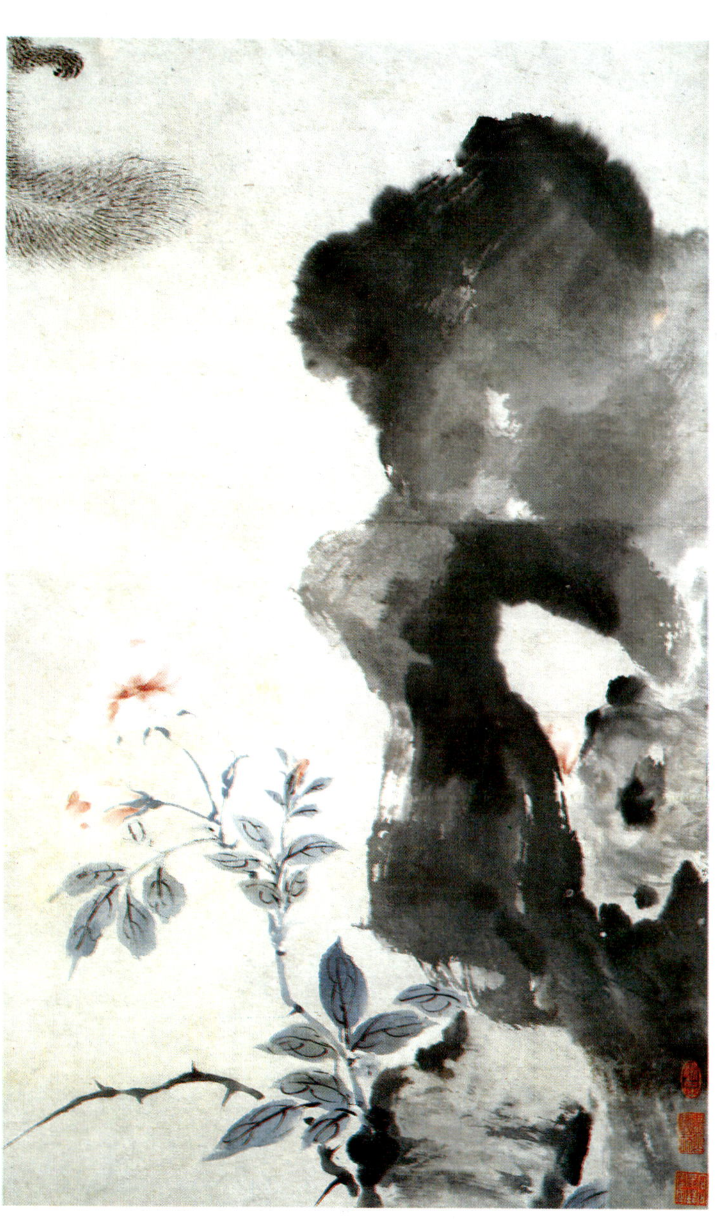

catalogue no. 71

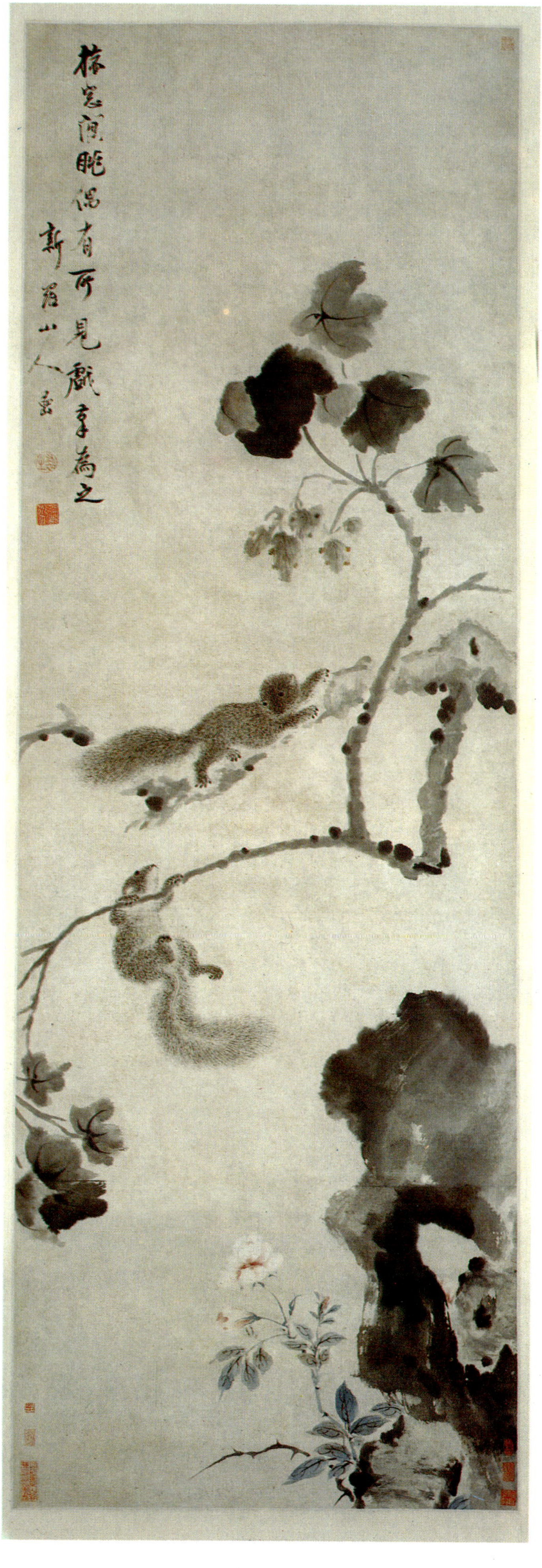

"Plum Blossom"
dated 1737 by Gao Fenghan (1683-1748)

Hanging scroll; ink and colour on paper. 83.9 x 40.9cm
Nanking Museum

The prunus (or blossoming plum), symbolising fortitude and rejuvenation, is depicted with great vigour and intensity. After surviving the cold winter, the prunus is one of the first trees to bloom in early spring, often before the last snow has melted. Even when apparently dead, it has the vitality to put forth new shoots and flowers each year. In this painting, new branches are represented shooting out of an old, broken stump and its claw-like roots. Sprouting from the brittle branches are clusters of exquisite white blossoms, which symbolise a kind of cool, pure beauty. The prunus and its misty surroundings appear almost scorched and charred with heavy, deep black ink. While a rugged, streaky brushwork expresses the enduring strength of the prunus, the feeling of rejuvenation is created by animated brushstrokes, fluttering and quivering with the subtle excitement of growing life.

The same shivering movement pervades the calligraphic inscription written in the cursive script, which becomes a part of the overall design of the painting. The characters are eccentric and appear slightly off-balanced. In the inscription, the indomitable human will and virtue are personified by the fortitude of the prunus that is strengthened by the harsh conditions of winter:
"Its fragrance comes from the
toughening experience [of cold winters].
Bitterly cold, emerging from layers of snow,
Piercing through a thousand **zhang** (approx. 3333m.) of ice.
Becoming as strong as a hundred **chi** (approx. 33cm.) of iron,
The indomitable will that survives the bitter cold winters
no cold wind can extinguish."
The inscription also tells us that the painting was done in winter, in the 12th lunar month of 1737, for a friend, who was highly respected for his stern integrity and high moral character.

Another inscription on the painting consists of the characters of "Virtues of a Recluse" written in seal characters; it was inscribed on the first day of the 12th lunar month.

Written with a nervous rhythm is a long piece of cursive calligraphy mounted above the painting on the same hanging scroll. It is actually a letter written to a close friend, as an accompaniment to the painting. In his letter, Gao relates how he and his friend, whom he had met only three or four times in Yangzhou, had reached the kind of empathy and understanding that their conversations just flow out, non-stop, and that they could simply bare their innermost thoughts and feelings to each others. He also tells us how when he fell ill while visiting Suzhou, he received the attention and care of his friend, in whose home he convalesced. In a quiet moment, he wrote this letter to accompany a small painting of blossoming plum, which he had painted with his left hand. He was hoping that his friend will keep the scroll as a witness to their strong and lasting friendship. He also tells his friend that the poem inscribed on the painting is not just conventional phrases praising the prunus, but is actually a portrait of his friend's character (i.e. his incorruptible virtues and high integrity).

Gao Fenghan was originally from Shandong province, but came to live in Yangzhou in about 1736. He passed the first degree (the **xiuzai** degree) in 1727 and was appointed to the position of a magistrate in Anhui province. But shortly afterwards, he was censured and sent away. As a result of severe rheumatism, he lost the control of his right arm, and started to paint and write with the left hand, which had a strong influence on the expressive and individualistic manner of his painting. He was occasionally numbered among the "Eight Eccentric Masters of Yangzhou".

The painting and calligraphy are signed by the artist and bear his seals.
Reproduced: **Nanking Museum Catalogue of Paintings,** vol. 2, p.90.

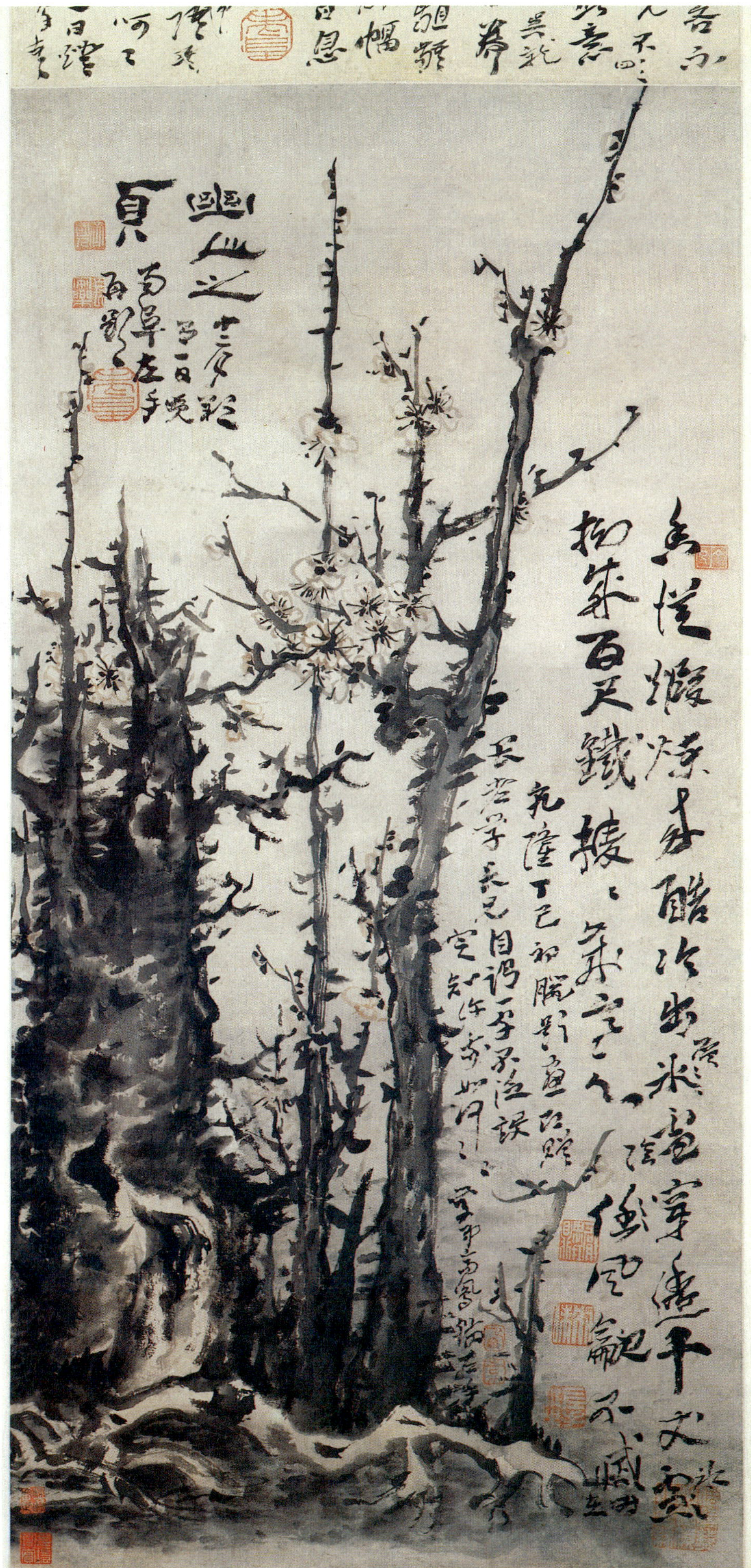

"Landscape"
by Gao Xiang (1688-1753)

3 album leaves; ink on paper, each leaf measures 28.5 x 38.8cm
Shanghai Museum

Leaf 1: "Village Dwellings in a Wintry Forest"
A child-like unassuming painting evocative of a quiet, dormant wintry landscape, is developed in a uniform brush manner. The snow-covered grassy knolls are depicted by a subtle repetition of a thin, dry brush line that resembles a drawing in soft pencil. The same brush line with a slight variation is used to draw the houses and the bare trees.

Reproduced: **Arts of China vol. 111: Paintings in Chinese Museums**, pl. 113.

Leaf 2: "Fishing Boat in Mountain Stream"
In this painting, the same brush manner has assumed an exuberant mood. A swirling movement of scribbly lines, resembling grass blowing in the wind, is suggestive of the irregular contours of a rocky outcrop. The impression of a waterfall is created with great subtlety. In the foreground, trees are depicted with the same quivering lines and clusters of vertical strokes which are repeated in the reeds on the edge of the river. The lonely fisherman and his boat are ingeniously described with a few simple lines. In a light-hearted, playful mood, the artist has shown great virtuosity in the handling of the brush.

The painting bears one seal of the artist.

Leaf 3: "Pavilions on the Bank of the Fan River"
Probably alluding to the style of Ni Zan, a quiet river landscape is depicted in a sparse, transparent manner; in the foreground are trees and pavilions on an island, and in the distance, rolling hills. The island is extended to the edge of the painting by the subtle touch of a bridge.

A slightly different brush manner has been used in this album leaf. The island in the foreground is sketched in a swift movement of long, relaxed, dry brushstrokes. Subtle motions in the trees are caught by short, animated brushes. In the distance, trees are simply repeated in horizontal strokes.

The painting has an inscription by the artist. Written in the archaic seal script are the words, "Lodging my feelings in the pavilions by the bank of the Fan river", which are followed by cursive writings in the following: "This phrase comes from my friend Ma Shejiang. Since it is in accord with the meaning of my painting, I inscribe it here". The inscription is followed by a seal of the artist.

Gao Xiang, a native of Yangzhou, is generally regarded as the ninth member of the Yangzhou group. He studied painting with Cheng Sui (active c. 1650-1680), who painted in a very dry manner. Gao was a personal friend of the Individualist painter Dao Ji (cat. no. 59) and also knew Jin Nong (cat. no. 80). He excelled in paintings of ink plum blossoms as well as landscapes.

Reproduced: **Shanghai Museum Catalogue of Paintings**, no. 88.

Leaf 1

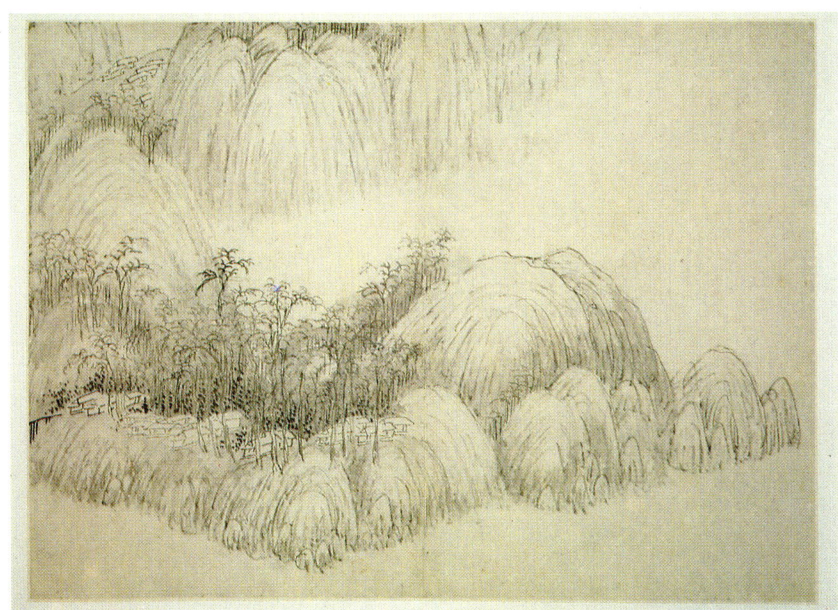

Leaf 2

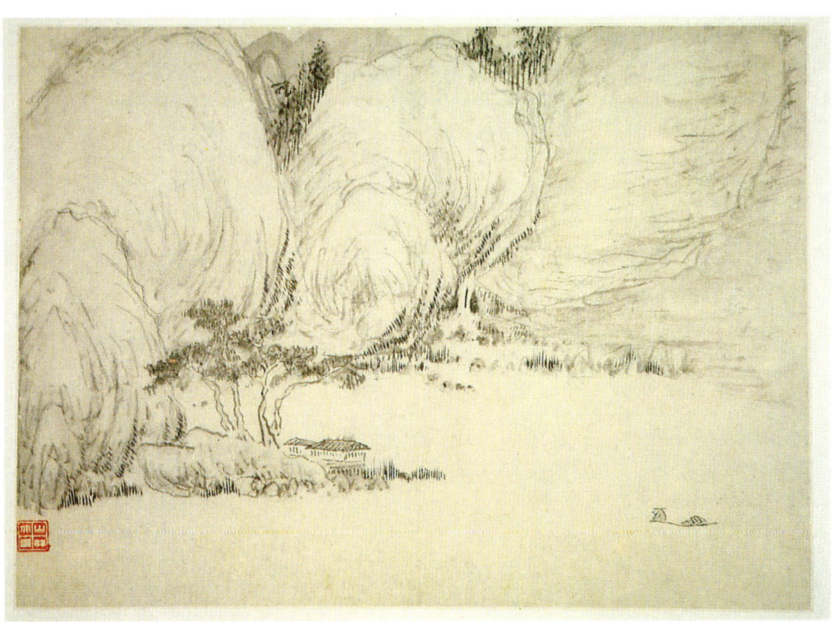

Leaf 3

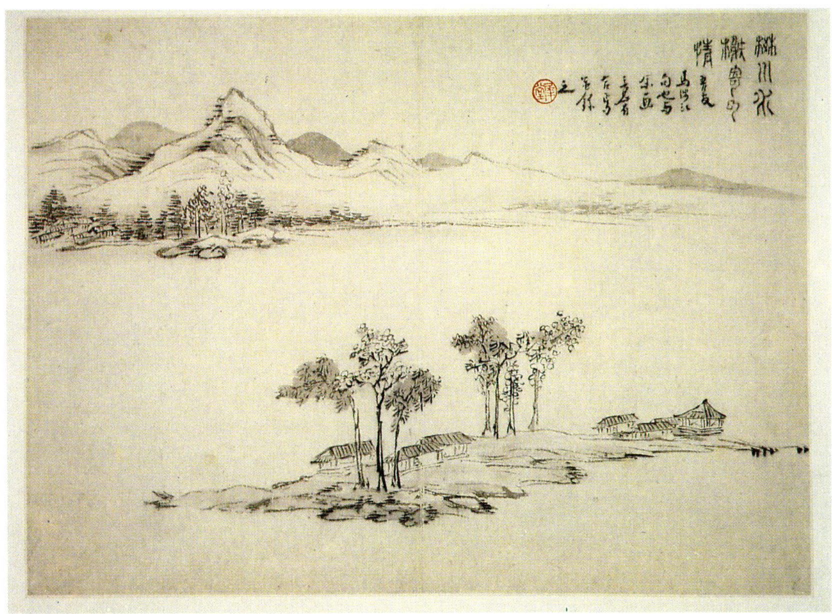

"Earthen Wall with Butterfly Orchids"
dated 1727 by Li Shan (1686-1762)

Hanging scroll; ink and colour on paper. 115 x 59.9cm
Nanking Museum

Perched lightly in the lichen and moss on top of an earthen wall are a group of blue butterfly orchids. The plants are delicately and naturally painted in light washes of blue that evoke a poetic mood. In contrast, the rammed earthen wall and the mosses are blotched with splashed, wet ink. A touch of brownish pink is applied on the earthen wall as well as on the leaves of the orchids.

As part of the compositional design, a calligraphic inscription in the running style occupies the upper part of the painting. In the inscription the artist tells us that this painting was inspired by a scene that he saw when he was travelling in Huzhou (present day Wuxing prefecture), Zhejiang province. He saw by chance a cluster of butterfly orchids growing on top of an earthen wall that enclosed a courtyard of spring flowers. The earthen wall, part of which had been washed away by heavy rainfall, and the butterfly orchids "appeared to have flown away together". This scene reminded him of scenery that he had seen in the Yangtze and Huai river regions during his former travels, where farmers are very fond of growing butterfly orchids on top of walls. When spring comes, the whole place is covered with orchids, like "purple clouds". Very quickly, he took hold of a brush and wrote down (i.e. sketched) this fleeting impression.

Li Shan came from Xinghua prefecture, Jiangsu province, the same locality as Zheng Xie (cat. no. 82) who became his close friend. When he was merely twenty-eight years old, he had already obtained both his first (**xiucai**) and second (**juren**) degrees. He studied painting with the famous bird and flower painter, Jiang Tingxi (1669-1732), who later became a high official in the imperial court, and was held in favour by the Kangxi Emperor. Probably through Jiang's influence, Li Shan became "painter in waiting" (**gongfeng**) at the court. There, he met the famous painter and high official, Gao Qipei (cat. no. 69), with whom he took up painting. Li was later involved in court intrigues and, as a result, he left Peking and went to Yangzhou in about 1725. He stayed in a monastery with his friends Zheng Xie (cat. no. 82) and Huang Shen (cat. no. 77), where they spent their time discussing painting and poetry. In Yangzhou, Li Shan became a famous painter, together with Jin Nong (cat. no. 80). Li was known for his paintings of flowers, birds, insects and at his best, paintings of orchids and bamboo.

The painting is signed by the artist, dating it to 1727, and bears seals of the artist.
Reproduced: **Nanking Museum Catalogue of Paintings** vol. 2, p. 97.

墨從夕賊作墻堆院
宇春光在此圍繞日
雨淋墻有缺蹺花和
土一齊飛去是莊
周夢裏身紫雲高
捲隔蒼苔奮半本
事住攔住盡良墻頭
玄趣人江滸楚人家土墻
頭喜植蝶花春來一片春
雲掩映一枝紅杏尋春
到五遠興遄飛天望酒帘
小愁頓忘歸去 雍正五年
中月湖州道中焦百此景
援筆寫之
懊儂袖人李鱓

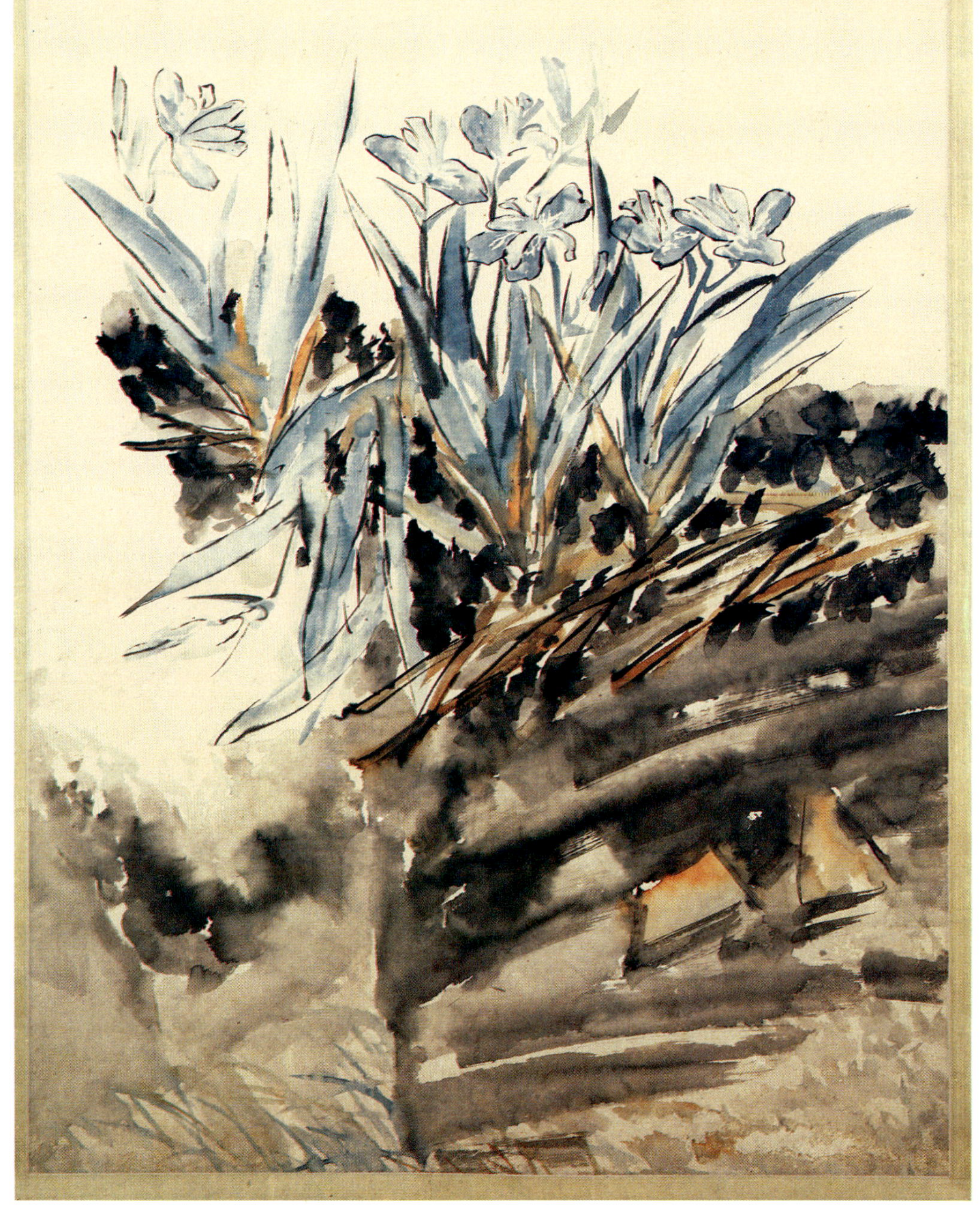

"Banana and Rock"
dated 1737 by Li Shan (1686-1762)

Hanging scroll; ink and colour on paper. 145 x 92cm
Nanking Museum

A dramatic banana palm is painted in bold, broad brushstrokes creating an ink pattern of strong tonal contrast, accented by swift calligraphic lines repeated in a backward-and-forward movement. The eccentric rock behind the palm is sketched in playful calligraphy; brisk, running and scribbly brushstrokes are applied over a subtle wash of light brown. Delicate day-lilies (**hemerocallis flava**) depicted with a few strokes in brown and light black ink, seem to be dancing in the air. The thin stem of the day-lilies is accomplished in a cursive line that moves in a fluent rhythm, following calligraphic rules of its own. Echoing the banana palm, the cluster of leaves of the day-lilies in the foreground is rendered in a rhythmic movement of calligraphic brushstrokes in deep black ink.

Li Shan's brush manner is described by Zhang Geng (1685-1760), a contemporary of Li, as "very free and quick, like a runaway horse, quite independent of all rules but nevertheless obtaining the effects of nature". A later critic, Qin Zuyong, writing in 1856, expressed a more critical opinion: "He was a man of considerable skill, but after all not quite satisfying, because his brushwork was reckless; he could not free himself from an air of vulgar audacity and traditional bad habits. In that kind of work only Jin Nong (cat. no. 80) reached the old masters. As to the others (of the Yangzhou group) they may have been wonderful, but they could not help being wild".

The painting is inscribed and signed by Li Shan dating it to 1737. It bears a seal of the artist.
Reproduced: **Nanking Museum Catalogue of Painting,** vol. 2, p. 96.

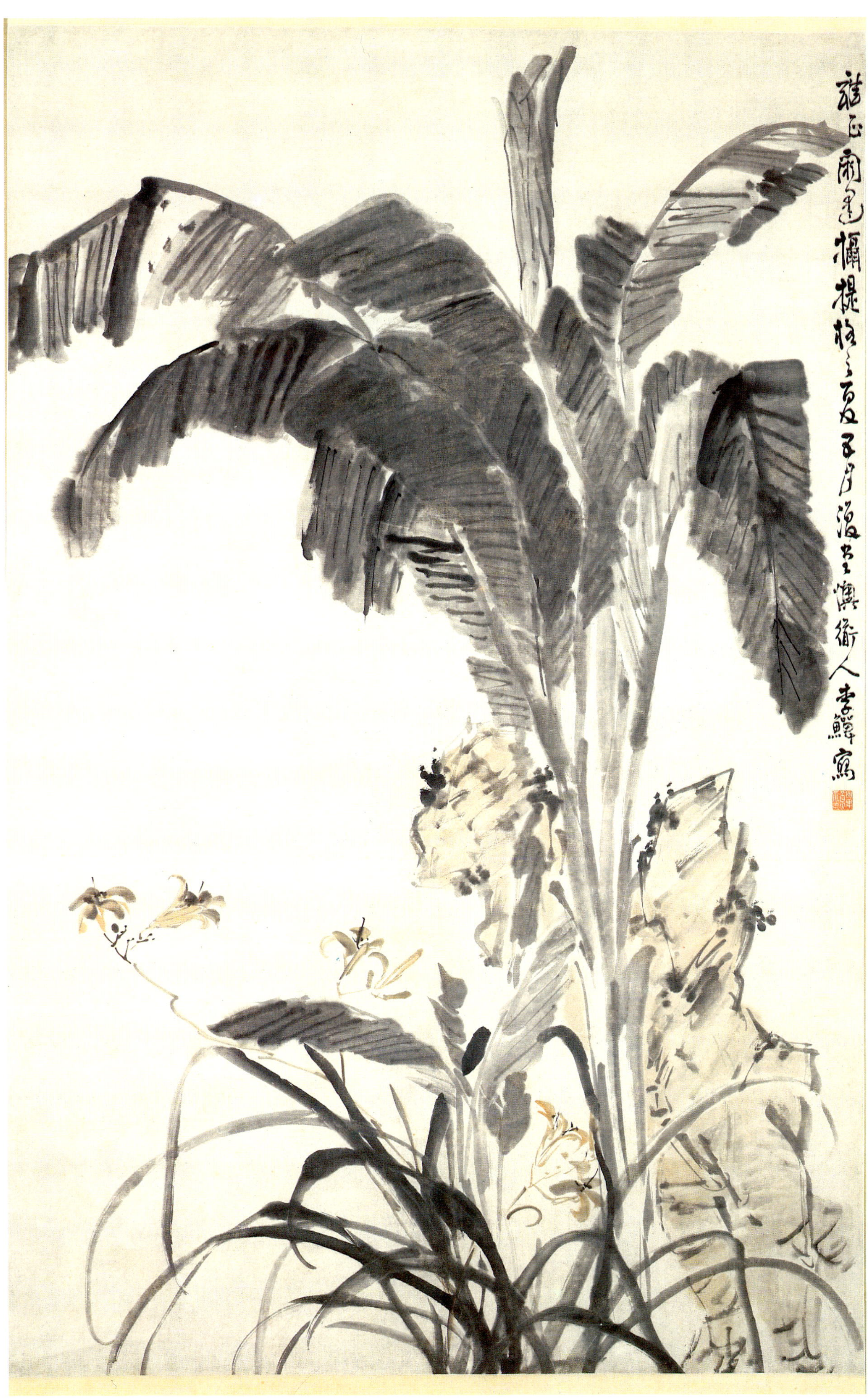
李鱓寫

"Treading on Snow and Looking for Plum Blossoms"
dated 1743 by Huang Shen (1687-1768)

Hanging scroll; colour and ink on silk. 167 x 95.8cm
Gugong Museum, Peking

In a snowy landscape, a scholar-traveller riding on a donkey is looking for plum blossoms, which flower in early spring, often before the last snow has melted. One of the servants is carrying a blossoming branch, while the other servant, a jar of wine. The sky is darkened by a light ink wash leaving the blank areas of the silk surface to convey the impression of snow. The feeling of cold wintry air is conveyed by the shivering posture of the servants and by the unhappy expression on the face of the donkey and by the wind-swept movements of the hat and beard of the scholar, who appears, however, comfortably warm. The scholar is portrayed with a well-rounded face with regular features. But one of the servants is caricatured with sharp, angular, bony features, and dressed in tattered clothes.

Besides the human interest created by the genre elements discussed above, the painting has also a calligraphic interest. The drapery folds of the servants and snow-covered landscape elements (i.e. rocks, bamboos, mountain cliffs and the contorted pine tree) are translated into swift, vigorous, brush movements that resemble the running and cursive scripts of calligraphy. The rhythmic movements of the brush are not only form-defining and descriptive of the objects depicted, but also constitute their very mass and substance. Such a brilliant brushwork performance by Huang Shen reveals technical training and discipline in both the representational skill of drawing and the mastery of calligraphy.

Huang Shen was a native of Fujian province. His father died when he was very young. After studying painting with a minor local painter of Fujian province, he took up painting to make a living and to support his widowed mother. As a conservative and popular artist, Huang specialized in figure painting, including genre subjects, but was also proficient in flowers and insects, as well as landscapes. The biographer of Huang Shen recounts how, when he turned eighteen, his mother showed concern that he would become nothing more than an artisan painter, and urged him to further his studies. She said to him with tears in her eyes: "You are doing this to earn your living, but I have heard that without immersing oneself in books and acquiring the spirit of a scholar, one can only reach the skill of an artisan; that would not enable you to distinguish yourself and comfort the departed spirit of your father". Huang Shen then began studying poetry and calligraphy in a Buddhist temple at night, using the light from lamps placed before the Buddhist statues. He then travelled to various parts of China and in 1727 settled in Yangzhou, where he met such scholar-painters as the famous Zheng Xie (cat. no. 82), Jin Nong (cat. no. 80), and Li Shan (cat. no. 75). From them, Huang acquired some of their taste and style of painting. In order to be taken seriously, he had to emulate the scholar-amateur painters; his technical training in painting became a liability. As one of the "Eight Eccentric Masters of Yangzhou", Huang Shen was known to excel in the three perfections of the scholar-artist, painting, poetry, and calligraphy.

The painting is inscribed and signed by Huang Shen, dating it to 1743. It bears seals of the artist.

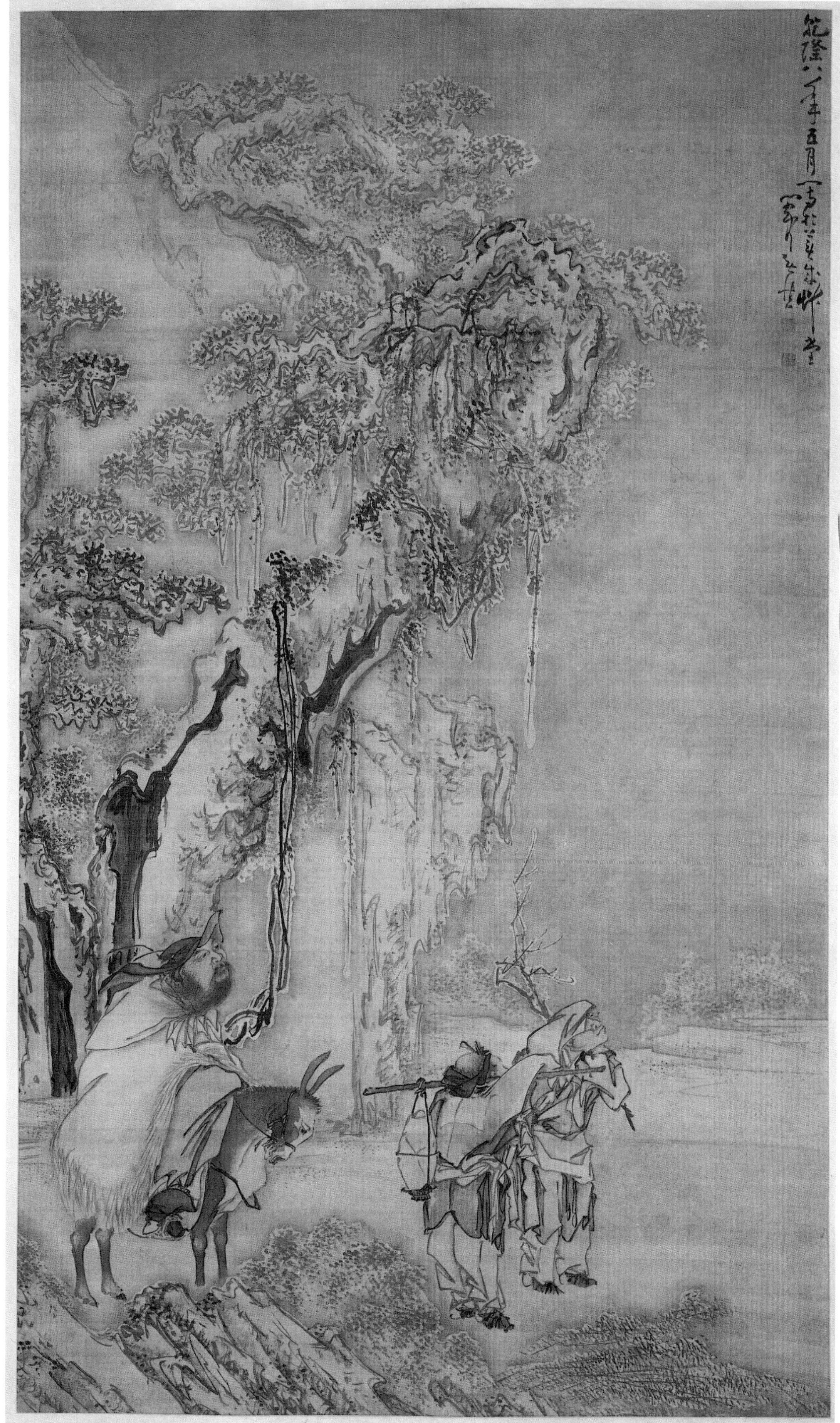

乾隆八十年五月

"Two Album Leaves"
by Huang Shen (1687-1768)

Each leaf measures: 29 x 25.3cm
Shanghai Museum

Leaf One: "Pomegranate", ink and colour on paper

In this album leaf, the three perfections of painting, poetry, and calligraphy, that are generally associated with the accomplishments of a cultivated gentleman, are integrated into an artistic whole. The branch of pomegranate and the poetic inscription written in cursive calligraphy are composed into a harmonious design. Calligraphy and painting are almost interchangeable in the sense that there are calligraphic elements in the painting and pictorial elements in the calligraphy. The pomegranate is simply suggested by a few broad, form-defining washes in light colour and ink. Its branches and leaves are quickly sketched in calligraphic brushstrokes. The characters in the inscription, which are exaggerated and abbreviated with a deliberate awkwardness, are composed into an abstract design. The couplet in the inscription, which according to Huang Shen quotes from works by Xu Wei (cat. no. 31), translates as follows:

"In the deep mountain and late autumn, no one comes to pick [the pomegranate];
Jumping out of their own accord, the bright pearls [i.e. seeds] are hitting
the sparrows.
A couplet from Xi Wenzhang [Xu Wei]".

The painting is signed by the artist and bear his seals.
Reproduced: **Shanghai Museum Catalogue of Paintings**, no. 84.

Leaf Two: "Calligraphy", ink on paper

The text is written rapidly in the cursive script of calligraphy. The brushwork is fluent and rhythmic and the turning strokes round and smooth. The pressure of the brush is relatively even. Highly simplified and abbreviated, the characters are barely legible; some are linked into continuous brush movements. Punctuated by interrupting pauses and gaps, the characters appear broken up, united by a scattering rhythm.

The calligraphy is followed by two seals of the artist.

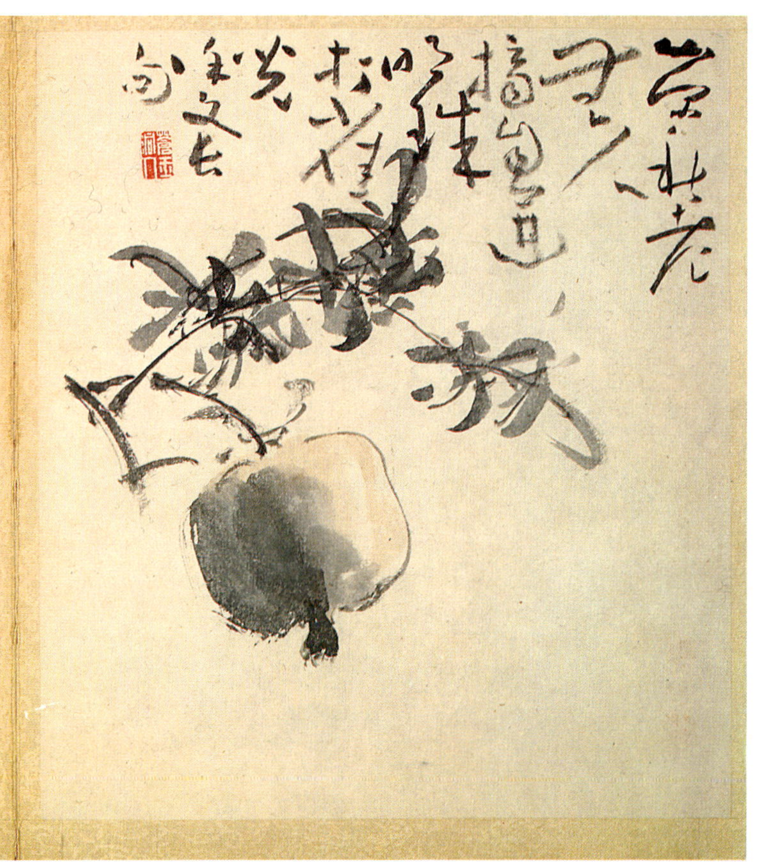

"Plum Blossom and Bamboo"
dated 1741 by Wang Shishen (1686-after 1762)

Hanging scroll; ink on paper. 86.5 x 30cm
Gugong Museum, Peking.

An attractive painting of plum blossoms, bamboo, and rock is painted with a soft and sensitive brush. Growing next to the rock are bamboos and a prunus tree which is partly cut off by the edge of the painting. Brushing gently against the bamboo are plum blossoms extending from the top of the painting. The stem and branches of the prunus are painted in wet ink with a fluctuating outline, and taper into thread-like thinness with a needle sharpness; they seem to be extremely delicate and fragile. Attenuated and bending at sharp angles, the meandering and quivering branches are interlaced into an elegant pattern, defining abstract empty areas. Completing the compositional design is a poetic inscription complementing the painting:
"With diluted ink, [I] sketch [lit. write] the outline of the cold
fragrance [i.e. plum blossom].
Like brothers the bamboo and rock are both free of restraint.
You may laugh at me for having nothing to do and simply growing old.
With the ink stone in the north and blossoms in the south, my quiet
pleasure is long and lasting".
Wang Shishen was originally from Anhui province. He moved to live in Yangzhou, where he made a living from his painting and calligraphy. Specialising in branches of blossoming plums and other flower and plant subjects, he gained his recognition as one of the Yangzhou masters. He made friends with the other scholar-amateur artists of Yangzhou including Jin Nong (cat. no. 80), Gao Xiang (cat. no. 74), and Hua Yan (cat. no. 71). In his old age, he became almost completely blind, but continued to paint with the remaining dim vision of his right eye.

The painting is signed by the artist and dated to 1741. It bears three seals of the artist.

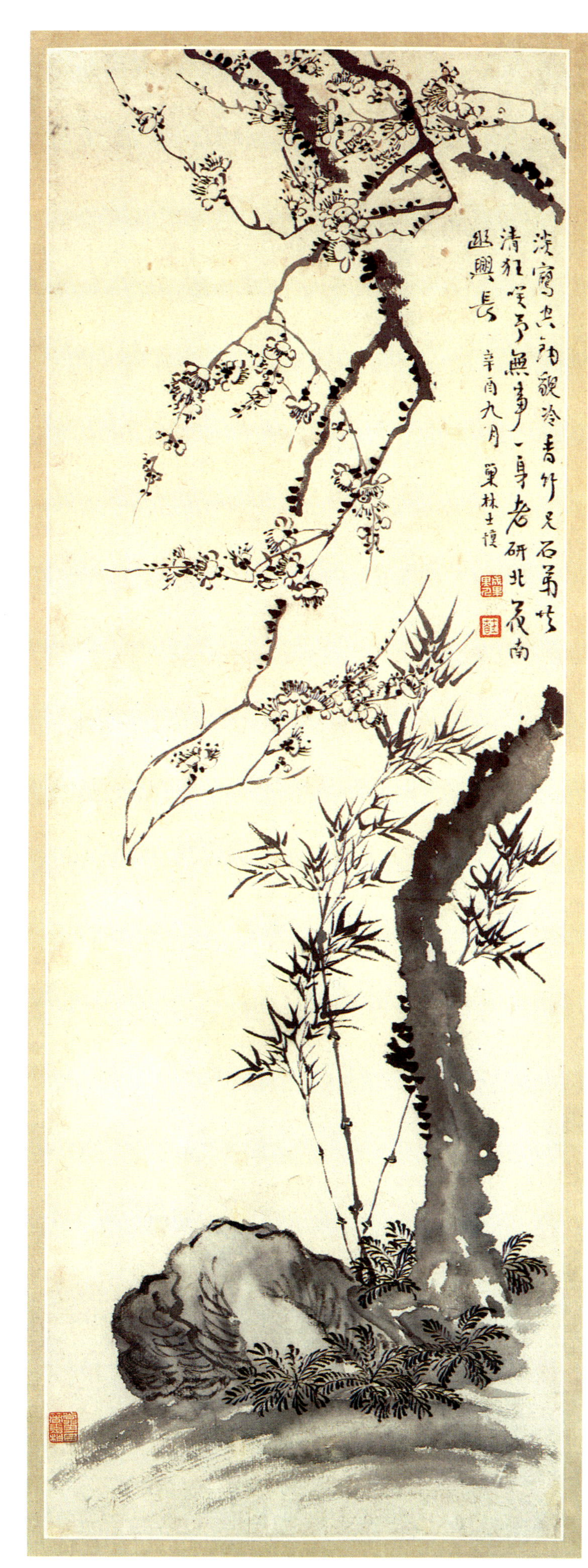

淡寫兼鶴冷香竹足石弟妹
清狂笑予無事一身老研北居南
幽興長　辛酉九月　翼林士楨

"Flowers and Plants"
dated 1761 by Jin Nong (1687-1763)

Album leaves; ink and colour paper, each leaf measures: 24.2 x 30.5cm
Liaoning Provincial Museum

Leaf One: "Red Bamboos"

The bamboos are painted in the simple manner of colour wash and ink outline that is evocative of the early method of painting as well as the style of a woodblock print. They are also rendered with a certain degree of freshness and originality; the very idea of painting bamboos in red (or pink) instead of black ink, for example, is refreshing. Moreover, the execution of the painting shows great sensitivity. The pink wash is subtly modulated in both intensity and tonal value. In some passages, the delicate ink-outline suffuses softly into the colour wash. The quiet delineation of the bamboo is free from the virtuoso brush performance (i.e. swift calligraphic brushstrokes) seen in paintings of some of the Yangzhou masters such as Gao Xiang (cat. no. 74), Li Shan (cat. no. 76), and Huang Shen (cat. no. 77).

Creating a great deal of artistic interest is the poetic inscription written in a distinct and individualistic manner of calligraphy. This unique style is based on the "standard" and the archaic "clerical" scripts of calligraphy, as well as on the stone-cut inscriptions of the Jin period (265-420). Square and blocklike, each individual character is a self-contained, structural unit. Written in deep black ink and hard-edged even lines, the characters are impressive as strong calligraphic images. As if chiselled out of stone, the even brushstroke begins with a slanted "cut" into the paper and ends with a slight upward hook. The characters are also infused with a deliberate child-like simplicity and awkwardness, which is manifested, for example, in their irregular size; some of them appear a little off-balance, with the right component raised slightly higher than the left. But all these are calculated with an innate sense of order and discipline to create a dynamic and individual quality.

The couplet in the inscription which refers to the red bamboos reads as follows:
"It is found only in [such regions] the Min [Fujian province]
and Yue [Guangdong province],
But not in other places".

The painting is signed by the artist and bears his seal.

Leaf Two: "Loquats"

Branches bearing loquats are softly painted in diluted ink and pale colours, in contrast to the sharp, clear-cut inscription in deep black ink. The inscription is written in the same "archaic standard" style of calligraphy as in leaf one. In the painting and in the calligraphy, Jin Nong emulates a child's drawing and writing, in cultivating a deliberate awkwardness. The loquat branches, leaves and fruits are rendered in flat washes of ink and colour with simple outlines. There is very little attempt to use shading and texturing. The branches turn at contrived and awkward angles. Under the appearance of awkwardness and blandness, there is a real sense of sophistication and refinement in the subtle use of colour and form. Cool, watery colours of pink and blue are merely suggested. Pale washes and outlines in blue and ink depicting the leaves are very sensitively modulated. Portrayed with a great simplicity of form, the pictorial images are superbly balanced. Finally, accenting the painting and relating it to the calligraphy are the deep black dots on the round loquats.

The accompanying inscription translates as follows:
"Enjoying the peach and plum blossoms that are everywhere,
With a thousand coins, we bought wines without credit.
Who is dragging a staff made from wisteria.
To come to look at the wild loquats
by the house of a monk?"

The painting is signed by the artist and bears his seal.

Leaf 1

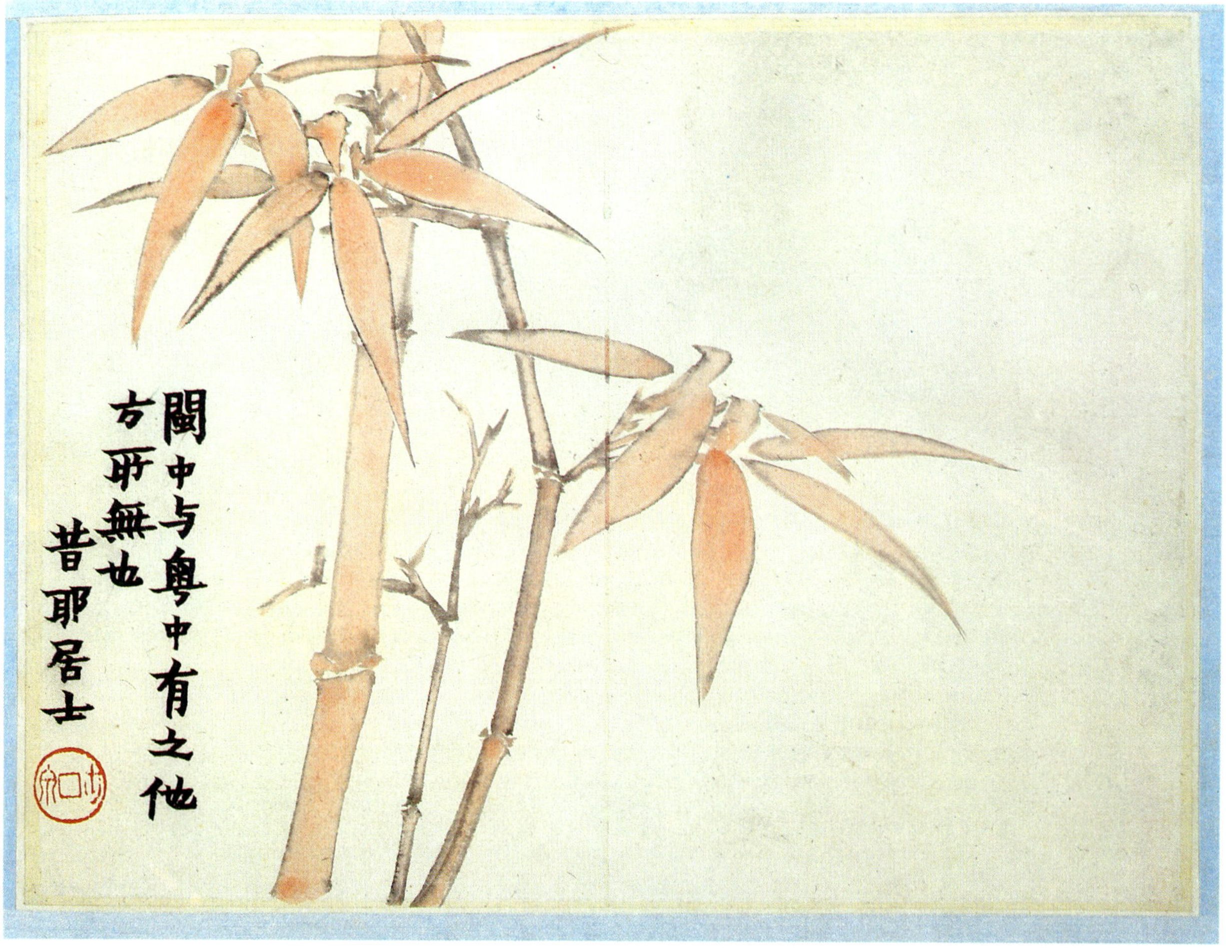

閩中与粵中有之他
方所無也
昔耶居士

Leaf 2

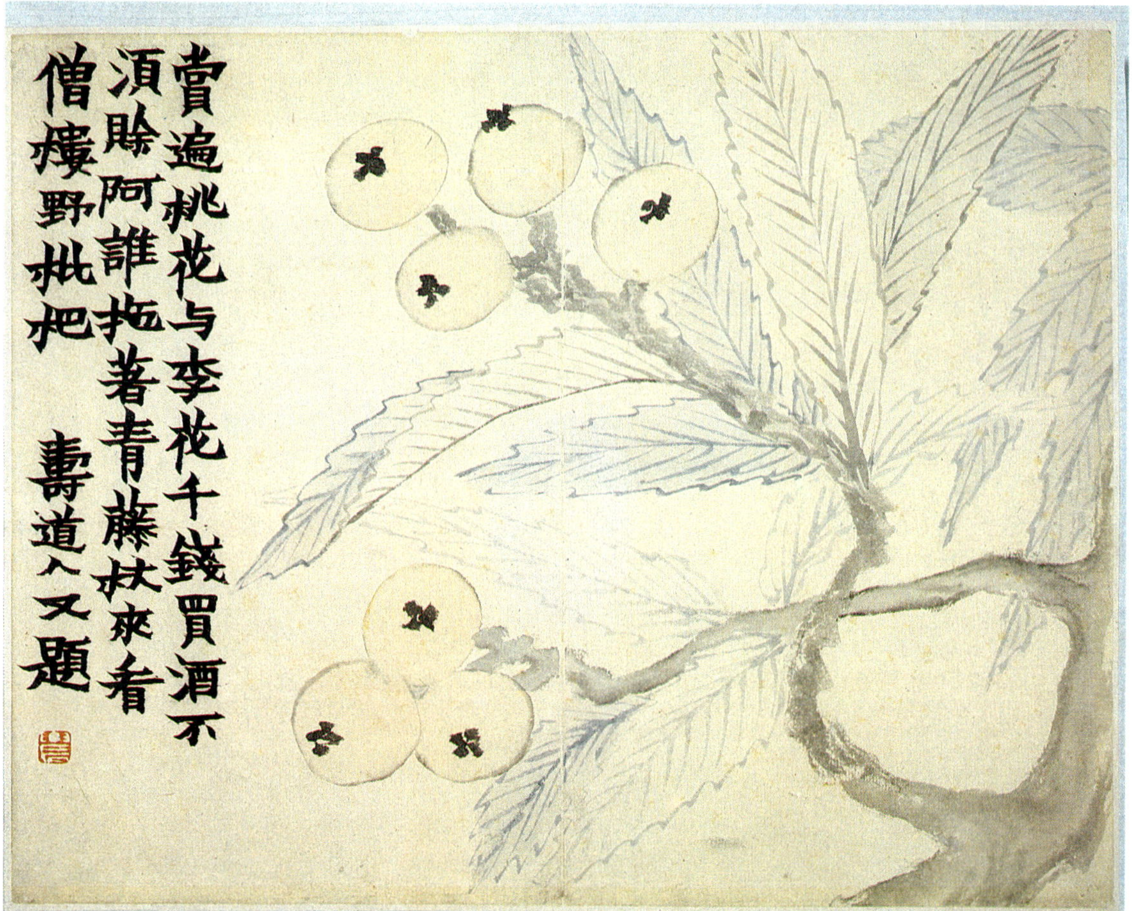

賞遍桃花与李花千錢買酒不
須賒阿誰拖著青藤杖來看
僧瘦野枇杷　壽道人又題

catalogue no. 80 continued

Leaf Three: "Butterfly Orchids"

Jing Nong has conceived a very original and eccentric painting. Dominating the composition is a full-blown butterfly orchid, painted in modulated washes of cool colours, pale blue and pink. The flower has a strange feminine beauty that is sensuous, delicate, and fragile. In contrast, the steel-blue leaves are portrayed with blade-like sharpness which thrust skywards. In their strong definitive outlines the leaves themselves resemble the brushstrokes of the characters. Like the characters, the plant is awkwardly balanced and held in tension. It is anchored by the curious, coral-like pitted rock in the background. The design of the painting is softened by the ground cover plants and strengthened by the calligraphy.

Commenting on the painting, the inscription says:
"Wild flower and small plants,
One finds such scenery in the garden of the Shen family.
Recorded by the seventy-five year old man, Jin Nong".

The inscription is followed by a seal of the artist.
Reproduced: **Arts of China vol. 111: Paintings in Chinese Museums**, pl. 24.

Jin Nong was born in Hangzhou, Zhejiang province and came from a gentry family which had declined during the Qing dynasty (1644-1911). He was well learned, accomplished in poetry and calligraphy. A connoisseur of art, he studied paintings of the ancient masters, and collected ink stones and rubbings of inscriptions on ancient bronzes and stone tablets. He did not take up painting seriously until late in life, after the age of fifty, and was probably self-taught for the most part. This was about the same time that he failed the examination for an advanced degree and gave up all hope of becoming an official. In his middle age, he travelled widely, and after the death of his wife, settled in Yangzhou in 1748. He lived in a Buddhist monastery and made a modest living from his professional career as an artist. Among the Yangzhou masters, Jin Nong was probably the most original and innovative. He was also the most influential, and was highly respected for both his erudition and innovation. As illustrated in these album leaves, Jin Nong pays homage to the scholar-artist's ideal of "amateurism".

catalogue no. 81

"Plum Blossom"
dated 1761 by Jin Nong (1687-1763)

Hanging scroll; ink and colour on silk. 130.8 x 42.2cm
Nanking Museum

A blossoming prunus tree is executed in the "boneless" (**mogu**) method of ink painting. With great mastery, Jin Nong painted the tree trunk with one broad brushstroke of ink wash without any linear definition. Undulating branches of plum blossoms caress the tree trunk, with white flowers dancing like snow. Accenting the painting are three columns of calligraphy in the "archaic standard" script.

In his inscription, Jin Nong tells us that this painting was inspired by a painting of plum blossoms that he had seen fifty years earlier and that he painted it at the age of seventy-five. The inscription is followed by the artist's seal.

Reproduced: **Nanking Museum Catalogue of Paintings**, vol. 2, p. 94.
Yiyuan Duoying, no. 5 (1979), p. 31.

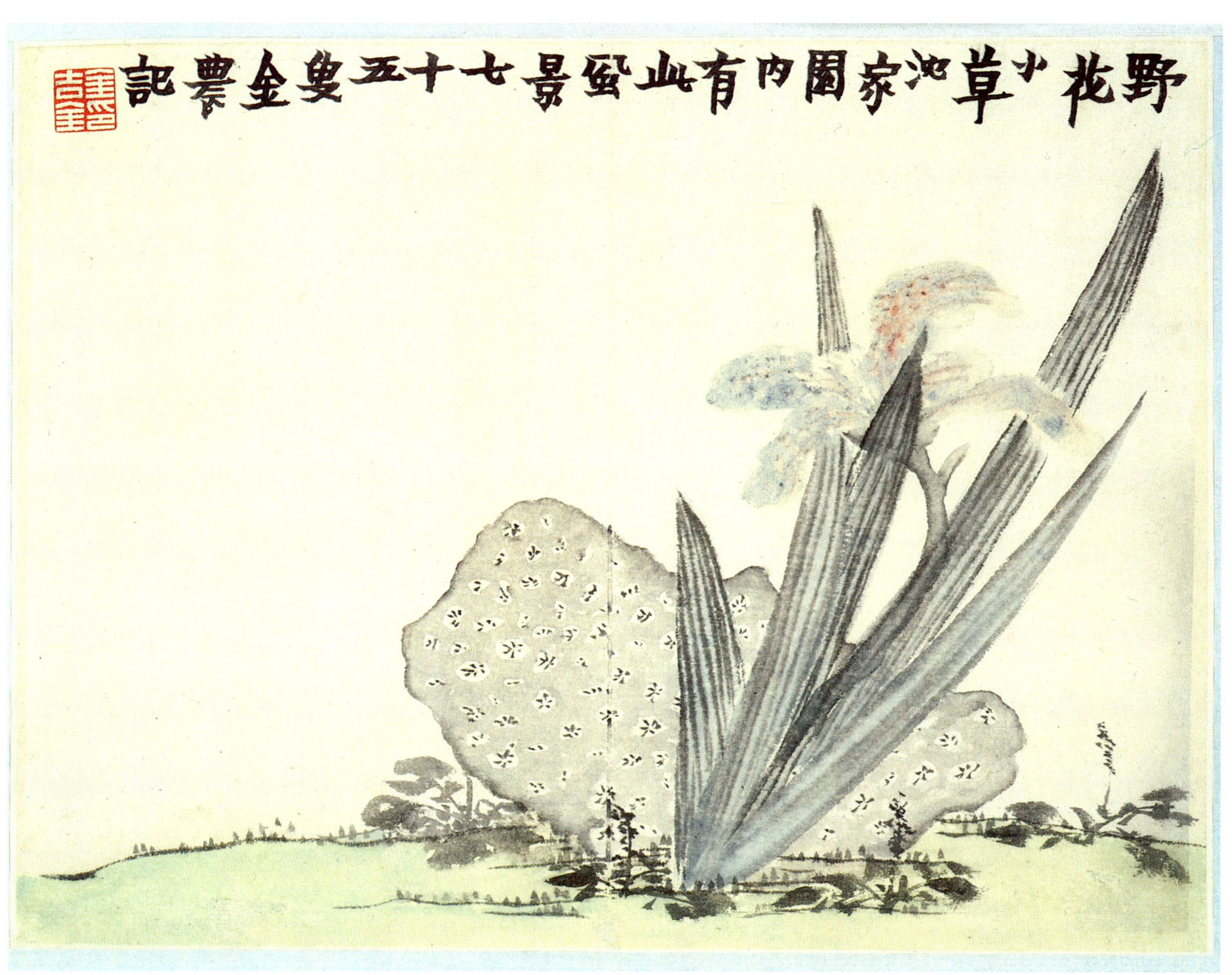

Leaf 3, cat. no. 80

catalogue no. 82

"Twin Pines"
dated 1758 by Zheng Xie (1693-1765)

Hanging scroll; ink on paper. 201.5 x 102cm
Shandong Provincial Cultural Relics Bureau

Two sturdy pine trees with twisting branches and dense clusters of luxuriant needles are depicted with strong calligraphic brushstrokes. The pine at the back painted in lighter ink tones not only creates a feeling of depth but also gives a sense of greater importance to the tree in front. Accompanying the pines are elegant bamboos rendered in beautiful brushstrokes.

In his inscription, Zheng Xie tells us that he painted this for an old friend whom he met in 1737, more than twenty years previously. He used the tree as a metaphor to describe his friend. The pine, which "does not compete with the other trees by flowering in the spring and summer" and "does not shed its leaves in the autumn and winter", is used to symbolize the admirable qualities of sincerity, vigour, steadfastness, and constancy. Zheng also comments how he found his friend remaining the same, when he met him again ten years after the first meeting. In another meeting three years later, his friend was still the same. Zheng Xie also tells us that the painting was done to commemorate the long lasting friendship between himself and his friend. Apparently, the two pines represent the two friends. Also according to the inscription, the bamboos were added to accompany the pines and to represent their many descendants, as nature's way of rewarding men for their virtues.

Zheng Xie combines the four major types of calligraphic scripts in his inscription: the archaic "clerical" (**li**), "standard" (**kai**), "running" (**xing**), and "cursive" (**cao**) scripts. With the different styles alternating throughout the inscription and the characters varying in size, speed, movement, and ink value, the abstract pictorial potential of calligraphy is fully explored. The horizontal and the flaring brushstrokes of the "clerical" style are emphasised. Some of the characters written in the "cursive"script are abbreviated and linked together. Probably referring to its irregular and unpredictable nature, Zheng's distinct style of calligraphy is commonly described as resembling "straying stones covering the streets". Some people called his style **Li-cao** ("the cursive style of the clerical script"). Zheng himself named it as "six-and-one-half tenths" (**liu-fen-ban-shu**), meaning six-and-one-half tenths of the "clerical"style.

Zheng Xie was known for his poetry, calligraphy, and paintings of bamboo and epidendrum He was a native of Xinghua near Yangzhou. Zheng received his education from his father who was a school teacher. In the Kangxi period (1662-1723) when barely twenty-two years old, he obtained his first degree, the **xiucai** degree. He then obtained the second (**juren**) degree in the following Yongzheng period (1723-1736), and the highest (**jinshi**) degree in the Qianlong period (1736-1796). He spent some time serving as district magistrate in Shandong province. He later retired to Yangzhou, and made his living on painting, although retaining in principle his amateur status. His painting and calligraphy were highly sought after. When he was too busy to meet the great demand, he posted on his door the prices for his work, which were established according to their size, adding: "Gifts and foods are not as good as cash, since what you give me might not necessarily be what I like. If you present cold, hard cash, then my heart swells with joy and everything I write or paint is excellent. Presents tend to get us all tangled up, and buying on credit, I fear, might end up not paying at all. In my old age when I get tired very easily, I cannot accompany you gentlemen in making useless talk…Even if you talk of old friendships and past companions, they are only taken as spring breeze blowing past my ear".What Zheng Xie says here would probably have shocked and horrified the scholar-amateur artists of the past centuries, who would never have openly sold their work but would have only given them away as presents, which were then reciprocated with gifts. But in 18th century Yangzhou, this was probably accepted as a form of eccentricity.

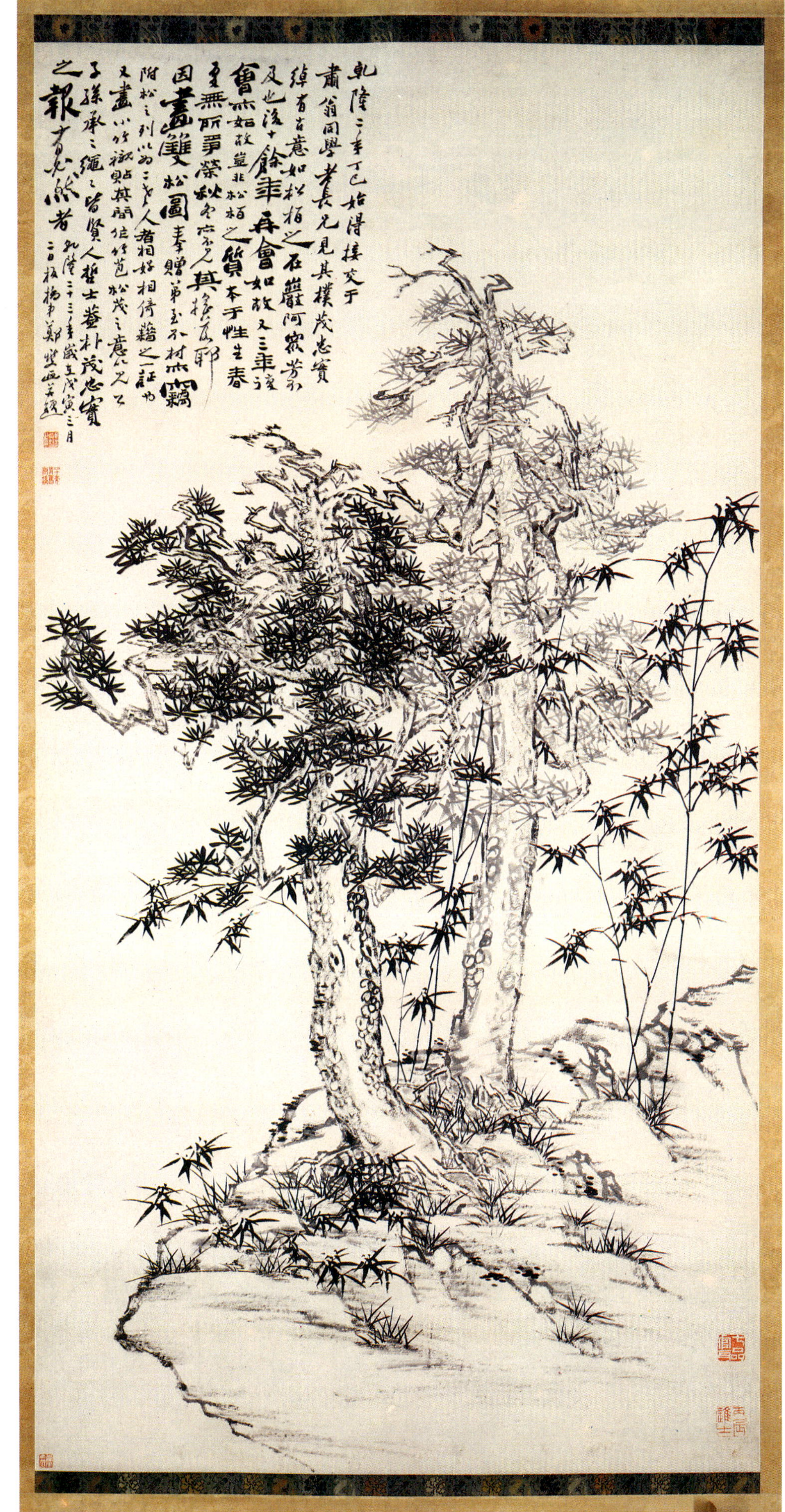

乾隆二年丁巳始得接交于
肅翁同學老長兄見其樸茂忠實
緯者古意如松柏之在巖阿眾芳菲
及此後十餘年再會如故又三年
會然如故豈非松柏之質本于性生生春
竟無所爭榮秋冬之茂其操履不改耶
因畫雙松圖奉贈弟玉不樹無隙
附松之列以為三公人者相好相倚藉之一証也
又畫小竹數枝貼其間使竹范松茂之意亦見之矣
子孫承之繩之當賢人哲士鑒朴茂忠實
之報方興未艾然者
乾隆二十三年歲在戊寅三月
板橋鄭燮畫并題

"Bamboo and Rock"
dated 1751 by Li Fangying (1695-1755)

Hanging scroll; ink on paper. 168 x 67.5cm
Nanking Museum

Growing beside an eccentric rock are bamboos caught in the wind. The bamboos are painted with clearly contrasting tones of dark and light ink. The lighter bamboos in silvery grey stand behind those in deep black ink, creating a shadowy and misty effect. The sweeping movement of wind is ingeniously evoked by the seemingly effortless configuration of thrusting, blunt strokes of bamboo leaves. The lyrical movements of the branches are echoed by the rock and grass, and stabilized by the sturdy stems, drawn in thick, even brushstrokes. Some of the leaves are stretching and extending themselves, conveying emotions of nostalgia and longing.

Also stabilizing the painting as part of the compositional design is the calligraphic inscription, which enlightens the viewer on the meaning of the painting:
"Painters have never [attempted to] depict the wind.
[But] I have undertaken the task to rival the skill of heaven.
If you look at this small painting of bamboos from Xiaoxiang [a river in Hunan province],
Your ears will be filled with the tinkering sounds of ten thousand hollow jades".

Thus, in the inscription the artist tells that he is portraying the wind and the rustling sounds of bamboo, which resemble the musical sounds of jade chimes.

Of all plants, bamboo was loved the most by the cultivated Chinese. It symbolized human virtues; the resilient stalk of the bamboo which bends with the wind but does not break, symbolised flexibility and inner strength. Ink-monochrome painting of bamboo became a favourite theme of the scholar-amateur artists, which was mostly due to its close affinity to calligraphy in brushwork and abstract design.

Li Fangying came from Tongzhou, Jiangsu province. He obtained his first (**xiucai**) degree when he was barely twenty, and served in several official posts, including one as District Magistrate in Hefei, Anhui province. He then retired to Yangzhou, where he had to sell his paintings to support himself and died there in 1754 as a poor man. He was regarded as one of the Yangzhou masters and excelled in the paintings of pine trees, bamboos, epidendrums and chrysanthemums.

This painting was signed and inscribed by Li stating that it was painted in Hefei in 1751.

It bears three seals of the artist.
Reproduced: **Nanking Museum Catalogue of Paintings,** vol. 2, p. 101.

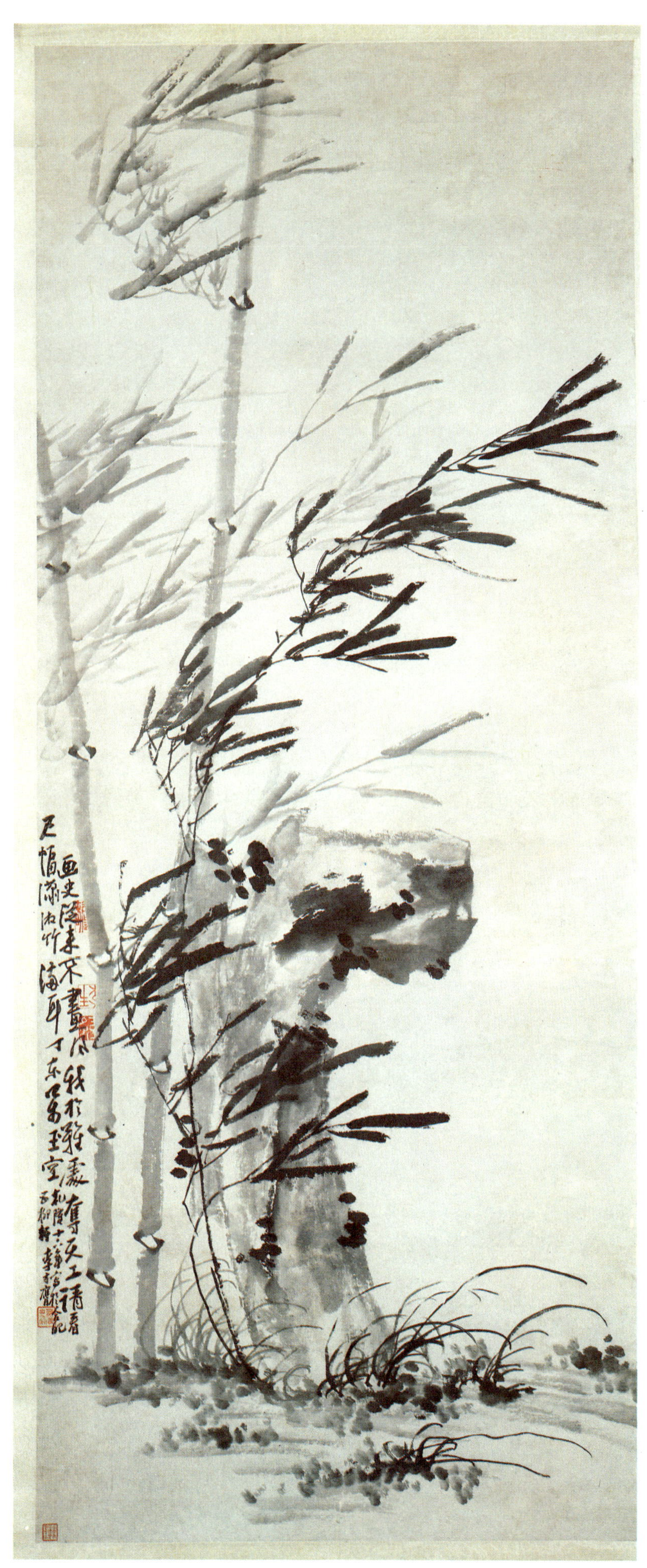
畫史隱來未畫竹
我於雜毫奪得天工請看
尺幅瀟湘竹海耳丁東寫至空

"Bamboo"
by Luo Pin (1733-1799)

Hanging scroll; ink on paper. 174 x 50.2cm
Gugong Museum, Peking

Silhouetting sharply against the paper surface are strong patterns of bamboos painted in deep black ink and rising from behind a rocky cliff. The bamboos are luxuriant with thick clusters. Abstract patterns of empty space are created by the interweaving movements of the leaves. Forceful and dynamic brushstrokes of spiky leaves express strong, powerful feelings. This reminds one of what a painter of the Yuan dynasty (1279-1368) is reported to have said about painting bamboo when he was angry, because the bamboo, "with its leaves sticking out like spears", is suited to the expression of anger. Finally, expressing the mood of the artist whilst executing this painting is his calligraphic inscription written on the surface of the wall-like cliff:
"I likewise wildly scribble the bamboos,
Fluttering the ink into (bamboo) tips.
But I cannot make use of the malachite green,
To draw minutely a parrot's feather".
What Luo Pin is saying here is that he painted the bamboo with ink in the free and spontaneous **xieyi** manner (a method associated with scholar-amateur painting), and that he could not paint with colour in the careful and meticulous **gongbi** manner (a technique employed in court academic and professional paintings).
Luo Pin was the youngest of the "Eccentric Masters of Yangzhou" and the last survivor of this major school in Chinese painting. He was born in Xiexian, Anhui province, but seems to have settled, while still young, in Yangzhou where he studied painting with Jin Nong (cat. no. 80). Compared to his master, he was technically more accomplished and versatile. What he learned from Jin Nong was probably his aesthetic ideas and taste. Regarded as Jin's artistic heir, Luo Pin became one of Yangzhou's most popular painters. Reflecting one of his eccentricities, Luo painted pictures of ghosts and claimed that he could actually see them.

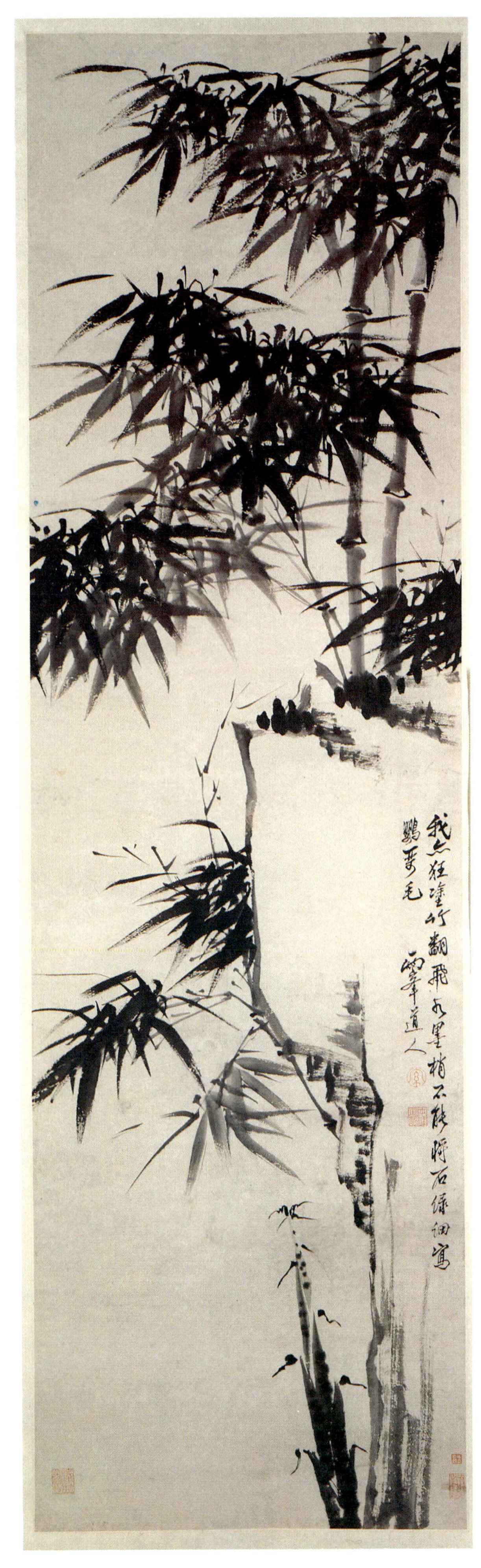

我亦狂塗竹翻飛五墨梢不能將石綠細寫
鸚䴉毛
雪峰道人

"Reeds and Wild Geese"
by Bian Shoumin (active c. 1725-1747)

Hanging scroll; ink and colour on paper. 85.4 x 34.9cm
Gugong Museum, Peking

In the foreground of a marshland, a goose is perched near the reeds while another goose is caught tumbling in mid-air. The geese are painted with even washes of ink. The reeds in the foreground are depicted in a few simple calligraphic brushstrokes. Rows of short, vertical strokes create the impression of recession in space.

Bian Shoumin came from Huaian, Jiangsu province. He was a professional painter and well known as a painter of geese.

The painting is signed by the artist and bears his seal. Above the painting on the same hanging scroll is an inscription written by Shen Zongqian (c. 1780-1794) in 1783, commenting on Bian Shoumin's painting of geese.

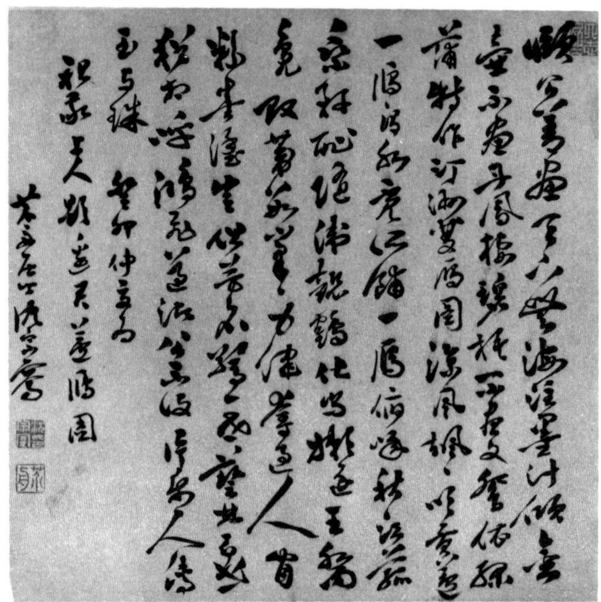

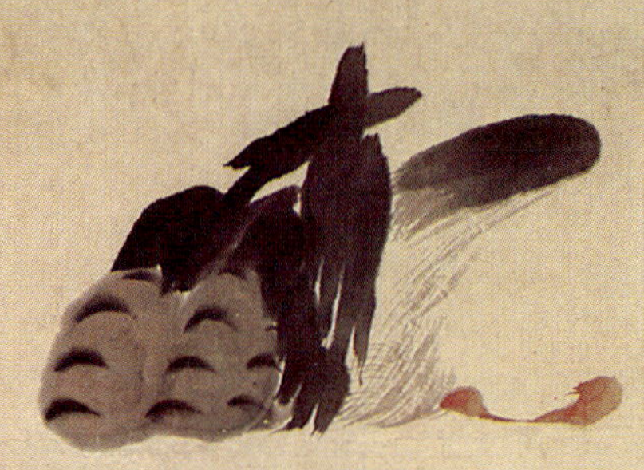

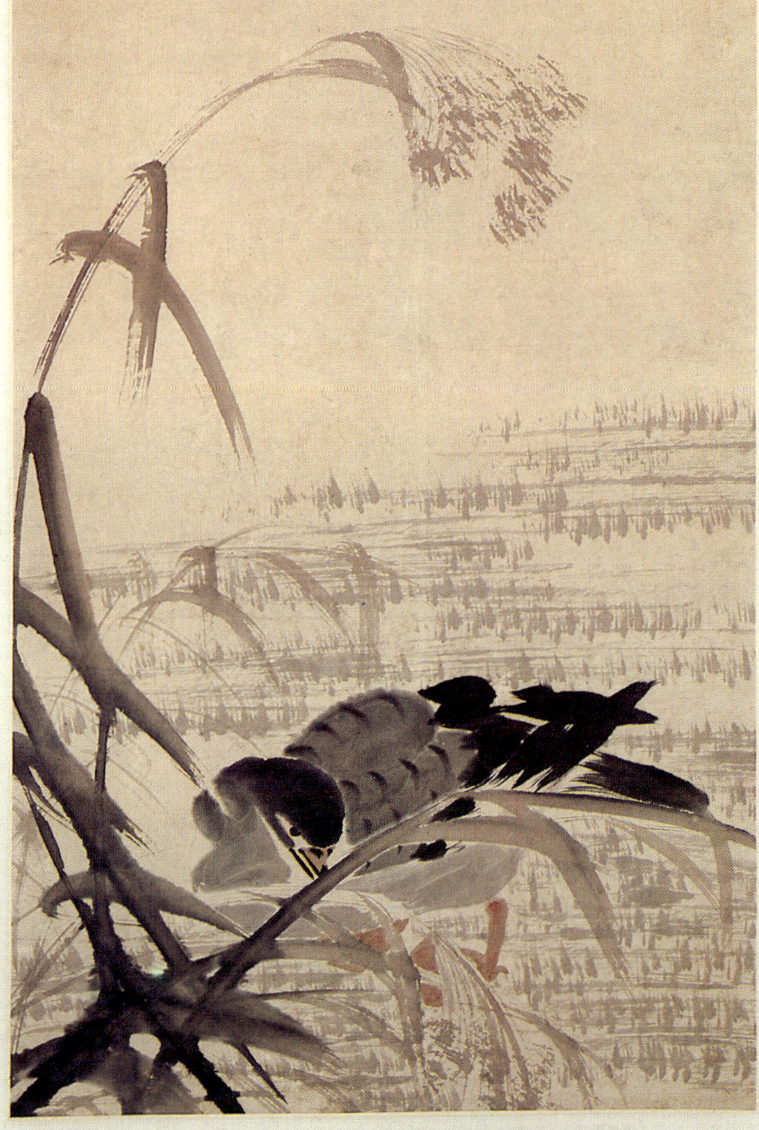
聲閒壽民

"Poetic Thoughts"
dated 1825 by Gai Qi (1774-1829)

Hanging scroll; ink and colour on paper. 99.3 x 32cm
Gugong Museum, Peking

A female figure is represented sitting in an eccentric chair and holding a book in her left hand. She is depicted in the traditional outline-and-colour manner that can be traced to the style of Qiu Ying (cat. no. 24) and even back to figure paintings of the Song (960-1279) and Tang (618-906) periods. The colours of red, blue, and turquoise blue are brilliant. The woman displays no individual characteristics but conforms to the ideal of feminine beauty current at the time. She is portrayed with a delicate oval face, narrow eyes and a small mouth, expressing a slight feeling of melancholy. Her hair is soft and cloud-like. Typifying the 19th century ideal of female beauty, she is willowy, with scarcely a suggestion of bodily form underneath her loose draperies. Her very qualities of appearing languid and helpless were found to be captivating.

Gai Qi was from Songjiang, Kiangsu province. He was educated but did not pursue official careers. Instead, he became a popular commercial artist in Shanghai, specialising in pictures of beautiful women.

The painting is inscribed by the artist, dating it to 1825 and telling us that it was painted in the poetic conception of the works of Yuanji. The inscription is followed by a seal of the artist. Commenting on the painting is a long colophon written by Shen Wu in 1871. Shen tells us that the female figure represents the poetess, Yu Yuanji of the Tang dynasty (618-906), a collection of whose poems has survived.

"The Seventh Day of the Seventh Moon"
by Fei Danxu (1802-1850)

Hanging scroll; ink and colour on paper. 120 x 52cm
Gugong Museum, Peking

The popular legend of the cowherd and the spinning-maid is depicted. There are differing versions of this legend. According to one of them, the cowherd (**Altair**) and the spinning-maid (**Vega**) were constellations. They were married when they visited the earth, and became so happy that they forgot their work when they returned to heaven. This angered the Emperor of Heaven, who decided to separate them so that they would continue their work. They were then ordered to live on either side of the Milky Way and were allowed to meet each other only once a year, on the seventh day of the seventh moon. On that evening, magpies from all over the world formed a bridge across the river in heaven so that the two lovers could meet.

Surrounded by stylised clouds, the cowherd is looking up at the spinning-maid floating with fluttering draperies. Both figures are painted with delicate outlines and soft colour washes. As in the painting by Gai Qi (cat. no. 86), the spinning-maid represents the then current idealisation of female beauty.

Fei Danxu was a native of Wu Cheng, Zhejiang province. Together with Gai Qi, he was one of the most popular commercial artists specializing in the genre of beautiful women.

The painting is signed by Fei Danxu and bears one of his seals.

"Wang Xizhi Watching Geese"
dated 1890 by Ren Bonian (1840-1896)

Hanging scroll; ink and colours on paper. 136 x 66.9cm
Gugong Museum, Peking

The 4th century scholar Wang Xizhi was the supreme master of the cursive or 'grass' script style of calligraphy and thereby gained an almost legendary status in literary circles. The popular theme of Wang watching geese derives from the inspiration he is known to have received from natural forms; in particular it is said that he solved some of the technical problems of rendering calligraphic line by studying the graceful movements of geese. Perhaps the most famous of such paintings is Qian Xuan's (Yuan dynasty) handscroll version now in the Metropolitan Museum of Art, New York. The inspiration of nature was of course a paramount theme to successive generations of Chinese painters, embodying as it does the literati ideal. Even in the late 19th century Ren Bonian adopted this archaic, but still pertinent, theme from this painting.

The master Wang is standing on a narrow bridge quietly observing the geese floating beneath beside a cluster of bamboo. Wang's attendant lounges peacefully on the bamboo handrail of the bridge. There is such tranquility and quiet concentration that one is acutely aware of the oblivion to the world beyond that the two figures are enjoying. Ren's strong sense of calligraphic line is well illustrated in the drawing of the figures, the robes and the geese. The brushstrokes are decisive, expressive, but subtle and forgiving. Even the heavier dark washes of the bamboo seem light and breezy.

Born in Zhejiang province Ren Bonian moved to Shanghai where he rapidly attained status as the most influential figure in the then dominant Shanghai school of painting, having originally served as an apprentice in a fan-painting workshop. Among the many anecdotes about Ren Bonian perhaps the most infamous describes how he met the master Ren Xiung (1820-1864). The younger Ren was studying painting by the time-honoured tradition of copying the popular and established masters and was, apparently, caught adding Ren Xiung's signature to one of his own works. Out of curiosity the elder Ren visited the younger 'forger' but so impressed was he that he immediately forgave him and accepted the young Ren as his pupil.

Ren Bonian's work displays a freshness and refreshing ease in the lack of traditional restraint, and yet there is still a poetic beauty to his figures. His popularity as a figure painter was greatly enhanced by his ability to represent even the most prosaic and down-to-earth subjects with the lyrical grace so evident in this painting. Wang Xizhi watching geese is one of the oldest recurring themes in the history of Chinese painting and yet it is rendered here with a distinctive contemporary flavour without any loss of poignancy. Ren Bonian illustrates the same capacity to combine a fresh naturalistic approach with the facility for updating traditional styles and techniques in his less well-known bird and flower paintings (see cat. no. 89).

Signed and dated in the inscription and seals of the artist.

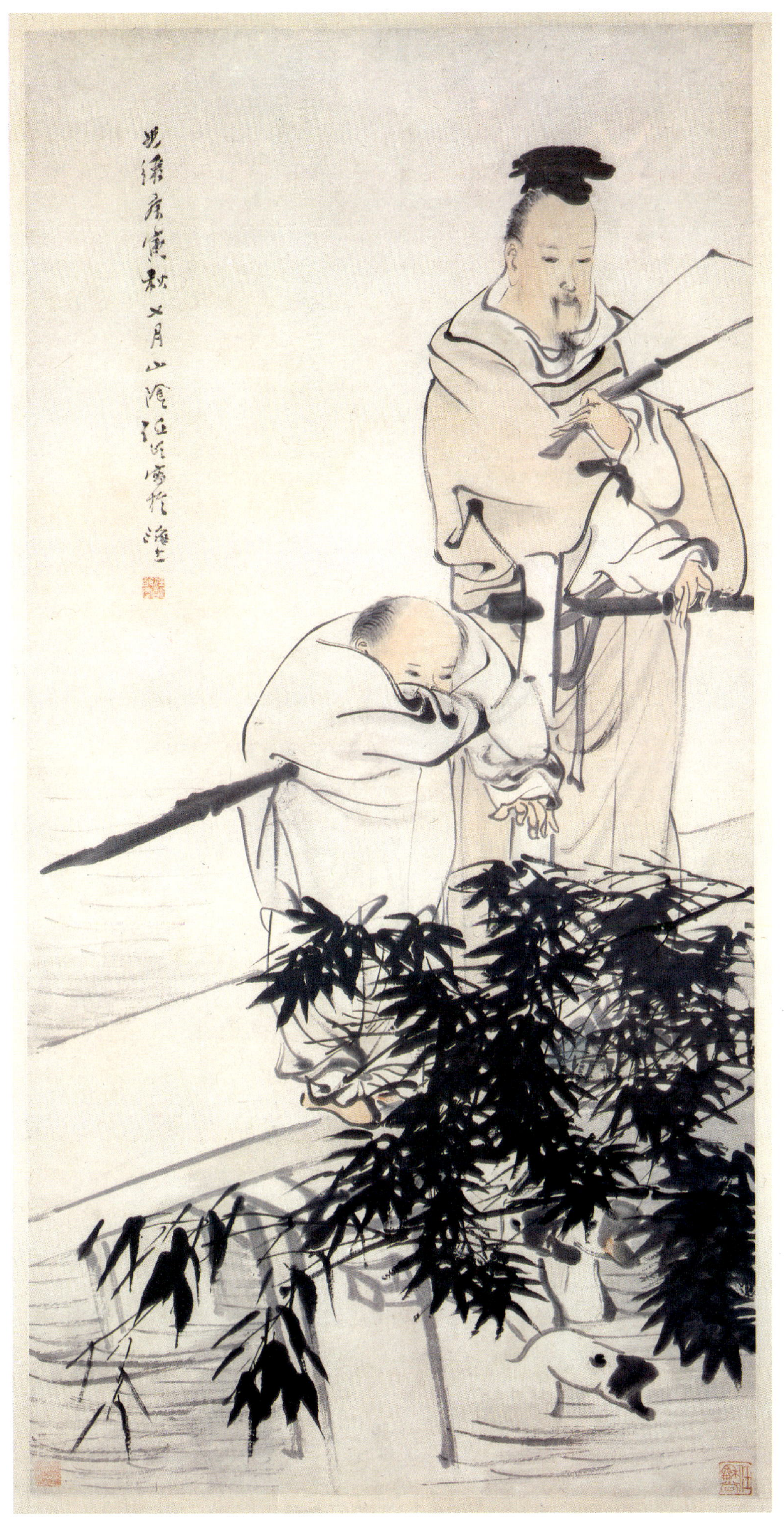
兆環庚寅秋七月山陰任頤寫於海上

"Birds and Flowers"
dated 1878 by Ren Bonian (1840-1896)

Four album leaves; ink and colours on paper, each leaf measures: 33.7 x 38.5cm
Zhenjiang City Museum

Leaf 1: "Flowering Peach"
Branches of a flowering peach tree twists from behind a rock on which is perched a colourful bird. Signed and dated in the inscription and with the seal 'Nian'.

Leaf 2: "Wisteria and Cockatoo"
A branch of blooming wisteria is suspended into the picture and from the branch hanging, in an eccentric if not entirely unnatural pose, is a cockatoo. Signed in the inscription and with the seal 'Nian'.

Leaf 3: "Swimming Duck"
A wild duck swims peacefully, but with a certain awareness, past reeds and lotus leaves which oddly cut across the image of the duck. The broad wet washes of the water seem absorbed by the paper as they gradually dissolve into the background. Signed 'Bonian' and with the seal 'Nian'.

Leaf 4: "Peach and Bird"
The branch of a fruit-bearing peach tree reaches across from a cliff face. On one of the branches is perched a small colourful bird. Signed in the inscription and with the seal 'Nian'.

Each leaf is painted entirely without the linear definition so much a feature of "Wang Xizhi Watching Geese". The sensitive colour and ink washes in the 'boneless' manner employed in these four leaves provide for an intimate immediacy and a lively, often fugitive, image.

For biographical notes see the entry for catalogue number 88.

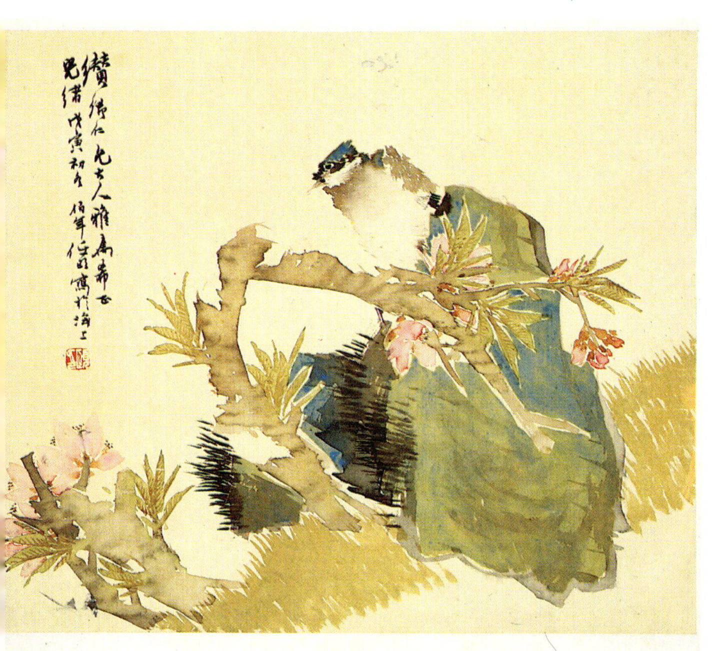

Leaf 1

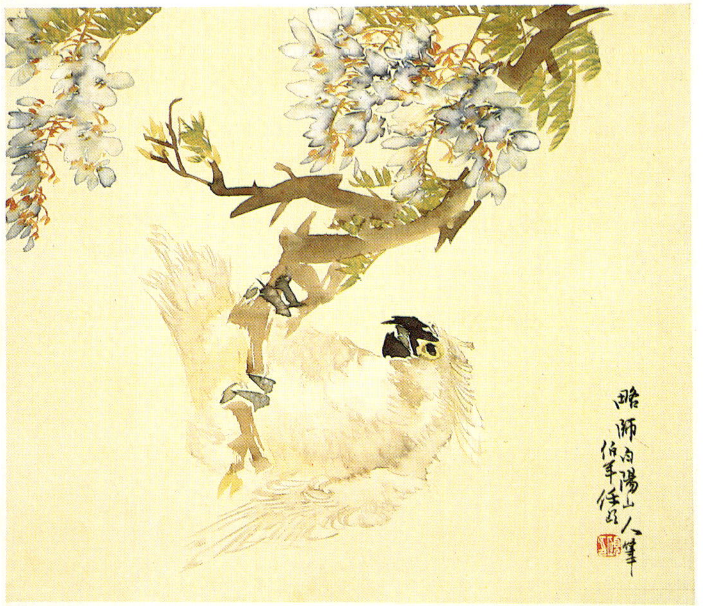

Leaf 2

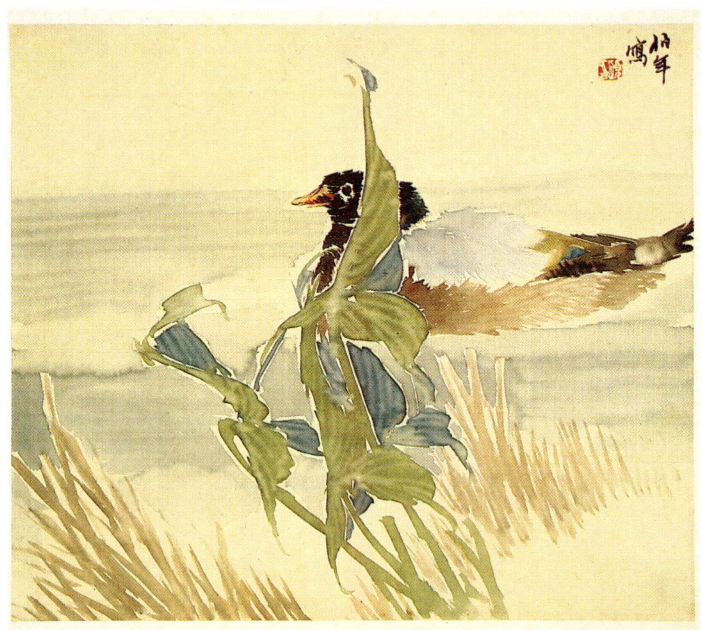

Leaf 3

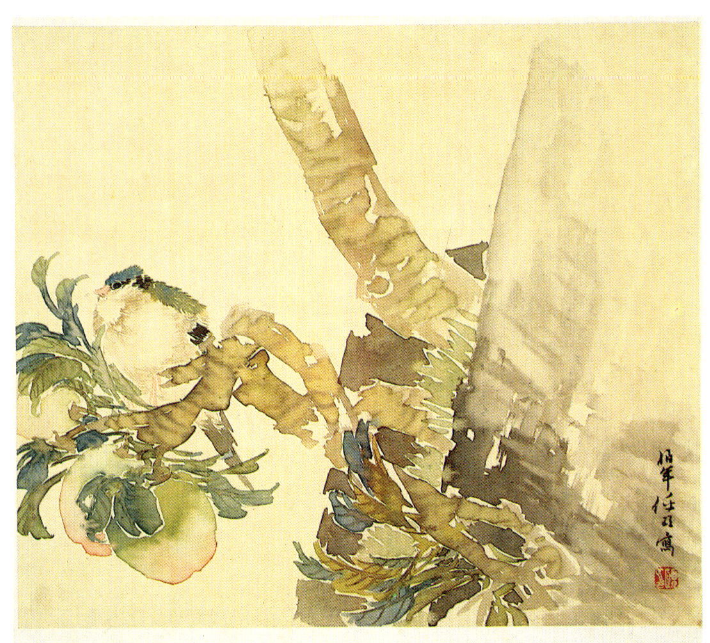

Leaf 4

catalogue no. 90

"Plum Blossom"
dated 1884 by Zhao Zhiqian (1829-1884)

Hanging scroll; ink and light colours on gold-flecked paper. 133.9 x 67cm
Gugong Museum, Peking

The traditional theme of the flowering plum tree, heralding the new Spring, is given an extraordinary vitality and robustness in this painting by Zhao Zhiqian. The trunk of the tree is rendered with ink and colour washes but outlined with brief, abrupt horizontal strokes producing a staccato effect that is both bold and aggressive. Similarly the branches, painted with a dense black ink brush, are given a harsh and abrasive quality by the abbreviated horizontal strokes. Although continuing in the literati tradition, the choice of subject too reflects this interest, Zhao's florid and emphatic style strikes a distinctly modern note. Zhao was at the centre of a small group of painters who in the mid 19th century rejected the strong traditionalist tendencies then current to seek fresh modes of expression. Like their **wenren** predecessors these painters found that means of individual expression in the use of brush and ink. Zhao's plum blossom is very much the work of an individual; it is full of agitation and restlessness, of emotion and anguish, whilst the sombre colouring evokes an unsettling melancholy. In discussing the work of Zhao and his contemporaries Takeyoshi Tsuruta identifies in their work "...a sense of dark hopelessness about the conditions of their time...If suffering is one condition of modern painting, we can say that modern Chinese painting begins with Zhao Zhiqian".

Zhao was born in Zheijiang province, and although he failed the examination for entry into official service in Peking, he obtained a provincial degree and was appointed a magistrate. Subsequently he went to Shanghai where he became a renowned poet, painter and calligrapher. In his day Zhao was probably more famous as a calligrapher than he was as a painter. In particular he was recognised as the master of the **jinshi** style – based on the robust calligraphy manner employed in engraving on stone and bronze. As a painter, Zhao's profoundly expressive style had its roots in the works of the Yangzhou Eccentrics and, in particular, Li Shan (see cat. nos. 75 and 76), whilst the pervasive gloom and threatening power of his paintings reflect the conditions of social and political turmoil that China was experiencing in the middle and later 19th century. It should be noted that this scroll was painted in the last year of his life.

Signed and dated in the inscription and seal of the artist.

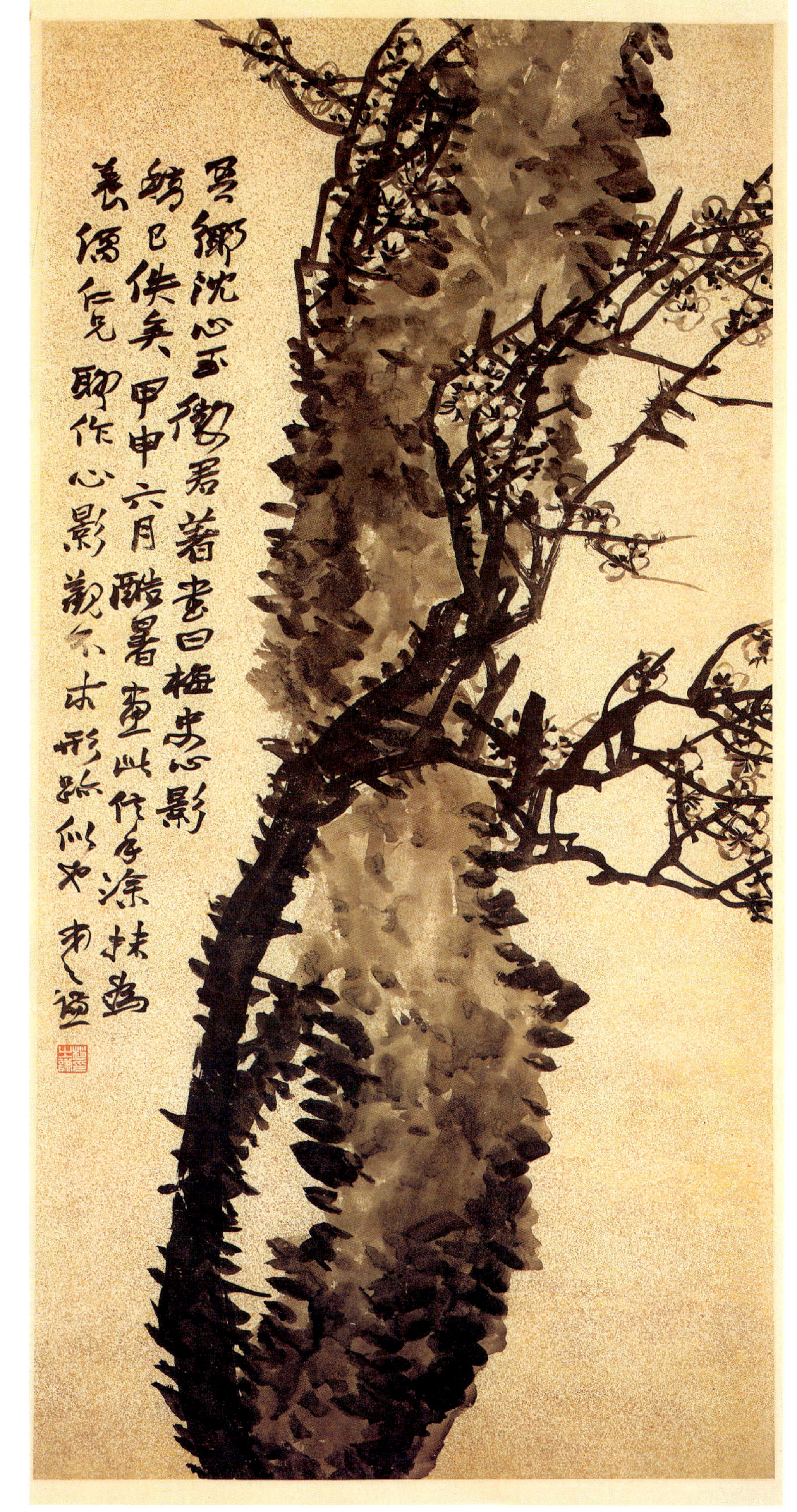

吾鄉沈心玉
衡君著雪日梅花心影
妙巳供矣、甲申六月酷暑畫此作手涂抹為
羲偶仁兄聊作心影觀不求形孤似也 虫逸

"The Jishu (Pile of Books) Cliff"
by Zhao Zhiqian (1829-1884)

Hanging scroll; ink and colours on paper. 69 x 35.3 cm
Shanghai Museum

The location of the Jishu Cliff is unknown, however, the peculiar rock structure clearly inspired Zhao to produce a painting with a touch of humour. Hidden within the busy and fragmented cliff face is a small hollow in which are placed neatly stacked piles of books echoing the complex stratification of the rocks. The subject is well suited to Zhao's active calligraphic style of brushwork and, although far less sombre than "Plum Blossom" there is the same concern for expression, vitality and movement in the busy brushwork. The general restlessness and energy of the painting is matched in the easily flowing lines of the rippling waters.

A brief inscription records that the painting was commissioned by a well-known collector of epigraphy, Pan Zuyin. Signed and with a seal of the artist. For biographical details see entry for catalogue number 90.

Reproduced: **Shanghai Museum Catalogue of Paintings;** no. 93
Arts of China: vol. 111: Paintings in Chinese Museums, pl. 115.

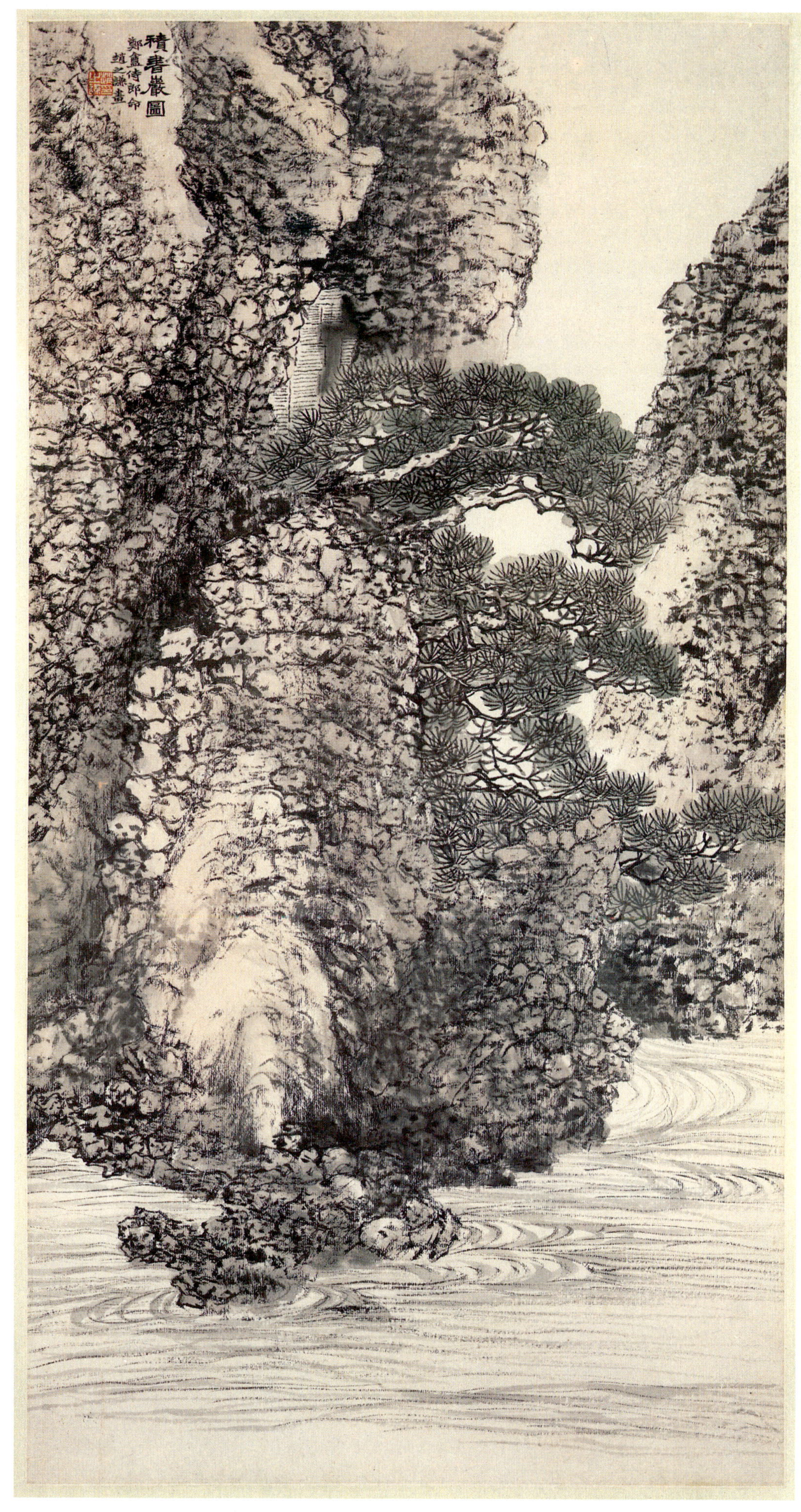

積書巖圖
鄭盦侍郎命
趙之謙畫

"Pine, Crane and Chrysanthemum"
dated 1887 by Xu Gu (1824-1896)

Hanging scroll; ink and colours on paper. 185.3 x 98cm
Suzhou Museum

Traditional symbols of longevity, the pine tree and the crane, and the chrysanthemum, the emblem of Autumn, are combined in an established form but with stunning modernity. The composition and the steeply sloping ground line represent a thoroughly established and traditional form in Chinese painting, but the energetic brushwork and vibrant colours place the picture firmly in a contemporary idiom.

Born in the same year as Zhao Zhiqian, Xu Gu too displays the same stirring and revolutionary qualities as his contemporary. Xu served as a military official under the ruling Manchus but during the Taiping rebellion abandoned government service to become a Buddhist monk. As a painter he worked in Yangzhou and Shanghai, and it was particularly in Shanghai that he gained his reputation as a member of that revolutionary group of artists which included Ren Bonian (cat. nos. 88 and 89) and Wu Changshuo (cat. nos. 94 and 95). He was particularly known for his paintings of goldfish, fruit, flowers and birds. His work is characterised by sharp and lively brushwork which is at times disciplined and forthright, for example the leg of the crane, and at times spontaneous and impressionistic, for example the dry grey and brown strokes of the pine tree branches. Among Xu's greatest admirers was Qi Baishi (see cat. no. 100).

Signed and dated in the inscription and with the seal of the artist.

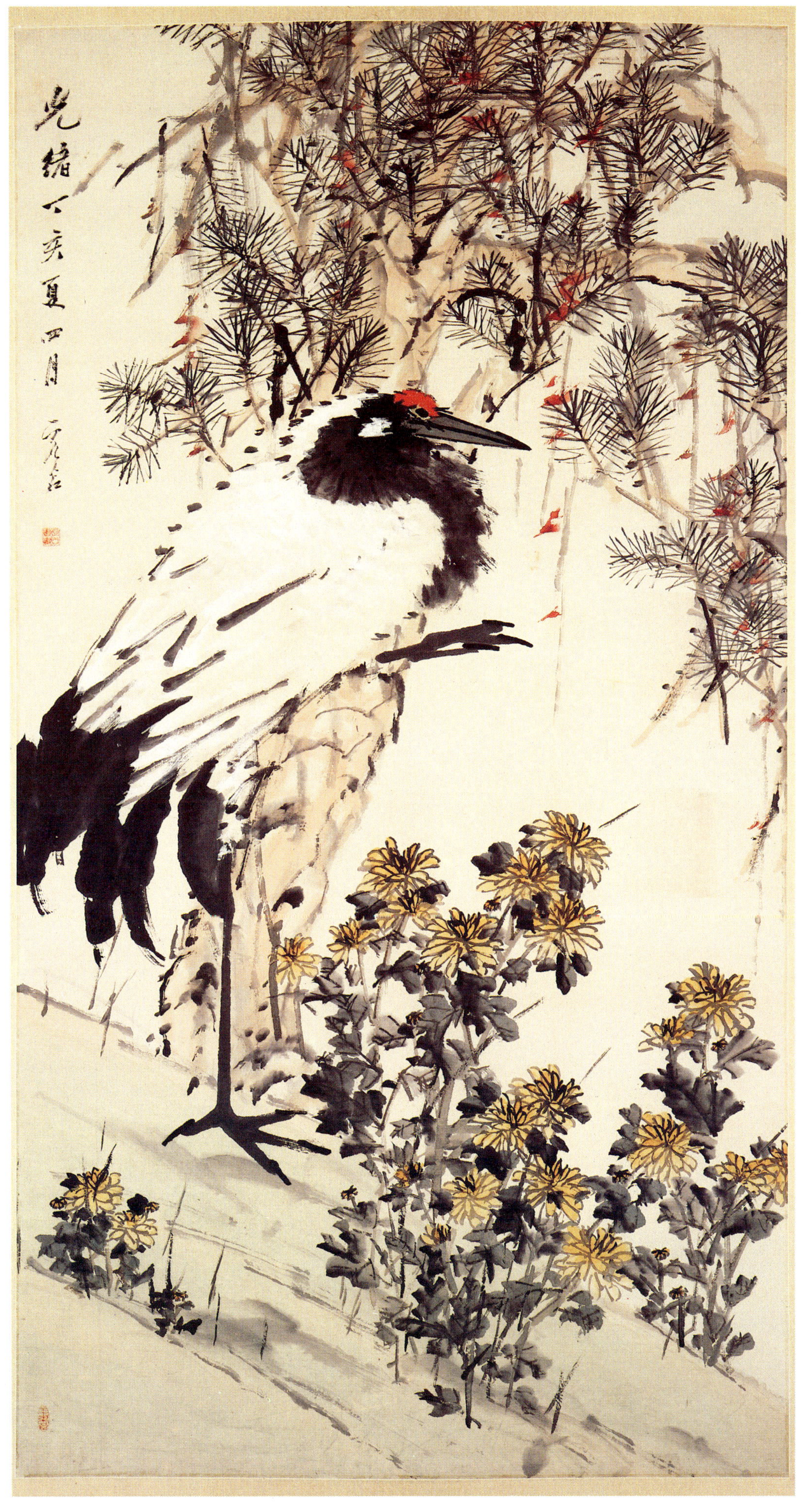

"Loquats"
by Xu Gu (1824-1896)

Handscroll; ink and colours on paper. 44.2 x 95.5 cm
Gugong Museum, Peking

Xu Gu's spontaneous and impressionistic style of brushwork is clearly illustrated in the sharp angular washes of the dark leaves and in the longer, but equally spontaneous, strokes of the branches. In some contrast, the fruits are painted with carefully modulated colour washes which provide them with a clarity of both form and volume. The fruits therefore seem to have a stabilising effect on the composition, although there is undoubted tension between them and the vivid expressionism of the leaves. Like "Pine, Crane and Chrysanthemum" the subject and the composition are traditional but the painting style contemporary.

The inscription is signed by the artist and followed by his seal.
For biographical details see entry for catalogue number 92.

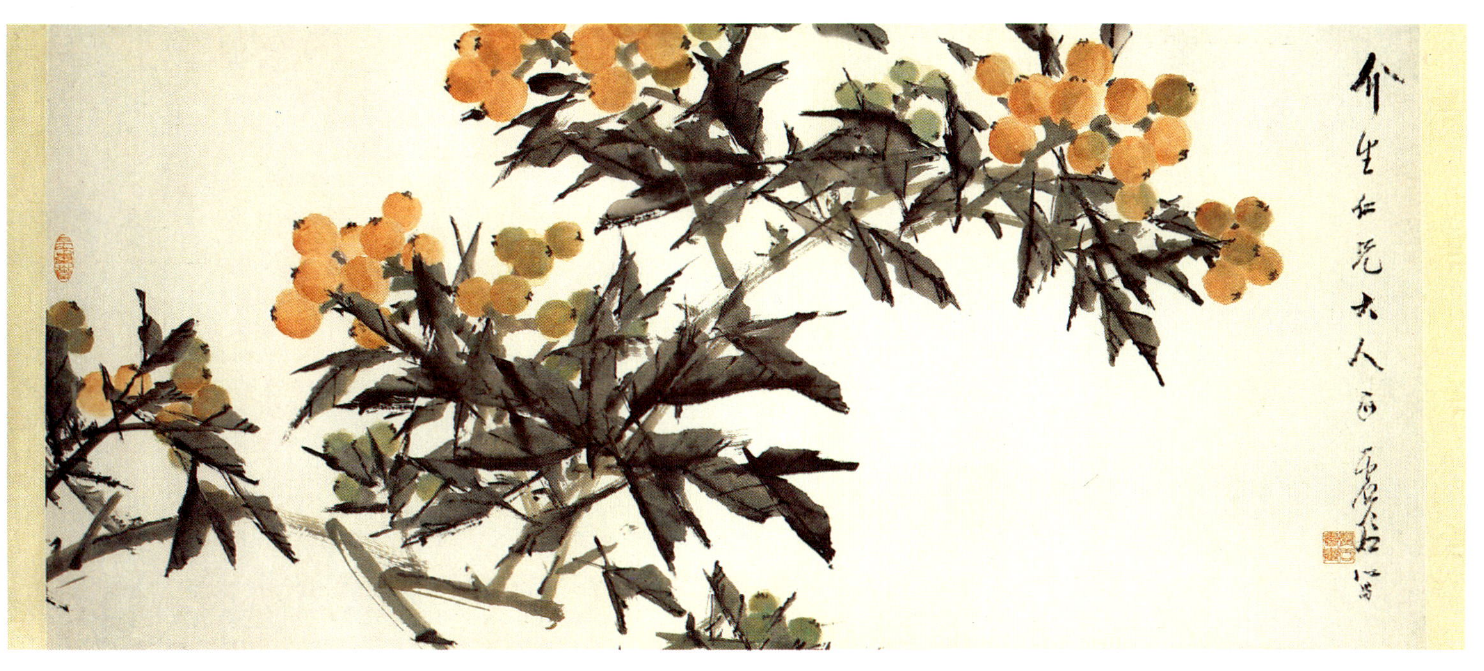

介生仁兄大人正
雷悳白寫

"New Year Flowers and Fruits"
dated 1915 by Wu Changshuo (1844-1927)

Hanging scroll; ink and colours on paper. 151.5 x 80.5cm
Gugong Museum, Peking

An eccentric rock is the focal point for this composition based on the fruit and flowers associated with the New Year celebrations. In his inscription Wu Changshuo echoes the tradition of the New Year:

One New Year's morning
by painting flowers and fruit set on their tables
our ancestors expressed the passing of time,
the impermanence of time.
So have I done…in the same spirit.

Behind the rock a tall-necked celadon vase holds a twig of blossoming prunus which twists dramatically across the scroll. In the foreground a bowl of narcissus with bright green leaves dominates the scattered pomegranates and persimmons. The selected objects are carefully composed in the traditional manner of Chinese flower paintings, even to the absence of a ground or base line and it is, therefore, the rock which anchors the composition. However, the bold brushwork and the emphatic and contrasting colours of this oddly sensitive, but at the same time aggressively styled, picture are characteristic of the new life and radicalism that was stimulating new directions in Chinese painting during the early years of the Republic.

Wu Changshuo is said to have taken up painting in his fifties but in all probability he had commenced studying at an earlier age, possibly as a consequence of his great interest in calligraphy and seal carving. During the later years of the Qing dynasty Wu served as a magistrate in his native Zhejiang province. As a painter and calligrapher, however, he gravitated towards Shanghai where he studied with Ren Bonian (cat. nos. 88 and 89) and was clearly influenced by Zhao Zhiqian (cat. nos. 90 and 91). Although he later dominated the Shanghai painting school, during his lifetime Wu was equally renowned for his calligraphy which, as we can see in the inscription to this painting, displays a sureness of hand, a confidence in its expression and a beautiful fluency. The long sweeping lines of the vase, the more rugged strokes of the rocks and the inflected lines of the narcissus leaves demonstrate the strength of Wu's capacity to define line in infinite variety. This fluency in calligraphy was surely the foundation of his distinctive, expressive and confident painting style. It has been said that once he had taken up the brush he wielded it with the speed of an arrow to create decisively drawn forms that reflected his rebellious spirit.

Signed and dated in the inscription and with seals of the artist.
Reproduced: **The Peking Museum: Paintings and Ceramics**, no. 50.

catalogue no. 95

"Red Smartweed and White Lotus"
dated 1923 by Wu Changshuo (1844-1927)

Hanging scroll; ink and colours on paper. 107 x 51.8cm
Gugong Museum, Peking

The large wet leaves of a lotus hang solemnly over plants of smartweed. The painting is executed with a full wet brush and the impression of leaves and flowers heavy with water is successfully achieved. The drama of this simple composition is heightened by the contrast between the dark and ominous colours of the flowers and the stark white of the untouched paper. Although painted in the 'boneless' style with colour washes Wu's characteristic calligraphic qualities are evident in the drawing of the lotus bloom and the smartweed.
Signed and dated in the inscription and with seals of the artist.
For biographical details see entry for catalogue number 94.

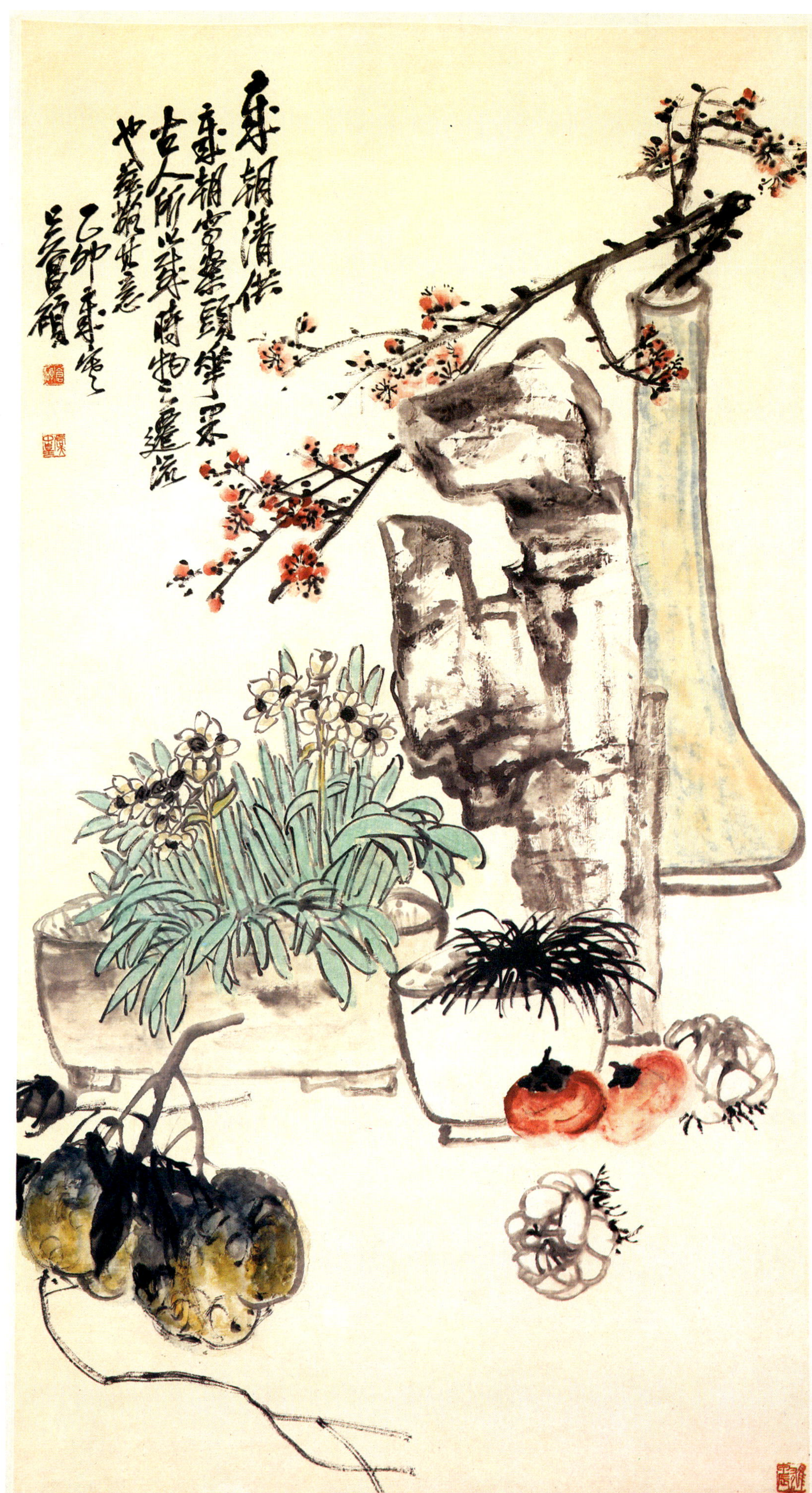

catalogue no. 94.

"Autumn Flowers"
dated 1922 by Chen Hengke (1876-1923)

Hanging scroll; ink and colours on paper. 178.5 x 89.7cm
Gugong Museum, Peking

The traditional floral emblem of autumn in China is the chrysanthemum which is held in great esteem, particularly in the north, for its variety and richness in colouring. The deep yellow of Chen's chrysanthemums in this painting is testimony to that tradition. More than any other flower in the history of China the chrysanthemum has been the subject of extraordinary investigation. The flower is mentioned in Tang and earlier texts not only for its beauty but also for its properties as a tonic, a sedative, a cosmetic and even, when taken in the form of a dry petal powder, as a means 'to recover the drunkard'. As early as the Song dynasty (960-1279) horticulturists, inspired by scholars, developed more and more unusual varieties through crossing and grafting. The chrysanthemum became an indispensable item in the decorative repertoire of Chinese art, not only as the emblem of Autumn, but as a purely decorative motif particularly in the Republican era.

Chen Hengke is said to have studied Western painting and sought to fuse Western and Chinese painting styles. Little obvious Western influence is evident in this painting which, in its spontaneous brushwork, broad colours and traditional format for flower compositions, conforms to the characteristics of the Shanghai School.

Although born in Jiangxi province, the son of a well-known poet, Chen established himself in the north. In particular he became a notable theoretician and art historian and was for many years a Professor at Peking University and at the Academy of Art. His wide education in both Chinese and Western artistic traditions combined with his own talents as a painter, calligrapher and seal engraver, made him a unique and interesting figure in the artistic circles of early 20th century China. His eclectic interests are reflected in the range of his paintings: flowers, landscapes, figures, miniatures and fans. It was probably in his figure paintings that Western influences are most evident. As the doyen of the painting fraternity in Peking it was Chen who recognised the great promise of Qi Baishi, with whom he became a great friend. Qi acknowledges the debt to his teacher in an inscription he appended to one of Chen's paintings: "Were it not for the Master, I would not have moved ahead; were it not for me, the Master would have gone back".

Signed and dated in the inscription and with seals of the artist.
Reproduced: **Arts of China vol. 111: Paintings in Chinese Museums, pl. 120.**

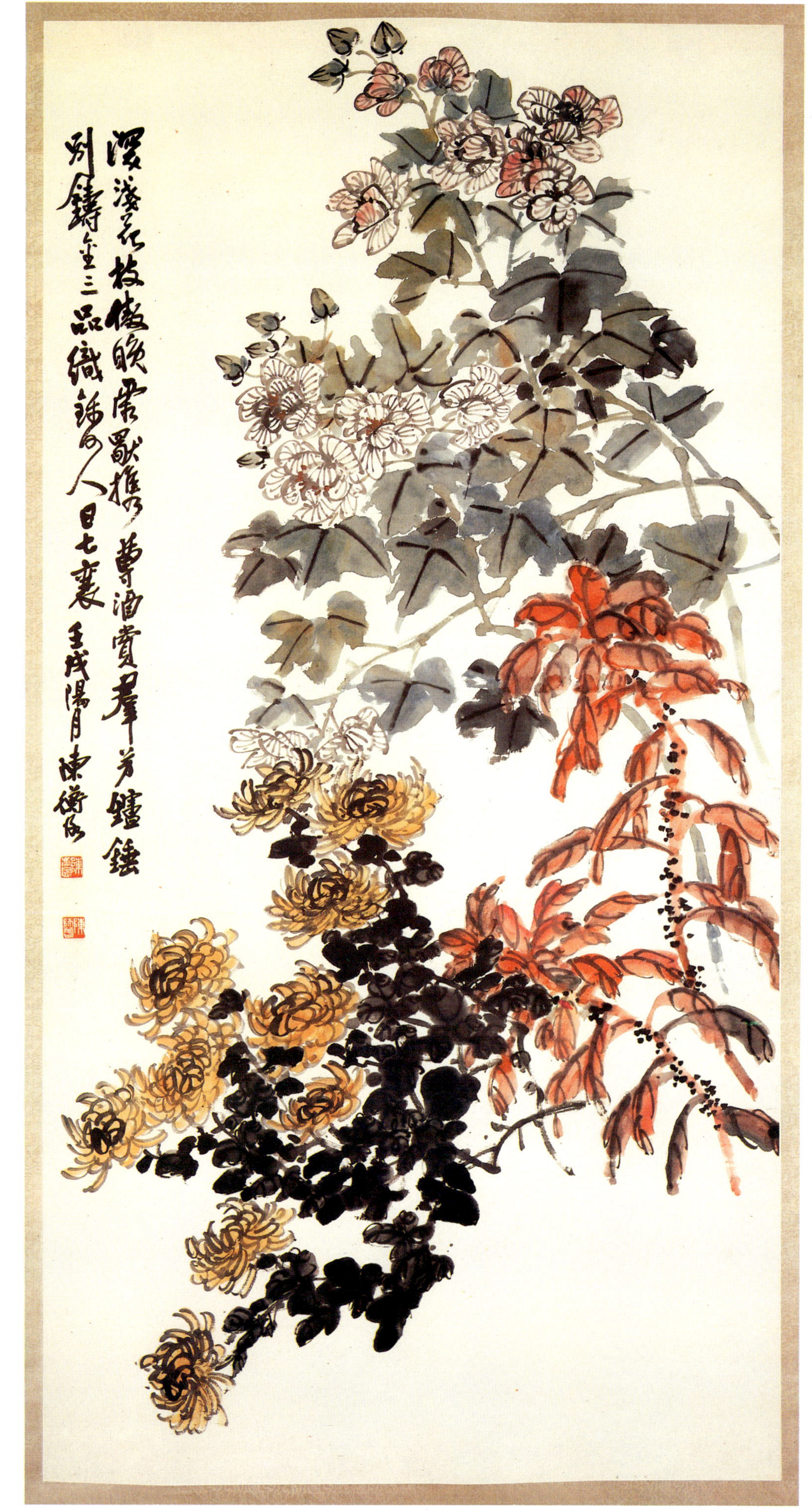

溪邊之花 枝叶偃晚
露歐攏 尊酒實羣芳鑑裏
別鑄金至三品織濃
人日七裹
壬戌陽月 陳衡恪

"Peony and Mandarin Fish"
by Cheng Zhang (1869-1936)

Hanging scroll; ink and colours on paper. 151.3 x 48.7cm
Gugong Museum, Peking

The Western influences to which China was subject in the early years of the Republican era were not strongly evident in painting traditions. Few artists made a conscious effort to study and assimilate Western styles but Cheng Zhang is one of these rare examples. The composition with a rocky cliff and flowering peonies overhanging a stream with leaping mandarin fish is in the established Chinese tradition. However, the careful drawing and shading of the petals of the flowers indicates a determined attempt to represent volume and depth in the Western manner. The colouring too, in soft tones of pink, white and green, echoes Western influences. The waters of the stream are shown by pale blue washes in place of the rippling strokes we might expect in a Chinese painting. The absence of calligraphic line, which we recognise as such an important constituent of any Chinese painting, and the use of modulated washes to describe both form and volume must be seen as distinct Western influences.

Cheng Zhang, from Anhui province, was attracted to the mecca of contemporary Chinese painting, Shanghai,where he studied with Wu Changshuo (see cat.nos. 94 and 95). He confined himself to paintings of birds, flowers and animals in which the Western influence and light, but clear and bright, colours are the characteristic features.

Inscription by the artist followed by his seal.

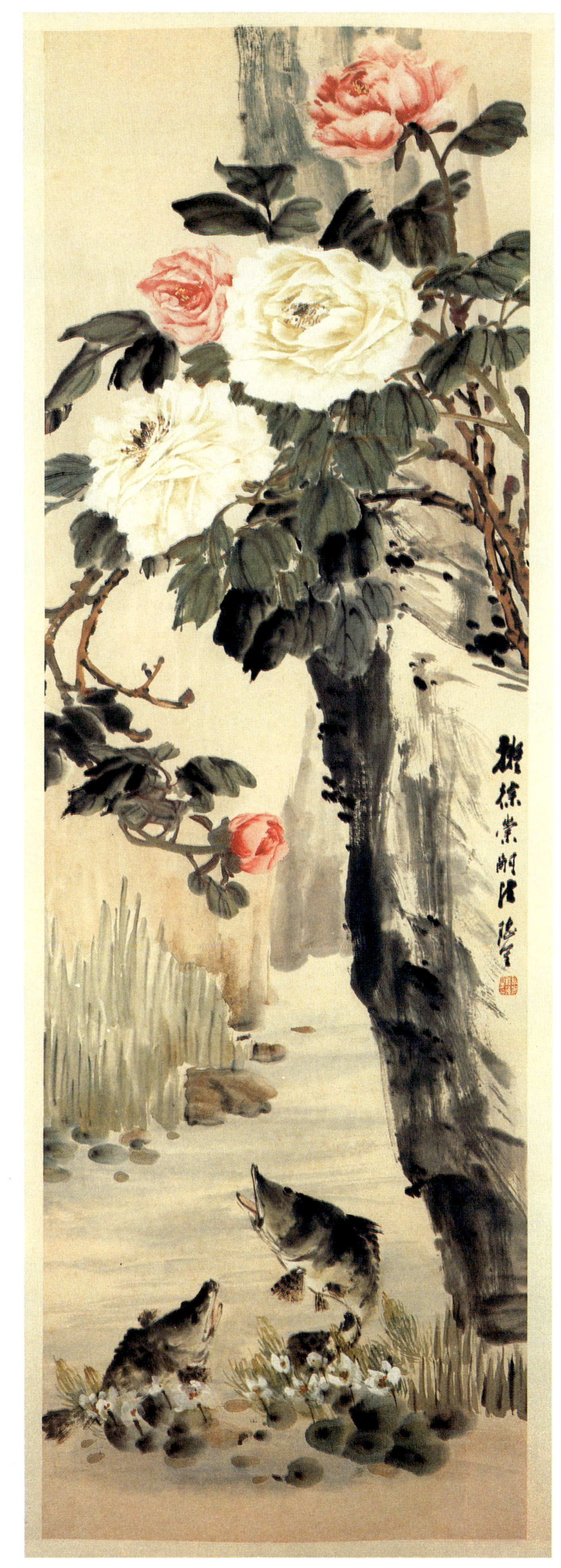
擬徐崇嗣法 陸恢寫

"Landscape"
dated 1922 by Huang Binhong (1864-1955)

Hanging scroll; ink and colours on paper. 110.7 x 44.3cm
Gugong Museum, Peking

At a time when Chinese painting was dominated by flower painters of the Shanghai School, Huang Binhong stands out as a landscape artist. This painting is composed upon well-established values and traditions in its clear definition into foreground, middleground and distant ground. Mists and valleys create space and depth whilst the ranging peaks create an harmonious and rhythmic composition. Huang's earlier landscapes illustrate a perhaps more individual interpretation, away from the articulate spatial relationships of landscapes in the **wenren** tradition towards a concern for pure textural qualities. This example, painted when the artist was fifty-eight years old, shows the beginnings of a more mature and settled style in its determined composition, although Huang's interest in texture and surface is still clearly evident. The range and variety of the brushstrokes employed create an excitement in both the form of the rocks and mountains and their textural qualities. The landscape in Huang's hands has a life and an energy which is reminiscent of Kun Can (cat. no. 51), the master whom Huang was known to have admired.

Huang Binhong was born in Anhui province into a family with long and established artistic traditions. He was brought up in a privileged environment devoted to literary and artistic pursuits. It was a background which nurtured and encouraged Huang's natural interests in painting and the history of art in China. Among his massive output of books and articles on art and literature probably his best known work is the Encyclopedia of Chinese Fine Arts (**Meishu congshu**) published in 1911 in no less than 120 volumes. The extensive knowledge and connoiseurship revealed in his writings ensured Huang a place in the official hierarchy. Among the many positions he held were Chairman of the Paintings Department of the Palace Museum in Peking in the late 1930s and, later, Professor at the Hangzhou School of Art.

Signed and dated in the inscription and with the seal of the artist.

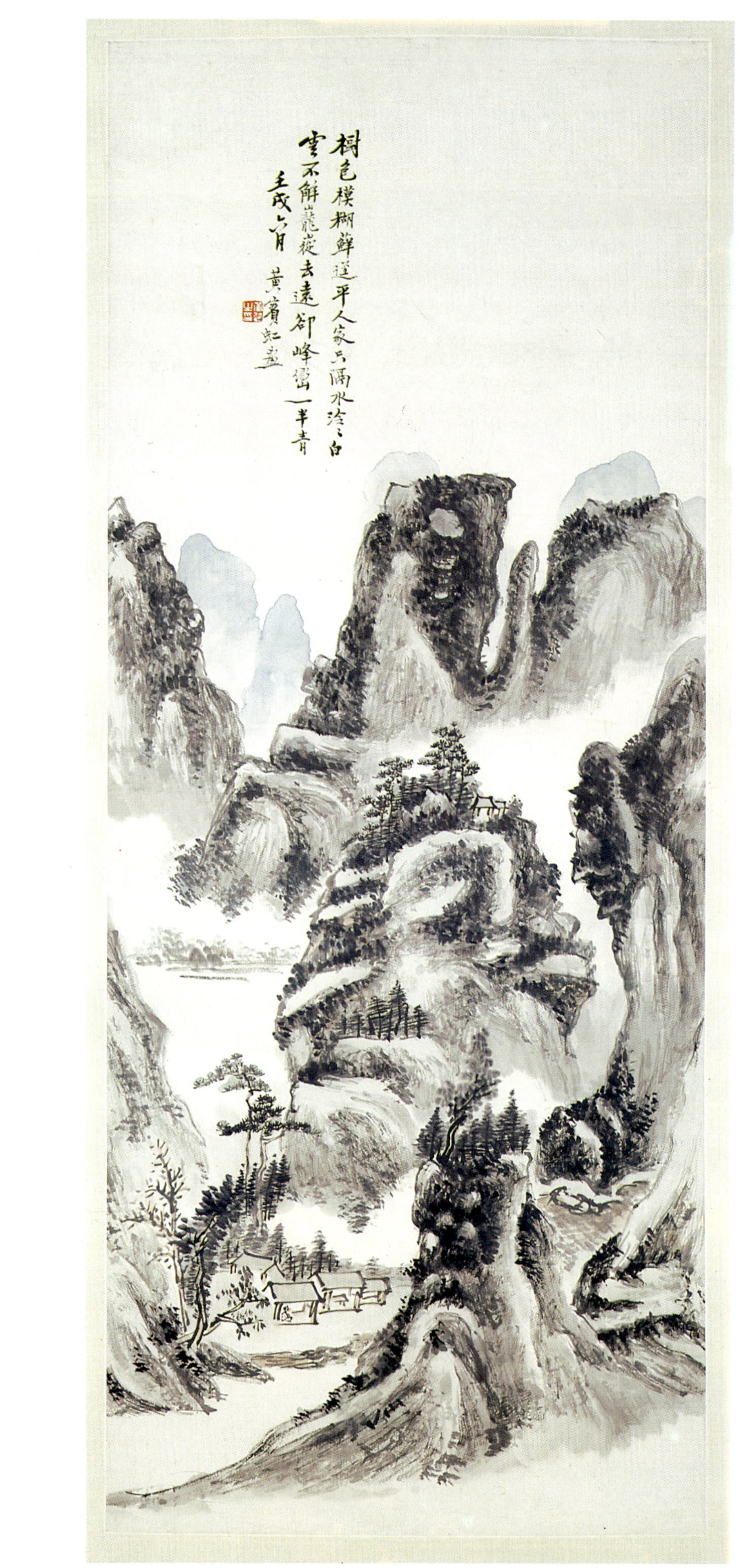

樹色模糊蘚逕平人家只隔水溶溶
白雲不解龍蛇去遠卻峰巒一半青
壬戌六月　黃賓虹畫

catalogue no. 99

"Two Cocks"
dated 1943 by Xu Beihong (1896-1953)
Hanging scroll; ink and colours on paper. 90 x 55.4cm
Shanghai Museum

The brilliance, humour and acute observation that characterises the work of Xu Beihong are fully expressed in this painting of two resplendent cocks perched on a wood fence. The two birds are proud and alert to the point of being wary, yet natural and almost playful. The dappled leaves and grasses rendered in colour washes with a deft lightness of touch combine with the stronger elements of the wood fence and the concentrated colour of the cocks to produce a painting of both vigour and sensitivity. We see in this scroll the same kind of modulated colour washes to define form and volume that Cheng Zhang used, although the delicacy of Xu's brushwork has ensured a more successful outcome.

From humble beginnings, as the son of a farmer and teacher in Jiangsu province, Xu strove to pursue a painting career. After initial setbacks his ability was recognised in Shanghai and this led to visits and studies abroad, firstly in Japan and thence to France where he studied at the École des Beaux Arts and at the Academie Julien. In France, Xu became the pupil of the realist painter Dagnan-Bouveret from whom he learnt to master the techniques of representational drawing in the realist manner and the unfamiliar art of painting in oils. For eight years Xu studied in Europe, spending most of his time in France but also visiting Germany, Switzerland and Italy. He returned to an unsettled China in 1927 and held a succession of appointments in Nanking, at the National University, in Shanghai at the Nanguo Art Academy and in Peking, at the National Academy of Art where he served as President. After the establishment of the People's Republic in 1949, Xu was appointed Chairman of the Artists Association of China. Xu's travels resulted in the first one-man show of a Chinese artist in Europe when he exhibited in Brussels in 1930. He also organised a major exhibition of modern Chinese painting, including works by Qi Baishi (cat. no. 100), to tour in Europe in the mid-1930s.

The experience that Xu had gained in his European studies, and moreover his exposure to totally different artistic traditions, influenced him greatly and we see in his work a strong sense of naturalistic representation that is quite unfamiliar in traditional Chinese painting. The vivacious galloping horse is the hallmark of Xu Beihong and, although painted with the flourishing brushwork we have come to expect in 20th century Chinese painting, there is a sense of naturalism that is new. The results of his studies of Western concepts of perspective, composition and even anatomy are obvious in Xu's horse paintings.

Having learnt and absorbed so much from Western art, Xu was critical of the Chinese tradition which he considered too imitative of the ancient masters. He sought to instil a new vigour into Chinese painting by close observation of the subject and analysis of its form and volume. All this is evident in his paintings, and yet, they remain firmly in the Chinese tradition. The qualities of brushwork are still the essence of Chinese painting, even of Xu Beihong.

Signed and dated in the inscription.

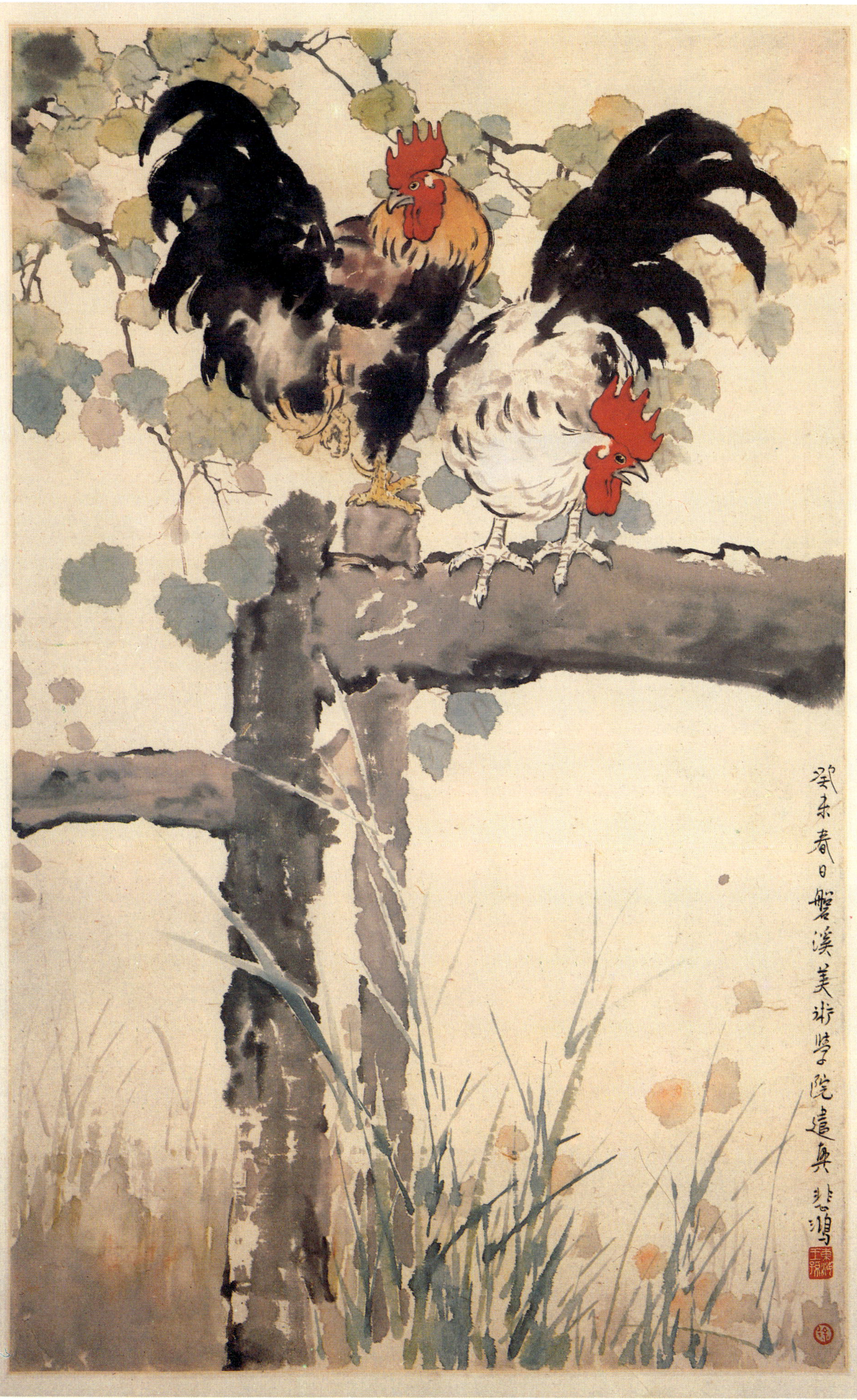

癸未春日磐溪美術學院遠奧
悲鴻

catalogue no. 100

"Lotus"
dated 1924 by Qi Baishi (1863-1957)
Hanging scroll; ink and colours on paper. 182.6 x 96.5cm
Shanghai Museum

Colour and vibrant activity characterise the style of Qi Baishi, arguably the most illustrious 20th century Chinese painter. In this painting a varied and colourful array of lotus plants sprout from a pool identified by sparse and dry horizontal strokes. The broad wet colour washes of the lotus leaves contrast with the spindly harsh black stalks and the sharply drawn lotus pods. It is a picture of movement, activity and apparent confusion; all of which are thrown into focus against the bright white of the untouched paper background. The work of Qi Baishi realises the peak of achievement in 20th century Chinese painting; it is strong, colourful and immediate in its impact, and yet, complex in composition and profoundly subtle in brush technique.

Born into a poor family in Hunan province Qi Baishi's early life was spent on the land as a farm labourer. He was then apprenticed to a local carpenter where he also painted portraits. At the comparatively late age of twenty-seven he began formal painting studies, adopting first the **gongbi** (fine brush) style before moving on to the more expressive calligraphic style that was to become the feature of his later works. Throughout his career Qi's painting was characterised by strong brushwork, bright colours and simple down-to-earth subject matter. His favourite themes included the lotus, the humble minnow, shrimp or crab; simple natural elements whose very essence he captured with warmth and humour in a few distinctive and expressive brushstrokes. Even at the age of sixty Qi was flattered to be compared with Wu Changshuo(cat.nos.94 and 95), although within a few years his fame was to eclipse that of his colleague.

At the age of fifty Qi moved to Peking. It is said that shortly after his arrival in the capital he was recommended for a minor official post. However, Qi declined, sending as his reply a painting of iris and crab, with a satirical inscription condemning those who 'ride with the tide', as does the crab. In his later years Qi Baishi was recognised in the People's Republic of China as a truly great, honest and original artist. He served as a delegate to the First People's Political Consultative Conference and as Chairman of the Artists Association of China.

The painting is signed and dated in the inscription and bears his seal.

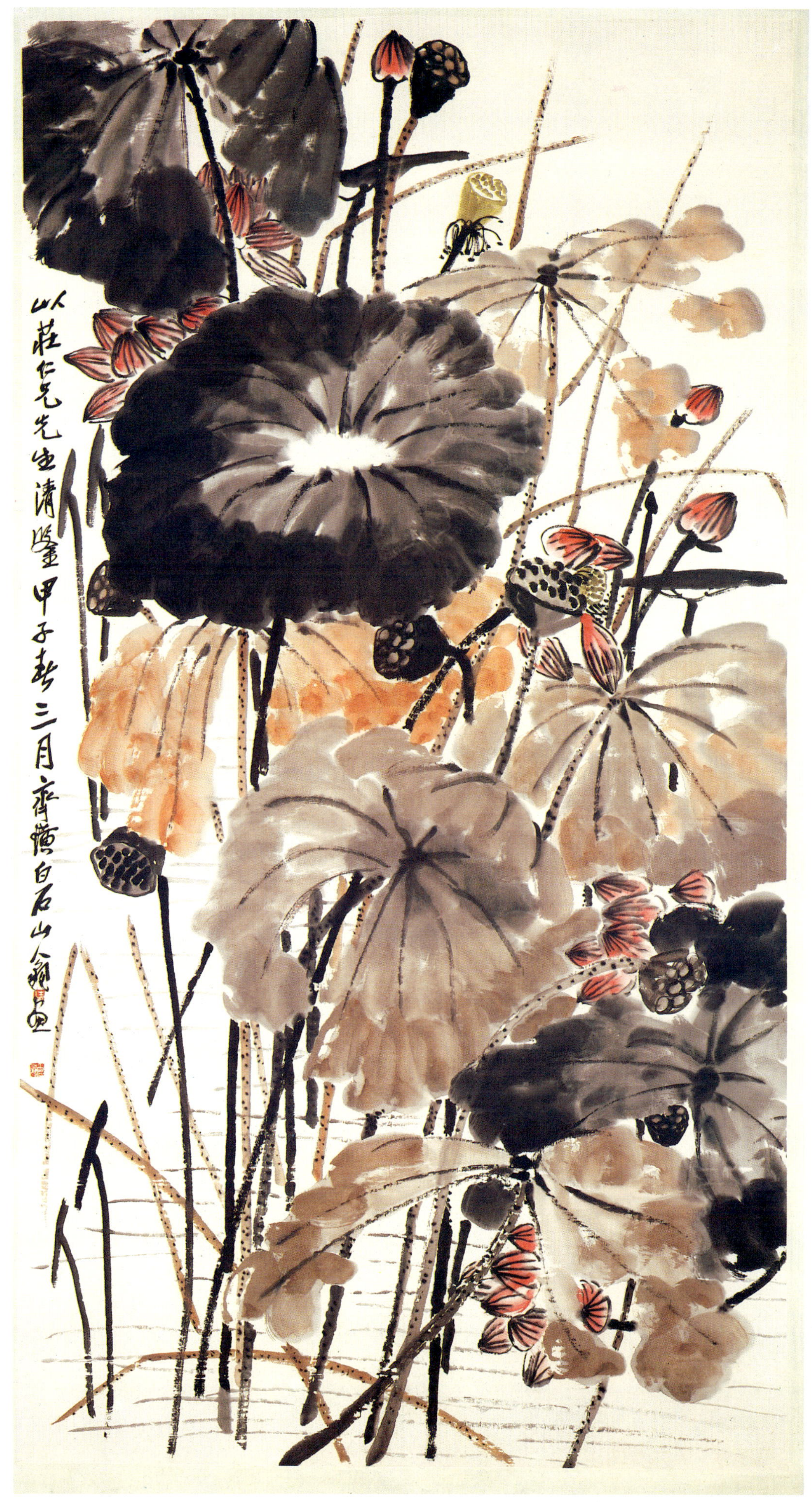

以莊冠先先生清鑒 甲子春三月齊璜白石山人畫

Chronological Table

XIA DYNASTY	c.2100 - 1600 BC	**MING DYNASTY REIGNS**		**QING DYNASTY REIGNS**
SHANG DYNASTY	c.1600 - 1027 BC	HONGWU	1368 - 1398	SHUNZHI 1644 - 1662
ZHOU DYNASTY	1027 - 221 BC	JIANWEN	1398 - 1403	KANGXI 1662 - 1723
QIN DYNASTY	221 - 206 BC	YONGLE	1403 - 1425	YONGZHENG 1723 - 1736
HAN DYNASTY	206 BC - AD 220	HONGXI	1425 - 1426	QIANLONG 1736 - 1796
THREE KINGDOMS AD	220 - 280	XUANDE	1426 - 1436	JIAQING 1796 - 1821
WESTERN JIN DYNASTY	265 - 316	ZHENGTONG	1436 - 1450	DAOGUANG 1821 - 1851
EASTERN JIN DYNASTY	317 - 420	JINGTAI	1450 - 1457	XIANFENG 1851 - 1862
NORTHERN AND		TIANSHUN	1457 - 1465	TONGZHI 1862 - 1875
SOUTHERN DYNASTIES	420 - 581	CHENGHUA	1465 - 1488	GUANGXU 1875 - 1908
SUI DYNASTY	581 - 618	HONGZHI	1488 - 1506	XUANTONG 1908 - 1912
TANG DYNASTY	618 - 906	ZHENGDE	1506 - 1522	HONGXIAN 1912
FIVE DYNASTIES	906 - 960	JIAJING	1522 - 1567	
SONG DYNASTY	960 - 1279	LONGQING	1567 - 1573	
YUAN DYNASTY	1279 - 1368	WANLI	1573 - 1620	
MING DYNASTY	1368 - 1644	TAICHANG	1620 - 1620	
QING DYNASTY	1644 - 1911	TIANQI	1620 - 1628	
REPUBLIC OF CHINA	1911 - 1949	CHONGZHEN	1628 - 1644	
PEOPLE'S REPUBLIC				
OF CHINA FOUNDED	1949			

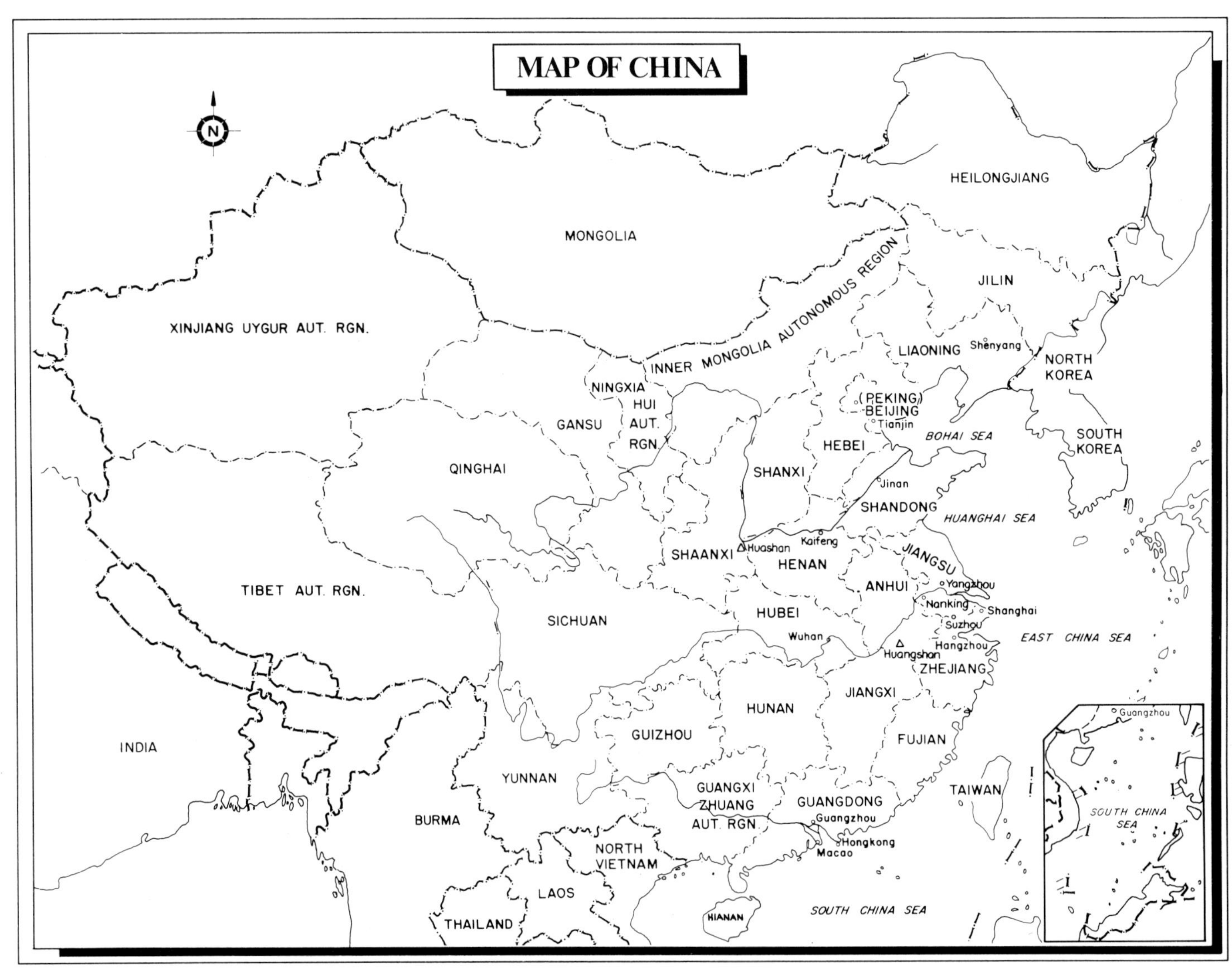

Index of Artists

Glossary of Terms

album (ce) A volume or book consisting of up to a dozen pages, occasionally more, and may include both paintings and examples of calligraphy, often with a picture facing a poem.

axe cut texture strokes (fupi cun) Broad sweeping brushstrokes creating a rocky surface resembling a block of wood hewn with an axe.

baimiao A method of drawing in fine ink line without colour.

blue and green landscape (qinglu shanshui) A mode of landscape painting which originated in the Tang Dynasty (618-906) or earlier. It took its name from the blue and green mineral pigments that were applied in colouring earth surfaces and rocks. Washes of blue and green were applied within forms outlined with a fine line drawing.

boneless manner (mogu fa) A technique of painting in ink and colour washes alone without a bounding outline and without linear definition.

broken ink (pomo) A means of "breaking" an ink wash by deeper toned accents.

brush (bi) A tuft of graded hair held together with adhesive and inserted in the end of a brush holder. The tuft is made of animal hair – most commonly from goats, deer, wolves, and hares; less frequently from horses, camels, pigs, rats, bird feathers, and humans; vegetable fibres were also used. Brush holders are generally made of bamboo or wood, but ivory, jade, lacquered wood, porcelain, or other valuable materials are also used. Brushes vary a great deal in size, both as to length and thickness. The brush has a central core formed by a bunch of bristles tied together; its thickness can be increased by adding layers of covering hair to the core. A layer of shorter hairs between the core and the outer layer of the brush create a small hollow space serving as a reservoir to enable the brush to hold a substantial quantity of ink. An extraordinary instrument of great sensitivity and flexibility, it responds to the slightest pressure of the hand, and is usually held perpendicular. Handling the brush involves the movements of fingers, wrist, arm and even the whole.body in the cae of writing large characters. Capable of producing a great variety of brushstrokes: dots, curves, vertical, horizontal and diagonal lines, it is used in both calligraphy and painting. In response to the pressure applied to the brush, a brushstroke fluctuates in thickness and varies in ink tonality. Infused with vital energy, it has a sense of direction, speed, and movement. Each line is made by a single stroke and each stroke is made in a single movement, with the brush travelling the full length in the right direction.

calligraphy (shufa) A nonrepresentational art, essentially an appreciation of the dynamic movements of a living line, independent of the meaning of the written character. It is believed that through its linear movement and abstract design, calligraphy could express and communicate the most subtle thoughts and feelings, and reveal the character and nature of the writer. Regarded as the highest form of visual art and executed with the same brush and ink as painting, calligraphy exerted a great deal of influence on painting. Major styles of calligraphy: seal script (zhuanshu), clerial script (lishu), cursive script (caoshu), running script (xingshu), standard script (kaishu).

colophon (tiba) An annotation or inscription in prose or poetry appended to a work of calligraphy or painting. It may be written by the artist himself or by some other person, a friend, collector, or a connoisseur, and gives general information on the painting, such as for whom and when it was painted, its source of inspiration and the meaning behind it, appreciation of the painting or even its history.

dot (dian) A type of brushstroke used on rocks and trees to suggest lichens or to suggest distant vegetation on hills and valleys.

examination system A means of recruiting officials in the civil bureaucracy, chosen on the basis of merit and talent, literary ability and knowledge of the classics. Three levels of examinations: prefectural level giving the Xiucai ("Flowering Talent") degree; provincial level giving the Juren ("Recommended Man") degree; metropolitan level giving the Jinshi ("Presented Scholar") degree. Success in the examinations which would qualify a degree holder to become a member of the ruling elite class, was the normal route to political power and financial success.

finger painting (zhihua) A technique of painting, employing the balls of the fingers and the side of the hand to apply broad streaks and washes of ink and colour, and using one fingernail grown to extra length to draw fine lines.

flying-white (feibai) A technique of brushwork used in calligraphy in which the brush hairs are made to separate by the pressure and swift movement of the brush, showing streaks of the white paper surface within the brushstroke.

gongbi A careful and meticulous manner of painting, associated with descriptive realism, and characterised by fine brushwork and close attention to detail.

hemp fibre texture strokes (pima cun) Long, thread-like brushlines resembling spread-out hemp fibres.

hua To paint, to draw boundaries, to outline forms, or to delineate.

ink (mo) Made of a mixture of lampblack and glue forming a clay-like paste, which is put into a wooden mould to be dried. The dry stick, or ink cake, that is removed from the mould, is ready to be ground on a stone or palette, and mixed with water. When the water turns black and reaches a creamy consistency, the ink is ready for use. By adjusting the amount of water in the ink, a wide range of tonal value ranging from deep black to light grey can be obtained. As early as the 9th century, ink was recognised as having colouristic qualities and fulfilling the representational function of colour.

Hanlin Academy (Hanlin Yuan) The Imperial Academy of Learning or the Board of Academicians. A carefully selected body of the most outstanding metropolitan graduates (Jinshi), whose function was to perform important literary tasks for the court, expounding the classics and drafting or compiling imperial utterances.

ink play (ximo) Painting in a very free and spontaneous manner, as a form of relaxation and self expression.

mountain and stream (shanshui) Landscape painting.

pingdan Plainness and blandness, qualities most highly prized in human personality and most praised in literaiti painting. Appreciative qualities stemming from the Confucian disapproval of ostentation, and the reserved, subtle taste of the cultivated scholar gentry class. Not to be equated with dullness, "plainness and blandness" are only apparent, a semblance of impoverishment concealing inner richness and brilliance.

qi Vital or life force, the creative and vital energy which, according to Taoist philosophy, permeates and animates all phenomena of the Universe. The presence of **qi**, the animating element, in an object, a brushstroke, or a painting would convey a feeling of vitality and dynamism.

qiyun Spirit resonance, vitality, a quality that appeared as the first of the Six Laws of Painting formulated by Xie He of the late 5th century. In later centuries, it became the most important element in painting and served as a criterion of excellence.

raindrop texture strokes (yudian cun) Small, fine dabs of ink resembling "rain drops".

scorched (or roasted) ink (jiaomo) Deep black ink applied dry and sparingly.

scrolls Rolled paintings. Painting in either paper or silk is mounted on a paper backing and framed by paper or silk margins. Two types of scrolls. The hanging scroll (zhou) has a vertical picture area, a roller at the bottom with, usually projecting ends of wood, ivory, jade, horn, porcelain or metal, and a slender bar at the top. It is usually hung on a wall for a short length of time and is then rolled up and stored away. The handscroll (juan) is a horizontal picture varying a great deal in length. It is intended to be unrolled on a table from right to left, with only a small section visible at a time. In a handscroll the roller is at the left end of the scroll. Its ends do not usually project but are commonly of jade.

seals (yinzhang or tuzhang) The vermilion signatures that are stamped on both painting and calligraphy. They may be affixed by the artist, or his friends or by collectors and connoisseurs. Sometimes they record the name of a person, studio, or place, and sometimes a commendatory phrase. They are generally square, but may be round or oval, or in the shape of a gourd. Seals are carved out of wood, ivory, jade, and stone.

splashed ink (pomo) A very wet application of ink. A means of spattering ink freely and spontaneously into ink blobs, broad brushstrokes, or suffused areas of ink wash.

texture strokes (cun) Brushwork within the outline or contour of a form. used to give distinctive shading, modelling, and texturing to rocks and mountains. Cun is literally translated as "wrinkles", meaning wrinkles on the face of a mountain, hill, or rock – inner markings representing clefts and fissures.

xie To write or sketch with descriptive and characterising calligraphic brushstrokes.

xieyi "Writing of ideas or "setting down the idea". To sketch freely with calligraphic brushstrokes (or washes) in ink (or colour) in order to capture the general conception (or the essentials) of an object depicted, or to express spontaneously the feeling of exhilaration within the artist.

wenren hua Paintings done by scholars who took on painting as a pastime, and as a means of self-expression. Like calligraphy, painting was believed to reveal the character of the man.

zhi To make as in in the making of beautiful and valuable objects. A term used by court academic and professional painters in signing a painting on commission which is usually characterised by great technical skill, fine details, and decorative colours.

zhuo Awkwardness, a quality admired in a Confucian personality and also in scholar-amateur painting. Not a real ineptitude but a child-like clumsiness, a natural, innate quality that is free of pretension and ostentation. In painting, it is opposite to technical facileness which carried the stigma of professionalism with a desire to please, a wish to sell one's painting.

Select Bibiliography

ACKER, William B. — Some Tang and pre-Tang Texts on Chinese Paintings. Leiden 1954

BARNHART, Richard — Wintry Forests, Old Trees: Some Landscape Themes in Chinese Painting. China Institute in America, New York 1973

BEURDELEY, Michel and Cécile — Guiseppe Castiglione: A Jesuit Painter at the Court of the Chinese Emperors. Rutland, Vermont and Tokyo 1971

CAHILL, James — Chinese Painting. Lausanne 1960

CAHILL, James — Fantastics and Eccentrics in Chinese Painting. New York 1967

CAHILL, James — Hills Beyond a River: Chinese Painting of the Yuan Dynasty 1279-1368. New York and Tokyo 1975

CAHILL, James — Parting at the Shore: Chinese Painting of the Early and Middle Ming Dynasty 1368-1500. New York and Tokyo 1978

CAHILL, James (Editor) — The Restless Landscape: Chinese Painting of the late Ming Period. Exhibition catalogue, Berkeley 1971

CAPON, Edmund — Chinese Painting. Oxford 1979

CHIANG Yee — Chinese Calligraphy, An Introduction to its Aesthetic and Technique. Cambridge, Massachusetts 1973

COHN, William — Chinese Painting. London 1948

CONTAG, Victoria — Chinese Masters of the 17th Century. Rutland, Vermont and Tokyo 1967

CONTAG, Victoria and WANG CHI-CH'IEN — Seals of Chinese Painters and Collectors of the Ming and Ch'ing Periods. Revised edition Hong Kong 1965

ECKE, Tseng Yu-ho — Chinese Calligraphy. Exhibition catalogue, Philadelphia Museum of Art 1971

EDWARDS, Richard — The Field of Stones: A study of the Art of Shen Chou. Washington DC 1962

EDWARDS, Richard et al — The Painting of Tao-chi (Daoji) 1641-c.1720. Exhibition catalogue, University of Michigan, Ann Arbor 1967

EDWARDS, Richard — The Art of Wen Cheng-Ming (1470-1559) University of Michigan, Ann Arbor 1974

FOURCADE, F. — Art Treasures of the Peking Museum. New York 1965

FU, Shen — Traces of the Brush: Studies in Chinese Calligraphy. Yale 1977

FU, Marilyn and Shen — Studies in Connoisseurship: Chinese Paintings from the Arthur M. Sackler Collection. Princeton 1974

GOEPPER, Roger — The Essence of Chinese Painting. London 1963

HEJZLAR, Josel — Chinese Watercolours. London 1978

LAI, T.C. — Treasures of a Chinese Studio (Ink Brush. Inkstone. Paper.) Hong Kong 1976

LAWTON, Thomas — Chinese Figure Painting. Washington DC 1973

LEE, Sherman — Chinese Landscape Painting. New York and Cleveland 1962

LEE, Sherman — The Colours of Ink. Asia House, New York 1974

LI, Chu-Tsing — A Thousand Peaks and Myriad Ravines: Chinese Paintings in the Charles A. Drenowatz Collection. Ascona 1974

LI, Chu-Tsing — Trends in Modern Chinese Painting. The Charles A. Drenowatz Collection. Ascona 1979

LIAONING MUSEUM — Liaoningsheng Bowuguan Canghuaji (Section of Paintings from the Liaoning Provincial Museum), Peking 1962

LIN Yutang — The Chinese Theory of Art. London 1967

LOEHR, Max — The Great Painters of China. Oxford 1980

LOVELL, Hin-cheung — An Annotated Bibliograpy of Chinese Painting Catalogues and Related Texts. Ann Arbor 1973

MURCK, Christian F. (ed.) — Artists and Traditions. Princeton 1976

NANKING MUSEUM — Nanjing Bowuguan Canghuaji. (Selection of Paintings in the Nanking Museum). Nanking 1966

PEKING MUSEUM — Gugong Bowuguan (The Palace Museum, Peking) Kodansha 1963

SHANGHAI MUSEUM — Shanghai Bowuguan Canghua. (Paintings in the Shanghai Museum). Shanghai 1959

SICKMAN, Laurence and SOPER, Alexander — The Art and Architecture of China. London and Baltimore 1956. Revised edition 1968.

SIREN, Osvald — The Chinese on the Art of Painting. Peking 1936; reprinted New York 1963

SIREN, Osvald — Chinese Painting: Leading Masters and Principles. 7 volumes. London and New York 1956-8

SIREN, Osvald — A History of Later Chinese Painting. 2 volumes. London 1938

SUZHOU MUSEUM — Suzhou Bowuguan Canqhuaji. (Selection of Paintings from the Suzhou Museum). Suzhou 1963

SULLIVAN, Michael — The Birth of Landscape Painting in China. London, Berkeley and Los Angeles 1962

SULLIVAN, Michael — Chinese Art in the 20th Century. London 1959

SULLIVAN, Michael — The Meeting of Eastern and Western Art. London 1973

SULLIVAN, Michael — The Three Perfections: Chinese Painting Poetry and Calligraphy. London 1974

SWANN, Peter C. — Chinese Painting. Editions Pierre Tisne, Paris 1958. (English and French editions)

TIANJIN MUSEUM — Tianjinshi Meishu Bowuguan Canqhuaji. (Selection of Paintings from the Tianjin Arts Museum). Peking 1959

WANG Shijie et al — I-yuan i-chen (Yiyuan yizhen) (Gems of Chinese Paintings) 5 volumes. Hong Kong 1967

WHITFIELD, Roderick — In Pursuit of Antiquity. Princeton 1969

WILSON Marc and WONG, Kwan S. — Friends of Wen Cheng-ming. China Institute in America, New York 1974

YONEZAWA Yoshiho — Arts of China Vol. III: Paintings in Chinese Museums, Tokyo 1970

Acknowledgements

PEOPLE'S REPUBLIC OF CHINA

Ministry of Culture
Bureau of Archaeological Relics
Gugong (Palace) Museum, Beijing
Guangzhou Museum
Hubei Provincial Museum
Jiangxi Provincial Museum
Liaoning Provincial Museum
Museum of Chinese History, Beijing
Nanjing Museum
Shandong Provincial Cultural Relics Bureau
Shanghai Museum
Suzhou Museum
Tianjin Arts Museum
Zhejiang Provincial Museum
Zhenjiang City Museum
Embassy of the People's Republic of China, Canberra

AUSTRALIA

Australia Council
Australia-China Council
Australian Embassy, Peking
BHP
Department of Home Affairs
Department of Foreign Affairs
Art Gallery of New South Wales
Art Gallery of South Australia
Art Gallery of Western Australia
Queensland Art Gallery
National Gallery of Victoria

International Cultural Corporation of Australia Ltd:

James Leslie: Chairman
Norman Baker: Deputy Chairman
Jean Battersby
Franco Belgiorno-Nettis
Graham Burke
Edmund Capon
Ann Lewis
John Lockhart
David Thomas
Robert Edwards: Executive Director.

Exhibition design: Greg Burgess, architect & designer.

Promotion, catalogue design and production:
Clemenger Harvie Pty. Ltd., Melbourne.

Photography: Supervised by John Delacour.